Control System Design Using MATLAB®

BAHRAM SHAHIAN

California State University, Long Beach

MICHAEL HASSUL

California State University, Long Beach

PRENTICE HALL, Englewood Cliffs, New Jersey 07632

Library of Congress Cataloging-in-Publication Data

Shahian, Bahram
Control system design using Matlab / Bahram Shahian, Michael Hassul
    p. cm.
    Includes bibliographical references and index
    ISBN 0-13-174061-X
1. Automatic control. 2. System design. 3. MATLAB.
I. Hassul, Michael. II. Title.
TJ213.S424 1993
629.8--dc20   92-42068
                        CIP

Acquisitions editor: Don Fowley
Editorial/production supervision and page make-up: Irwin Zucker
Copy editor: Brenda Melissaratos
Cover design: Patricia McGowan
Prepress buyer: Linda Behrens
Manufacturing buyer: David Dickey
Supplements editor: Alice Dworkin
Editorial assistant: Phyllis Morgan

© 1993 by Prentice-Hall, Inc.
A Simon & Schuster Company
Englewood Cliffs, New Jersey 07632

Printed in the United States of America

10 9 8 7 6 5 4 3 2 1

ISBN 0-13-174061-X

Prentice-Hall International (UK) Limited, *London*
Prentice-Hall of Australia Pty. Limited, *Sydney*
Prentice-Hall Canada Inc., *Toronto*
Prentice-Hall Hispanoamericana. S.A., *Mexico*
Prentice-Hall of India Private Limited, *New Delhi*
Prentice-Hall of Japan, Inc., *Tokyo*
Simon & Schuster Asia Pte. Ltd., *Signapore*
Editora Prentice-Hall do Brasil, Ltda., *Rio de Janeiro*

*To my parents, Saleh and Mahin,
and my wife and children, Farahnaz, Bita,
and Nima*

B. Shahian

To Laurie J. Spector

M. Hassul

Contents

10 Algebraic Design   308

11 Random Signals and Systems Analysis   343

12 Linear Quadratic Control   366

13 Robust/H_∞ Control   395

Preface

This book has evolved both as an attempt to fully integrate Computer-Aided Control System Design (CACSD) tools into our control curriculum and to devise an exciting and meaningful control system design course at California State University at Long Beach (CSULB).

Evolution of a Control Design Course

Just a few years back, when we taught our design course, we would assign different textbook design problems to students. Most of the design work was done by hand. The difficult part was verification. Very few diligent students would actually compute the step response and plot it point by point using a calculator. Problems had to be limited to 2nd or 3rd order systems for obvious reasons. From the instructor's point of view, checking the results was also very tedious.

We then decided to ask the students to write computer programs to verify their work. This almost made things worse. We found that the students were spending most of the time writing, debugging, and perfecting their programs. The control design aspects faded into the background. Good programmers turned in nice reports (although we do not know if they learned any control design), while those who were weak in programming were very frustrated. On our side, we still had problems with verification. Students were writing programs in different languages, so you had to check their results along with their programs.

Next, we decided to remove some of the programming burden on the students. We put together a collection of programs from Melsa's famous book [MJ73] and handed them out. Although this helped, it still was not very efficient. The Fortran programs were not user friendly, to say the least, and students were still wasting a lot of their valuable time on the computer.

The situation remained the same for several terms until we discovered MATLAB®. Our gut reaction to our first session with MATLAB can be summarized as *"where have you been all these years ?!"*

The rest is history, as MATLAB based programs have become the *de facto* language and tools for control systems engineers worldwide. We were now able to assign more challenging problems, compare different design techniques, and expect better performance and full verification. On our side, we were able to write simple routines that would automatically regenerate the students' results and verify their work. We noticed improved performance in designs, better prepared reports, and better grasp of concepts.

The only problem was that students were still complaining about spending too much time paging through manuals (or looking for them because they were constantly disappearing). Valuable class time (or our own personal time) had to be spent answering questions about various commands. We sensed a need for a condensed book/manual to support our classes. The present book is the result of our efforts towards that goal.

Finally, we came to the conclusion that since we now have the computational tools, we can add a dimension of realism to our class by requiring full-scale hardware designs. The motivation behind this is that we believe that no amount of lecturing can substitute for the real experience of design. There are analysis and design issues that simply cannot be taught in the real sense in a traditional lecture format. Issues such as modeling, model uncertainties including nonlinearities and component tolerances, noise and disturbance effects, and a host of other implementation problems are issues that have to be experienced head-on and dealt with. Too many students leave the classroom without really knowing the true properties of feedback. If they do, they usually think that we use feedback to stabilize systems, not realizing that feedback itself can be a source of instability. Moreover, the interdisciplinary nature of control systems and control technology issues such as sensor and actuator technologies are subjects that can be better learned through actual experience.

We have selected for assignment some traditional problems in control: inverted pendulum on a cart, magnetic levitation of a globe, balancing a ball on a beam, and the sun tracking control system. Other feasible projects might be the double tank problem or the cruise control system. Samples of the projects are usually demonstrated at the beginning of the term to motivate the students. Groups of one to three (the larger the group size, the less likely they will finish the task) students pick any project they find interesting. Appropriate references and some good reports from previous years are made available to them. Students are expected to derive the mathematical models, gather data to obtain the parameters, search for and purchase the necessary parts (lists of local vendors are available; we also recycle some components from unsuccessful projects from previous terms to reduce out-of-pocket expenditures), set the specifications, design the compensator, simulate, implement, test, prepare a report, and finally demonstrate their projects at the end of the term. Biweekly progress reports are also collected to obviate any future problems. A variety of designs from simple lead compensators to LQG type designs have been reported. After weeks of frustration over globes that defy stability, beams that over-react and hurl a metal ball into your face, carts that dance around the room, fried transistors and motors, the final day is a day to remember. The joy of learning and accomplishment, or the joy of learning and at least attempting to accomplish something real, is the true result of the course experience. A sense of appreciation for giving them the opportunity to prove their ingenuity and engineering skills has been the typical response from most students. This has been our reward.

Why We Wrote this Book

Our experience has indicated that we cannot spend valuable class time to discuss various commands or idiosyncrasies of any particular program. On the other hand, it is neither fair nor practical to expect students to pour over voluminous manuals (which are written to be comprehensive) when they have to study their main text, as well as study for other courses they happen to be taking. Therefore, we decided to write a user-friendly textbook that would include elements of a program manual and a control systems design book. It is not as comprehensive and thorough as a manual, but it has more examples targeted to a control audience. It is not a regular control text, because most concepts are not fully motivated or developed and there are virtually no theorems or proofs. It instead is written in tutorial format. This should take the burden of teaching software off the instructor's shoulders without expecting too much of the students either. Most design techniques from classical to modern optimal control techniques, including the more recent H_∞ control, are discussed, with an example for every method. We show, step by step, how the designs can be performed on the computer and how to verify them.

The book covers almost 90 percent of MATLAB commands, all of the commands in the Control System Toolbox, almost half of the commands in the SIMULINK manual, some of the commands in the Signal Processing Toolbox, and some references to the Robust Control and μ-Tools Toolboxes. In summary, all of the commands needed to support the topics in the book are covered. Because the present book covers a wide range of topics in control, we dare say that it is the most comprehensive introduction to MATLAB and its toolboxes in the market.

Recently, some control textbooks either contain a general description of MATLAB, or have a brief summary of commands in an appendix. In our opinion, this may be adequate for a first course in control systems, but it is not sufficient for more advanced courses. Performing comprehensive analysis, data analysis and visualization, and studying novel or advanced design techniques (such as adaptive, or fuzzy control) requires a more comprehensive knowledge of MATLAB.

The book is divided into two parts. Part I is a quick, yet thorough introduction to MATLAB, the Control Systems Toolbox, and SIMULINK. Most of the commands that we thought to be relevant to students in the systems area are quickly introduced and illustrated. Basic commands are covered in Part I; more advanced commands are introduced when needed in Part II. For example, commands for state space design, optimal control, digital control, and signal processing are discussed in the appropriate chapters. The assumed background for the reader is knowledge of classical control and some basic matrix theory. We have included a review of classical control in Chapter 1, and, for completeness, a brief introduction to state space in Chapter 5. Part II is a collection of lessons in tutorial form for control design from classical to modern optimal control-based techniques. We wanted the book to retain its usefulness for those students taking more advanced courses in controls and for the working engineer.

How this Book Can Be Used

We envision the following uses for this text.

1. As a supplement to any control or signal processing course. Our experience has shown that the majority of students understand the basics in 5–8 hours (Chapters 2, 3 and 4). They learn the programming, MATLAB commands, classical control, graphics and state space commands (Chapters 1–5) in 3–4 weeks. The use of SIMULINK (Chapter 6) for block diagram simulation of linear/nonlinear systems takes 1–2 weeks. Within one semester, 15 weeks, Chapters 1–8 and 10 can be covered. Within that period, they will have mastered most aspects of the program. For signal processing courses, Chapter 11 should also be covered.

2. As a textbook for a Control Systems Laboratory course. Part I of the book is fully covered. This is how we use the book at CSULB. The problems in Chapters 2, 3, 4 and 6 are intentionally written in Lab format to facilitate this use. Most of these problems are divided into two parts (Preliminary analysis and Lab work). All problems have a two-fold purpose: to practice using the program and to amplify important concepts in control. The approach is to learn and discover concepts and properties via simulation. Since many problems involve repeated computations and simulations, programming is introduced early.

The following concepts and properties are studied via simulation in the problems (problem numbers are indicated).

- dominant poles (3.3)

- s-plane regions satisfying transient response specifications (3.5)

- properties of the exponential map for s-plane to z-plane (3.6)

- effects of moving poles in a second order system (4.1)

- effects of adding poles and zeros to a second order system (4.2)

- effects of nonminimum phase zeros on the step response (4.3)

- effects of lead/lag compensators (4.4)

- disturbance rejection properties of feedback (4.5)

- effects of PI control (4.6) and PID control (4.7)

- differences between cascade and feedback compensators (4.8)

- discovering the problems faced using Bode plots for nonminimum phase systems (4.9)

By judiciously choosing problems in Chapters 2–4, one can clarify some properties that may be difficult to grasp for some students. At our school, we devote two thirds of a semester to PC-based simulations and the remaining one third to analog servomotor control. Since the Control Systems Lab is a prerequisite to all subsequent control courses, we assume a working knowledge of the program in our control sequence.

3. As a handy reference for working engineers. The tutorial format provides quick reviews without getting bogged down on theoretical details. This does not mean that theoretical issues are not important, but rather we assume that the reader is either familiar with them or can refer to any number of excellent controls textbooks. It has not been our intent to de-emphasize the importance of these books in the study of control theory. Important design formulas and equations are provided, and properties are explained and demonstrated by examples. All design techniques are demonstrated by examples. We also verify the results by providing appropriate plots, data, and tables. For instance, we have found that when some people perform state space design, they frequently have problems verifying the frequency response properties of their system or misinterpret the results, or use the wrong transfer function (mixing up open loop and closed loop transfer functions). We have tried to point these out and explicitly derive the appropriate transfer functions. Most of the examples (like the problems) serve a two-fold purpose: to demonstrate the use of various commands, and to amplify important concepts in control.

Organization of the Book

Part I of the book is devoted to familiarizing the reader with MATLAB. Chapter 1 is a review of classical control. We also set our notation and terminology there.

Chapter 2 introduces a selection of MATLAB commands, data structures, input/output, graphics, and some math commands.

Chapter 3 discusses programming structures; sample programs are provided to illustrate the procedures. The programs can be used for data analysis in later chapters.

Chapter 4 introduces classical control commands for tasks such as step response, root locus, and frequency response analysis.

Chapter 5 is a quick introduction to state space analysis followed by appropriate commands. The packed matrix notation for system representation, which is becoming popular in the robust control literature, is also introduced. This is used to derive system interconnection commands. We also discuss how to deal with multi-input multi-output systems.

Chapter 6 is a brief introduction to the SIMULINK. This is one of the most important and useful tools of MATLAB. Thorough discussion of all simulation features would double the size of the book, but we believe that this chapter will get the reader started. Several examples from simple lead compensation to simulating the chaotic behavior of the nonlinear Lorenz system are discussed.

Part II starts with Chapter 7, Classical Design. Design using root locus, Bode plots, and analytical formulas for PID, lead and lag compensation are discussed. All methods are demonstrated by examples. Simple programs that can be modified by the user are provided for all techniques to insure that the user concentrates on design rather than on programming. We give an example of *ad hoc* design so the reader knows that classical design is also an art and not a cook book procedure that works for all systems. There is a unique section on interpreting stability margins for nonminimum phase systems. This is one of the more troubling areas in control. We frequently encounter systems that are closed loop stable with multiple positive and negative gain and phase margins. Compensators of unstable systems, obtained via state space methods, are frequently nonminimum phase. Most textbooks do not discuss these cases, perhaps, because they could totally confuse the students. Moreover, different computer programs produce different numbers in such cases. We have tried to shed some light on this issue and interpret the results.

Chapter 8 discusses state feedback, observers, and reduced-order observers. We briefly introduce concepts of controllability and observability. The same example is used throughout for comparison. The chapter ends with programs for design and verification.

Chapter 9 is a self contained and brief introduction to discrete systems and digital control. Appropriate commands are introduced and the effects of sampling, different discretization methods, and frequency warping are discussed. Classical digital design techniques are presented. The chapter ends with design programs.

Algebraic, or polynomial, design is introduced in Chapter 10. Various methods for choosing desired closed loop transfer functions are discussed. The standard unity feedback, RST (two-parameter), and controller-observer (Input/Output) configurations are presented. Sample programs to implement various techniques are given at the end of the chapter.

Chapter 11 is intended to prepare the reader for an introduction to Kalman-Bucy filtering, and to introduce various signal processing commands. We summarize basic terminology, facts, and important results from stochastic processes. An example is worked out in detail to demonstrate the signal processing commands and to show how to interpret the results of the analysis.

Optimal control methods (LQR/LQG) and the Kalman-Bucy filter are discussed in Chapter 12. Formulas and classical properties of LQ methods are presented and verified by examples. The famous stability margins of LQR and their subsequent loss when estimators are introduced are demonstrated by an example. These concepts and properties are usually discussed and proved in classroom lectures. We assign additional simulation homework. Our experience indicates that students retain the material better when they verify it by simulation.

Chapter 13 is a brief introduction to robust control. The chapter starts by a critique of LQG and its lack of robustness. Performance specifications of feedback systems, including their robustness is discussed. Model uncertainties, and measures of determining stability robustness, for SISO and MIMO systems, are presented. The loop transfer recovery (LTR) and H_∞ control techniques are introduced and demonstrated by examples.

The chapter ends with sample programs and an appendix on singular values and norms for systems.

The Appendix at the end of the book covers hardware design projects. The magnetic levitation of a ball, the ball on beam, and the inverted pendulum on a moving cart are presented. Although, these problems are discussed in various texts, their hardware implementation does not appear anywhere. The issues of mathematical modeling, parameter determination, compensator design, and full implementation including the circuit diagrams are presented. It is our intent that this chapter will serve as a model so more students will build these projects. Because this Appendix is based on student reports of these projects (successfully demonstrated), they may still contain some errors. We have tried to remove the ones we discovered, but the original circuit diagrams are shown as they were presented in the reports. Sometimes, students make last minute changes to the actual system without reporting those changes. For these reasons, we emphasize that the designs are not meant to be taken as recipes that could be duplicated; rather, they should be used as models to follow. We hope that this Appendix will prove useful in encouraging more hardware designs.

Typography

Books that involve the use of computers require special attention with respect to typography. Please read this section so you can identify various changes from regular text to command entry to computer response. We have used the following typefaces in the book.

> regular text is shown in 10 point Times font.
> ```
> commands you enter following the MATLAB prompt >> are shown in 8
> point Courier font.
> ```
> MATLAB response to your commands are shown in 8 point Helvetica font
> MATLAB command names and new words are shown in *italics*.
> Example text is shown in 9 pont Times font.

Acknowledgments

We wish to acknowledge our debt to all those who have somehow contributed to our knowledge and efforts. The first author wishes to thank Baxter Womack, who first introduced him to the subject of control; David Luenbeger, who showed him the beauty and magic of dynamic systems; Gene Franklin, who showed him that great teachers are not made overnight; Thomas Kailath, whose great classic book has had, and still has, a great deal of influence on him; Cornelius Leondes, who gave him the opportunity to explore and selflessly shared his years of experience with him. The second author wishes to thank his teachers in systems and controls: Leonard Shaw, Eliahu I. Jury, Pravin Varaiya, and particularly Ronald A. Rohrer, his graduate advisor who gave him his appreciation for computer-aided design. He also wishes to thank his university and industrial colleagues: Robert N. Clark, Wendy Svitil, Joseph Anselmi, Gerry Manke, and Eugene A. Lee.

We thank M. Hasan AlHafez, a former student at CSULB, who contributed some of the programs in Chapters 7 and 10, and worked on a solutions manual.

From Prentice Hall, we thank Gerry Johnson, who encouraged us to write this book and wholeheartedly supported us throughout; Tim Bozik, who initially approved our project; Irwin Zucker, the production editor; and finally Don Fowley, who supported us and put up with long delays.

Our thanks to the people at The MathWorks, Inc., especially Liz Callanan, who provided us with MATLAB and all of its toolboxes in a timely fashion and supported us in every way they could.

The authors would like to acknowledge that the helicopter example used in Chapters 7, 8, 10 and 12 is taken from:

G. Franklin, J. D. Powell, A. Emami-Naeini, *Feedback Control of Dynamic Systems,* © 1991, by Addison-Wesley Publishing Company, Inc. Reprinted with permission of the publisher.

We also would like to acknowledge the source for Example 6.3:

Thomas Kailath, *Linear Systems,* © 1980, pp. 31–34. Adapted by permission of Prentice Hall, Englewood Cliffs, New Jersey.

An early version of Chapter 13 was reviewed by Peter Thompson of Systems Technology, Inc. We are greatly indebted to him for his comments and suggestions. B. Shahian has also benefited from lectures by M. Safonov of the University of Southern California; V. Manousiouthakis of University of California, Los Angeles (UCLA), and Frank Hauser of UCLA Extension.

Finally, we thank our wives who gave us a generous "sabbatical" or leave of absence from home, and all the sacrifices they have made over the time period we were working on this book.

Bahram Shahian

Michael Hassul

1

Review of Classical Control

1.1 Introduction

The *Encyclopedia of Science and Technology* (6th ed., McGraw-Hill, 1987) defines control systems as "interconnections of components forming system configurations which will provide a desired system response as time progresses." This definition is all encompassing, covering just about everything in the natural and man-made world. The universe, for example, is a system of planets, gasses, stars, etc. The desired response of the planetary system is a question best left for philosophers, however. Of more immediate concern to engineers are the systems composed of manufactured physical components (e.g., machines, electronics, and chemical processes) and to biomedical engineers, the biological processes.

Control system design began in antiquity. The first cave man or woman who designed the bow and arrow combined two components to achieve the desired response of a more efficient means to hunt and to protect. This type of system is known as a ballistic, or open loop, system. Once set in motion, there is no further control of the behavior of the arrow. Feedback control is more sophisticated. System response is monitored and compared with the desired response. Corrective action can then be taken to minimize the difference between desired and actual response. The governor of a steam engine is an early example of feedback control.

Until this century, control systems were designed by artisans and crafts-people. They used their experience and insight. Mathematical modeling of the components of a system and their interconnections brought the engineer into the picture. With mathematics came predictability and increased sophistication of control system design.

The first great impetus that drove the development of control system mathematics was the telephone. Electronic feedback amplifiers were required to amplify the signals in a telephone system. World War II saw the extension of these feedback control techniques to the mechanical world. Oliver Heaviside (1850–1925) provided a mathematical framework that allowed the analysis and design of control systems. His technique, similar to the Laplace transform, takes the analysis and design of dynamic systems from the time domain of the differential equation and the convolution integral into the frequency domain of the

1

transfer function. Transfer function techniques are to this day a mainstay in control system analysis and design.

An nth order linear time invariant (LTI) system can be described by a linear constant coefficient differential equation of the form

$$y^{(n)} + a_{n-1} \, y^{(n-1)} + \ldots + a_1 \, \dot{y} + a_0 \, y = b_m \, u^{(m)} + b_{m-1} \, u^{(m-1)} + \ldots + b_1 \, \dot{u} + b_0 \, u$$

where appropriate initial conditions are specified for the output, $y(t)$, of the system. Laplace transforming the above equation, we get

$$Y(s) = \frac{N(s)}{D(s)} \, U(s) + \frac{IC(s)}{D(S)} = G(s) \, U(s) + \frac{IC(s)}{D(s)}$$

where

$$G(s) = \frac{b_m \, s^m + b_{m-1} \, s^{m-1} + \ldots + b_1 \, s + b_0}{s^n + a_{n-1} \, s^{n-1} + \ldots + a_1 \, s + a_0} = \frac{N(s)}{D(s)}$$

and $IC(s)$ is a polynomial in s, a complex variable, containing the terms arising from the initial conditions. As you can see, the total response is the sum of the contributions from the initial conditions and the system input. If the system is unforced (i.e., the input is zero), we call the resulting response the *zero-input response* (ZIR) of the system. Likewise, if all initial conditions are zero, the forcing function produces the *zero-state response* (ZSR). The ratio of transform of output over transform of input of the system under zero initial conditions is the *transfer function*, denoted by $G(s)$ above.

Note that both terms in the output equation contain the same denominator polynomial, which is known as the *characteristic equation*. The roots of the common denominator $D(s)$ are the characteristic roots or the system *modes*.

The term *classical control* is applied to the body of techniques developed from the beginning of control theory to the early 1960s. It is characterized chiefly by the use of algebraic and graphical frequency domain techniques applied to single input–single output (SISO) systems. The use of computers was very limited. Classical control techniques are still in widespread use today. We will briefly review some of these methods in the following sections.

1.2 Transfer Functions

An open loop control system is composed of an input signal, a component that conditions the input signal (the controller), an actuator, the plant (or process), and the output signal. The control law, $G_1(s)$, the actuator, $G_2(s)$, and the plant, $G_3(s)$, are each modeled with transfer functions. The overall transfer function, $G(s)$, is given by

$$\frac{Y(s)}{X(s)} = G(s) = G_1(s)\, G_2(s)\, G_3(s)$$

Each individual transfer function is represented as a ratio of polynomials (or a rational function) in s, where s is a complex variable (interpreted as complex frequency). For example, $G(s)$ may be represented as

$$G(s) = K\,\frac{(s-z_1)(s-z_2)\,\ldots\,(s-z_m)}{(s-p_1)(s-p_2)\,\ldots\,(s-p_n)}$$

where we have assumed for simplicity that the polynomials have no repeated factors. If $\lim_{s \to \infty} G(s) = C < \infty$, $G(s)$ is said to be *proper*; otherwise, it is called *improper*. If $C = 0$, $G(s)$ is *strictly proper*. Most physical systems have strictly proper transfer functions.

   The set of frequencies at which a transfer function "blows up" (i.e., approaches infinity) is the transfer function *poles*. The set of frequencies at which the transfer function approaches zero is the *zeros*, of the transfer function. As you know, the numerator roots are the finite zeros, and the denominator roots are the finite poles of $G(s)$ as long as there are no common factors among the numerator and denominator. Strictly proper transfer functions have $(n - m)$ zeros at infinity, and improper transfer functions have $(m - n)$ poles at infinity.

   If there are no common roots between the numerator and denominator of $G(s)$ (i.e., there are no pole-zero cancellations), we say $G(s)$ is *coprime* (or *irreducible*). Most properly modeled physical systems have strictly proper and coprime transfer functions; nevertheless, these definitions are needed later as constraints on physically realizable compensators or as mathematical solvability conditions.

1.2.1 Frequency Response

Because s is a complex variable ($s = \sigma + j\,\omega$), transfer functions like $G(s)$ are also complex. A complex number can be expressed with a magnitude and angle. Graphs of magnitude and angle of $G(s)$ versus s are three dimensional. Although it is possible to draw such graphs, particularly with the help of a computer, we typically limit ourselves to considering only values of s on the imaginary axis. This gives us the *sinusoidal steady state response*, which fully characterizes the system. Plots of magnitude and phase of a transfer function versus frequency are called *frequency response* plots.

   At Bell Labs in the 1930s, H. W. Bode (1906–1982) developed a new method for displaying gain and phase. He plotted the logarithm of the gain (multiplied by 20) versus the logarithm of frequency and phase versus the logarithm of frequency. These plots have two immediate advantages over the linear plots. One is that using the log of frequency compresses that scale so that greater detail is available over a very wide range of frequencies.

More important, we are often analyzing systems in which transfer functions are multiplied together. A product of gains can be turned into a sum by taking logarithms. This is how we find the Bode magnitude plot of a product of transfer functions. We simply add the individual gain plots. Because the total phase of a product of complex numbers is already the addition of the individual phases, linear phase is plotted versus log frequency. The Bode magnitude and phase plots of the following transfer function are shown in Figure 1-1:

$$G(s) = \frac{1}{s\,(s+1)\,(s+2)}$$

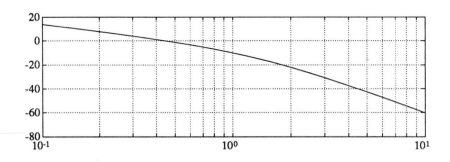

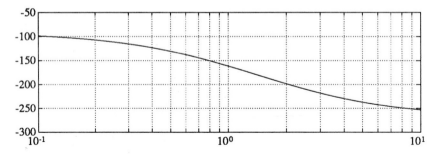

Figure 1-1 Bode magnitude and phase plot of $G(s)$.

Bode plots require two separate plots for each transfer function. If frequency is eliminated as a variable, then gain and phase can be shown on the same plot. There are many ways to present such data. Plots can be rectilinear or polar; gains can be linear or logarithmic. Before Bode's contribution, H. Nyquist (also of Bell Labs) published a paper on the use of linear magnitude polar plots in systems analysis. The polar, or Nyquist, diagram shows the frequency variations of the magnitude and phase of a transfer function as an ordered pair on the complex plane. At a given frequency, the gain and phase are found. The gain determines the distance from the origin of the complex plane, and the phase determines the angle from the positive real axis. Figure 1-2 shows the Nyquist plot for $G(j\omega)$. The Nyquist plot can also be constructed by plotting $\mathrm{Im}G(j\omega)$ versus $\mathrm{Re}G(j\omega)$, where $G(j\omega) = |G| \cos \angle G + j\,|G| \sin \angle G$.

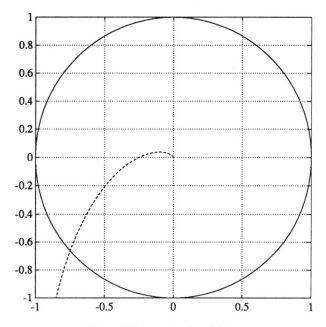

Figure 1-2 Nyquist plot of $G(s)$.

We will discuss other plots as appropriate. A major benefit of the Bode and Nyquist plots is that they allow us to predict closed loop behavior by examining the open loop system. This will be discussed in Section 1.8.

1.3 Convolution and the Impulse Response

Convolution is a fundamental concept in systems analysis. It is a time domain technique that provides the basis for transfer function analysis. Its use in a system of any complexity requires a computer; for this reason convolution has not been greatly used in classical control. Convolution is the basis for modern control analysis, however, and so will be reviewed here.

The zero-state response of a linear time invariant system can be represented as

$$Y(s) = H(s)X(s)$$

where $H(s)$ is the system transfer function. The output, $Y(s)$, is the Laplace transform of

$$y(t) = \int_{-\infty}^{\infty} h(\tau)\, x(t-\tau)\, d\tau = \int_{-\infty}^{\infty} x(\tau)\, h(t-\tau)\, d\tau$$

The right-hand sides of the above equation are both known as the convolution integral. The equation can be abbreviated as

$$y(t) = h(t) * x(t) = x(t) * h(t)$$

where $x(t)$ is an arbitrary input (we will discuss $h(t)$ shortly). The convolution integral can also be used in time-varying systems. Remember, we cannot use Laplace transforms for time-varying systems. This makes the convolution integral more applicable than transform techniques. For a time-varying system, the convolution integral becomes

$$y(t) = \int_{-\infty}^{\infty} h(t, \tau) \, x(\tau) \, d\tau.$$

If we limit our discussion to time invariant systems, we can find $h(t)$ for a given system by using Laplace transforms. If the input to the system is an impulse, $\delta(t)$, then $X(s) = 1$ and

$$Y(s) = H(s) \cdot 1$$

The inverse Laplace transform leads to the impulse response

$$y(t) = h(t)$$

This leads to the very powerful conclusion that for a linear time invariant system, the system transfer function is the Laplace transform of its impulse response. This property is used in system identification. As an example of the use of the impulse response and the convolution integral, we will find the step response of the first order system represented by

$$H(s) = \frac{100}{s + 3}$$

The impulse response of the system is $100 \, e^{-3t} \, u(t)$. The step response is found as

$$y(t) = e^{-3t} u(t) * u(t) = \int_{-\infty}^{\infty} e^{-3\tau} u(\tau) \, u(t - \tau) \, d\tau$$

The unit steps change the limits of integration to 0 and t, so we get

$$y(t) = \int_{0}^{t} e^{-3\tau} \, d\tau = \frac{1}{3}(1 - e^{-3t}) \quad t \geq 0$$

The output of this system to any input can be found in a similar manner by replacing the unit step with the input of interest and using a table of integrals or a computer simulation program.

Higher order systems can also be analyzed using this technique. The transfer function of an nth order system can be expanded as

$$H(s) = \frac{R_1}{s - p_1} + \dots + \frac{R_n}{s - p_n}$$

where p_i may be complex, and we assume, again for simplicity, that there are no repeated roots. The impulse response is, therefore,

$$h(t) = (R_1 e^{p_1 t} + \dots + R_n e^{p_n t}) u(t)$$

As you know, if there is a complex pair of poles, the corresponding impulse response is a damped sinusoid. Because integration is additive, it is a relatively simple matter to extend the first order example to the nth order example. An alternative approach is to represent the nth order system with a first order matrix equation. In this case, the impulse response is an exponential raised to a matrix power and, with certain modifications, similar equations discussed here can be used. This is the basis of state space analysis and will be discussed further in Chapter 5.

1.4 Stability

A control engineer must always consider the stability of a system under study or design. There are many definitions of stability; the *IEEE Standard Dictionary of Electrical and Electronics Terms* has two and a half pages of definitions for stability. For now, however, we define a stable system as one in which the output of the system does not grow without bound for any initial condition (natural response) or for any bounded input. To avoid confusion, we will use stability to refer only to the behavior of the natural response. The second type is commonly known as *bounded input–bounded output* (BIBO) stability.

1.4.1 Stability of the Zero-Input Response: Asymptotic Stability

Consider the ZIR of a system. This is determined only by the system's characteristic equation and its initial conditions. That is,

$$Y(s) = \frac{IC(s)}{D(s)}$$

Recall that the roots of the characteristic equation are called system modes. There are three possibilities.

    1. $\text{Re}(p_i) < 0$ for all i

where p_i are the roots of the characteristic equation. In this case, $y(t) \to 0$ as $t \to \infty$ and the system is *asymptotically stable*.

    2. $\text{Re}(p_i) > 0$ for any i

Now, $y(t) \to \infty$ as $t \to \infty$, and the system is *unstable*.

    3. $\text{Re}(p_i) = 0$ for any i

This means that a root of the characteristic equation is zero or purely imaginary. In this case, the output either remains constant or is sinusoidal. Therefore, the output neither returns to zero nor goes to infinity. This is known as *marginal stability*. If the roots are repeated and have zero real parts, the system is unstable. This can be seen from the following examples:

$$H_1(s) = \frac{1}{s} \qquad\qquad H_2(s) = \frac{1000}{s^2 + 100} \qquad\qquad H_3(s) = \frac{1}{s^2}$$

Because the behavior of the ZIR is similar to the system's impulse response, we can examine stability by finding the impulse response of each system:

$$h_1(t) = u(t) \qquad\qquad h_2(t) = 100 \cos 10t u(t) \qquad\qquad h_3(t) = tu(t)$$

The systems represented by $H_1(s)$ and $H_2(s)$ are marginally stable because their impulse responses neither decay nor grow without bound. Conversely, the system represented by $H_3(s)$ is clearly unstable. This leads to the following: A system with a simple mode at the origin or single pairs of complex modes on the $j\omega$ axis is marginally stable. Multiple modes at the origin or on the $j\omega$ indicate an unstable system.

1.4.2 Stability of the Zero-State Response: BIBO Stability

We now consider the stability of ZSR of systems. The output of a linear time invariant system with general input $x(t)$ is given by the convolution integral

$$y(t) = \int_{-\infty}^{\infty} h(\tau) x(t - \tau) \, d\tau$$

If the input is bounded (i.e., $|x(t)| \leq M < \infty$), then

$$|y(t)| = |\int_{-\infty}^{\infty} h(\tau) \, x(t - \tau) \, d\tau \,| \leq M \,|\int_{-\infty}^{\infty} h(\tau) \, d\tau \,| \leq M \int_{-\infty}^{\infty} |h(\tau)| \, d\tau$$

Therefore, the system is BIBO stable if and only if

$$\int_{-\infty}^{\infty} |h(\tau)| \, d\tau < \infty$$

Mathematically this means the impulse response is absolutely integrable (also known as an L_I function).

We state, without formal proof, that a system is BIBO stable if and only if all poles of the system lie in the open left half plane (LHP). If any pole lies in the right half plane (RHP), the system is unstable. Poles on the $j\omega$ axis require special attention. Is a marginally stable system BIBO stable? The answer is no. Consider the step response of $H_1(s)$:

$$\frac{1}{s} H_1(s) = \frac{1}{s^2} \rightarrow tu(t)$$

Because the unit step is bounded and this system's output is unbounded, $H_1(s)$ is not BIBO stable.

It appears that the two definitions of stability (asymptotic and BIBO) are the same. This is a subtle point and needs some care. Asymptotic stability is determined by the modes, which are the roots of the characteristic equation. BIBO stability depends on the poles, however. In some cases, we may encounter a transfer function that is not coprime (i.e., there are pole-zero cancellations). Technically, poles are computed after the transfer function is reduced and any common terms are canceled out. Therefore, some of the modes may not appear as poles. We conclude that asymptotic stability implies BIBO stability but not vice versa. The definitions are equivalent only in the case of coprime transfer functions. The next example illustrates the point:

$$H(s) = \frac{(s - 1)}{(s - 1)\,(s + 2)}$$

The modes are at $\{1, -2\}$, but the system has only one pole at $\{-2\}$. By the way, if you think the system has a pole at $\{1\}$, use L'Hospitals's Rule to verify that such is not the case. Therefore, the system is BIBO stable. Because of the RHP mode at $\{1\}$, however, it is not stable in the asymptotic stability sense. Such contradictory answers are common whenever we encounter transfer functions that are not coprime. We will see later that such cases are rare and pathological.

1.5 First and Second Order Systems

We will discuss time and frequency response characterization of first and second order systems in this section.

1.5.1 First Order Systems

The normalized (low frequency gain = 1) first order transfer function is

$$G(s) = \frac{a}{s + a}$$

This system has a single real pole at $(-a)$ and has the frequency response shown in Figure 1-3. The *bandwidth* of a low pass system (control systems are essentially low pass) is defined as the frequency where the magnitude drops by a factor of ($\frac{1}{\sqrt{2}} = 0.707 = -3$ dB) of its DC value (i.e., gain at zero or low frequency). As you can see from Figure 1-3, the bandwidth of the first order system is equal to the magnitude of the pole:

$$BW = |a|$$

The time response of the output, $y(t)$, can be found by taking the inverse Laplace transform of $Y(s)$. When done by hand, we use the partial fraction expansion technique. The first order step response is given by

$$Y(s) = \frac{1}{s} \frac{a}{s+a} = \frac{1}{s} - \frac{1}{s+a}$$

The inverse Laplace transform yields the step response

$$y(t) = (1 - e^{-at}) \, u(t)$$

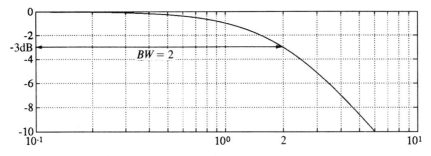

Figure 1-3 Magnitude response of first order system for $a = 2$.

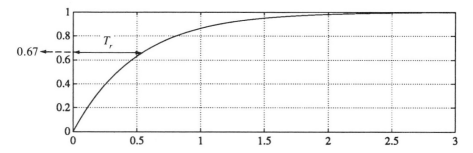

Figure 1-4 Step response of first order system for $a = 2$.

The first order step response is plotted in Figure 1-4. We can see that the time constant of the first order step response ($\tau = 1/a$) is the inverse of the system bandwidth. The larger (smaller) the bandwidth, the faster (slower) the step response. Bandwidth is a direct measure of system susceptibility to noise. It is also an indicator of the system speed of response. The inverse relationship between bandwidth and speed of response also holds approximately for higher order systems. This demonstrates a design tradeoff. A very fast system requires a large bandwidth. This means the system will be quite susceptible to high frequency noise, and unless additional filters are placed at appropriate points in the system, the noise may cause havoc in the system.

There are two additional performance criteria that are used to describe the step response: *rise time* and *delay time*. Rise time, T_r, is a measure of the initial speed of the transient response and is defined as the time it takes the step response to go from 10% to 90% of its final, or steady state value. Delay time, T_d, is defined as the time it takes the step response to reach 50% of its final value. Do not confuse delay time with a pure time delay [$f(t) = g(t - T)$]. For the first order step response we can derive the following simple formulas for rise time and delay time:

$$T_r = \frac{2.2}{a} = 2.2\,\tau \quad \text{and} \quad T_d = \frac{0.69}{a} = 0.69\,\tau$$

1.5.2 Second Order Systems

The second order transfer function is very important in control design. System specifications are often given assuming that the system is second order. For higher order systems, we can often use dominant pole techniques to approximate the system with a second order transfer function. Let us assume that

$$G(s) = \frac{\omega_n^2}{s^2 + 2\,\zeta\,\omega_n\,s + \omega_n^2}$$

where ζ is the damping ratio and ω_n is the natural frequency of the system. The poles are at

$$s_{1,2} = -\zeta\,\omega_n \pm j\,\omega_n\,\sqrt{1-\zeta^2}$$

Note that the poles can either both be real ($\zeta > 1$, overdamped), real and identical ($\zeta = 1$, critically damped), or complex conjugates ($0 < \zeta < 1$, underdamped).

The Bode magnitude plot of the underdamped case is shown in Figure 1-5. The plot shows a peak resonance at $\omega = \omega_r$, with a peak magnitude of M_r, where

$$\omega_r = \omega_n\,\sqrt{1-2\,\zeta^2} \quad \text{for } \zeta \le \frac{1}{\sqrt{2}}$$

$$M_r = \frac{1}{2\,\zeta\,\sqrt{1-\zeta^2}} \quad \text{for } \zeta \le \frac{1}{\sqrt{2}}$$

Note that the peak magnitude depends only on ζ.

The bandwidth, or 3-dB frequency, of the second order system is

$$BW = \omega_n\,[1 - 2\,\zeta^2 + (2 - 4\,\zeta^2 + 4\,\zeta^4)^{1/2}]^{1/2}$$

As ζ varies from 0 to 1, BW varies from $1.55\omega_n$ to $0.64\omega_n$. Control engineers, however, usually try to keep the damping ratio of their systems at approximately 0.707; for this value of ζ, $BW = \omega_n$. In fact, for most design considerations, we assume that the bandwidth of a second order all pole system can be approximated by ω_n.

The general all pole second order step response is

$$Y(s) = \frac{1}{s}\,G(s) = \frac{1}{s}\,\frac{\omega_n^2}{s^2 + 2\,\zeta\,\omega_n s + \omega_n^2}$$

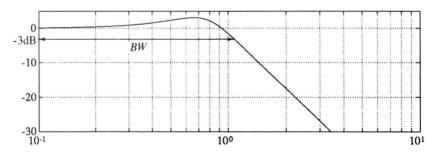

Figure 1-5 Bode magnitude plot of second order system, $G(s) = \dfrac{1}{s^2 + 0.6s + 1}$.

Partial fraction expansion yields

$$Y(s) = \frac{1}{s} - \frac{s + 2\,\zeta\omega_n}{(s + \zeta\omega_n)^2 + \omega_n^2\,(1 - \zeta^2)}$$

This leads to the step response of $y(t)$:

$$y(t) = 1 - \frac{e^{-t/\tau}}{\sqrt{1 - \zeta^2}}\,\cos(\omega_d\,t - \varphi_d), \qquad t \geq 0$$

where

$$|\sigma| = \zeta\,\omega_n \text{ and } \tau = 1/|\sigma|, \quad \omega_d = \omega_n\,\sqrt{1 - \zeta^2}, \quad \varphi_d = \sin^{-1}\zeta$$

Figure 1-6 shows an underdamped second order step response with some important design criteria: overshoot, settling time, rise time, and delay time. To find overshoot (usually described as percent overshoot), determine the time of the first peak, T_p. The peak value of $y(t)$ is then found (denoted by M_p); finally the percent overshoot, POS, is calculated as $100\,[(M_p - y(\infty))/y(\infty)]$. The results are

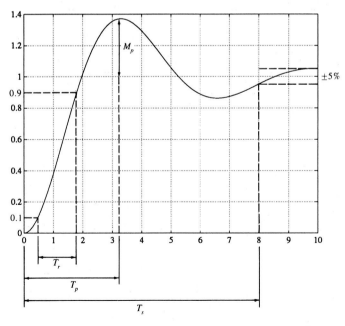

Figure 1-6 Step response of second order system, $G(s) = \dfrac{1}{s^2 + 0.6s + 1}$.

$$T_p = \frac{\pi}{\omega_d} = \frac{\pi}{\omega_n \sqrt{1-\zeta^2}} , \quad M_p = 1 + \exp\left(\frac{-\zeta\pi}{\sqrt{1-\zeta^2}}\right)$$

$$POS = 100 \exp\left(\frac{-\zeta\pi}{\sqrt{1-\zeta^2}}\right)$$

The overshoot is strictly a function of ζ; remember peak resonance in the magnitude frequency plot is also a function of ζ. The settling time is determined by the time constant of the envelope ($\tau = 1/\zeta\omega_n$). If we use the rule of thumb that an exponential decays in four to five time constants, then

$$T_s(\pm 2\%) \approx 4\tau = \frac{4}{\sigma} \quad \text{and} \quad T_s(\pm 1\%) \approx 4.6\tau = \frac{4.6}{\sigma}$$

If, as is often the case, overshoot and settling time are both given as desired system specifications, we first determine ζ from the allowable overshoot and then find ω_n from the settling time. There are no simple formulas for rise time and delay time; they are dependent on both ζ and ω_n. In addition, delay time is a function of the initial value of $\dot{y}(t)$; an output with an initial velocity will begin to rise before an output with zero initial velocity. For a damping ratio of 0.5, however, rise time is approximately equal to [FPE91]

$$T_r \approx \frac{1.8}{\omega_n} \quad \text{for} \quad \zeta = 0.5$$

Other approximations can be used also, but, as a general rule, we note that rise time is inversely proportional to ω_n.

Now that we have seen how ζ and ω_n affect such parameters as overshoot and settling time, we turn to the complex plane. In Figure 1-7, the vertical line is the contour of constant damping σ. Because the step response settling time is inversely proportional to σ, all second order systems that have poles along this contour will have the same settling time. To decrease (increase) the settling time, we must move the real part of the poles to the left (right).

The horizontal line in Figure 1-7 is the contour of constant ω_d, the oscillation frequency. It is sometimes important to control this variable to avoid exciting a resonant frequency of the structure being controlled.

The angle θ of the line from the origin through the pole in Figure 1-7 is the contour of constant ζ. This is easily shown by finding θ:

$$\theta = \tan^{-1}\frac{\sqrt{1-\zeta^2}}{\zeta} = \sin^{-1}\sqrt{1-\zeta^2} = \cos^{-1}\zeta$$

$$\zeta = \cos\theta$$

To increase (decrease) the damping of a second order system, decrease (increase) θ.

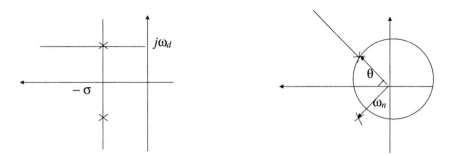

Figure 1-7 Complex plane showing different contours.

The radius in Figure 1-7 can be found from simple trigonometry to be ω_n. Therefore, the constant contour for ω_n is the circle shown. To increase (decrease) ω_n, increase (decrease) the radius of the circle.

To demonstrate the effects of varying pole locations in a canonical second order underdamped system, we consider the following:

$$G(s) = \frac{\omega_n^2}{s^2 + 2\zeta\omega_n s + \omega_n^2} = \frac{\omega_d^2 + \sigma^2}{s^2 + 2\sigma s + (\omega_d^2 + \sigma^2)}$$

Case I: Effects of σ $\omega_d = 1, \sigma = \{0.5, 1, 5\}$

The poles move horizontally deeper into the LHP while keeping their imaginary parts fixed. We expect the following effects:

- Settling time decreases because it is inversely proportional to σ.
- Rise time decreases because the distance of the pole to origin increases and rise time is inversely proportional to this distance.
- Overshoot decreases because θ decreases, which means that ζ increases.
- Peak time remains fixed because ω_d is fixed.
- Bandwidth increases because it is proportional to ω_n . Note that bandwidth and rise time are inversely proportional.

The relevant step responses and Bode magnitude plots are shown in Figure 1-8.

Case II: Effects of ω_d $\sigma = 1$, $\omega_d = \{0.5, 1, 5\}$

The poles move up vertically, whereas their real parts remain fixed at 1. In this case, settling time is fixed. Overshoot and bandwidth increase; peak time and rise time decrease. The plots are shown in Figure 1-9.

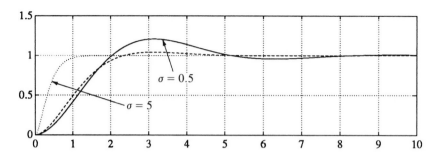

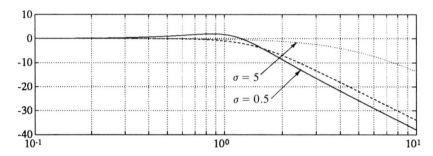

Figure 1-8 Step and magnitude responses for case I.

Case III: Effects of ω_n $\zeta = \dfrac{1}{\sqrt{2}}$, $\omega_n = \{\dfrac{\sqrt{2}}{2}, \sqrt{2}, 5\sqrt{2}\}$

The poles are moved radially outward along a line with angle of 45 degrees. Overshoot remains fixed while rise time, peak time, and settling time decrease. The bandwidth will increase. The plots are shown in Figure 1-10.

Case IV: Effects of ζ $\omega_n = \sqrt{2}$, $\theta = \{30, 45, 60 \text{ degrees}\}$

The poles are rotated along the perimeter of a circle of a fixed radius $\sqrt{2}$. Rise time is fixed, whereas overshoot and settling time increase and peak time decreases. The plots are shown in Figure 1-11.

1.5.3 Effects of Adding Poles and Zeros

The effects discussed earlier are limited to the case of second order systems in canonical form. It also holds for higher-order systems with zeros as long as the system has a pair of dominant complex poles; i.e., all other poles and zeros are located deep in the LHP. Note that a system with RHP poles is unstable, and RHP zeros will cause

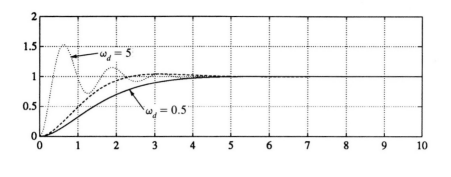

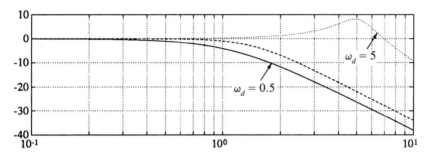

Figure 1-9 Step and magnitude responses for case II.

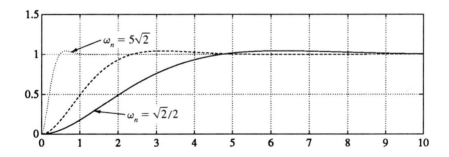

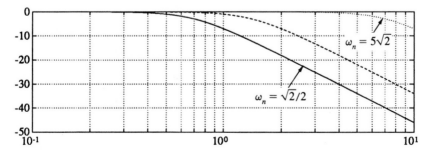

Figure 1-10 Step and magnitude response for case III.

17

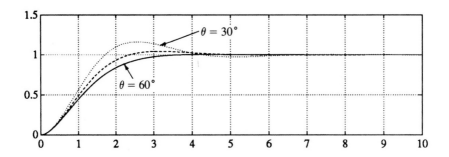

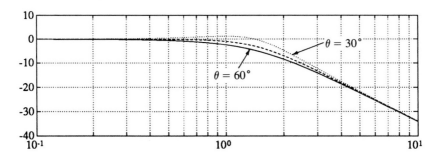

Figure 1-11 Step and magnitude response for case IV.

spurious effects. What effect does a zero have on the second order step response? To determine this, we have plotted the step response of the following transfer function:

$$G(s) = \frac{z\,s + 1}{s^2 + s + 1}$$

where values for z are $\{0.2624, 0.6122, 1.4286, 3.3333\}$. As you can see in Figure 1-12, as the zero approaches the origin (i.e., z approaches infinity), overshoot is increased dramatically, rise time and peak time decrease, and bandwidth and the resonant peak increase. The effects of an added pole can be seen by examining

$$G(s) = \frac{1}{(p\,s + 1)\,(s^2 + s + 1)}$$

The values of p are the same values as z earlier. As the pole approaches the origin, the real pole will dominate the response, and the system effectively behaves like a first order system. The overshoot decreases to zero, whereas rise time and peak time increase.

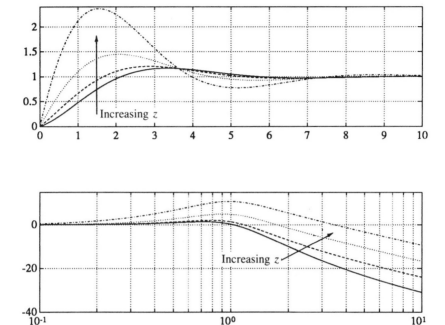

Figure 1-12 Step and magnitude response showing the effects of an added zero.

The system bandwidth decreases, and the resonant peak disappears. These effects are shown in Figure 1-13.

It is important for a control engineer to have a very good understanding of the effects of pole-zero locations in systems. A more extensive discussion of the effects of adding zeros and poles to transfer functions will be presented in Chapter 4 in problem 4.2.

1.6 Feedback Control

Open loop systems perform adequately only if the model of the plant or process is very accurate, if plant parameters change in a predetermined manner, and if there are no external disturbances. Because these conditions are rarely met, most systems use feedback control. Feedback has many properties, some of which will be discussed in this section.

1.6.1 Feedback Properties

Simple feedback control systems are modeled in Figure 1-14. The controller is denoted by $K(s)$, and $G(s)$ denotes the plant. Models for actuators and other components in the forward path can be included in the plant model. The forward path transfer function, KG, is the

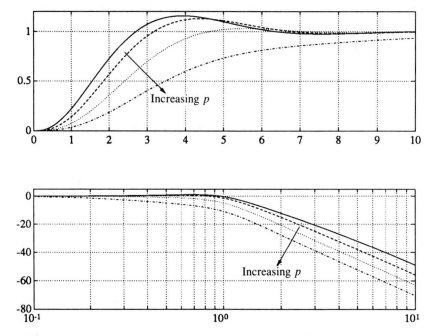

Figure 1-13 Step and magnituded response showing the effects of an added pole.

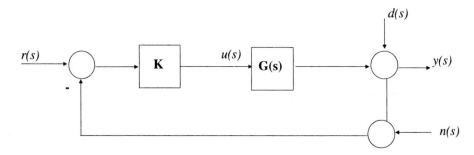

Figure 1-14 Block diagram feedback system containing disturbance and noise.

loop gain (also called the *open loop transfer function* or *return ratio*). The system in general has several inputs:

   r = reference input, which the system is desired to follow or track

   d = disturbance inputs, known or unknown inputs that could be random or deterministic

   Disturbances may represent actual physical disturbances acting on the system such as wind gusts disturbing aircrafts, disturbances owing to actuators such as motors, or uncertainties resulting from model errors in plant or actuator. Model uncertainties include neglected nonlinearities in plant or actuator, and neglected or unknown modes in the system.

n = sensor or measurement noise, which is introduced into the system via sensors and are usually random high frequency signals

A properly designed control system must track reference inputs with small error and reject disturbance and noise inputs. The contribution of general disturbances to the output must be small. The output of the closed loop system is

$$y(s) = \frac{K\,G(s)}{1 + K\,G(s)}\, r(s) + \frac{1}{1 + K\,G(s)}\, d(s) - \frac{K\,G(s)}{1 + K\,G(s)}\, n(s)$$

If we define the tracking error as $e = r - y$, we get

$$e(s) = \frac{1}{1 + K\,G(s)}\, r(s) - \frac{1}{1 + K\,G(s)}\, d(s) + \frac{K\,G(s)}{1 + K\,G(s)}\, n(s)$$

Finally, the actuator output (i.e., the plant input) is given by

$$u(s) = \frac{K}{1 + K\,G(s)}\, (\, r(s) - d(s) - n(s)\,)$$

Several quantities appear frequently in the above relationships and are defined subsequently:

$$J(s) = 1 + K\,G(s) \qquad \textit{Return Difference}$$

$$S(s) = \frac{1}{1 + K\,G(s)} = \frac{1}{J(s)} \qquad \textit{Sensitivity}$$

$$T(s) = \frac{K\,G(s)}{1 + K\,G(s)} \qquad \textit{Complementary Sensitivity}$$

It can be seen that for all frequencies: $S(s) + T(s) = 1$

To understand the concept of return difference, consider the block diagram in Figure 1-14. Break the loop at any point, and apply a unity input. At the output of the loop breaking point, we measure the returned signal as $- KG(s)$. The difference between the injected signal and the returned signal is the return difference, which is $1 - (-KG(s)) = 1 + KG(s)$. Bode introduced it as a quantitative measure of the amount of feedback. Using the above notation, we can rewrite the output relationships as

$$y(s) = S(s)\, d(s) + T(s)\, [\, r(s) - n(s)]$$

$$e(s) = S(s) \, [\, r(s) - d(s) \,] + T(s) \, n(s)$$

$$u(s) = K \, S(s) \, [\, r(s) - d(s) - n(s) \,]$$

We are now ready to draw some general conclusions.

1. *Disturbance rejection*: The sensitivity must be small to reduce the effects of disturbances. This can be accomplished by keeping the loop gain large; i.e., $|KG(s)| \gg 1$.

2. *Good tracking*: To keep e small, sensitivity must be small. Therefore, tracking and disturbance rejection are compatible specifications.

3. *Noise immunity*: For proper suppression of noise, we need to keep the complementary sensitivity small. Because S and T must add to unity, we conclude that noise immunity and the previous requirements are conflicting objectives.

4. *Bounded actuator signals*: All physical systems have limits on their inputs and outputs. Actuator outputs must be limited to avoid damage to the plant. Also, actuators produce limited outputs (motors can produce a limited amount of torque, and amplifiers will saturate beyond certain limits). So generally, the signal $u(s)$ must be kept within certain specified limits. To keep the controller output within specified limits to prevent saturation problems, we need to limit $|K \, S(s)|$. If the loop gain is large, however, we get

$$K \, S(s) = \frac{K}{1 + K \, G(s)} \approx \frac{1}{G(s)}$$

Because most physical systems are strictly proper, their transfer functions roll off at high frequencies. This means that at high frequencies, $|G(s)|$ is small so the actuator signals can be large. Hence the gain at high frequencies must be adjusted to prevent saturation.

Typically we require the loop gain to be large at low frequencies to satisfy tracking requirements and rejection of low frequency disturbances. At high frequencies, the loop gain is kept low to suppress high frequency noise. Over the mid-frequency range, the gain is shaped to satisfy stability margin requirements. The process of adjusting the loop gain to satisfy the above objectives is called *loop shaping*.

Sensitivity of the overall system to specific parameter changes can also be defined. This is called *differential sensitivity* and is defined by

$$S_x^y = \frac{\partial y / y}{\partial x / x} = \frac{x}{y} \frac{\partial y}{\partial x}$$

which is read as "the sensitivity of y with respect to x." This function measures the relative change in y owing to a relative change in x. For example, suppose we want to find the differential sensitivity of the closed loop system in Figure 1-14 with respect to changes in gain K.

The closed loop transfer function (same as complementary sensitivity defined earlier) and its sensitivity are given by

$$T(s) = \frac{K\,G(s)}{1 + K\,G(s)}$$

$$S_K^T = \frac{K}{T}\frac{\partial T}{\partial K} = \frac{1}{1 + K\,G} \rightarrow 0 \quad \text{for } |K\,G| \text{ large}$$

Note that this quantity is the same as the sensitivity transfer function defined earlier. If K is located in the feedback path instead of the forward path, we get

$$S_K^T = \frac{K}{T}\frac{\partial T}{\partial K} = \frac{-K\,G}{1 + K\,G} \rightarrow -1 \quad \text{for } |K\,G| \text{ large}$$

We conclude that feedback reduces the effects of parameter variations with respect to elements in the forward path. The overall system is still very sensitive to elements in the feedback path, however.

Another property of feedback is linearization. Given a nonlinear system, we can use feedback control to reduce the effects of nonlinearities within the system. If the nonlinearity is perfectly known, we can use a nonlinear controller to linearize the system and then use a linear controller to shape its response. This is called *feedback linearization*. Consider the example

$$\dot{x} = x^2 + x + u$$

using the following nonlinear controller

$$u = -x^2 + \bar{u}$$

we get a linear system

$$\dot{x} = x + \bar{u}$$

using the linear control law

$$\bar{u} = -k\,x \quad \rightarrow \quad \dot{x} = (1 - k)\,x$$

we obtain a stable system for $k > 1$.

Feedback is also frequently used to stabilize unstable systems. You have to be aware, however, that feedback itself can destabilize otherwise stable systems. So use it with caution.

In summary, we emphasize that even though feedback has many other properties as well (modifies system gain, bandwidth, speed, etc.), the main reasons it is generally used are stabilization, disturbance rejection, and protection against model uncertainties.

1.6.2 Closed Loop Stability

We have already seen how the stability of a system depends on the location of the system's poles. The closed loop poles can be found using the computer. In parametric cases, in which the location of the closed loop poles depends on some parameter like K, we can use root locus (described later) to find all of them for all values of the parameter. The *Routh–Hurwitz* test is a technique for determining how many closed loop poles are located in the RHP. Although its use is outdated if control system computer programs are available, it is still an effective and easy method for hand calculations.

Routh–Hurwitz Stability Test

We demonstrate the Routh–Hurwitz technique with the following example:

$$K\,G(s)\,H(s) = \frac{K}{s^4 + s^3 + 11\,s^2 + s + 0.5}$$

The characteristic equation is given by

$$s^4 + s^3 + 11\,s^2 + s + K + 0.5 = 0$$

The Routh array is

$$
\begin{array}{c|ccc}
s^4 & 1 & 11 & K+0.5 \\
s^3 & 1 & 1 & \\
s^2 & 10 & K+0.5 & \\
s^1 & -K+9.5 & & \\
s^0 & K+0.5 & &
\end{array}
$$

The number of poles in the RHP is equal to the number of sign changes in the first column. For stability, there must be no sign changes. From row 4, $K < 9.5$, whereas from row 5, $K > -0.5$. Therefore, $-0.5 < K < 9.5$ would lead to a stable system. If $9.5 < K$, there would be two sign changes and, therefore, two poles in the RHP. If, conversely, $K < -0.5$, there would be one sign change and one pole in the RHP. The Routh array occasionally leads to zeros in the first column or an all-zero row. Consult a control textbook in the references to see how to deal with these situations.

1.6.3 Steady State Error

In many control system designs, we are specifically interested in the final, or steady state, value of the output. This is known as steady state accuracy. Ideally, in the steady state, the output, $y(t)$, equals the command signal, $r(t)$, and the error is zero. This ideal situation is rarely met, and so we need to be able to determine the steady state error for any system. The steady state error is defined as

$$e_{ss} = \lim_{t \to \infty} e(t) = \lim_{t \to \infty} [r(t) - y(t)]$$

For unity feedback systems, and only for unity feedback systems, the error is the comparator output signal. For nonunity feedback systems, this is not the case. For unity feedback systems, we can determine the steady state error by examining the open loop transfer function $KG(s)$. For unity feedback, we can write

$$E(s) = R(s) - Y(s) = R(s) - G(s)E(s)$$

so

$$E(s) = \frac{1}{1 + G(s)} R(s)$$

The final value theorem tells us that (assuming closed loop stability)

$$e_{ss} = \lim_{s \to 0} sE(s) = \lim_{s \to 0} \frac{s}{1 + G(s)} R(s)$$

We are interested in the steady state error for step, ramp, parabolic, and higher order polynomial inputs, i.e.,

$$r(t) = \frac{t^n}{n!} \rightarrow R(s) = \frac{1}{s^{n+1}} , \quad n = 0, 1, 2, \ldots\ldots$$

Therefore,

$$e_{ss} = \lim_{s \to 0} \frac{1}{s^n + s^n G(s)}$$

For a unit step input ($n = 0$), $e_{ss} = \dfrac{1}{1 + G(0)}$

For higher order polynomial inputs, $e_{ss} = \lim_{s \to 0} \dfrac{1}{s^n G(s)}$

The steady state error obviously depends on the structure of $G(s)$. For example, if $G(s)$ has no poles at the origin, then $G(0)$ is finite, which means that the step response error is finite, and all other response errors are infinite. We define the system *Type* as the order of the input polynomial that the closed loop system can track with finite error. If $G(s)$ has no poles at the origin, the closed loop system is Type 0 and can track a constant; one pole at the origin results in a Type 1 system that can track a ramp; two poles at the origin result in a Type 2 system that can track a parabola, etc.

Because we deal with many electromechanical systems, control engineers also define position, velocity, and acceleration error constants as follows:

$$K_p = G(0), \quad K_v = \lim_{s \to 0} sG(s), \quad K_a = \lim_{s \to 0} s^2 G(s)$$

Table 1-1 shows the steady state errors for Type 0, 1, and 2 systems.

Table 1-1 Steady State Errors for Polynomial Inputs			
System Type ⇒ Polynomial Degree ⇓	0	1	2
0	$\dfrac{1}{1+K_p}$	0	0
1	∞	$\dfrac{1}{K_v}$	0
2	∞	∞	$\dfrac{1}{K_a}$

System type and steady state errors can also be found directly from the closed loop transfer function. If the closed loop transfer function is given by

$$T(s) = \frac{b_m s^m + b_{m-1} s^{m-1} + \ldots + b_1 s + b_0}{s^n + a_{n-1} s^{n-1} + \ldots + a_1 s + a_0}$$

then the steady state error to a unit step is given by

$$e_{ss} = \lim_{s \to 0} [1 - T(s)] = \left| \frac{a_0 - b_0}{a_0} \right|$$

For a Type 1 system, $e_{ss} = 0$, so $a_0 = b_0$. Likewise for a Type 2 system we can find the condition to be : $a_0 = b_0$ and $a_1 = b_1$.

1.7 Root Locus

Let us examine the effect of feedback on pole and zero location. We assume that $G(s) = N_1(s)/D_1(s)$ and $H(s) = N_2(s)/D_2(s)$ so that the closed loop transfer function can be written as (refer to Figure 1-15)

$$T(s) = \frac{KN_1(s)/D_1(s)}{1 + K[N_1(s)/D_1(s)][N_2(s)/D_2(s)]}$$

or

$$T(s) = \frac{K N_1(s) D_2(s)}{D_1(s) D_2(s) + K N_1(s)N_2(s)}$$

The poles of the closed loop system, therefore, are found from

$$1 + K G(s) H(s) = D_1(s) D_2(s) + K N_1(s) N_2(s) = 0$$

We will be describing several techniques to find information about closed loop behavior given the open loop transfer function. The closed loop zeros are another matter. They are clearly the zeros of the plant and poles of the feedback transfer functions assuming there are no pole-zero cancellations.

The root locus is a plot of the poles of closed loop transfer function, $T(s)$, as any parameter; e.g., K, varies from 0 to ∞. The most straightforward method, used by many computer programs, is to simply vary K and use a polynomial root solver to find the poles. Techniques developed early in control analysis history, however, still give important insights into the design of closed loop systems. For this reason, we will describe some of them here.

The characteristic equation of $T(s)$ is

$$1 + K G(s) H(s) = 0 \quad \rightarrow \quad D_1(s) D_2(s) + K N_1(s) N_2(s) = 0$$

For K small, the right side yields

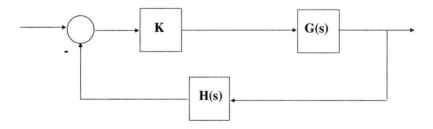

Figure 1-15 Block diagram of a feedback control system.

$$D_1(s)D_2(s) = 0$$

These solutions are the poles of $G(s)H(s)$. For K large, we get

$$KN_1(s)N_2(s) = 0$$

The solutions of which are the zeros of $G(s)H(s)$. Hence, we have our first rule. The root locus begins at the poles of $G(s)H(s)$ and ends at the zeros of $G(s)H(s)$. The obvious starting point, therefore, is the pole-zero plot of the loop gain $G(s)H(s)$. Most of the other rules can be derived if we first rearrange the characteristic equation as

$$KG(s)H(s) = -1$$

This implies that

$$|KGH| = 1 \quad \text{and} \quad \angle GH = \pm(2k+1)\pi$$

The properties in this equation are the basis of most stability studies. For a point, s^*, in the s-plane to be part of the root locus, the total angle from the poles and zeros of $G(s)H(s)$ to s^* must be $\pm(2k+1)\pi$. The gain K that corresponds to this point is found by $K = 1/|G(s^*)H(s^*)|$.

A partial listing of root locus rules sufficient for quick sketches is given subsequently for $0 < K < \infty$.

1. Loci start at poles and end at zeros of $G(s)H(s)$, where poles and zeros at infinity are also included.

2. Loci exist on the real axis only to the left of an odd number of poles and zeros.

3. Loci approach asymptotes with angles of $\dfrac{(2k+1)\pi}{(n-m)}$, where n is the number of finite poles, and m is the number of finite zeros of $G(s)H(s)$.

4. The asymptotes originate from a centroid on the real axis, σ, where

$$\sigma = \frac{\sum_i p_i - \sum_j z_j}{n-m}$$

As an example, the root locus of the open loop transfer function of the system shown below appears in Figure 1-16:

$$K\,G(s) = \frac{K}{s\,(s+1)\,(s+2)}$$

For $K > 6$, the root locus is in the RHP, indicating closed loop instability for these gains.

The changes in closed loop pole locations owing to changes in other system parameters can also be analyzed with the root locus technique. Consider a unity feedback system with a second order closed loop transfer function:

$$T(s) = \frac{10}{s^2 + bs + 20}$$

We can rearrange $T(s)$ as

$$T(s) = \frac{10}{s^2 + 20 + bs} = \frac{10/(s^2 + 20)}{1 + bs/(s^2 + 20)}$$

We can now treat $bs/(s^2 + 20)$ as $KG(s)H(s)$ and plot the root locus with b as the gain parameter.

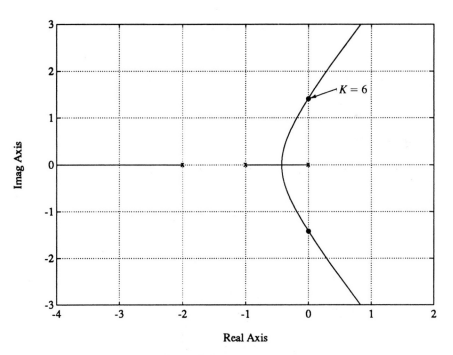

Figure 1-16 Root locus of $K\,G(s)$.

$$\boxed{\textbf{WARNING}}$$

It is important to note that the correct pole-zero plot that is used to construct the root locus is the pole-zero plot of the open loop transfer function (i.e., the loop gain) *KGH* and not the closed loop transfer function (*T= KG/*(1+*KGH*)). It has been observed many times that students learn the mechanics of root locus plotting, but do not quite understand the concept behind it and, hence, use the wrong transfer function. These types of conceptual errors may become accentuated when computer programs are used to plot root locus. An important aspect of classical control is to use the open loop transfer function to predict closed loop behavior.

1.7.1 Zero Degree Root Locus

There are instances in which we are interested in the closed loop poles as a parameter ranges over negative numbers. An equivalent situation is when we have positive feedback loops where the characteristic equation becomes

$$1 - KG(s)H(s) = 0$$

Rearranging this, we get

$$KG(s)\, H(s) = 1$$

Hence, the angle of *GH* becomes 0 or any multiple of 2π. This changes rules 2 and 3 and all other rules related to the angle criterion. Loci on the real axis now exist to the left of an even number of poles and zeros. Poles or zeros at positive infinity are now numbered as the zero position where zero is considered as an even number.

1.8 Frequency Response Analysis

Frequency response analysis has been at the heart of classical control. The fact that frequency response can be measured in the laboratory and used for analysis without relying on mathematical models (empirical models are frequently obtained from frequency response data) has been their traditional advantage. Time delays, ever present in process control applications, can also be easily handled by these techniques. Their graphical nature together with physical and intuitive appeal, their ability to predict closed loop response from open loop analysis, and many years of successful applications are the primary reasons frequency response techniques have survived and have now been generalized to handle multivariable systems.

1.8.1 Bode Plot

Bode plots have several uses. They are used to determine stability and relative stability, and are also used for design purposes. Again, the warning about the use of root locus is in order here. We can obtain the Bode plot of any transfer function, but we distinguish between open loop and closed loop Bode plots. You have to know how to interpret each plot and use them correctly. The Bode plot of the open loop transfer function (i.e., *KGH*) can be used to determine relative stability margins of closed loop stable systems. For ease of use, it is necessary that the open loop system itself be stable and *minimum phase*. By minimum phase, it is meant that the system has no zeros in the RHP (some authors define it as no poles or zeros in the RHP). The Bode plot should not be used to determine closed loop stability for nonminimum phase systems.

System Type can be determined by looking at the low frequency slope of the magnitude plot. For example, if the initial slope is −20 dB/dec, then the system is Type 1 (assuming unity feedback). Open loop Bode plots are also used for compensator design as described in Chapter 7. In fact, this is one of their main uses in control systems. Because gain and phase plots are additive, the effects of a compensator, *H*, can easily be determined. The Bode plots are shaped until desired specifications are met.

Bode plots of the closed loop transfer function [$T = KG/(1+KGH)$] can be used to determine the system bandwidth, which is a measure of both the filtering properties and speed of response of the system. The peak in the closed loop Bode plot is a reliable indicator of relative stability. The use of closed loop Bode plots in classical design has been very limited, however, because of the way *H* enters the equation.

The open and closed loop Bode plots provide complementary information, provided they are interpreted correctly.

1.8.2 Nyquist Plot and Stability Criterion

The Nyquist plot provides a powerful tool for determining the stability of systems. It is the plot of imaginary versus the real part (or a polar plot of magnitude and phase) of the *open loop transfer function*. However, the derivation of this technique is quite involved. We will present a brief review here.

Consider the gain *D(s)*. Without proof, we state the following:

$$Z_D = P_D + \vec{N}$$

where $\vec{N}$ is the number of *clockwise* encirclements of the origin, P_D is the number of poles of *D(s)* in the RHP, and Z_D is the number of zeros of *D(s)* in the RHP. For a counterclockwise traversal of the origin, $\vec{N}$ is negative. You should be aware that some authors reverse this definition. Note that poles and zeros of *D(s)* that are in the LHP, or on the $j\omega$ axis, do not affect the above equation.

Now, reconsider the closed loop transfer function (with $K = 1$):

$$T(s) = \frac{G(s)}{1 + G(s)\,H(s)}$$

Define the denominator of $T(s)$ as

$$T(s) = \frac{G(s)}{D(s)} \quad \text{so} \quad D(s) = 1 + G(s)\,H(s)$$

The poles of $T(s)$ are equal to the zeros of $D(s)$. We can now use the Nyquist plot of $D(s)$ and the previously stated result to find the zeros of $D(s)$. Note that the poles of $G(s)H(s)$ are the same as the poles of $D(s)$. We can now rewrite our result as

$$P_T = P_{GH} + \overrightarrow{N}$$

Rather than examine $D(s)$, we can examine $G(s)\,H(s) = D(s) - 1$. The point of interest is shifted from the origin to the $(-1,0)$ point. We draw the Nyquist plot of $G(s)H(s)$ and count the number of clockwise encirclements of the $(-1, 0)$ point. The number of poles of $T(s)$ in the RHP is equal to the number of encirclements plus the number of RHP poles of $G(s)H(s)$. We remind you that N is positive for a clockwise traversal and negative for a counterclockwise traversal.

Figure 1-2 shows the Nyquist plot for our example transfer function:

$$K\,G(s) = \frac{1}{s\,(s + 1)\,(s + 2)}, \quad K = 1$$

For this system, there are no open loop RHP poles, so that any clockwise encirclement of $(-1,0)$ indicates an unstable closed loop system. As you can see, for $K=1$ there is no encirclement of $(-1,0)$ so the closed loop system is stable.

1.8.3 Gain and Phase Margins

Because of model uncertainties, it is not merely sufficient for a system to be stable, but rather it must have adequate stability margins. Stable systems with low stability margins work only on paper; when implemented in real time, they are frequently unstable. The way uncertainty has been quantified in classical control is to assume that either gain changes or phase changes occur. Typically, systems are destabilized when their gain exceeds certain limits or if there is too much phase lag (i.e., negative phase associated with unmodeled poles or time delays). These tolerances of gain or phase uncertainty are called gain and phase margin.

Suppose a system is stable for $K < K_{max}$, then *gain margin* (GM, or more properly *upper* GM) is defined as

$$GM \mid _{dB} = 20 \log \frac{K_{max}}{K}$$

In some cases, such as systems that are open loop unstable, the system may become destabilized for low gain, so for stability we may have $K > K_{min}$. We can likewise define a *lower gain margin* (or *gain reduction margin* [GRM]) as

$$GRM \mid _{dB} = 20 \log \frac{K_{min}}{K}$$

Note that according to our definition, GM is positive, and GRM is negative for stability. GM is the factor by which the gain can be increased before the onset of instability. These measures can be computed using the Routh–Hurwitz test or found from the root locus. They can also be measured from open loop Bode and Nyquist plots, as shown for our example plant in Figures 1-17 and 1-18. The GM can be read off the Bode plot by measuring the distance to unity gain (i.e., 0 dB) when the phase is −180 degrees. The frequency where the phase is −180 degrees is called the *phase crossover frequency* and is denoted by ω_{pc}.

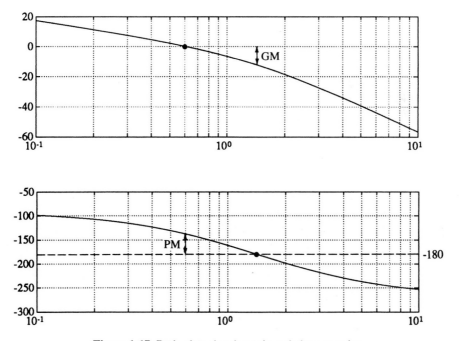

Figure 1-17 Bode plots showing gain and phase margins.

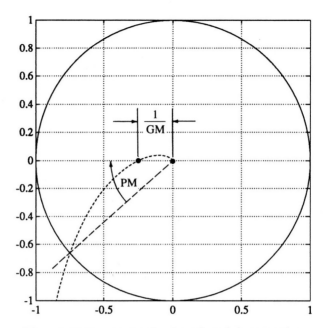

Figure 1-18 Nyquist plot showing gain and phase margins.

Phase margin is defined as the minimum amount of phase lag that can be added to the system to destabilize it. This happens when

$$1 + KG(s)H(s) = 0 \text{, or } KG(s)H(s) = -1$$

$$\text{i.e., } |KG(j\omega)H(j\omega)| = 1 \quad \text{and} \quad \angle KG(j\omega)H(j\omega) = \pm \pi$$

The angular distance to $-\pi$ when the magnitude is unity is the phase margin; i.e.,

$$PM = \pi + \angle KG(j\omega_{gc})H(j\omega_{gc}) \quad \text{when} \quad |KG(j\omega_{gc})H(j\omega_{gc})| = 1$$

where ω_{gc} is the *gain crossover frequency*. The gain crossover frequency is the frequency at which the magnitude of the loop gain is unity. On the Bode plot, we can determine the phase margin at the frequency where the gain crosses the 0 dB line. On a Nyquist plot (Figure 1-18), we look at the point where the plot intersects the unit circle. For a stable minimum phase system, the system is closed loop stable if the gain is below the 0 dB line (i.e., GM > 0), and the phase is above the −180 degree line (i.e., PM > 0).

1.8.4 Relationship between Open and Closed Loop Behavior

Unless otherwise noted, we assume that $H(s) = 1$; i.e., unity feedback. For the first order case, $KG(s) = Ka/(s + a)$. The open loop Bode magnitude plot is shown in Figure 1-3. We already know that the open loop bandwidth is a and the open loop gain is K. We define the *gain-bandwidth product* for this system as

$$GBW = Ka$$

The closed loop transfer function for this system is

$$T(s) = \frac{KG(s)}{1 + KG(s)} = \frac{Ka}{s + a\,(1 + K)}$$

The closed loop gain is $K/(1 + K)$, and the closed loop bandwidth is $a(1 + K)$. We can see that the closed loop gain is lower than the open loop gain, and the closed loop bandwidth is greater than the open loop bandwidth. Because of the increased bandwidth, the closed loop system is faster than the open loop system (closed loop $\tau = 1/a(1 + K)$). The closed loop gain-bandwidth product is still Ka! In fact, for first order systems, the gain-bandwidth product is a constant.

What can we tell about the closed loop system from the open loop plot of Figure 1-3? To find out, let us solve for the gain crossover frequency, $\omega_{gc} = a\,K$. Comparing this answer to the closed loop bandwidth of $a(1 + K)$, we see that for large K, $\omega_{gc} \approx BW_{CL}$.

We now assume that

$$K\,G(s) = \frac{K\,\omega_n^2}{s^2 + 2\,\zeta\,\omega_n\,s + \omega_n^2}$$

The open loop Bode magnitude plot for $K = 1$ is shown in Figure 1-5. If we assume that $BW \approx \omega_n$, then the open loop gain bandwidth product for this system is

$$GBW = K\omega_n$$

The closed loop transfer function is

$$T(s) = \frac{K\,\omega_n^2}{s^2 + 2\,\zeta\,\omega_n\,s + (K + 1)\,\omega_n^2} = \frac{K\,\omega_n^2}{s^2 + 2\,\zeta_{CL}\,\omega_{n_{CL}}\,s + \omega_{n_{CL}}^2}$$

Therefore, the closed loop natural frequency, damping ratio, and gain-bandwidth product are given by

$$\omega_{n_{CL}} = \omega_n \sqrt{K+1} \, , \qquad \zeta_{CL} = \frac{\zeta}{\sqrt{K+1}} \, , \qquad GBW_{CL} \approx \frac{\omega_n K}{\sqrt{K+1}}$$

Note that the gain bandwidth product is not constant for a second order system. We can still make the general statement, however, that as the gain is decreased, the bandwidth is increased. Also, the gain crossover frequency ($\omega_{gc} \approx \omega_n \sqrt{K}$ for K large) still gives an accurate measure of the closed loop bandwidth.

The damping ratio of the closed loop system is approximately $1/\sqrt{K}$ of the open loop damping ratio. The closed loop system will therefore be faster and have greater overshoot than the open loop system. Can the closed loop damping ratio (ζ_{CL}) be predicted from the open loop frequency response? From the definition of phase margin in the Nyquist plot, using simple geometry, we obtain

$$PM = 2 \sin^{-1} \frac{1}{2 \, | \, T(j \, \omega_{gc}) \, |}$$

Because $\omega_{gc} \approx \omega_n \sqrt{K}$, then

$$PM \approx 2 \sin^{-1}(\zeta_{CL}) \quad \text{or} \quad \zeta_{CL} \approx \sin\left(\frac{PM}{2}\right)$$

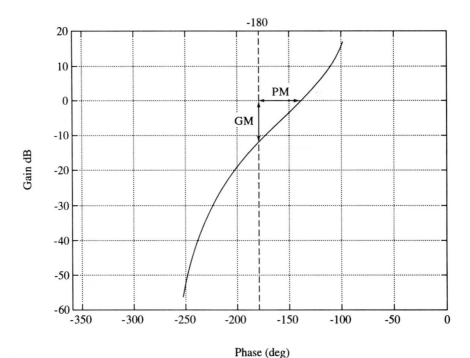

Figure 1-19 Nichols plot showing gain and phase margins.

Some authors [FPE91] use the following approximation:

$$\zeta_{CL} \approx .01 \; PM \; \text{(degrees)}$$

If we are just interested in stability, rather than compensator design, the *Nichols plot* is very convenient (see Figure 1-19 on page 36). As you can see, the 180 degree point, the gain margin, and phase margin are quite clear. Neither ω_{gc} nor ω_{pc} are obvious, however. The Nichols plot is actually more sophisticated than shown in this figure and can be used to determine closed loop behavior. Consult the references for more details on the use of the Nichols plot.

Remember, neither the Bode nor Nichols plot should be used to determine stability if the system is nonminimum phase. In this case, use either the root locus or Nyquist plot.

1.9 Computer-Aided Control System Design

Engineers and physicists have been using mechanical and electrical aids for the analysis and design of systems since William Thompson (Lord Kelvin) invented a mechanical integrating device (a primitive analog computer) in 1876 that could be used to solve ordinary differential equations. The mechanical analog computer was greatly improved during World War I and was successfully applied to naval gunfire control systems. The electronic differential amplifier was invented in the early part of the twentieth century, was improved during World War II, and led to the development of the operational amplifier in 1947. The operational amplifier made possible the development of electronic circuits that would add, subtract, multiply, and integrate. Thus was born the electronic analog computer, which can be used for the simulation of a vast class of systems.

With the introduction of digital computers and languages such as FORTRAN and BASIC, the engineer was able to write numerical routines to simulate integration. One could, therefore, model and simulate dynamic systems. The earliest prewritten, or canned, programs such as CSMP were based on these techniques. Additional programs increased the efficiency of the control engineer, which led to the tackling of ever more complex systems using more sophisticated techniques.

As systems grew in complexity from single-input single-output to multi-input multi-output systems, the classical techniques became cumbersome, or even impossible, to use. In the 1960s, control engineers turned to linear algebra techniques of state space modeling for these systems. The matrix-based mathematics of state space analysis and design drove the need for more sophisticated computer analysis. Fortunately, the numerical analysis community had been busy. Packages such as LINPACK and EISPACK were made commonly available. It was still left to the mathematician or engineer, however, to write the main body of the analysis program, while making subroutine calls to LINPACK or EISPACK.

To relieve some of this burden, C. B. Moler of the University of New Mexico wrote an interactive program called MATLAB, which provided easy access to the routines of LINPACK and EISPACK. The introduction of MATLAB was a phenomenal success, as it revolutionized computer-aided analysis and design of control systems. Although MATLAB provided an easy-to-use environment for mathematics, especially matrix-based mathematics, it still lacked the additional algorithms needed for control system analysis and design. Soon after its introduction, many companies developed commercially available software for control systems based on the MATLAB environment; e.g., MATRIX$_X$ (by Integrated Systems, Inc.), MATLAB (by The Mathworks, Inc.), and Ctrl-C (by Systems Control Technology). All of the preceding programs provide easy access to control, signal processing, and mathematics algorithms.

Programs based on the MATLAB environment can be considered as sophisticated matrix calculators with specialized toolboxes or modules for control systems. There are also other programs available, not based on MATLAB, that are more specialized. Program CC (by Systems Technology Inc.) and EASY5 (by Boeing Computer Services) are control systems programs. SIMNON (by Lund Institute of Technology), a differential equation calculator (according to its manual), is suited more for simulation of linear and nonlinear systems. ACSL (by Mitchell & Gauthier Associates, MGA) and CSMP are among other simulation programs. There are many other programs, and we refer the reader to [JH85], [F91].

Further progress in computer hardware and software, along with recent developments in control theory, are bringing in new tools. For instance, new generations of EISPACK and LINPACK are being made available that take advantage of parallel processing capabilities of computers. Object-oriented programming (OOP) has been incorporated into Xmath. New data types are also being introduced into MATLAB for expert system development (see [P91]) and μ-synthesis (see [CS91] and [BPDGS 91]).

1.10 Problems

1.1 Consider a system represented by the following differential equation:

$$\ddot{y} + \dot{y} - 2y = \dot{u} - u \qquad \text{with} \qquad y(0^-) = a \ , \ \dot{y}(0^-) = b \ , \ u(0^-) = c$$

a. Find the characteristic equation and the system modes. Determine asymptotic stability.

b. Find the system transfer function and its poles. Determine BIBO stability.

c. Find the zero-input response (ZIR).

d. Find the zero-state response (ZSR).

e. Determine for what set of initial conditions the ZIR approaches zero. Conclude that for all other initial conditions, the ZIR goes to infinity.

f. Explain the specific feature of this system that has resulted in conflicting answers relating to stability.

1.2 Find and sketch the impulse and step responses of the following transfer functions.

a. $G_1(s) = \dfrac{1000}{5s + 20}$

b. $G_2(s) = sG_1(s)$, compare to part a

c. $G_3(s) = \dfrac{1}{s}G_1(s)$, compare to part a

d. $G_4(s) = \dfrac{100}{s^2 + 20s + 100}$

e. $G_5(s) = \dfrac{100}{s^2 + 4s + 100}$

f. $G_6(s) = (s + 5)G_5(s)$

g. $G_7(s) = (s^2 + .2s + 100)G_4(s)$

1.3 Consider the system, $G(s)$, and a cascade compensator, $K(s)$, in unity feedback:

$$G(s) = \frac{1}{s + 2}, \qquad K(s) = k\,\frac{s + a}{s}$$

a. Discuss the effects of $K(s)$ on the steady state error properties of the system.

b. Consider three range values for a: $a < 0$, $0 < a < 2$, and $a > 2$. Draw the root locus for each range and decide which ones are stabilizing.

c. Which range gives the fastest settling time? Why?

1.4 Consider the following transfer functions (assume unity feedback):

$$G_1(s) = \frac{1}{s} \;,\quad G_2(s) = \frac{1}{s(s+1)} \;,\quad G_3(s) = \frac{1}{s(s+1)(s+5)}$$

$$G_4(s) = \frac{1}{s^3} \;,\quad G_5(s) = \frac{s+1}{s^3} \;,\quad G_6(s) = \frac{(s+1)(s+5)}{s^3}$$

Note that in the first set of transfer functions (G_1, G_2, G_3), poles are added to G_1, whereas in the second set, zeros are added to G_4.

a. Obtain the root locus in each case.

b. How does adding poles affect the shape of the root locus and stability?

c. Same question as in part b, but now comment on the effects of adding zeros.

1.5 Repeat the preceding problem using Bode plots. Obtain gain and phase margins in each case, and comment on how adding poles and zeros affects the margins.

1.6 In this problem, you will compare the differences between cascade and feedback compensation. Consider the plant $G(s)$ and compensator $K(s)$:

$$G(s) = \frac{4}{s(s+2)} \quad,\quad K(s) = \frac{s+1}{s}$$

a. Show that if $K(s)$ is in series with $G(s)$, with unity feedback, the system will be stable and can track step and ramp inputs with zero error. Find the closed loop zeros.

b. Show that if $K(s)$ is placed in the feedback path, these properties are lost, even though both systems have the same closed loop poles. Find the closed loop zeros, and compare with part a.

c. Show that we can recover the tracking properties of part a using feedback compensation, by placing an additional compensator outside the loop. Find this compensator and call it $K_{f(s)}$.

d. Suppose during implementation, or due to component tolerances, we instead use

$$K_2 (s) = \frac{s+0.5}{s}$$

Repeat part a with this incorrect compensator. Are the tracking properties lost?

e. Repeat part b with the incorrect compensator.

f. Use the same $K_f(s)$ as in part c, show that you lose the tracking properties of part c.

1.7 Consider the following plant, $G(s)$, and compensator, $K(s)$. Assume the plant and compensator are in series with unity feedback around them.

$$G(s) = \frac{1}{s^2} \quad , \quad K(s) = K_c \frac{s+a}{s+b} \quad \text{and} \quad a > 0, b > 0, K_c > 0$$

a. Use the Routh-Hurwitz test to determine for what values of a and b the system will be stabilized.

b. Verify your answer in part a using root locus with K_c as the root locus parameter.

c. Set $b = 5$ and $K_c = 1$. Obtain the root locus with a as the root locus parameter. Confirm the conclusion in part a by determining for what values of a the system will be stable.

d. Draw the Nyquist plot for value of K_c in part b, and show that the system is stable. Also find the gain crossover frequency, gain margin and phase margin.

1.8 Consider the plant $KG(s)$ in unity feedback:

$$KG(s) = \frac{K(s+0.8)}{s(s-1)}$$

a. Find the stabilizing value of K.

b. Find value of K for a critically damped response.

c. Using the value of K in part b, find the steady state errors to unit step and ramp inputs.

1.9 The purpose of this exercise is to show how closed loop bandwidth and gain crossover frequency can be estimated by the location of dominant closed loop poles. Consider the plant, $KG(s)$, in unity feedback:

$$KG(s) = \frac{K}{s(s+1)}$$

a. Find exact analytical formulas for ω_n, ω_d, BW, ω_{gc}, T_p.

b. Using your formulas, what are the effects of increasing K on the system?

c. Compute the above quantities for $K = 1, 10$.

d. Determine how well BW and ω_{gc} are approximated by ω_d and ω_n.

1.10 Consider a plant containing time delay in unity feedback; i.e.,

$$K\,G(s) \;=\; \frac{K\,e^{-Ts}}{s+1}$$

Analytically find the gain crossover frequency of the system, and determine for what value of T = time delay, the system becomes unstable for a given gain.

1.11 The open loop transfer function of a system is given by

$$K\,G(s) = \frac{K}{(s+2)^2\,(s+3)}$$

Find an acceptable range of values for K to simultaneously satisfy the following specifications:

$$K_p \geq 2 \quad \text{and} \quad GM \geq 20 \log_{10} 3 \text{ dB}$$

1.12 Consider the following plant in unity feedback:

$$G(s) \;=\; \frac{1}{(s-1)^2}$$

The specifications are closed loop stability and zero steady state error to unit step input. Discuss in each case, using root locus, whether both specifications can be met by a cascade compensator. Give full explanations. If any of the compensators work, you must specify for what range of values the specifications are met. Remember that the system must be stabilized first before you consider steady state errors.

a. Proportional control: $K(s) = k$

b. PI : $K(s) = a + (b/s)$

c. PD : $K(s) = a + bs$

d. Lead : $K(s) = (s+a)/(s+b)$, $a < b$

e. Lag : $K(s) = (s+a)/(s+b)$, $a > b$

f. PID : $K(s) = a + (b/s) + cs$

g. Suppose, in addition, all closed loop poles are to be placed at $s = -1$. Determine the compensator parameters to achieve this. Also, plot the root locus and step response for the compensated system for this case.

1.13 The system $G(s)$ in unity feedback is

$$G(s) = \frac{1}{s^2+1}$$

a. Draw the root locus and discuss the system's stability.

b. Suppose we try to compensate the system using $K(s) = k \dfrac{s+a}{s+b}$

Using root locus or the Routh–Hurwitz test, determine for what values of a and b the system is stable.

c. Let $a = 1$, $b = 5$, find k to get less than 10% steady state error to a unit step input.

d. Discuss the effects of increasing k on the following system characteristics:

i. Relative stability measured by the distance of the closest pole to the $j\omega$ axis

ii. Percent overshoot

iii. Sensitivity with respect to modelling errors

iv. Steady state errors

v. Frequency of oscillation in the transient step response

vi. Settling time

In each case, give adequate reasons for your answer.

1.14 Consider the following plant, $G(s)$, and assume unity feedback:

$$G(s) = \frac{1}{s\,(s+1)}$$

It is desired to track unit ramp inputs with a maximum steady state error of 10%. This must be achieved while maintaining an overshoot of less than 20%.

a. Suppose an amplifier with gain K is placed in series with the plant. Determine the value of K that meets the tracking requirement. Find the closed loop transfer function and estimate the resulting overshoot. Is the design satisfactory? Explain.

b. Suppose a compensator of the form $K(s) = (s+a)/(s+b)$ is proposed. This compensator will be placed in series with the plant. Determine the ratio a/b that meets the tracking requirement.

c. Set $a = 0.1$ and find the value of b (this is called a *lag* compensator). Find the closed loop transfer function; plot the root locus; find the closed loop poles; and estimate the resulting overshoot. Is this design satisfactory? Explain.

d. Compare the design in part a with part c. Compare other step response characteristics such as settling time and peak time.

1.15 This problem will take you through the steps for lead compensation using root locus. Consider the plant, $G(s)$, and the following specifications:

$$G(s) = \frac{1}{s^2} \qquad \text{specifications: } T_s \le 4 \text{ sec and POS} \le 20\%$$

a. Show that if the dominant closed loop poles of the system are at $s^* = -1 \pm j\,2$, the system will meet the specifications.

b. Find the angle of $G(s)$ at s^*.

c. Suppose a compensator of the form $K(s) = K_c(s+a)/(s+b)$ is placed in series with the plant in a unity feedback configuration. Compute the angle of $K(s)$ such that the root locus of $K(s)G(s)$ passes through the point s^*.

d. Set $b = 3$. Find the value of a such that $K(s)$ will have the angle obtained in part c.

e. Determine the value of K_c for the compensated system at the point s^*.

f. Find the closed loop transfer function, closed loop poles, and determine if the specifications are met. If the specifications are not met, explain why.

Notes and References

The recent survey by A. Feliachi [F91] reports the following as the most frequently used textbooks (in frequency of usage) in a first course in automatic control (we are listing the latest editions): [Do89], [K91], [O90], [PH88], [HSS88], [FPE91], [M84], [DH88], [SM67], [H88]. For further study, we refer the reader to any of the above texts. See the Bibliography for more details.

2

Introduction to MATLAB

MATLAB is a sophisticated mathematics and simulation environment that can be used to model and analyze dynamic systems. It handles continuous, discrete, linear, or nonlinear systems. As the name implies, it has extensive features for matrix manipulations. MATLAB is an open environment for which many specialized toolboxes have been developed: Control Systems, Signal Processing, Optimization, Robust Control, μ–analysis and synthesis (μ-Tools), Spline, System Identification, MMLE State-Space Identification, Neural Networks, and Chemometrics. Simulink (formerly known as Simulab) is a graphical environment for modeling and simulating block diagrams and general nonlinear systems. The emphasis of this textbook is on the basic MATLAB, and the Control Systems and Signal Processing toolboxes. A brief introduction to Simulink is also given in Chapter 6. The Control Systems Toolbox contains classical and modern control commands. This toolbox is completely covered in Chapters 4 and 5. Selected commands of general interest from the Signal Processing toolbox are also covered in the present chapter and Chapter 11.

The basic MATLAB and the toolboxes are command driven; hence, you have to know the various commands that are available. Because on-line help is available and the syntax structures of most commands are very similar, there is no need to memorize the commands. You will learn them very quickly as you use the program. In this chapter, we will introduce most of the basic MATLAB commands.

The MATLAB prompt is `>>` and the command you enter is shown in COURIER font.

2.1 On-screen Help

You can get on-screen information about MATLAB commands with `help`. Typing

```
>> help
```

produces a listing of all HELP topics and MATLAB commands (includes commands related to all the toolboxes available on the path), as shown subsequently.

MATLAB built-in functions: Copyright (c), The MathWorks, Inc.

help	l	conj	exp	ident	matlabpa	rand	string
[	~	contour	expm	i	max	rcond	subplot
]	abs	cos	eye	ieee	memory	real	sum
(	all	cumprod	feval	if	mesh	relop	svd
)	ans	cumsum	fft	imag	meta	rem	tan
.	any	dc2sc	filter	inf	min	return	text
,	acos	delete	find	input	nan	round	title
;	asin	det	finite	inquire	nargin	save	type
%	atan	diag	fix	inv	norm	sc2dc	what
!	atan2	diary	floor	isnan	ones	schur	while
:	axis	dir	flops	isstr	pack	script	who
'	balance	disp	for	j	pause	semilogx	xlabel
+	break	echo	format	keyboard	pi	semilogy	ylabel
-	casesen	eig	fprintf	length	plot	setstr	zeros
*	ceil	else	function	load	polar	shg	
\	chdir	elseif	getenv	log	polyline	sign	
/	chol	end	ginput	loglog	polymark	sin	
^	clc	eps	global	logop	prod	size	
<	clear	error	grid	ltifr	prtsc	sort	
>	clg	eval	hess	ltitr	qr	sprintf	
=	clock	exist	hold	lu	quit	sqrt	
&	computer	exit	home	magic	qz	startup	

Directory of M-files in c:\matlab

acosh	cov	flipud	hex2dec	log10	nersolv	quad8	sqrtm
angle	cplxpair	fmin	hex2num	logm	nestop	quad8stp	stairs
asinh	date	fmins	hilb	logspace	nextpow2	quadstp	std
atanh	dec2hex	fminstep	hist	lscov	nnls	quiver	strcmp
backsub	deconv	foptions	ifft	mean	null	rank	subspace
bar	diff	fplot	ifft2	median	num2str	rat	table1
bessel	ellipj	fsolve	info	menu	ode23	readme	table2
bessela	ellipk	fsolve2	int2str	meshdom	ode45	reshape	tanh
besselh	erf	funm	interp1	mkpp	orth	resi2	toeplitz
besseln	errorbar	fzero	interp2	nebroyu	pascal	residue	trace
blanks	etime	gallery	interp3	nechdcmp	pinv	roots	tril
cdf2rdf	expm1	gamma	interp4	neconest	polarbar	roots1	triu
clabel	expm2	gammac	inverf	nefdjac	poly	rose	unmkpp
compan	expm3	gammai	invhilb	nefn	polyder	rot90	unwrap
compass	feather	gpp	isempty	neinck	polyfit	ref	vander

cond	fft2	gradient	kron	nelnsrch	polyval	rsf2csf	zcheck
conv	fftshift	gtext	laguer	nemodel	polyvalm	sha	
corrcoef	fitfun	hadamard	length	neqrdcmp	ppval	sinh	
cosh	fliplr	hankel	linspace	neqrsolv	quad	spline	

Directory of M-files in c:\matlabl\control

abcdchk	ctrb	dinitial	dsigma3	jetdemo	mulresp	reg	stepfun
acker	ctrbf	diskdemo	dsort	kalmdemo	nargchk	ric	tf2ss
append	ctrldemo	distsl	dstep	lab2st	ngrid	rlocfind	tf2z
are	d2c	dlqe	dtimvec	logm2	nichols	rlocus	tfchk
augstate	d2cm	dlqew	esort	lqe	ryquist	model	timvec
balreal	damp	dlqr	estim	lqe2	obsv	schord	tzero
blkbuild	dbalreal	dlqry	exresp	lqed	obsvf	series	tzero2
bode	dbode	dlsim	fbode	lqew	ord2	sgrid	tzreduce
bodeu	dcgain	dlyap	feedback	lqr	pade	sigma	vsort
boildemo	dcovar	dmodred	fixphase	lqr2	parallel	sigma2	zgrid
c2d	ddamp	dmulresp	freqint	lqrd	perpxy	sigma3	zp2ss
c2dm	ddcgain	dnichols	freqint2	lqry	place	ss2ss	zp2tf
c2dt	destim	dnyquist	freqresp	lsim	poly	ss2tf	
canon	dexresp	dreg	givens	lyap	poly2str	ss2zp	
chop	dfrqint	dric	gram	lyap2	printmat	ssdelete	
cloop	dfrqint2	drmodel	housh	margin	printsys	sselect	
connect	dgram	dsigma	impulse	minreal	pzmap	stairs	
covar	dimpulse	dsigma2	initial	modred	readme3	step	

Information about a specific command is obtained by typing

```
>> help command name
```

For example, note the result of typing

```
>> help impulse
```

IMPULSE Impulse response of continuous-time linear systems.
IMPULSE(A,B,C,D,IU) plots the time response of the linear system
$$x = Ax + Bu$$
$$y = Cx + Du$$
to an impulse applied to the single input IU. The time vector is automatically determined.
IMPULSE(NUM,DEN) plots the impulse response of the polynomial transfer function G(s) =
NUM(s)/DEN(s) where NUM and DEN contain the polynomial coefficients in descending powers of
s.
IMPULSE(A,B,C,D,IU,T) or IMPULSE(NUM,DEN,T) uses the user-supplied time vector T which
must be regularly spaced. When invoked with left hand arguments,
        [Y,X,T] = IMPULSE(A,B,C,D,...)
        [Y,X,T] = IMPULSE(NUM,DEN,...)

returns the output and state time history in the matrices Y and X. No plot is drawn on the screen. Y has as many columns as there are outputs and length(T) rows. X has as many columns as there are states.
See also: STEP,INITIAL,LSIM and DIMPULSE.

The general syntax of MATLAB commands is the following:

[output1, output2, ...] = command name (input1, input2, ...)

where the command outputs are enclosed within square brackets and inputs within parentheses. If there is only one output, brackets are optional.

If you type demo, a list of demos will appear that will demonstrate how to use MATLAB and will show off some of its features and capabilities. The demos are very instructive, and if you have the patience, you can learn many features of MATLAB from the demos.

2.2 File Management

To create a record of all inputs and outputs in a MATLAB session, and to save the record under a given name in ASCII format, use the *diary* command below. Note that this command does not save your data, just what you type and what you see on screen. It is used for report generation and writing programs. It is strongly recommended that you use it at the start of every session to keep track of your work. To save your session record, you should close the diary. For different diaries, use different names; otherwise, you will write over the previous one.

```
>> diary filename
```

Opens a diary with a given name (the name can include drive and directory paths). When you are done, you can close the diary file using

```
>> diary off          % close the diary
```

Typing *diary* by itself toggles diary on and off, and saves the record under the filename "diary".

The symbol % used in the above allows you to add comments to your programs. To enter comment lines, type

```
>> %    (everything to its right on that line is ignored and is not executed)
```

```
>> save filename
```

Saves the data to a file with the given name in the binary MATLAB format. If no extension is specified, MATLAB adds the extension .MAT to the filename. If no filename is specified, your file will be saved under MATLAB.MAT. Note that this command saves the workspace (variables you have defined or results of operations), while *diary* saves input and output records only and not the actual data. You can also perform a partial save; i.e., save some of the data. For example,

```
>> save filename  x y z        (save variables x, y, and z to file)
>> save filename x /ascii /double
```

Using the *ascii* and/or *double* options allows you to save the data or some of the variables in 8-digit (16-digit for *double*) ASCII format. This allows you to transfer data from MATLAB to other programs.

```
>> load filename
```

loads a data file with the given name. If the file is an ASCII *flat file* (this means fixed-length rows terminated by carriage returns, and numbers separated by spaces), all variables will be loaded but will appear under the name of the file (without the extension). No options are available for *load*; you cannot do a partial load.

```
>> what
```

shows the MATLAB files and the MAT data files under the current directory.

```
>> dir
```

shows all the files under the current directory. You can also delete files using the *delete* command (similar to DEL in DOS), or change directory using the *chdir* command. Pathnames and wildcards are supported. You can also view the contents of ASCII files using the *type* command.

```
>> clear  a b c
```

clears specified variables (a, b, c) from the workspace. Typing *clear* by itself clears the entire workspace. You have to use this with caution or you will lose all your data.

```
>> !
```

allows you to access the operating system. If you have enough memory, you can launch other programs (e.g., an editor) within MATLAB. This is a temporary leave from MATLAB, and you will not use your data. This command is not available (nor needed) under windowing environments such as Macintosh or Microsoft Windows.

There are two ways to correct data entry mistakes. If you have not yet hit the RETURN (ENTER or ↵) key, use the BACKSPACE (←) key. More generally you can use the *multiline buffer* to correct errors in lines above (below) your present line. Simply press the UP or DOWN ARROW (↑ or ↓) key until you reach the line of interest.

MATLAB is case sensitive. All commands must be entered in lower-case letters. MATLAB distinguishes between the variable X and x. The command *casesen* can be used to switch off case sensitivity. This is a toggle command; every time you issue it, you change the case sensitivity. It is best not to use *casesen* because some toolboxes use both upper- and lower-case letters.

To exit MATLAB, type

```
>> exit   or   quit
```

2.3 Data Structures: Vectors and Matrices

The basic element in MATLAB is a double-precision complex matrix. This representation is quite general and includes real and complex vectors and scalars. It indirectly includes polynomials and transfer functions. Row vectors are entered using square brackets where you can separate the elements using either blanks or commas. To create a column vector, transpose the vector using the apostrophe (') key. Examples of row vectors are

```
>> x=[1,2,3], y=[1+j, 2+pi*i, -sqrt(-1)]

x =
      1     2     3
y =
   1.0000 + 1.0000i    2.0000 + 3.1416i       0 - 1.0000i
```

Note that we can create several vectors on a single line of code separating them with commas or semicolons.

Some often-used quantities with special values have special names, such as *pi* (=3.1416...) and *j* or *i* (= $\sqrt{-1}$). Other special functions are: *Inf* (∞ ; result of division by 0) and *NaN* (stands for Not-a-Number; result of indeterminate forms such as 0/0). The last two special functions are useful because they prevent programs from crashing. You will get a warning instead of an error message. You can still use these names for other variables if you wish, or assign other names to these special numbers. Note that when you define elements of a vector, you can use any number of mathematical functions or expressions. For instance, in the vector y above we have used the *sqrt* function for $\sqrt{-1}$.

```
>> z=[1+j, 2+pi*i, -sqrt(-1)]'

z =
   1.0000 - 1.0000i
```

```
      2.0000 - 3.1416i
      0 + 1.0000i

>> z.'

ans =
      1.0000 - 1.0000i    2.0000 - 3.1416i         0 + 1.0000i
```

When you transpose complex vectors, you get the *conjugate transpose* as can be seen from the signs of the imaginary parts of z. To get the unconjugated transpose, use a dot before the transpose symbol as shown above. Note that we have not assigned any name to the result of the last operation. In such cases the permanent variable name *ans* will be automatically assigned by MATLAB. Permanent variables are like any other variable except that they cannot be cleared from the workspace. Another permanent variable is *eps*. It stands for the smallest machine number.

```
>> eps

eps =
   2.2204e-016
```

The *colon* " : " is one of the most powerful commands in MATLAB and has many uses. For example, it can be used to generate sequential data such as

```
>> t=[0:0.1:10];
```

which generates a row vector t, that increases from 0 to 10 in increments of 0.1. If the increment is negative, you will get a decreasing sequence. You can also generate sequential data using the *linspace* and *logspace* commands.

```
>> t=linspace(n1,n2,n)
>> w=logspace(n1,n2,n)
```

The *linspace* command generates a vector from n1 to n2 with length n (the number of points, n, is optional; its default value is 100). The *logspace* command produces a logarithmically spaced vector from 10^{n1} to 10^{n2} with n points (the number of points, n, is optional; its default value is 50). These commands are typically used to create a time axis and a frequency axis for time and frequency response calculations, respectively. For example, logspace(-1,2) gives 50 points from 0.1 to 100; logspace(0,pi) gives 50 points from 1 to π. The latter example demonstrates an exceptional case; if n2=pi, then pi is treated as the final point rather than a power. This special case has been created for digital signal processing applications.

To suppress the immediate display of data, end each command with a semicolon:

```
>> ;
```

You will soon discover that if you forget to end your commands with the semicolon, you will be forced to watch lines and lines of data. So, use it often. You can always examine the value(s) of a variable by simply typing its name. Alternatively, you can use the *disp* command, which displays a variable.

Very long variables or commands may require more than a single line for data entry. To continue a long command to the next line, type

```
>> ...
```

at the end of the current line.

Matrices are entered row by row, separated by semicolons (you can also hit the RETURN key). To enter the matrix

$$A = \begin{pmatrix} 1 & 2 & 3 \\ 4 & 5 & 6 \\ 7 & 8 & 9 \end{pmatrix}$$

type

```
>> A=[1 2 3;4 5 6;7 8 9]
```

During data entry, you can put as many spaces as you wish between data elements. You have to be careful, though, when there is an operator between the data elements or when you have complex data. Note the difference among the elements of the following vector:

```
>> [1, 1+ 2, 1 +2, 1 + 2]

ans =
     1       3       1       2       1       2
```

Four commands, *who*, *whos*, *size*, and *length* provide information about the variables in use in the workspace.

```
>> who       and      whos
>> size(a)
>> length(a)
```

The command *who* lists all the variables currently in memory. In addition, *whos* displays the variables, their sizes, how many bytes they occupy, and whether they are real or complex; *size* returns the number of rows and columns of a as a row vector; *length* returns the dimension of a vector. If the argument is a matrix, *length* returns the larger dimension. These are very useful commands because matrix algebra requires that dimensions of vectors and matrices satisfy certain compatibility conditions.

The display format of data can be modified using the *format* command. For example,

```
>> format long
```

displas the output in 15 digit scaled fixed point. Another format available is *long e,* which displays in scientific notation (15 digit floating point). This is useful when small numbers appear as zeros, and switching to long format will display the correct value. To get back to the default format, use *format short* or *format short e.* You can also enter data in scientific notation; e.g., 2000 is entered as 2E3. For displaying large matrices, use the *format +* option. This option displays positive numbers using +, negative numbers using− and zeros as blanks.

2.3.1 Matrix Addressing and Subscripting

Because a matrix is the basic data type in MATLAB, you need to become very fluent in manipulating matrices. In addition, MATLAB is able to perform operations on matrices that are not available in other languages; some of these operations are not even defined (or are even illegal) in linear algebra. Elements of matrices are addressed by A(m,n). For example, A(2,3) gives the (2,3) element; A(:,2) gives the second element in all rows (i.e., the second column); A(1:2,1:3) gives rows 1 through 2 and columns 1 through 3. Note the use of " : " as a wildcard in these cases.

If you assign a number to a nonexisting address in a matrix, the matrix grows to fit the new element while filling the unspecified locations with zeros. Try the following:

```
>> a=[11 12;21 22]

a =
      11      12
      21      22


>> a(3,3)=33

a =
      11      12       0
      21      22       0
       0       0      33
```

Subscripts of a matrix do not have to be integers (even irrational subscripts are acceptable). For example, A(2.2,3) refers to the (2,3) element; A(2.6,3), A(2.5,3), and A(pi,3) all refer to the (3,3) element. Subscripts have to be positive, though. Entering A(:) returns a long column vector, elements of which are the columns of A stacked one by one under each other. This operation is defined in matrix algebra and is known as the *vec* operation. For example,

```
>> a=[1 2;3 4]; a(:)
```

```
ans =
     1
     3
     2
     4
```

Subscripts of a matrix can be vectors. For example,

```
>> b=a(x,y)
```

creates the matrix b by taking elements of a with row subscripts from the vector x and column subscripts from the vector y. For example, suppose a matrix has n columns, then

```
>> b=a(:,n:-1:1)
```

will reverse the columns of a. This is because the first column of b is the nth column of a, the second column of b is the $(n-1)$th column, etc. If you understand this feature, you can write powerful programs with a few lines of code. Here is another example:

```
>> a=[11 12;21 22]

a =
    11      12
    21      22

>> x=[1 2]; y=[2 1]; c(x,y)=a

c =
    12      11
    22      21

>>  d(x,y)=a(y,x)

d =
    22      21
    12      11
```

2.3.2 Special Matrices

Some often-used matrices are available as utility functions.

```
>> eye(m)
```

returns an m by m *identity* matrix, eye(a) returns an identity matrix the same size as the matrix a, and eye(m,n) creates the largest identity matrix it can and fills the rest of the matrix with zeros.

```
>> ones(n)
```

returns an n by n matrix of "1's"; ones (m, n) returns an m by n matrix of "1's"; and
ones (a) returns a matrix of "1's " the same size as the matrix a. These functions are
quite useful; e.g., *ones (t)*, where *t* is a vector generates the *"unit step "* function. The *zeros*
command has the same syntax but creates a matrix of 0's. The *rand* command has similar
syntax and returns a uniformly distributed random number (vector or matrix) between 0
and 1.

For example, to create the function y(t) = 3 + t , for t = 0, 1, 2, ... , 10, enter

```
>> t=[0:1:10]; y=3*ones(t)+t
```

Alternatively, we can use

```
>> t=[0:1:10]; y=3+t
```

Yes! In MATLAB you can add scalars to vectors (or matrices); the scalar gets added to
every element. This, of course, is illegal in linear algebra.

Sooner or later, you will run into the following difficulty. Suppose a=2, and you
enter ones (a). Is the result equal to 1 or a 2 by 2 matrix of 1's? The answer is that you
will get a 2 by 2 matrix of 1's. This is fine, but what if a = 0? You will get an error message.
To get around this, first you will need to determine the size of a; then use the *ones*
command. The same comment applies to the *zeros* and the *eye* commands.

Another special matrix that does not exist in matrix algebra is the *empty* (or *null*)
matrix:

```
>> q=[]
```

The matrix q exists on the workspace, but it has zero size. It allows you to define matrices
that are needed as inputs for certain commands without specifying what they are. You can
delete rows and columns of matrices by assigning them to the empty matrix. For example,

```
>> a=rand(5,5); a(:,1:3)=[]
```

creates a 5 by 5 random matrix and removes the first three columns.
Another useful matrix command is

```
>> diag(v)
```

which returns a *diagonal matrix* with elements of the vector *v* on its diagonal. If *v* is a
matrix, then this command returns the diagonal of *v* as a column vector; *diag(v,1)* returns
the first superdiagonal, and *diag(v,- 1)* returns the first subdiagonal. Other related commands are *triu* and *tril* ,which return the upper and lower triangular portions of a matrix.

2.3.3 Strings

Text strings are entered by placing them within single quotes:

```
>> disp('text string')

text string
```

Text strings can be assigned to vectors or matrices entered inside single quotes. A text string can be displayed using the *disp* command or by typing its name. For example,

```
>> a=['this is a';'text string']

All rows in the bracketed expression must have the same number of
columns.
```

The above error message means that a matrix of strings is treated like any other kind of matrix. We will add two spaces to fix the problem:

```
>> aa=['this is a  ';'text string']

a =
this is a
text string
```

There are several string manipulation commands that can be used to label and title plots, among other things. Some of them are *num2str*, *int2str*, *fprintf*, and *sprintf*.

2.4 Mathematical Operations and Functions

Basic algebraic operations +, −, *, \ , /, ^(^ stands for power), standard trigonometric functions, hyperbolic functions, transcendental functions (*log* = natural log, *log10* = base 10 log, *exp*), and *sqrt* ($\sqrt{}$) are supported. Other functions such as *det* (determinant), *inv* (inverse), *eig* (eigenvalue), *rank*, *trace*, and *norm* are standard matrix operations. Advanced matrix computations are, of course, at the heart of MATLAB. Other functions are *real*, *imag*, *abs* (absolute value or magnitude of complex quantities), and *conj* (complex conjugate). There are also element-by-element operations that are very useful but are not part of standard linear algebra. A complete list is available using the *help* command.

2.4.1 Elementary Operations

MATLAB has two types of mathematical functions and operations: matrix type and array (or element-by-element) type. Because array type operations are not part of standard linear algebra, you may not be familiar with them. You will find out, however, that they are very useful for data analysis.

Matrix addition, subtraction, and multiplication are done according to basic linear algebra rules. Matrix exponentiation will be defined shortly. Matrix inversion (or division) is defined by

```
>> A\B
>> B/A
>> inv(A)
```

$A \backslash B$ is equivalent to $A^{-1}B$ or $inv(A)*B$. It solves the problem $Ax = B$. B/A is equivalent to BA^{-1} or $B*inv(A)$. It solves the problem $xA = B$. If A is rectangular, $A \backslash B$ and B/A automatically find the least squares solution, whereas $inv(A)$ is only valid for square matrices.

Array addition (+), subtraction ($-$), multiplication (.*), division (./ , .\\), and exponentiation (.^) are performed element by element. All array type operations require that the arguments have the same dimension. Some array operations are preceded by a dot (.) before their names.

A.*B is the element-by-element product and returns a matrix $c_{ij} = a_{ij} b_{ij}$.

A./B, A.\\B, and A.^B return $\dfrac{a_{ij}}{b_{ij}}$, $\dfrac{b_{ij}}{a_{ij}}$, and $a_{ij}^{b_{ij}}$, respectively. For example,

```
>> a=[1 2;3 4]; b=[5 6;6 8];
>> a.*b

ans =
      5     12
     18     32

>> a.\b

ans =
      5      3
      2      2

>> a.^b

ans =
         1            64
       729         65536
```

You can verify the identity { $\sin(2t) = 2 \sin(t) \cos(t)$ } by

```
>> t=[0:100]'; x=sin(2*t); y=2*sin(t).*cos(t); [x  y]
```

Another type of product is the *Kronecker tensor product* of matrices. It is defined by

```
>> C=kron(A,B)
```

$C = kron\ (A,B)$ is a matrix where the ij-th partition is $C_{ij} = a_{ij} B$. For A and B given previously we get

```
>> a=[1 2;3 4]; b=[5 6;6 8];
>> kron(a,b)

ans =
     5     6    10    12
     6     8    12    16
    15    18    20    24
    18    24    24    32
```

2.4.2 Elementary Mathematical Functions

All trigonometric, hyperbolic, and transcendental functions are performed on an element-by-element basis. For angles, MATLAB operates in radian mode. Another function of interest is *angle* (angle of a complex number between $-\pi$ to π). For example,

```
>> x=[1+j , -1-j]; angle(x)*180/pi

ans =
    45   -135
```

Matrix functions (if they exist) are defined in linear algebra by

$$f(A) = M\, f(\Lambda)\, M^{-1}$$

where Λ is the matrix of eigenvalues and M is the modal matrix (matrix of eigenvectors of A). The following matrix functions are available: *expm*, *logm*, *sqrtm*, and *funm*. The function *funm* computes a matrix function of any elementary math function. Its syntax is

```
>> fa=funm(a,'fun')
```

where the option `fun` is any elementary function such as *sin*, *cos*, *log10*, etc.

2.4.3 Data Analysis: Column-Oriented Functions

The following functions operate on vectors. If they are applied to matrices, they are computed on a column-by-column basis. The functions *min, max, mean, median, std, sum, prod, cumsum*, and *cumprod* are among them. They find the minimum, maximum, mean, median, standard deviation, sum, product, cumulative sum, and cumulative product, respectively, of elements of vectors. Again, for matrices, they operate columnwise (the result is presented as a row vector). To find the smallest element in the matrix a, we cascade the command; i.e., sum(sum(a)). The commands *min* or *max* also return the corresponding index (or location) of the minimum or maximum value, respectively, when used with two output arguments. For example, we can find the peak value and the peak time in a step response from

```
>> [Mp,Tp]=max(ystep)
```

The *sort* command sorts each column of a matrix in ascending order. For complex data, the sorting is done according to the magnitudes of the elements:

```
>> [sx,indx]=sort(x)
```

The output, sx, is the sorted input; the second output, indx, is the indices used in the sort.

The *spline* command uses cubic splines for data interpolation; it has the syntax

```
>> yi=spline(x,y,xi)
```

Suppose $y=f(x)$ has been computed for a range of x. The *spline* command gives the value yi at the point xi. The following example demonstrates an application. First, we generate logarithms of 1 to 5. We then use interpolation to find logarithm of 2.5. The correct value is also shown.

```
>> x=[1:5]; y=log10(x);
>> y2=spline(x,y,2.5)

y2 =
     0.3993

>> log10(2.5)

ans =
     0.397
```

2.5 Polynomials

Polynomials are represented as vectors containing the polynomial coefficients in descending order. The *roots* command finds roots of polynomials. For example, the roots of the polynomial $s^3 + 2 s^2 + 3 s + 4$ are found by

```
>> p=[1 2 3 4]; roots(p)
```

```
ans =
  -1.6506
  -0.1747 + 1.5469i
  -0.1747 - 1.5469i
```

The *poly* command is used to form a polynomial from its roots. It returns the coefficients of the polynomial as a row vector:

```
>> p2=poly([-1 -2])

p2 =
     1     3     2
```

If the input argument of *poly* is a matrix, the command returns the characteristic polynomial of that matrix (characteristic polynomial of $A = \det |\lambda I - A|$) as a row vector.

A polynomial can be evaluated at a point using the *polyval* command. Its syntax is

```
>> ps=polyval(p,s)
```

where p is a polynomial and s is the point at which the polynomial is to be evaluated. The input s can be a vector or a matrix. In such cases, the evaluation is done element by element. For example, consider the polynomial $p(s) = (s + 1)(s + 2)$:

```
>> p2=[1 3 2]; a=[1 2;3 4]; polyval(p2,a)

ans =
      6    12
     20    30
```

The command *polyvalm, evaluates polynomials in the matrix sense. Given the matrix A and the polynomial matrix p(A)*, we get

$$A = \begin{bmatrix} 1 & 2 \\ 3 & 4 \end{bmatrix}, \qquad p(A) = A^2 + 3A + 2I$$

```
>> polyvalm(p,a)

ans =
     12    16
     24    36
```

Polynomials are multiplied and divided using the *conv* and *deconv* commands, respectively.

```
>> c=conv(a,b)
>> [q,r]=deconv(a,b)
```

Actually, *conv* performs discrete convolution, which is equivalent to polynomial multiplication; *deconv* performs long division where q is the quotient and r is the remainder.

```
>> conv([1 1],[1 2])

ans =
     1     3     2

>> deconv([1 3 2],[1 1])

ans =
     1     2
```

The *residue* command performs partial fraction expansion:

```
>> [r,p,k]=residue(num,den)
```

The outputs r, p, and k are the partial fraction coefficients, poles, and the direct term:

```
[r,p,k]=residue(1,[1 3 2])

r =
    -1
     1
p =
    -2
    -1
k =
    [ ]
```

Note that the direct term is the empty matrix because the transfer function is strictly proper. The *residue* command can also be used to form the (num,den) polynomials from its partial fraction expansion:

```
>>  [n,d]=residue(r,p,k)

n =
     0     1
d =
     1     3     2
```

MATLAB has several commands for numerical solution of calculus-type problems. They are: *quad* (numerical integration), *ode23* (ordinary differential equation solver), *fzero* (finding zeros of a nonlinear function), *fmin* (minimization of functions), and *fsolve* (solving systems of nonlinear algebraic equations). Use *help* for further information about these commands after reading Chapter 3.

2.6 Plotting and Graphics

MATLAB has a very strong graphic capability that is well suited to scientific and engineering applications. We will demonstrate some of these options and features. The basic commands are *plot, loglog, semilogx, semilogy,* and *polar*. They are all used the same way, although the axis scaling is different. The *plot* command uses linear axes. In the *loglog* command, both axes are logarithmic. In *semilogx* (*semilogy*), the X axis (Y axis) is logarithmic, and the other axis is linear. (The *semilogx* command is used to draw Bode plots; the frequency axis must be generated using the *logspace* command. See Chapter 4 for examples.) Finally, *polar* uses polar coordinates.

```
>> plot(x,y)
```

Plots the vector y versus the vector x. The vectors must have the same length. If one of the input arguments is a matrix, the vector is plotted against the row or columns of the matrix (whichever lines up). If both arguments are matrices, the columns of x will be plotted against the columns of y.

If y is a complex vector, then `plot(y)` will plot the imaginary versus the real part of y. This is useful for Nyquist plots.

2.6.1 Multiple Curves

If multiple curves (with the same number of data points) are to be plotted against the same axis, you can form a matrix from the data and use (shown for three sets of data)

```
>> plot(t,[x1 x2 x3])
```

If the curves are plotted against different vectors, use (shown for three sets of data)

```
>> plot(t1,x1,t2,x2,t3,x3)
```

This command plots $x1$ versus $t1$, $x2$ versus $t2$, etc. In this case, $t1$, $t2$, and $t3$ can have different sizes, so long as $x1$, $x2$, and $x3$ are compatible with their time axes.

You can display multiple curves on the same screen by splitting the screen. The screen can be split into a maximum of four windows. This is done using the *subplot* command:

```
>> subplot(rcp)
```

The screen is broken into r by c windows and p is the window for the present window. For example, *subplot*(212) splits the screen into two windows and puts the current plot in the second window (`subplot (211)` and `subplot (212)` are appropriate for Bode plots). Windows are numbered from left to right and top to bottom.

After the plot is drawn, we can add title, labels, text, and grid lines to it by issuing the following commands:

```
>> title('My Title'), xlabel('My X-axis Label')
>> ylabel('My Y-axis label), gtext('Text for annotation')
>> text(x,y,'Text for annotation'), grid
```

The command *gtext* is for mouse-positioned text. You will get a mouse cursor that allows you to position the text anywhere on the graph screen (some figures in this book are annotated using *gtext*). The text command writes the specified text string in the position specified by coordinates x and y. These coordinates are in units from the last plot.

The commands *shg* and *clg* will show and clear the graph screen, respectively. The *hold* command is a toggle (*hold on* or *hold off*); it keeps the present graph on screen, with its scaling and axis, so other graphs can be overlaid on it.

MATLAB automatically chooses its own axis scaling. You can override this using the axis command.

```
>> axis([x_min, x_max, y_min, y_max])
```

sets the axes to the specified settings. The plot must be redrawn for the new axis setting to take effect. Typing *axis* by itself freezes the current setting for subsequent plots. Typing *axis* again resumes auto-scaling. Another use of the *axis* command is to control the aspect ratio. Typing `axis ('square')` creates a square box so that a circle will be displayed as a true circle (normally it appears as an oval due to screen irregularities). To return to the normal mode, type `axis ('normal')`.

Line styles (-, —, :, -.), symbols (+, *, o, ., x), and colors (r=red, g=green, b=blue, w=white, i=invisible) used for the plots can also be modified. For three-dimensional plots and other features, follow the examples.

2.7 Examples

Example 2.1 Mercury's Orbit about Earth

The equations for Mercury's orbit about earth are given by the following parametric equations [EP88].
$$x(t) = 93 \cos t + 36 \cos 4.15t$$
$$y(t) = 93 \sin t + 36 \sin 4.15t$$

After $7\frac{1}{3}$ revolutions we get the following curve called an *epitrochoid*. The vectors x and y
are computed and plotted against each other. The plot is shown in Figure 2-1.

```
>> t=[0:pi/360:2*pi*22/3];
>> x=93*cos(t)+36*cos(t*4.15); y=93*sin(t)+36*sin(t*4.15);
>> axis('square'), plot(y,x), axis('normal')
```

Try the command worm(x,y) for an interesting and animated plot of this figure

Example 2.2 Polar Plots

The equation of a four-leaf figure in polar coordinates is $r = \cos(2\theta)$.

The angle must be in radians for the *polar* command. The figure is plotted in polar
coordinates in Figure 2-2. The *grid* command adds polar grid lines in this case.

```
>> th=[pi/200:pi/200:2*pi]'; r=cos(2*th); polar(th,r), grid
```

The equation for the Archimedes spiral is given by $r = k\,\theta$, $k > 0$.

The plot is shown in Figure 2-3.

```
>> sa=th/(2*pi); polar(th,sa), grid,pause
```

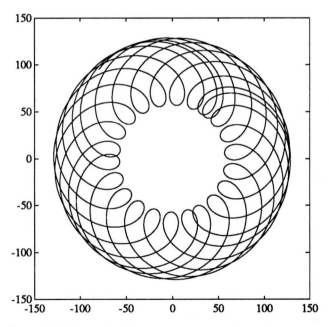

Figure 2-1 Mercury's orbit about earth. Linear plots of two vectors.

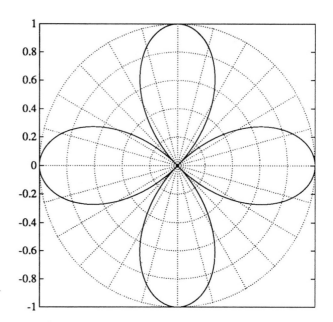

Figure 2-2 The four-leaf figure. A polar plot example.

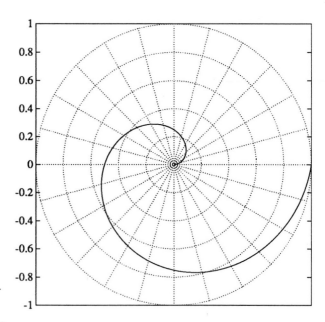

Figure 2-3 Archimedes spiral. A polar plot example.

Example 2.3 Drawing Circles

A circle, centered at the origin with radius r, is given by: $z = re^{j\theta}$.
Figure 2-4 shows five concentric circles using five different point types (symbols).

```
>> th=0:pi/10:2*pi; x1=exp(j*th);
>> plot(real(x1),imag(x1),'.',real(2*x1),imag(2*x1),'o',...
real(3*x1),imag(3*x1),'+',real(4*x1),imag(4*x1),'*',...
real(5*x1),imag(5*x1),'x')
```

Note the line continuation command (...) for long command lines. Also note that this method
of plotting multiple graphs allows changing line styles and symbols.
    The parametric equations of a circle with radius r and center at (a, b) are given by

$$x(t) = r\ cos\ (t) + a \quad , \quad y(t) = r\ sin\ (t) + b$$

$$(x - a)^2 + (y - b)^2 = r^2$$

We will plot two unit circles, one centered at the origin and the other centered at (1,1). Plotting
x versus y produces the circles

```
>> tt=[0:0.1:2*pi]'; x=cos(tt); y=sin(tt);
>> axis('square'), axis([-2 3 -2 3]);
>> plot([x x+1],[y y+1]), grid, axis('normal')
```

Note the manual and square axis settings. Do not forget to reset the axis to normal for future
plots. The plot is shown in Figure 2-5.

Example 2.4 Generating a Pulse Train

The Kronecker product is used here to duplicate a long series of 1's and –1's for the pulse
train. The plot is shown in Figure 2-6. Some of the graph characteristics can be modified
directly from pull-down menus in the Macintosh version of MATLAB. We have used that
here to change the axis setting (y_min=-2, y_max=2).

```
>> u=[1;-1;1;-1]; u=kron(u,ones(30,1));
>> ttt=0.1*[0:length(u)-1]'; plot(ttt,u)
```

Example 2.5 Drawing Geometric Figures: Triangles

It is possible to draw lines and generate geometric figures. All one needs to do is to enter the
X coordinates in one vector and the Y coordinates in another, and plot Y versus X. To produce
closed figures like triangles, the first and last coordinates must be the same.

```
>> a=[1;1]; b=[3;1]; c=[2.5;2];        % the vertices
>> tx=[a(1) b(1) c(1) a(1)];            % X coordinates
>> ty=[a(2) b(2) c(2) a(2)];            % Y coordinates
```

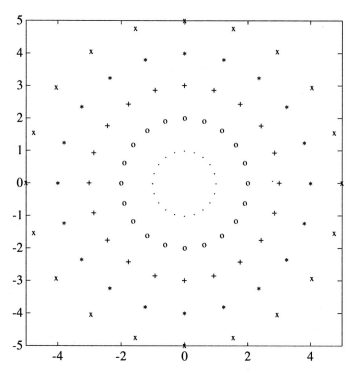

Figure 2-4 Concentric circles showing different plot symbols.

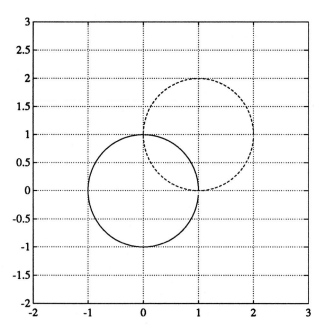

Figure 2-5 Two circles. Example showing axis settings and plotting a matrix versus another matrix.

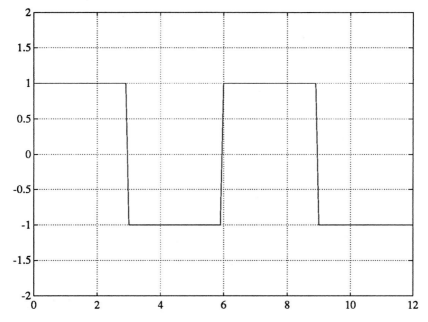

Figure 2-6 Pulse train.

We will now define a rotation matrix, which will rotate the vertices of the triangle by 45 degrees, and plot the rotated triangle (see problem 2.7).

```
>> aa=[cos(pi/4) -sin(pi/4); sin(pi/4) cos(pi/4)];  //rotation matrix
>> b1=aa*b; a1=aa*a; c1=aa*c;    % new vertices
>> tx1=[a1(1) b1(1) c1(1) a1(1)];  % new X coordinates
>> ty1=[a1(2) b1(2) c1(2) a1(2)];   % new Y coordinates
>> axis('square'), axis([0 3.5 0 3.5]), plot(tx,ty), hold on,...
plot(tx1,ty1),hold off, axis('normal')
```

Note the use of the *hold* command to retain the first triangle. The plot is shown in Figure 2-7.

Example 2.6 Three-Dimensional Plots

The commands *mesh* and *meshdom* are used to create mesh surfaces for functions of two variables. Typing mesh(z), where z is a matrix, is an interesting way to visualize large matrices. Suppose you want to plot $z=f(x,y)$ where x and y define the domain of f. First, we define the vectors x and y over their range. Make sure their size is not very large or you will run out of memory (creating 3-D surfaces consumes a lot of memory and time). Then, we need to generate a plane corresponding to the domain. The mesh surface is constructed on top of this plane with heights determined by the function values. The *meshdom* command produces

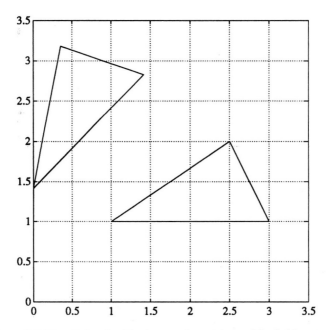

Figure 2-7 Plot of triangles. Plotting matrices and use of the *hold* command.

this plane by creating two matrices with repeated rows and columns of the x and y vectors. Finally the function is evaluated over the elements of the resulting matrices.

We will demonstrate the process by creating the frequency response surface of a second order system. Consider the system

$$G(s) = \frac{\omega_n^2}{s^2 + 2\zeta\omega_n s + \omega_n^2}$$

Letting $s = \sigma + j\omega$ we get

$$G(\sigma + j\omega) = \frac{\omega_n^2}{(\sigma^2 - \omega^2 + 2\zeta\sigma\omega_n + \omega_n^2) + j(2\sigma\omega + 2\zeta\omega\omega_n)}$$

For $\zeta = 0.5$ and $\omega_n = 1$

$$G(\sigma + j\omega) = \frac{1}{(\sigma^2 - \omega^2 + \sigma + 1) + j(2\sigma\omega + \omega)}$$

This function of two variables will now be plotted for: $-3 \leq \sigma \leq 3$ and $-3 \leq \omega \leq 3$.

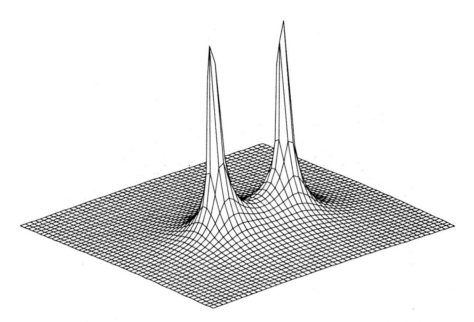

Figure 2-8 Mesh plot of the frequency response surface. An example of 3-D plotting.

```
>> w=linspace(-3,3,50); s=linspace(-3,3,50);
>> [W,S]=meshdom(w,s);
>> re=S.^2-W.^2+S+1; im=2*S.*W+W; den=re+j*im;
>> z=ones(den)./abs(den); mesh(z)
```

Note the use of element-by-element operations for matrices. The plot is shown in Figure 2-8.
You can view mesh surfaces from specified viewpoints.

```
>> mesh(z,[azimuth  elevate])
```

allows you to specify the azimuth (horizontal rotation) and elevation angles (in degrees).
Positive angle for the azimuth rotates the object clockwise, and positive value for the elevation
views the object from above (90 degrees is directly overhead). The default viewing angles are
[–37.5 30].
The next example creates the domain matrices directly (demonstrating the *meshdom*
command); we will also view the object from different angles. We will plot

$$z = \sin \sqrt{x^2 + y^2}$$

```
>> x=[-3:.1:3];
>> y=x'; x2=ones(y)*x; y2=y*ones(x);    % this is what meshdom does
>> r=sqrt(x2.^2+y2.^2);
```

```
>> z=sin(r); mesh(z)
```

The plot is shown in Figure 2-9.

```
>> mesh(z,[-30 +70])
```

rotates the plot and views it from above, as shown in Figure 2-10.

```
>> mesh(z,[-30  -70])
```

rotates the plot and views it from below, as shown in Figure 2-11. In the course of this example we created an interesting optical illusion. Look at the two views again. The *mesh* command can easily become a pleasing pastime.

Besides the basic plot types that we have discussed, MATLAB has some additional plot types. Bar charts can be drawn using the *bar* command; for sampled-data systems, the *stairs* command produces staircase-type plots; the *contour* command gives level curves for 3-D surfaces. Other fancier plot types such as *quiver, rose, compass,* and *feather* produce plots of complex data using arrows. As our final example, we will demonstrate the *compass* command.

Complex numbers can be represented using points or vectors in the complex plane. The Nyquist plot of a system is simply the plot of the frequency response (complex numbers) in the complex plane. The *nyquist* command (discussed in Chapter 4) produces the frequency response as two sets of vectors; the real parts, and the imaginary parts of the frequency response. Normally, a computer-generated (or hand-drawn) Nyquist plot is a plot of these complex numbers as points. The points are attached to each other to create a smooth-looking plot. The vectorial representation of complex numbers (and, hence, the Nyquist plot) can be very revealing and informative. Too often, this revealing representation is missed by students. We will use the *compass* command to show this vectorial representation along with the Nyquist plot of

$$G(s) = \frac{2}{s^2 + 3s + 2}$$

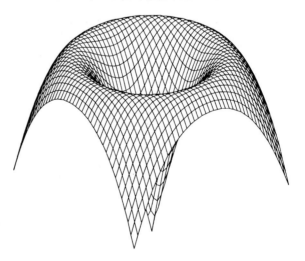

Figure 2-9 Mesh plot of a surface. Example of 3-D plotting.

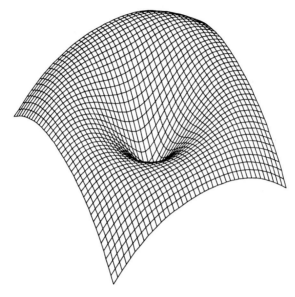

Figure 2-10 Mesh plot of Figure 2-9 viewed from above.

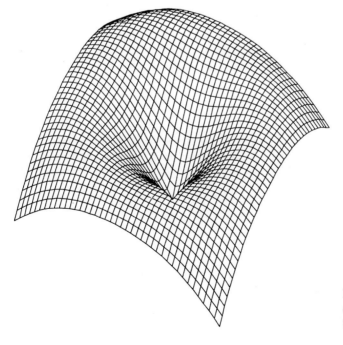

Figure 2-11 Mesh plot of Figure 2-9 viewed from below.

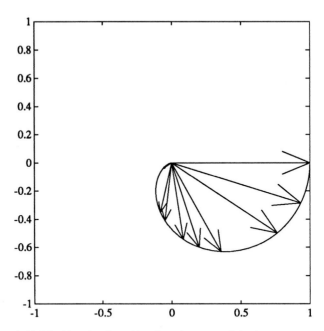

Figure 2-12 The Nyquist plot with selected vectors of the frequency response.

First, we obtain the data for the Nyquist plot. For a smooth-looking plot we use 100 points.

```
>> w1=logspace(-2,2,100); [re,im]=nyquist(2,[1 3 2],w1);
```

Because 100 vectors displayed with arrows will appear too cluttered, we will re-create some of the data using selected frequency points:

```
>> w2=[0 0.2 0.4 0.8 1 1.2 1.6 1.8 5 10];
>> [re2,im2]=nyquist(2,[1 3 2],w2);
```

In each case, the real and imaginary parts are added to create complex vectors. We then set a square grid for the plot; draw the vectors using *compass*; hold the plot; and draw the Nyquist plot overlaid on the vectors. The resulting plot is shown in Figure 2-12.

```
>> nyq=re+j*im;; z=re2+j*im2;
>> axis('square'), compass(z), hold on, axis('square'), plot(nyq)
```

2.8 Problems

2.1   The purpose of this exercise is to demonstrate different ways of addressing elements of matrices. Consider the following matrix A:

$$A = \begin{bmatrix} 11 & 12 & 13 & 14 \\ 21 & 22 & 23 & 24 \\ 31 & 32 & 33 & 34 \\ 41 & 42 & 43 & 44 \end{bmatrix}$$

You are to predict the result of the following operations and later check your predictions on the computer.

a. Use minimum number of operations to enter the matrix A.

b. A(: , 1)

c. A (2 , :)

d. A (: , 2 : 3)

e. A (2 : 3 , 2 : 3)

f. A (: , 1 : 2 : 3)

g. A (2 : 3)

h. A (:)

i. A (: , :)

j. ones (2 , 2)

k. eye (2)

l. B = [A , [ones (2 , 2) ; eye (2)]]

m. diag (A)

n. diag (A , 1)

o. diag (A , -1)

p. diag (A , 2)

2.2 The purpose of this exercise is to demonstrate matrix functions; e.g., the matrix sine function.

a. Enter the following matrix A:

$$A = \begin{bmatrix} 0 & \dfrac{\pi}{3} \\ \dfrac{\pi}{6} & \dfrac{\pi}{2} \end{bmatrix}$$

b. Find the sine of the individual elements; call this B1.

c. Find the cosine of the individual elements; call this B2.

d. Find B1^2 + B2^2. Note that this is not the identity matrix.

e. Find the eigenvalues and eigenvectors of A; call the eigenvector matrix M and the eigenvalue matrix L.

f. Find M sin(L) M^{-1}.

g. Find the matrix sine function of A using the *funm* command. You must get the same answer as in part *f*.

h. Find cos(A).

i. Show sin(A)^2 + cos(A)^2 = I.

2.3 The purpose of this exercise is to demonstrate the use of the matrix division (\) command.

a. Use the *rand* command to generate five random 2 by 2 matrices, A, B, C, D, E.

b. Without the use of the *inv* command, compute F in one line.

$$F = A^{-1} \, [\, B + C^{-1} (D^{-1} E) \,]$$

c. Without the use of the *inv* command, find the first column of A^{-1} using one command. Check your answer in both parts using the *inv* command.

2.4 The purpose of this exercise is to demonstrate the use of element-by-element operations and Kronecker products. Do each part by hand, and compare your answer with the computer.

$$A = \begin{bmatrix} 1 \\ 1 \\ 1 \end{bmatrix} \quad \text{and} \quad B = [\, 2 \ \ 3 \ \ 4 \,]$$

a. kron(A , B')
b. kron(A , B)
c. kron(A' , B)
d. kron(A' , B')
e. A .* B'
f. A .\ B'
g. A' .\ B

2.5 The purpose of this problem is to practice some of the graphic features.

a. Plot the following in polar coordinates for $0 \le \theta \le 2\pi$.

   i. $r = 3 \, (1 - \cos \theta)$ cardioid

   ii. $r = 2 \, (1 + \cos \theta)$

   iii. $r = 2 \, (1 + \sin \theta)$

   iv. $r = \cos 3 \, \theta$ three-leaf rose

   v. $r = e^{\frac{\theta}{4\pi}}$ logarithmic spiral

b. Obtain the three-dimensional plot of the function z for the given range of values $-5 \le x \le 5$, $-5 \le y \le 5$.

$$z = \frac{1}{(x+1)^2 + (y+1)^2 + 1} - \frac{1.5}{(x-1)^2 + (y-1)^2 + 1}$$

2.6 The purpose of this problem is to practice graphics along with some MATLAB math functions.

a. Obtain a plot of

$$y(t) = 1 - 2\,e^{-t}\sin(t), \quad \text{where } 0 \le t \le 8$$

Label the X axis "Time", the Y axis "Amplitude", and title the graph "Decaying-oscillating Exponential".

b. Obtain a plot of

$$y(t) = 5e^{-0.2t}\cos(0.9t - 30°) + 0.8e^{-2t}, \quad \text{where } 0 \le t \le 30$$

c. For $0 \le t \le 10$, obtain a graph of

$$y(t) = 1.23\cos(2.83t + 240°) + 0.625 \quad \text{and} \quad x(t) = 0.625$$

Plot the functions on the same graph, and find $y(t=0)$ and $y(t=10)$. Watch out for radians and degrees.

d. For $0 \le t \le 20$, plot the following functions on the same graph.

$$y_1(t) = 2.62\,e^{-0.25t}\cos(2.22t + 174°) + 0.6$$
$$y_2(t) = 2.62\,e^{-0.25t} + 0.6$$
$$y_3(t) = 0.6$$

Limit your graph to values of y between -2 and $+3$. Find the minimum value of y_1, the maximum value of y_1, and the values of the second maximum and minimum of y_1.

e. For $0 \le t \le 25$, plot the following functions on the same graph.

$$y_1(t) = 1.25\,e^{-t}$$
$$y_2(t) = 2.02\,e^{-0.3t}$$
$$y_3(t) = 2.02\,e^{-0.3t}\cos(0.554t - 128°) + 1.25\,e^{-t}$$

Limit the Y axis to -0.2 and $+1$ and your X axis to 0 and 16. Also find the following values for $y_3(t)$: $y(t=0)$, y_{max}, y_{min}, and $y(t=12)$.

2.7 The purpose of this problem is to demonstrate the effects of linear transformations. A point in the two-dimensional plane can be represented as a vector (an element of R^2 vector space). A matrix is geometrically a linear transformation or a map from R^2 to R^2. Therefore, $y = A\,x$ is another point or vector in the plane. Different matrices have different effects. They may expand, shrink, reflect, rotate, or perform other geometric operations on the vector.

You are to consider the following matrices and determine by analysis their effects on the triangle shown in the examples and then check your work using the computer. In each case, plot the original triangle and the transformed triangle on the same plot using appropriate scales for the x and y axis. (In MATLAB: issue the *plot* command for the first triangle, and use the *hold on* command.)

a. $A1 = \begin{bmatrix} 1 & 0 \\ 0 & -1 \end{bmatrix}$

b. $A2 = \begin{bmatrix} -1 & 0 \\ 0 & 1 \end{bmatrix}$

c. $A3 = \begin{bmatrix} 2 & 0 \\ 0 & 1 \end{bmatrix}$

d. $A4 = \begin{bmatrix} 1 & 2 \\ 1 & 0 \end{bmatrix}$

e. $A5 = \begin{bmatrix} \cos\left(\dfrac{\pi}{2}\right) & -\sin\left(\dfrac{\pi}{2}\right) \\ \sin\left(\dfrac{\pi}{2}\right) & \cos\left(\dfrac{\pi}{2}\right) \end{bmatrix}$

Note: Make sure you use appropriate scaling for the axes to fit both plots on the same screen.

2.8 Create a vector (with 101 elements) whose elements are alternating 1's and −1's. Plot the vector using the *plot* command. Replot it using the *comb* command (instead of the *plot* command). Repeat using the *stairs* command.

3

Programming in MATLAB

MATLAB supports some basic programming structures that allow looping and conditioning commands along with relational and logical operators. The syntax and use of some of these structures are very similar to those found in other high level languages such as C, BASIC, and FORTRAN. These new commands combined with ones we have discussed earlier can create powerful programs or new functions that can be added to MATLAB. These features are discussed in this chapter.

3.1 Relational and Logical Operators

Relational operators allow the comparison of scalars (or matrices, element by element). The result of relational operators is scalars (or matrices of the same size as the arguments) of either 0's or 1's (we refer to them as binary or 0-1 matrices). If the result of comparison is true, the answer is 1; otherwise, it is 0. The following operators are available.

< less than	<= less than or equal	== equal
> greater than	>= greater than or equal	~= not equal

For complex data, "==" and "~=" compare both the real and imaginary parts; other operators compare only the real part. You can also compare a scalar with a matrix, in which case all elements of the matrix are compared with the scalar. The result is a matrix of 1's and 0's. Let us try some examples. Note that we may occasionally add some spaces for clarity. You have to be careful with spaces, however. For example, x >= y is correct, but x> =y is wrong.

```
>> a=[1+j  pi  2  3.14  1-i]; b=[1-i  3.14  2  3.14  1+i];
>> c= a > b

c =
   0   1   0   0   0
```

```
>> c= a == b

c =
   0   0   1   1   0

>> c= a >= b

c =
   1   1   1   1   1

>> c= a ~= b

c =
   1   1   0   0   1
```

There are three logical operators available; they are

&   logical AND | logical OR   ~   logical NOT

X&Y returns a binary (0-1) matrix the same size as X and Y. In locations where X **and** Y have nonzero elements, 1 is returned (otherwise, 0 is returned); X|Y returns 1 in locations where X **or** Y have nonzero elements (otherwise, 0 is returned); ~X returns 1 where X has nonzero elements (otherwise, 0 is returned). For example,

```
>> X=[0, 2;pi, 0]; Y=[0, 0;j, 0];

>> X & Y

ans =
   0   0
   1   0

>> X|Y

ans =
   0   1
   1   0
```

The precedence of operators are arithmetic, relational, and logical. For instance in (X&Y+X>Y), X and Y are added, the result is then compared with Y, and the result of the comparison is then ANDed with X.

```
>> z= X & Y + X > Y

z =
   0   1
```

```
    1   0

>>   z= X > Y + X & Y

z =
   0   0
   0   0
```

There are two logical commands in MATLAB that also produce binary (0-1) matrices. They are *any* and *all*.

```
>> any(x)
```

Returns 1 if any of the elements of the vector argument is nonzero. It returns 0 otherwise. For matrix arguments, the operation is done columnwise, and the command returns a row vector. For example, the following command compares two matrices and returns 1 if they are not equal:

```
>> any(any(A~=B))
```

The command *all* returns 1 if all of the elements of the vector argument are nonzero. It returns 0 otherwise. For matrix arguments, the operation is done columnwise:

```
>> all(x)
```

For example, the following command returns 1 if two matrices are equal to each other:

```
>> all(all(A==B))
```

A matrix is *symmetric* if it is equal to its own transpose. The following command determines if a matrix is symmetric, returning 1 if it is:

```
>> all(all(A==A'))
```

Finally, we introduce a very useful command that returns the index (location) of nonzero elements in a vector (or matrix). The command name is *find*.

```
>> find(x)
```

Returns the location (index) of nonzero elements in a vector. If the argument is a matrix, MATLAB converts it to a long column using x(:). For example, suppose you have a vector that starts with leading zeros that you would like to remove (some commands in MATLAB and its toolboxes produce vectors with leading zeros that may cause problems in other commands). The following commands will remove the leading zeros:

```
>> ind=find(p~=0); p_=p(ind(1):length(p));
```

The first command finds the location of the nonzero elements; the next command redefines the vector. Let us test it.

```
>> p=[0 0 1 3 2]; ind=find(p~=0); p_=p(ind(1):length(p)); p_
```

```
p_ =
   1   3   2
```

The following command finds the number of nonzero elements in a vector or matrix:

```
>> nonzer=length(find(x))
```

MATLAB has commands for detection of NaNs (defined in Section 2.3), empty matrices, infinities, and strings. The commands *isnan, isempty,* and *isstr* return 1 when they find NaNs, empty matrices, and strings; the command *finite* returns 0 when it finds infinities.

The following command finds the location of the largest element in a vector (useful if you are trying to find the peak time in a step response). Assume the vector x is already defined.

```
>> peaktime=find(x==max(x))
```

3.2 Loops and Conditional Structures

Three commands are available that allow you to write loops, conditional loops, and conditional statements. They are *for, while,* and *if-else* commands. The loops can be nested and the statements can continue across lines; you can also use indentation for clarity. All commands, however, must terminate with an *end*. In nested loops, every occurrence of the above commands requires its own *end* statement.

for

The *for* command is used to execute a series of statements iteratively. Its syntax is shown below:

```
>> for  variable=expression, statement,..., statement, end
```

The expression is a vector or matrix, or valid MATLAB command resulting in a vector or matrix. *The statements are executed once for each element of the row vector or column of the matrix.* Loops tend to be slow and error prone; instead, wherever possible, take advantage of vector and matrix operations like *sort, find, any, all*, and various matrix-addressing operations. In short, try to vectorize statements.

The following example computes logarithms of numbers from 1 to 10,000. We do this in different ways for comparison. The commands *clock* and *etime* are used to time the operations (although not shown, we used *clear* at the beginning of every line).

```
>> t1=clock;for i=1:10000, a(i)=log(i);end; e1=etime(clock,t1);
>> t1=clock; ind=[1:10000]; for i=ind, a(i)=log(i); end;...
e2=etime(clock,t1);
>> t1=clock; a=zeros(1,10000); ind=[1:10000];...
for i=ind, a(i)=log(i); end; e3=etime(clock,t1);
>> t1=clock; ind=[1:10000]; a=log(ind); e4=etime(clock,t1);
>> t1=clock; ind=[1:10000]; a=zeros(1,10000); a=log(ind);...
e5=etime(clock,t1);
```

The following are the computation times for the different methods:

86.1700   86.5600   2.4200   0.2700   0.2800

The first method (first line) is a straightforward *for* loop. In the second method, the index of the loop is predefined as a row vector and the loop runs over its columns. In the third method, the vector a , which stores the output result, is preallocated. We now see a drastic reduction in computation time. The reason for this reduction is that in the previous methods, MATLAB has to resize the vector a each time it goes through the loop; with preallocation, this step is eliminated. In the fourth method, we eliminate the *for* loop and instead use MATLAB's built-in matrix calculation capabilities. This is what is meant by *vectorization*. Again, the reduction in computation time is significant. In the last method, we use both vectorization and preallocation. We notice a slight increase in computation time. This is because we do not have a loop anymore, and there is no resizing; hence, preallocation is unnecessary in such cases. The MATLAB User's Guide points out that preallocation of output variables reduces memory fragmentation and uses memory more efficiently. There-fore, preallocation of output variables is recommended when working with large matrices, especially on computers with limited memory.

The following example demonstrates elimination of *for* loops by vectorization. Suppose we wish to exchange elements between two matrices systematically (a very common operation). In particular, given matrices A and B, we wish to set every other row of A equal to the last seven elements of every other row of B.

```
>> a=[1:2:13]; am=ones(7); for i=1:7, am(i,:)=a; end; am
am =
    1   3   5   7   9   11   13
    1   3   5   7   9   11   13
    1   3   5   7   9   11   13
    1   3   5   7   9   11   13
    1   3   5   7   9   11   13
    1   3   5   7   9   11   13
    1   3   5   7   9   11   13
```

```
>> b=0:2:18; bm=ones(10); for i=1:10, bm(i,:)=b; end; bm
```

bm =

0	2	4	6	8	10	12	14	16	18
0	2	4	6	8	10	12	14	16	18
0	2	4	6	8	10	12	14	16	18
0	2	4	6	8	10	12	14	16	18
0	2	4	6	8	10	12	14	16	18
0	2	4	6	8	10	12	14	16	18
0	2	4	6	8	10	12	14	16	18
0	2	4	6	8	10	12	14	16	18
0	2	4	6	8	10	12	14	16	18
0	2	4	6	8	10	12	14	16	18

The following is how **not** to solve the problem!

```
>> a2=am; for i=1:2:7, for j=1:7, a2(i,j)=bm(i+1,j+3); end; end; a2
```

a2 =

6	8	10	12	14	16	18
1	3	5	7	9	11	13
6	8	10	12	14	16	18
1	3	5	7	9	11	13
6	8	10	12	14	16	18
1	3	5	7	9	11	13
6	8	10	12	14	16	18

The following command uses matrix addressing and produces the same result:

```
>> a2=am; a2([1:2:7],[1:7]) = bm([2:2:8],[4:10])
```

while

This command allows conditional looping in which statements within the loop are executed as long as the condition is true. Its syntax is

```
>> while  expression,  statement,  . . ,statement,end;
```

The "expression" is of the form: X operator Y, where X and Y are scalars or expressions that yield scalars. The "operator" is usually a relational operator.

The following example uses *while* to search for a random and stable matrix (i.e., the real part of its eigenvalues are negative):

```
>> rand('normal'); a=rand(2);
>> while max(real(eig(a))) >= 0, a=rand(2); end; eig(a)
```

```
ans =
 -0.2185 + 1.0137i
 -0.2185 - 1.0137i
```

To compute and display the famous Fibonacci numbers, defined by

$$f(n+2) = f(n+1) + f(n) \qquad f(0) = 1, \; f(1) = 1$$

we write

```
>> f=[1 1]; i=1; while f(i+1)+f(i)<100;
f(i+2)=f(i+1)+f(i); i=i+1; end; f

f =
   1   1   2   3   5   8   13   21   34   55   89
```

if, else, elseif

These commands are also used for conditional execution of a set of commands. The syntax is

```
>> if   expression1, statement,...statement,...
        elseif  expression2,  statement,...,  statement ,... ,
        else  statement,... ,
     end
```

If expression1 is true (i.e., it has all nonzero elements), the first set of statements is executed; if expression2 is true, then the next set of statements is executed; otherwise, the statements after *else* are executed. Expression has the same form as the *while* statement; i.e., it is usually a relational operator. The *elseif* (this is one word; do not insert a space) or the *else* portions are optional. Note that all the three commands above can also be nested. Remember that the *end* statement is mandatory. Here are two examples.

This example will remove leading zeros from a polynomial. We previously used the find command to perform the same task.

```
>> p=[0 0 0 1 3 0 2 0 0 9];
>> for i=1:length(p), if p(1)==0, p=p(2:length(p));
end;
end; p
p =
   1   3   0   2   0   0   9
```

In the following example, we perform the opposite task. We compare the dimension of two vectors; if they are different, the vector with the smaller dimension will be padded

with enough zeros to make it the same size as the other vector; if the vectors have the same
dimension, the program should return with the vectors unchanged.

```
>> p=[1 2 3]; q=[1 2 3 4 5 6];
>> lp=length(p); lq=length(q);
>> if lp == lq, break
        elseif lp > lq
        q=[zeros(1,lp-lq) q]
        else p=[zeros(1,lq-lp) p]
     end

p =
   0   0   0   1   2   3

>> p=[1 2 3 4]; q=1;      % try the program on these vectors


q =
   0   0   0   1
```

Note the use of the *break* command that terminates the execution of the rest of the
statements if its condition is met.

3.3 M-files: Scripts and Function Files

In its normal mode, MATLAB is command-driven. You type in the commands and
MATLAB responds (unless you forget to close a loop by an *end* statement, or worse, you
write a never-ending loop!). MATLAB is also capable of executing programs that are
stored in files. There are two conditions: the program (as an ASCII file) must reside in a
directory that is in MATLAB's path; the file must have an extension of ".m". For example,
the previous commands in our last example that pads vectors with zeros can be stored in
a file called "zeropad.m". This is why MATLAB programs are called M-files. The
restriction on filename extension is not needed in the Macintosh version of MATLAB.
M-files are usually created using any text editor that produces ASCII format files, such as
the MS-DOS Editor. Almost any word processor also has this feature, although with
advanced word processors you have to make sure that your file is saved as an ASCII file;
otherwise, word processors add non-ASCII characters and codes to the file and make it
unreadable by MATLAB.

There are two types of M-files: *script files* (or *scripts*) and *function files* (or
functions).

3.3.1 Scripts

Long sequences of MATLAB commands can be placed in a script file and executed. To
execute a script file, simply type its filename (without its extension) at the prompt. Scripts

operate globally on the data in the workspace. For example, if the variable x is on the workspace, and you run a script that redefines x, the value of x will change. All variables referenced in the script must either be available on the workspace or defined within the body of the script.

For example, consider the following script file called "padzer.m":

```
lp=length(p); lq=length(q);
if lp == lq, break
        elseif lp > lq
        q=[zeros(1,lp-lq) q]
        else p=[zeros(1,lq-lp) p]
end
```

To use this program, first define the vectors p and q; then execute the script as shown:

```
>> p=[1 2]; q=[1 2 3 4 5];
>> padzer
```

3.3.2 Functions

Functions are M-files that extend the capabilities of MATLAB. Many of MATLAB's and all of the Toolboxes' commands are in the form of functions. The main differences between scripts and functions are: functions allow parameter passing by values, and functions use local variables and do not operate globally on the workspace. Another difference is that the first line of a function file must contain the word "function". The following is a typical function file:

```
function [out1,out2,...]=filename(in1,in2,...)
%  optional comment lines for documentation
 MATLAB commands
```

A function can have multiple input and output arguments. Similar to other MATLAB functions, the inputs are placed within parentheses and outputs within square brackets (not necessary if there is only one output). After the first header line, you can include comments for documentation purposes. These lines will be displayed when *help* is requested. All variables defined within the body of the function are local, and will be destroyed once the function is executed. The only variables passed on to the workspace are the ones that are assigned as the function outputs. Local variables in a function will not affect the global workspace. Functions can be used like any other MATLAB command.

The following is a simple function, called " cltf ", that assumes transfer functions G(s) and K(s) are in series in unity feedback configuration. It gives the open loop, GK(s), and closed loop, T(s), transfer functions.

```
function [ngk,dgk,nt,dt]=cltf(ng,dg,nk,dk)
ngk=conv(ng,nk); dgk=conv(dg,d);
```

```
dimngk=length(ngk); dimdgk=length(dgk);
nc=[zeros(1,dimdgk-dimngk),ngk];
dt=nc+dgk;
nt=ngk;
```

We will use this function to find the closed loop transfer function for (unity feedback) $G(s) = \dfrac{1}{s^2}$ and $K(s) = \dfrac{s+5}{s+10}$:

```
>> ng=1; dg=[1,0,0]; nk=[1,5]; dk=[1,10];

>> [ngk,dgk,nt,dt]=cltf(ng,dg,nk,dk)

ngk =
   1    5
dgk =
   1   10    0    0
nt =
   1    5
dt =
   1   10    1    5
```

3.3.3 Creating M-files

In Macintosh MATLAB, select New under the File Menu; a File window will be opened where you can type your program. When you are done, select Save and Go to save and execute the script; switch back and forth between the Command and the File windows until you have an error-free program. In Windows MATLAB, you may use the Notebook icon; type your program and save it. You can switch back and forth between the MATLAB and the Notebook windows until you have a working program. In the DOS version of MATLAB, use either the *edit* command or the "!" character to invoke your text editor. If you use the *edit* command, the MATLAB.BAT file must contain a line to invoke your text editor. Using the "!" command, you temporarily leave MATLAB; use your favorite editor to type your program. When you exit the editor, you automatically return to MATLAB.

Sometimes, you may not know how to proceed to solve a problem. Most people have to use some trial and error or "poking around" until they get a working program. In such cases, it may be faster to turn *diary* on. The *diary* command stores your session inputs and outputs in a file; you can then use your text editor to remove your errors and the MATLAB responses to get a clean working program.

3.4 Text Strings as Macros

Macros are a short sequence of MATLAB commands that are used often in a session. They can be saved for use in future sessions as part of other M-files. Macros are created as *text strings* and are executed using the *eval* command. The next example uses a macro to compute factorials:

```
>> fct= 'prod(1:n)';
```

We will now use the macro to find 10!

```
>> n=10; eval(fct)
```

```
ans =
   3628800
```

3.5 Programming Utilities

MATLAB has several commands that allow you to make your programs interactive, and help with debugging your programs. We will briefly discuss some of these commands.

```
>> pause
```

stops an M-file until any key is pressed. It is useful after plotting commands; *pause(n)* will pause for *n* seconds and *pause(-2)* cancels all subsequent pauses.

```
>> echo    or    echo on    or    echo off
```

displays the program contents while an M-file is being executed. It is a toggle command, so typing *echo* by itself will change the echo state. If *echo* is on, it affects all script files; it affects function files differently, though. To turn *echo* on for a particular function file, use *echo filename on*; *echo on all* turns it on for all functions (functions are interpreted instead of compiled when *echo* is on; hence, they become considerably slower).

```
>> keyboard
```

stops an M-file and gives the control to the keyboard. You can view and change all variables as you wish. Typing *return* and pressing the return (or ENTER) key allows the M-file to continue. It is useful for debugging programs.

```
>> x=input('prompt')
```

The *input* command displays the text string as a prompt, waits for the user to enter a response, evaluates the expression entered by the user and assigns it to x. It is the input command that lets you create interactive programs. For example, we now write an interactive factorial macro:

```
>> f1='prod(1:n)';
```

```
>> f2='n=input(''enter number:__''); z=eval(f1); disp(''n! is''), disp(z)';
>> eval(f2)
```

> enter number:__5
> n! is
>   120

Note the following points. The interactive macro, f2, can call another macro, f1. When you use strings containing apostrophes ('), you must double the apostrophes (do not use quotation marks) . For instance, the f2 macro is enclosed by apostrophes; the strings within the *input* and *disp* commands are also enclosed by apostrophes; the apostrophes for these strings are doubled.

```
>> exist('item')
```

checks for the existence of a variable in the workspace or a file in MATLAB's path. It returns 1 if the variable exists; it returns 2 if the file exists; it returns 0 otherwise.

3.6 Program Examples

Example 3.1

The following is a simple script that will compute the step response of a second order system for values of ζ ranging from 0.1 to 1 and will create a mesh plot of the step responses.

```
n=1; y=zeros(200,1); i=1;
for del=0.1:0.1:1
        d=[1, 2*del, 1];
        t=[0:0.1:19.9]';
        y(:,i)=step(n,d,t);
        i=i+1;
end
mesh(fliplr(y),[-120 30])
```

The output of the program is shown in the Figure 3-1. The *fliplr* command flips a matrix from left to right. This along with the view angle change is done to re-create the plot on the cover of the Control System Toolbox User's Guide.

Example 3.2

This program is a slight generalization of the first program. Suppose we want to obtain the step response of a system for three different values of damping ratio and undamped natural frequency; i.e.,

$$G(s) = \frac{b}{s^2 + a s + b}$$

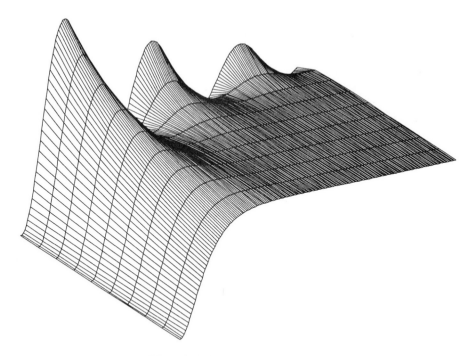

Figure 3-1 Family of step responses.

where a = { 1, 2, 4 } and b = { 1.25, 2, 29 }. The following program accomplishes the task:

```
a=[1 2 4]; b=[1.25 2 29];
y=zeros(100,3); t=linspace(0,10,100)';
for j=1:3,
        num=b(j), den=[1 a(j) b(j)],
        y(:,j)=step(num,den,t);
end
```

Example 3.3

This program is a function that will compute the step response characteristics of a system. It computes percent overshoot (POS), rise time (T_r), peak time (T_p) and 2% settling time (T_s). You can modify it for your own use. It is also meant to demonstrate the use of *for, if,* and *while* structures. You will find this program useful for many of the exercises and simulations in Chapter 4 because it simplifies data analysis by automating it.

```
function [pos,tr,ts2,tp]=stepchar(t,y)
% Finding POS and Tp
[mp,ind]=max(y); dimt=length(t);yss=y(dimt);
pos=100*(mp-yss)/yss; tp=t(ind);
```

```
% Finding rise time Tr
i=1; j=1; k=1; q=1;
while y(i)<0.1;
  i=i+1;
end;
t1 = t(i);
while y(j)<0.9;
  j=j+1;
end;
t2 = t(j); tr= t2 -t1;
% Finding settling time (two percent) Ts
i = dimt + 1; n = 0;
while n==0,
    i = i - 1;
            if i == 1,
                    n = 1;
            elseif y(i) >= 1.02,
                    n = 1;
            end;
end;
t1 = t(i); i = dimt + 1; n = 0;
while n == 0,
  i = i - 1;
            if y(i) <= 0.98,
                    n = 1;,
            end;
  t2 = t(i);
            if t1 > t2,
                    ts2 = t1;
            else
                    ts2 = t2;
            end
end
```

Example 3.4

Here is the same program using the *for* and *if-elseif* structures.

```
function [pos,tr,ts,tp]=stpchar2(t,y)
dimt=length(t); [mp,ind]=max(y); yss=y(dimt);
pos=100*(mp-yss)/yss; tp=t(ind);
for i=1:dimt,
        if y(i) > 1.02*yss,
                ts=t(i);
        elseif y(i) < 0.98*yss,
                ts=t(i);,
        end
```

```
        end
    for i=1:dimt
            if y(i) < 0.1*yss,
                    t1=t(i);
            elseif y(i)==mp,
                    break;
            end
    end
    for i=1:dimt;
            if y(i) < 0.9*yss,
                    t2=t(i);
            elseif y(i)==mp,
                    break
            end;
    end
    tr = t2 - t1;
```

3.7 Problems

Note: The problem denoted by * requires many simulations and is time-consuming.

3.1 The purpose of this problem is to illustrate the use of *for*, *sum*, and *prod* commands.

a. Use the *prod* command to generate and list N factorial (N !) and test it for N ranging from 1 to 10.

b. Repeat part *a* using the *for* command instead of *prod* command.

c. Use the *sum* command to find and list in tabular form the consecutive sum of N numbers and test it for N ranging from 1 to 10.

d. Repeat part *c* using the *for* command instead of the *sum* command.

e. Write a program to generate and tabulate the sum of the squares for the first N integers and test it for N ranging from 1 to 10.

Note: For the following problems, you might note that the step response and frequency response of a transfer function, $G = num/den$, are obtained as shown below.

```
>> t=linspace(0,tmax,Npts)';
>> vy=step(num,den,t);
>> [mag,phase,w]=bode(num,den);
```

3.2 Modify the program in Example 3 or 4 so that the function computes characteristics of several step responses simultaneously. Note that in the examples, the step response data are a column vector; here you want to feed in several responses simultaneously, so the response data are a matrix (each column corresponds to a different step response data).

3.3 The purpose of this problem is to compare the step response of a system with a pair of dominant complex poles versus systems that have nondominant poles.

a. Find the poles of the following transfer functions. Use the program developed in Problem 3.2 to compute the step response characteristic features (POS, T_r, , T_s, T_p) of the following systems.

$$T_1 = \frac{2}{s^2 + 2s + 2} \quad , \quad T_2 = \frac{4s + 2}{s^2 + 2s + 2} \quad , \quad T_3 = \frac{1}{2s^3 + 3s^2 + 3s + 1}$$

b. Write a program that will take as its inputs the closed loop frequency response data (ω, Mag, Phase) and will output its characteristic features (M_r, BW). Test it on the above systems.

c. Use the above programs and tabulate the required data.

d. Comment on the effects of an added zero (as in T_2) or an added pole (as in T_3) on the time and frequency response characteristics of the systems.

3.4 Write a program that will take the numerator and denominator of a transfer function as its input and that finds its poles, isolates the *dominant* complex poles, and computes its step response characteristic features. Note that in the program of Problem 3.2 you used actual data to find response features, whereas here you use the dominant poles and *formulas* (see Chapter 1). It is expected that while the poles are dominant, the results of both programs should be fairly close; otherwise, the formulas give inaccurate results. Use the transfer function in Problem 3.3 for data. Note that T_2 and T_3 have an extra pole or zero, and it is expected that the results will be inaccurate for these cases.

*3.5 Write a program that will take two step response specifications and produce a set of five desirable complex pole locations that meet the specifications. It should also compute the other remaining features and tabulate them along with the pole locations. Note that this program is almost " inverse" of the program you prepared for Problem 3.4. For example, the inputs might be $10 \le POS \le 30$, and $1 \le T_r \le 3$. Your program should search over the appropriate region of the complex plane and choose five pole locations, and for each pole it should compute the expected T_r, T_s, T_p and tabulate them alongside the corresponding poles. Test your program for the following specifications and tabulate your results. Before writing the program, show geometrically in the complex plane the regions satisfying the following specifications. You should also obtain the step response of a canonical second order transfer function having your computed poles and actually verify that your poles meet the specifications by finding the resulting step responses and their characteristics.

a. $10 < POS < 30$, $5 < Tr < 10$

b. $5 < POS < 15$, $1 < Tr < 2$

c. $5 < POS < 20$, $2 < Tp < 3$

d. $1 < Tp < 2$, $5 < Ts < 10$

For example, our program produced the following outputs for part *d*.

POLE_LOC =   Computed using formulas for pole locations

Real	Imag	POS	Ts	Tr	Tp
-0.4000	1.5708	44.9329	10.0000	1.1105	2.0000
-0.5000	1.9635	44.9329	8.0000	0.8884	1.6000
-0.6000	2.3562	44.9329	6.6667	0.7403	1.3333
-0.7000	2.7489	44.9329	5.7143	0.6346	1.1429
-0.8000	3.1416	44.9329	5.0000	0.5552	1.0000

POLE_LOC =   Computed from acrual data

POS	Ts	Tr	Tp
44.7869	6.8182	0.9091	1.9697
44.4832	5.4545	0.6061	1.6667
44.7966	4.5455	0.4545	1.3636
44.0916	3.9394	0.4545	1.2121
44.0948	3.3333	0.4545	1.0606

3.6 Consider the exponential mapping between two complex planes: $z = e^{sT}$

This map plays an important part in digital control (see Chapter 9); e.g., it shows the relation between poles of a continuous system and its sampled version. Let $T = 1$ for simplicity. Remember, the complex variable of the Laplace transform, s, is

$$s = -\sigma + j\,\omega_d \quad \rightarrow \quad z = e^{-\sigma + j\omega_d} = e^{-\sigma} e^{j\omega_d} \quad \text{where} \quad \sigma = \zeta\,\omega_n \;, \;\; \omega_d = \omega_n \sqrt{1 - \zeta^2}$$

We would like to investigate how various lines in the *s*-plane are mapped into the *z*-plane. For example, lines of constant σ are mapped into circles of radius e^{σ} as shown next.

When σ is fixed, $|z| = e^{\sigma}$ and $\angle z = \omega_d$. Therefore, as ω is varied, a circle is swept out. In particular, the $j\omega$ axis ($\sigma = 0$) is mapped onto the unit circle.

a. Let $\omega_d = [0 : 0.1 : 2]$, plot the map of constant σ for $\sigma = [1 : 5]$. Use the *hold* command to get five concentric circles in one plot.

b. Let $\sigma = [0 : 0.05 : 5]$, plot the map of constant ω_d, for $\omega_d = [0 : \pi/6 : \pi]$. Use the *hold* command to get seven lines emanating from the origin in one plot.

c. Let $\zeta = [0 : 0.05 : 1]$, plot the map of constant ω_n, for $\omega_n = [\pi/20 : \pi/10 : \pi]$. Use the *hold* command to get ten logarithmic curves in one plot.

d. Let $\omega_d = [0 : \pi/60 : \pi]$, plot the map of constant ζ, for $\zeta = [0 : 0.2 : 0.8]$. Use the *hold* command to get five spirals in one plot.

To get the correct plots, you will have to express z in terms of the appropriate sweep variables. For instance, in part *c*, you have to write z in terms of ζ and ω_d.

Refer to [FPW91], [O87], or other references given in Chapter 9 to see samples of these contours.

4

Classical Control

Commands

In this chapter we will demonstrate some of the MATLAB commands available for classical control analysis. These commands are available in the Control System Toolbox. We are interested in finding impulse response, step response, response to general inputs, frequency response, and root locus of a system represented by a transfer function. A transfer function $G(s)$ is entered by defining separately its numerator and denominator as polynomials. MATLAB commands interpret these polynomials internally as a transfer function.

4.1 Time Domain

Many of the control system commands automatically generate plots if invoked without left-hand arguments. Based on the locations of poles and zeros, the auto-selection algorithms find the best set of time or frequency points. The auto-plot option does not produce any data, however. It is best used for initial analysis and design. For comparative studies and record keeping, you should use the syntax form that includes left-hand arguments.

The step response, $y(t)$, of a single-input single-output system with transfer function $G(s) = num(s)/den(s)$, can be obtained by the *step* command. Its syntax is

```
>> y=step(num,den,t)
```

Note that the time axis, t, must be generated first as a vector. The step response will have the same dimension as the vector t. For single input–multioutput (SIMO) systems, the output will be a matrix with the same number of columns as the number of outputs. The *step* command has other syntax forms that require the state space notation (see Chapter 5).

For example, to compute and plot the step response from $t = 0$ to $t = 10$ of

$$G(s) = \frac{10}{s^2 + 2\,s + 10}$$

enter

```
>> num=10; den=[1,2,10];
>> t=[0:0.1:10]'; y=step(num,den,t); plot(t,y)
```

This produces two columns, with 101 elements; one for the time axis and one for the step response.

The impulse response is obtained by the *impulse* command. Its syntax is similar to the *step* command; i.e.,

```
>> y=impulse(num,den,t)
```

The system response to general inputs can also be obtained. The appropriate command is *lsim* and has the following syntax:

```
>> y=lsim(num,den,u,t)
```

The input is the vector *u*. The number of rows of *u* determines the number of output points computed. For single-input systems, *u* is a column vector. For multi-input systems the number of columns of *u* equals the number of inputs. For example, to compute the ramp response, use the vector t as the input:

```
>> ramp=t; y=lsim(num,den,ramp,t)
```

We can find the response to random uniform noise using the *rand* function. Note that *rand(m, n)* generates an *m* by *n* matrix of uniformly distributed random numbers between 0 and 1. The noise response of the system is found for a 10-sec record as shown below:

```
>> noise=rand(101,1); y=lsim(num,den,noise,t);
```

4.2 Frequency Domain

The frequency response of systems can be obtained using the *bode, nyquist,* and *nichols* commands. These commands automatically generate plots if they are used without left-hand arguments. The various syntaxes for the *bode* command are

```
>> bode(num,den)
>> [mag,phase,w]=bode(num,den)
>> [mag,phase]=bode(num,den,w)
```

The first syntax produces, on a split screen, the Bode magnitude (in dB) and phase (in degrees) plots. In the alternate syntaxes, magnitude and phase are returned as column vectors. The magnitude is not now in dB, however. The second form automatically generates the frequency points as a row vector. In the third form, the user supplies the frequency points. If you are comparing frequency responses of various transfer functions, the third form may be more convenient. For other options and syntactical information, get on-line help on *bode*.

To generate plots, issue the following commands:

```
>> subplot(211), semilogx(w,20*log10(mag)),
>> subplot(212), semilogx(w,phase)
```

the first command splits the screen in two halves and places the magnitude plot in the top half. The second command uses the *semilogx* command to produce a semilog plot (logarithmic frequency axis) and converts the magnitude to dB. The second line places the phase plot in the bottom half. If you wish the frequency axis to be in Hz, use w/(2*pi) instead of w. If you want to specify the frequency points, use the *logspace* command:

```
>> w=logspace(m,n,npts)
```

This command produces a row vector of logarithmically spaced points from 10^m to 10^n, the number of points (npts) is optional. For example, the following produces points from 0.01 to 1000 rad/sec:

```
>> w=logspace(-2,3);
```

The *nyquist* and *nichols* commands have the syntaxes

```
>> [re,im]=nyquist(num,den,w)
>> [mag,phase]=nichols(num,den,w); magdb=20*log10(mag);
```

The *nyquist* command computes the real and imaginary parts of $G(j\omega)$. To obtain the plot, simply plot the imaginary versus the real part. The *nichols* command computes the magnitude and phase (in degrees). If you have already issued the *bode* command, you can get the same result by plotting magnitude versus phase directly. A Nichols Chart grid can be overlaid on the plot using the *ngrid* command; i.e., enter *ngrid* at the prompt.

4.2.1 Stability Margins

Classical notions of relative stability, as measured by gain and phase margins, are obtained using the *margin* command. Its syntaxes are

```
>> [gm,pm,wpc,wgc]=margin(mag,phase,w)
>> margin(mag,phase,w)
```

The inputs are the magnitude (not in dB), phase, and frequency vectors obtained from the *bode* or *nichols* command. The outputs are the gain margin (not in dB), phase margin (in degrees), and their corresponding frequencies. The second syntax form, without left-hand arguments, generates the Bode plots with the margins marked with vertical lines. If there are multiple crossings of the frequency axes, the plot marks the worst margins. The first form does not necessarily give the worst margin. In fact, our experience has shown that the results of the *margin* command may not be accurate. It is important that these numbers be accepted cautiously and interpreted correctly. This can be done by obtaining the Nyquist plot and examining the encirclements.

4.3 Root Locus

Root locus of continuous SISO systems can be obtained using the *rlocus* command. There are two basic varieties of this command:

```
>> rlocus(num,den)    or   rlocus(num,den,k)
```

In these forms, the root locus plot is automatically generated. If the third input argument (the vector k) is specified, the root locus for those gains will be plotted; otherwise, the gain is automatically determined.

The following syntax generates the closed loop poles. You can obtain a root locus plot using a symbol of your choice by plotting the imaginary versus the real parts of the closed loop poles.

```
>> clpoles=rlocus(num,den)   or   clpoles=rlocus(num,den,k)
>> plot(real(clpoles),imag(clpoles),'*')
```

The *axis* command allows you to zoom on a particular region. Lines of constant damping ratio (ζ from 0 to 1 in 0.1 increments) and natural frequency can be overlaid on the root locus by using the *sgrid* command:

```
>> sgrid   or   sgrid(zeta,wn)
```

The second form allows you to specify particular ranges for the damping ratio and natural frequency. The following commands plot the root locus of *G(s)*, zoom on the upper half of the plane in the vicinity of the imaginary axis, and overlay the damping ratio lines from 0.5 to 0.7 and natural frequency line at 0.5 rad/sec:

```
>> ng=1; dg=[1 3 2 0]; axis([-1 1 0 3]); rlcous(ng,dg)
>> sgrid([0.5:0.1:0.7],0.5)
```

It is frequently desired to find the gain at a given point on the root locus. This can be accomplished using the *rlocfind* command. First, obtain the root locus; then issue the following command:

```
>> [k,poles]=rlocfind(num,den)
```

This will put a crosshair in the graphics window. Using a mouse, point to the desired location and click the mouse button. The gain at that point and the closed loop poles will be returned. If the selected point is not on the locus, the gain will be returned; if it is close to the locus, the gain and the closed loop poles nearest the selected point will be returned.

This command can also be used without doing the root locus first, provided you use the following alternate form

```
>> [k,poles]=rlocfind(num,den,p)
```

The input argument p is a vector of specified poles. Suppose, for G(s), you want to find the root locus gains and all closed loop poles for the pole locations –0.5 and –0.6; the following command can be used:

```
>> ng=1; dg=[1 3 2 0];
>> [k,clpoles]=rlocfind(ng,dg,[-0.5 -0.7])
```

The outputs are

```
k =
    0.3750   0.3360

clpoles =
   -2.1514   -2.1381
   -0.5000   -0.6000
   -0.3486   -0.2619
```

4.4 Transfer Function Utilities

There are other commands available for analysis and manipulation of transfer functions. A transfer function can be displayed using the *printsys* command. Its syntax and an example are shown next:

```
>> printsys(num,den)

>> ng=[1 1];dg=[1 3 2 0];
>> printsys(ng,dg)

num/den =
   s + 1
  ---------------
  s^3 + 3 s^2 + 2 s
```

Poles and zeros of transfer functions can be found in different ways. For example, we can use the *roots* command to find the roots of the numerator and denominator.

Alternately, we can use the *tf2zp* or *pzmap* commands. The syntax of the *tf2zp* command is

```
>> [z,p,k]=tf2zp(num,den)
```

This returns the zeros and poles in the column vectors z and p; the gain is the scalar k. The inverse of this command is the *zp2tf* command, which is useful for creating a transfer function with known poles and zeros.

The syntax of the *pzmap* command is

```
>> [p,z]=pzmap(num,den)
```

If the left-hand arguments are omitted, the pole-zero plot of the system will be displayed. This command can also be used to plot previously computed poles and zeros (input arguments are poles and zeros entered as column vectors).

When a transfer function is not coprime (i.e., it has pole-zero pairs that cancel), we can cancel the common terms using the *minreal* command and obtain a lower order model. The syntax is (the pole-zero form of the syntax is also available)

```
>> [numr,denr]=minreal(num,den,tol)
```

The third input argument (optional) is the tolerance level for cancellation. When the pole-zero pair are not exactly equal but close to each other, we can still force them to cancel out by changing the tolerance parameter.

Some of the most common operations with transfer functions are multiplication, addition, and feedback connection of transfer functions. Block diagrams can be analyzed and simulated using SIMULINK (Chapter 6), or by state space commands (Chapter 5). Simple block diagrams can be handled using the transfer function forms of the *series*, *parallel*, *feedback*, and *cloop* commands. The syntaxes for these commands are given by

```
>> [nums,dens]=series(num1,den1,num2,den2)
>> [nump,denp]=parallel(num1,den1,num2,den2)
>> [numf,denf]=feedback(num1,den1,num2,den2,sign)
>> [numc,denc]=cloop(num,den,sign)     % for unity feedback systems
```

The resulting transfer function, in each case, is given by

Series : $G_s(s) = G_1(s)G_2(s)$

Parallel : $G_p(s) = G_1(s) + G_2(s)$

Feedback : $G_f(s) = \dfrac{G_1(s)}{1 + G_1(s)G_2(s)}$

Unity feedback (using *cloop*) : $G_c(s) = \dfrac{G(s)}{1 + G(s)}$

The optional parameter, sign, is -1 for negative feedback and $+1$ for positive feedback. The default is negative feedback.

4.5 Examples

Example 4.1

To demonstrate how the above commands can be used in analysis of control systems, we will consider the following third order plant with unity feedback configuration (see Figure 4-1):

$$G(s) = \frac{1}{s\,(s+1)\,(s+2)}\ , \qquad K = 1.5$$

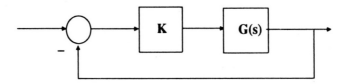

Figure 4-1   Block diagram for Example 4.1.

Frequency response analysis

First, we enter the open loop transfer function, $G(s) = ng/dg$, and obtain the Bode plot with gain $K = 1.5$. The *logspace* command is used to generate the frequency axis with 100 points:

```
>> k=1.5; ng=1; dg=poly([0 -1 -2]); w=logspace(-1,1,100)';
>> [m,p]=bode(k*ng,dg,w);
>> subplot(211); semilogx(w,20*log10(m)); subplot(212);semilogx(w,p)
```

From the plots in Figure 4-2, we observe that the gain and phase margins are approximately 10 dB and 45 degrees. We can verify this using the *margin* command:

```
>> [gm,pm,wpc,wgc]=margin(m,p,w)
```

gm =
    4.0002
pm =
    41.5332
wpc =
    1.4142
wgc =
    0.6118

The value of the *gm* indicates that we can increase the gain by a factor of 4 before the system becomes unstable. This is actually 12 dB, which can be determined directly from the data. This will be verified later.

The Nyquist plot, with the unit circle superimposed on it, is obtained next. To generate the unit circle, we create a linearly spaced vector from 0 to 2π using the *linspace* command. The circle is then obtained by plotting the imaginary versus the real part of $e^{j\omega}$:

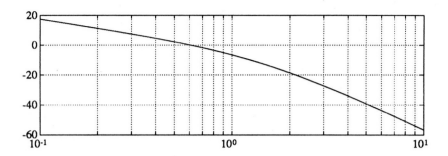

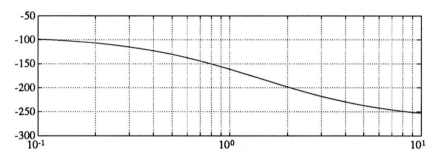

Figure 4-2   Bode magnitude and phase plot of *KG (s)*.

```
>> w2=linspace(0,2*pi,100)';ejw=exp(j*w2);r2=real(ejw);i2=imag(ejw);
>> [r,i]=nyquist(k*ng,dg,w);
>> axis('square'); plot(r2,i2); axis
```

The last statement sets up a square box for a round circle, draws the unit circle, and freezes the axes. The following line overlays the Nyquist plot and the circle:

```
>> plot(r2,i2,r,i); grid;
```

Because there are no encirclements of the (-1) point, the Nyquist plot in Figure 4-3 confirms closed loop stability.

    We will obtain the Nichols plot next. This can be done using either the *nichols* command or by plotting magnitude versus phase. Note that the plot shown in Figure 4-4 confirms the 12 dB gain margin.

```
>> nichols(k*ng,dg,w)    or    plot(p,20*log10(m))
```

The closed loop Bode plot is also obtained to find the bandwidth and the peak resonance. Let *T(s)* denote the closed loop transfer function. We use the *cloop* command to find the closed loop transfer function:

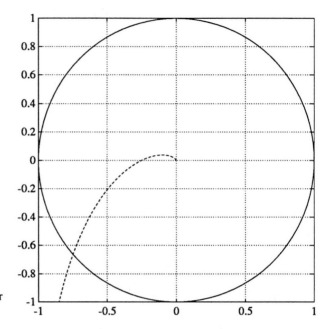

Figure 4-3 Nyquist plot for Example 4.1.

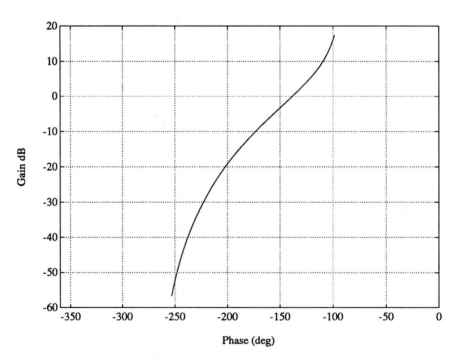

Figure 4-4 Nichols plot of *KG(s)*.

```
>> [nt,dt]=cloop(k*ng,dg);
>> mc=bode(nt,dt,w); subplot(211), semilogx(w,20*log10(mc)); grid
```

From Figure 4-5, we observe a peak resonance of 3 dB and a bandwidth of about 1 rad/sec.

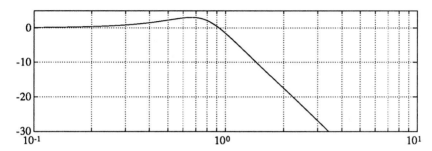

Figure 4-5   Closed loop Bode magnitude plot.

Root locus analysis

Next we will use root locus to predict the response for various gains. The plot is shown in Figure 4-6.

```
>> rlocus(k*ng,dg)
```

Using the *rlocfind* command, we note that system becomes unstable for values of *K* larger than 6. We can get a more accurate answer by finding the closed loop poles for a range of gains.

```
>> clpole=rlocus(ng,dg,[0.3:.1:7])
>> range=[0.3:.1:7]';[range clpole]
```

ans =

0.3000	-2.1254	-0.6611	-0.2135
0.4000	-2.1597	-0.4201 - 0.0932i	-0.4201 + 0.0932i
5.9000	-2.9909	-0.0046 - 1.4045i	-0.0046 + 1.4045i
6.0000	-3.0000	0.0000 - 1.4142i	0.0000 + 1.4142i
6.1000	-3.0090	0.0045 - 1.4238i	0.0045 + 1.4238i

The above data show a partial listing of the gains and the closed loop poles. The following conclusions can be drawn.

Case 1: For $0 < K < 0.4$, the poles are distinct and real, implying an overdamped response.
Case 2: The breakaway point occurs for $K = 0.4$; the response is critically damped.

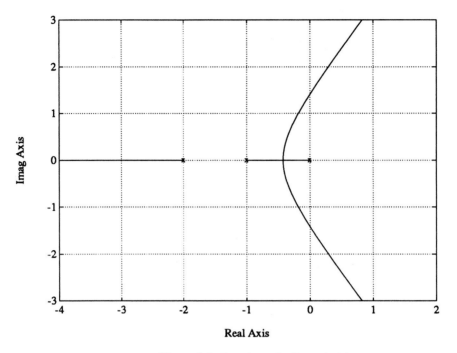

Figure 4-6   Root locus for Example 4.1.

Case 3: For $0.4 < K < 6$, the dominant poles are complex, resulting in an underdamped response.

Case 4: For $K = 6$, the system has a pair of imaginary poles and is marginally stable.

Case 5: For values of $K > 6$, the poles enter the RHP, and the system is unstable.

To verify the above observations, we will find the closed loop transfer function and obtain the five step responses. Instead of repeating this procedure five times, we use a *for* loop to find the closed loop step response. The values of K for the simulations are { 0.25, 0.4, 1.5, 6, 8}.

```
>> rangek=[.25 .4 1.5 6 8]; t=[0:.2:20]';
>> for j=1:5
>> [ntc,dtc]=cloop(ng*rangek(j),dg);
>> y(:,j)=step(ntc,dtc,t); end
>> subplot(211), plot(t,y(:,1:3)), grid
>> subplot(212), plot(t,y(:,4:5)), grid
```

The plots for the three stable and two nonstable responses are shown in Figure 4-7.

From now on, we will concentrate on the underdamped response; i.e., $K=1.5$. We can compute the percent overshoot as the percentage difference between peak value M_p (maximum value) and the steady state response *yss*:

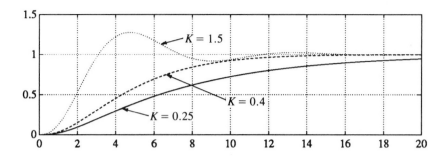

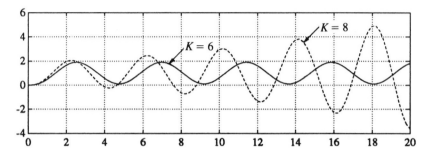

Figure 4-7 Step responses for Example 4.1.

```
>> y3=y(:,3); mp=max(y3); yss=y3(length(t)); pos=100*(mp-yss)/yss
```

pos =
   27.9035

Steady state error analysis

Because the unity feedback system has a pole at the origin, it is Type 1, and the steady state error (e_{ss}) to a step input is zero. The error to a unit ramp input is given by ($1/K_v$), where K_v is the velocity error coefficient

$$K_v = \lim_{s \to 0} s\ G(s) = \frac{1.5}{2} = 0.75 , \quad \text{hence,} \quad e_{ss} = 1.33$$

We will use the *lsim* command to find the ramp response and verify our result (see Figure 4-8). An easy way to find the ramp response is to find the step response of the closed loop system multiplied by 1/s. This is done by adding an extra 0 to the denominator polynomial vector as shown below:

```
>> dtt=[dt , 0]; t2=[0:0.1:10]';
>> yramp=step(nt,dtt,t2);
>> subplot(211), plot(t2,[t2 yramp]), grid
```

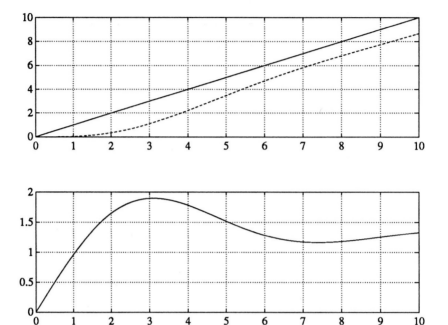

Figure 4-8   Ramp response and the error for Example 4.1.

We can verify the steady state error from

```
>> ess=t2-yramp; subplot(212), plot(t2,ess), grid, ess(length(ess))
ans   =
   1.3307
```

Filtering properties

From the closed loop Bode plot (Figure 4-5), we can see that the system acts as a low pass filter. Most control systems have low pass characteristics. This means the system rejects high-frequency signals outside of its bandwidth. We will verify this by finding the response of the underdamped system to random noise. The *rand* command is used to add uniform noise to a step input, and the *lsim* command is used to find the response.

```
>> noise=ones(t2)+rand(t2);
>> ynoise=lsim(nt,dt,noise,t2);
>> subplot(211), plot(t2,[noise ynoise])
```

Note that t2 is a vector, ones(t2) creates a step input of the same size, and rand(t2) creates a random vector of the same size with elements between 0 and 1, so the input is a noisy step. For comparison, we have overlaid the input and output on the same plot in Figure 4-9. As

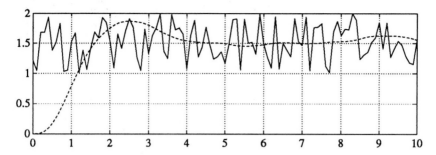

Figure 4-9   Response of the system in Example 4.1 to random noise.

expected, the system suppresses high-frequency signals such as noise. Noise creates an offset error in this case. The offset occurs because the noise has an average magnitude of 0.5. Usually random noise has smaller magnitude relative to the input; in this case its effect is barely noticeable.

Example 4.2 Effects of Time Delay

Time delays exist in many applications of control systems such as, process control, manufacturing systems, transportation, and deep space applications. In linear time invariant continuous systems, time delay is represented by e^{-sT}. Systems with time delay can be conveniently analyzed using frequency response methods.

Note that $e^{-j\omega T} = 1 \angle -\omega T$. Therefore, time delay leaves the magnitude unchanged and simply adds phase lag. The phase lag associated with time delay tends to be destabilizing. For simulation purposes, if we use the *bode* command, all we have to do is subtract the phase of time delay from the phase of $G(s)$.

Let $G(s) = \dfrac{2}{s+1}$ and $T = 1$, the Bode plot of the system is obtained as follows:

```
>> n=2; d=[1    1]; del=1;
>> w=logspace(-2,0.7,100)'; [m,p]=bode(n,d,w);
>> pd=p-(del*w*180/pi);       // subtract the phase in degrees
>> subplot(211), semilogx(w,20*log10(m)), grid;
>> subplot(212), semilogx(w,[p pd]), grid
```

Observe from Figure 4-10, that even though the original system has infinite gain margin and about 120 degrees of phase margin, time delay reduces these margins to almost 2 dB and 30 degrees. Hence, the destabilizing effects of time delay can be quite drastic. The Nyquist plot can be obtained by observing that

$$G(jomega)e^{-j\omega T} = [R(\omega) + j\,I(\omega)]\,e^{-j\omega T} \quad \text{where} \quad R(\omega) = \text{Re}\,[\,G(j\omega)\,]\ ,\ \ I(\omega) = \text{Im}\,[\,G(j\omega)\,]$$

Therefore, we can compute the real and imaginary parts of the frequency response of the system with time delay. The plot of the imaginary versus the real part is the Nyquist plot:

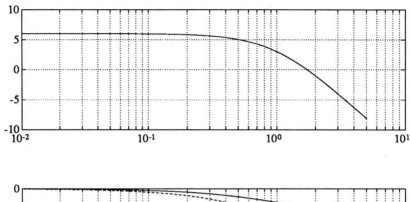

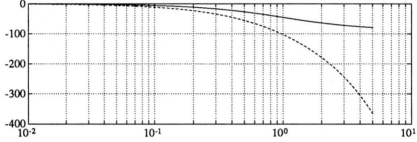

Figure 4-10 Bode plot of the system showing the effects of time delay.

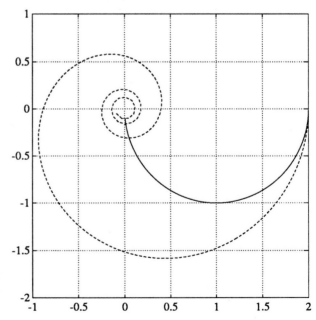

Figure 4-11 Nyquist plot of the system showing the effects of time delay.

```
>> w2=logspace(-2,1.3,200)'; [r,i]=nyquist(n,d,w2);
>> rd=real((r+j*i).*exp(-j*w2*del));
>> id=imag((r+j*i).*exp(-j*w2*del));
>> clg, axis('square'), plot([r, rd],[i, id]), grid
```

Note the use of *real*, *imag*, and *exp* commands. The Nyquist plot in Figure 4-11 clearly shows the small stability margins.

4.6 Problems

*4.1 The purpose of this exercise is, to investigate the effects of varying the pole locations of a second order underdamped system, and to observe some well-known relationships between the step response and Bode plot of the system.

The canonical form of an underdamped second order system is

$$G(s) = \frac{\omega_n^2}{s^2 + 2\zeta\omega_n s + \omega_n^2} = \frac{(\omega_d^2 + \sigma^2)}{s^2 + 2\sigma s + (\omega_d^2 + \sigma^2)}$$

where the poles are located at

$$s = -\sigma \pm j\,\omega_d \quad \text{where} \quad \sigma = \zeta\,\omega_n \;, \quad \omega_d = \omega_n \sqrt{1 - \zeta^2} \quad \text{and} \quad \zeta = \cos(\theta)$$

Preliminary analysis

Using the properties and formulas for second order systems, discuss the effects of varying each parameter, σ, ω_d, ω_n, and ζ (the other three fixed) on the step response parameters (POS, T_r, T_s, T_p) and Bode plot parameters (M_r, BW). For terminology, formulas, and notation, refer to Chapter 1.

Laboratory

For each of the following parts, the step responses are from $t = 0$ to 10, plotted simultaneously, and Bode plots are from $\omega = 0.1$ to 10. Magnitude plots are log-log, plotted in the upper half of the screen, simultaneously; phase plots are semi-log, plotted on the lower half of screen, simultaneously. You must turn in a total of 12 plots containing the results of 36 simulations (there are some duplications, only 27 simulations are needed). Because of the large number of repetitive simulations, you are far better off writing a simple program using *for* loops (see Chapter 3) to automate the process and save a lot of time.

a. Let $\omega_d = 1$, obtain the step response and Bode plots when $\sigma = 0.5, 1, 5$.

b. Repeat part *a* for $\sigma = 1$ and $\omega_d = 0.5, 1, 5$.

c. Repeat part *a* for $\zeta = \dfrac{1}{\sqrt{2}}$ and $\omega_n = \dfrac{\sqrt{2}}{2}, \sqrt{2}, 5\sqrt{2}$.

d. Repeat part *a* for $\omega_n = \sqrt{2}$ and $\theta = 30, 45, 60$ degrees. Note $\zeta = \cos(\theta)$.

e. From your data and the plots, compute all of the above six response parameters, and tabulate your results. Use the data to draw conclusions about the effects of varying the parameters on response characteristics (increase, decrease, or no change).

The following questions are about some relationships between step and frequency responses.

f. What relation do you observe between M_r and POS? Can you obtain a numerical relation between them?

g. What about T_r and BW?

h. What about ω_n and BW? Can BW be approximated by ω_n?

*4.2 The purpose of this exercise is to investigate the effects of adding poles and zeros to a second order transfer function. The pole and zero are added separately. We also distinguish two cases: adding a pole (or zero) within the loop, or outside the loop. Because in classical design using Bode or root locus we usually add poles and zeros—lag-lead compensators—to modify system dynamics, it is important to have a good understanding of these effects.

The nominal system is $G(s)$ in unity feedback structure with a closed loop transfer function given by $T(s)$.

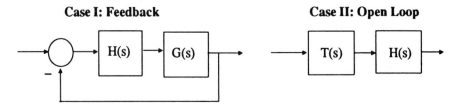

Case I: Feedback   **Case II: Open Loop**

Preliminary analysis

Using rough manual root locus and Bode sketches and some analysis, predict the effects of adding pole (or zero) in both cases I and II. Comment on any increase or decrease in speed of response, overshoot, bandwidth, and relative stability of the system (gain and phase margins).

Laboratory

Let $H(s) = \dfrac{1}{p\,s + 1}$ for the case of adding a pole and $H(s) = z\,s + 1$ for the zero case. Note that the actual pole and zero locations are $1/p$ and $1/z$, respectively. Similar to problem 4.1, you will obtain some plots (16 of them) and perform data analysis. Plots are again simultaneous with the same format as before. Since the number of simulations are large (43), it is important to choose good mnemonic names for variables and jot them down for later reference. Also since the number of data vectors generated are large, you may run out of memory locations depending on your hardware platform. To solve this problem, you may have to do the experiment in two steps. For example, do the simulations for the case of adding pole, save your data, and clear the workspace. Then do the case of adding zero and save it under a different name. All step response simulations are from $t = 0$ to 10. Bode plots are from $\omega = 0.05$ to 20. A simple program is a must because of the large number of simulations. Both p and z take the following values: {0.2624, 0.6122, 1.4286, 3.3333}. These values can be generated by the following commands:

```
> b=log(7/3);a=(10/3)exp(-4*b);
>> for i=1:4,p=a*exp(b*i),end;
```

For each case, the following simulations and the corresponding data must be obtained and tabulated.

Case I: Closed loop step response (POS, T_r, and T_s), open loop Bode plot (ω_{gc} and PM), closed loop Bode plot (M_r and BW).

Case II: Step response and Bode plot (since there is no loop, there is only one kind of Bode plot).

a. Obtain the step response and Bode plot of $T(s)$, and Bode plot of $G(s)$. Note that this is the nominal system; i.e., no pole or zero added, against which all other responses are compared.

b. Case I, add a pole to $G(s)$: let p take the specified values, obtain the appropriate responses. Plot the responses simultaneously with the one in part a for comparison. For instance, your step response plot should consist of five plots, four of them generated here; the fifth one was obtained in part *a*.

c. Case II, add a pole to $T(s)$: same comments as in *b*.

d. Case I, add a zero to $G(s)$: same comments as in *b*.

e. Case II, add a zero to $T(s)$: same comments as in *b*.

You should now be able to answer the following questions. Note that adding a pole or zero to the transfer function, $T(s)$, does not change its stability; it changes its other properties, however. Adding a pole or zero to the open loop transfer function, $G(s)$, changes both the stability and other response parameters. In general, adding zeros has stabilizing effects, and adding poles may be destabilizing. This is one of the reasons compensators are added inside the loop. We will see later how to choose these pole and zero locations to satisfy certain specifications.

f. Based on analysis of your data, what is the effect of adding a pole to $G(s)$ on POS, T_r, PM, and BW?

g. What about adding a pole to $T(s)$?

h. What about adding a zero to $G(s)$?

i. What about adding a zero to $T(s)$?

These questions relate to some correspondence between step response and frequency response parameters.

j. What relation do you observe between POS and PM?

k. What about ω_{gc} and BW ?

4.3 This problem investigates the effects of nonminimum phase zeros (i.e., zeros in the right half plane). Systems with RHP zeros or time delays are commonly referred to as nonminimum phase systems. Consider the system

$$G(s) = \frac{n(s)}{s^2 + 0.5\,s + 1.5}$$

a. Let $n(s) = 1.5$, using formulas for step response of a second order system, estimate POS, peak time, and settling time of the system. Find the step response using the computer and compare your results.

b. Let $n(s) = (-s + \alpha)/\alpha$, find the step response for $\alpha = \{1, 3, 6\}$.

c. Let $n(s) = (s + \alpha)/\alpha$, find the step response for $\alpha = \{1, 3, 6\}$.

Report your work in two plots and tabulate your results. Each plot in case *a* is overlaid with the simulation plots on *b* and *c*.

d. Based on your data, what are the effects of LHP and RHP zeros on the step response? Observe that when the system has RHP zeros the step response "goes in the wrong direction" first. This phenomenon can be shown to occur whenever the system has an odd number of RHP zeros.

4.4 The purpose of this problem is to introduce *lag* and *lead* compensators and show their effects on an unstable system. Consider the following double integrator system, $G(s)$, and the proposed compensators. $G(s) = \dfrac{1}{s^2}$

I) *Proportional* compensator: $K(s) = K_c$

II) *Lead* compensator: $K(s) = K_c \dfrac{s+1}{s+5}$

III) *Lag* compensator: $K(s) = K_c \dfrac{s+5}{s+1}$

Preliminary analysis

Using both root locus and Bode plots, drawn manually, answer the following questions.

a. Can the system be stabilized in case I? What are the effects of increasing K_c on the step response in case I?

b. Can the system be stabilized in case II? What are the effects of increasing K_c on the step response in case II?

c. Can the system be stabilized in case III? What are the effects of increasing K_c on the step response in case III?

Laboratory

d. Simulate the step response in each case using three values for $K_c = \{0.1, 0.5, 1\}$.

Three simultaneous closed loop step response plots in each case are required. Analyze the plots and confirm your conclusions with your preliminary analysis. Convenient final times for simulation in each case are {10, 50, 5}.

4.5 The purpose of this problem is to demonstrate disturbance rejection properties of feedback systems as compared with open loop systems. You must first analyze the problem and answer the questions; then confirm your results via simulations.

Preliminary analysis

Consider the first order system: $G(s) = \dfrac{1}{s+1}$

a. Open Loop Control: Find a compensator, $K(s)$, that has poles at $\{-1 \pm j\}$ and achieves zero steady state error to step and ramp inputs.

b. Feedback Control: Assume the compensator is in series with the plant in a unity feedback configuration. Find the compensator to satisfy the specifications in part *a*.

c. Assume that there is a unit step disturbance entering between $K(s)$ and $G(s)$. Find the steady state response of both systems to this disturbance. Which one is suppressing the disturbance better?

d. Determine the filtering properties of each case by looking at rough Bode plots. Which system is better able to suppress high-frequency noise or disturbance?

Laboratory

e. Find the step response in each case to verify your results in part *c*. Make sure you use the correct transfer function.

f. Generate "normal/Gaussian" noise and let the input be $n(t) = 0.01*rand(t)$. Simulate the noise response using *lsim* command. In each case, plot the noise input and its response together. Does your simulation confirm your analysis? Does there seem to be a conflict between suppressing low-frequency disturbance and high-frequency noise?

4.6 The purpose of this problem is to introduce *Proportional plus Integral (PI)* control, and investigate its effects. Consider a canonical second order system $G(s)$ and a cascade PI compensator $K(s)$:

$$G(s) = \frac{\omega_n^{\,2}}{s(s + 2\,\zeta\,\omega_n)} \quad , \quad K(s) = K_p + \frac{K_I}{s} = K_c\,\frac{s+z}{s}$$

Preliminary analysis

a. Determine for what values of K_c and z the closed loop system is stable.

b. What are the effects of PI on the steady state error properties of the system?

c. Let $\zeta = 0.5$, $\omega_n = 2$, $K_c = 1$, and $z = 1$. Draw the root locus before and after compensation; determine the effects of PI on rise time and POS.

d. Using open and closed loop Bode plots, determine the effects of PI on peak resonance, closed loop bandwidth, and phase margin.

Laboratory

e. Use root locus to find closed loop poles for the values specified in part c.

f. Obtain step response before and after compensation. Compare rise time and POS.

g. Obtain open loop Bode plots before and after compensation and compare phase margins and gain crossover frequencies.

h. Obtain closed loop Bode plots before and after compensation to compare bandwidths and peak resonance values. *Note*: All before and after plots must be displayed together for comparison.

4.7 The purpose of this problem is to introduce *Proportional plus Integral plus Derivative (PID)* control and perform a simple ad-hoc design. Consider the following unstable plant:

$$G(s) = \frac{1}{(s-1)^2}$$

The specifications are: closed loop stability and zero steady state error to unit step inputs.

Preliminary analysis

a. Use the Routh-Hurwitz test and root locus arguments to show that a cascade PID compensator, $K(s)$, can meet both specifications. Remember that the system must be stabilized first before you consider steady state errors. Assume unity feedback configuration.

PID compensator: $K(s) = K_p + \dfrac{K_I}{s} + K_D s$

Laboratory

b. Use trial and error to select the PID parameters to meet the above specs. Obtain the step response of the system and plot it. Note that the PID introduces two zeros. These zeros can be complex or real. Try both cases.

c. Suppose, in addition, all closed loop poles are to be placed at $s = -1$. Determine the compensator parameters to achieve this. Also, plot the root locus and step response for the compensated system for this case.

4.8 The purpose of this problem is to compare cascade and feedback compensation. Consider the plant $G(s)$ and a PI compensator $K(s)$

$$G(s) = \frac{4}{s\,(s+2)}, \qquad K(s) = \frac{s+1}{s}$$

Preliinary analysis

a. Show that if $K(s)$ is in series with $G(s)$ with unity feedback, the system will be stable and can track step and ramp inputs with zero error.

b. Show that if $K(s)$ is placed in the feedback path, these properties are lost, even though both systems have the same closed loop poles.

c. Show that we can recover the tracking properties of part a using feedback compensation by placing an additional compensator outside of the loop. Find this compensator and call it $K_f(s)$.

d. Suppose that during implementation, or due to component tolerances, we instead use the following incorrect compensator, $K_2(s) = \dfrac{s+0.5}{s}$. Repeat part a with this compensator. Are the tracking properties lost?

e. Repeat part b with the incorrect compensator.

f. Using the same $K_f(s)$ as in part c, show that the tracking properties of part c are now lost.

There are three lessons here. First, the location of the compensator (i.e., cascade or feedback), seriously affects the tracking properties of the system. Second, tracking requirements can be met by using compensators outside of the feedback loop; i.e., you do not need feedback to satisfy tracking, or even response shape requirements. The third lesson is that feedback reduces the sensitivity of the closed loop system with respect to changes in elements in the forward path. That is why tracking properties of part a are maintained in part d, but they are lost in part f. When properties of the system are maintained in spite of parameter variations, we call that system property *robust*. Hence, using a PI cascade compensator is a robust method of meeting tracking requirements while the design procedure in part c is not. The actual robustness comes from the fact that PI increases the system Type. If instead, we had used another compensator, such as lag (i.e., a pole at 0.001 instead of at the origin), the steady state error to ramp would also increase in part c but not as much as in part f.

Laboratory

g. Obtain and plot the step and ramp responses in each case (there are a total of eight plots). In all cases, find the steady state errors to step and ramp inputs, and compare with the results of your preliminary analysis.

*4.9 The purpose of this problem is to show that using Bode plots can lead to misleading or confusing answers when applied to nonminimum phase systems. The plants to be studied in the problem are

i. $KG_1(s) = \dfrac{10K\,(-1+s)}{s\,(1+10\,s)}$ $K = -0.05$.

ii. $KG_2(s) = \dfrac{K\,(s-1)}{s\,(2\,s+1)}$ where $K = -0.5, -1,\ 1$

iii. $KG_3(s) = \dfrac{K\,(4s-1)}{(10s-1)\,(2s+1)\,(s+1)}$ where $K = -1.5, -1,\ 1$

iv. $KG(s) = \dfrac{7\,K}{(s-1)\,(s+2)\,(s+4)}$ for $K = 2$

Preliminary analysis

a. Use the Routh-Hurwitz test and root locus to find the stable range of K. Use this information to find the lower and upper gain margin(s) for the specified gain(s).

b. Obtain the Nyquist plots and use Nyquist stability criterion to verify your answer in part *a*. In addition, find the phase margin(s).

Laboratory

c. Obtain the Bode plot(s) for the specified gain(s) and use the *margin* command to find the gain and phase margins. Compare the results with parts *a* and *b*. Comment on the validity of using Bode plots to determine stability of nonminimum phase systems.

4.10 Consider the following plants, and in each case perform the requested analysis:

i. $G_1(s) = \dfrac{0.485}{s^2 + 0.3s + 1}$

ii. $G_2(s) = \dfrac{7\,(s+2)}{s\,(s^2 + 2s + 12)}$

a. Use the open loop Bode plots to obtain the gain and phase margins.

b. Use the closed loop Bode plot to obtain the peak resonance.

c. Find the closed loop poles (unity feedback) and compute the damping ratio.

d. Obtain the closed loop step response; find POS, T_r, and T_s; comment on the quality of the transient response.

e. Based on the information from the above data, which quantity best describes the poor quality observed in the step response?

5

Introduction to State Space Analysis

5.1 Introduction

Mathematical analysis of systems requires that the system be represented by a mathematical model that captures its essential features. An electrical circuit can usually be adequately modeled using Kirchoff's laws, whereas mechanical systems can be modeled by Newton's laws. These models are combinations of algebraic and differential equations. A linear time invariant (LTI) system can be represented equivalently by its impulse response or its Laplace transform, the transfer function. We may also use graphical models such as circuit diagrams, free body diagrams, block diagrams, or signal flow graphs. These different "realizations" of the same system are equivalent means of system representation. In the early 1960s, a new system representation was developed: the state space representation. Roughly speaking, any N*th order* differential equation can be converted to *N* simultaneous *first order* differential equations. Some of the advantages of state space representation over transfer function models are the following:

- The equations are written directly in the time domain and, hence, are more amenable for computer solutions.
- The equations are first order and, therefore, conceptually simpler. Simultaneous equations involve the use of matrix algebra for which a wealth of robust numerical routines such as EISPACK/LINPACK are available. Programs such as MATLAB and MATRIX$_X$ are based on these core of routines.
- Multiple input–multiple output (multivariable or MIMO) systems and advanced optimal and robust control techniques are usually formulated in state space and use state space based algorithms for their numerical solutions.
- Time varying and nonlinear systems are more naturally represented in state space.

5.2 State Space Realizations

We will demonstrate the idea of state space realizations with a simple example. Consider the following second order differential equation (possibly representing an RLC circuit):

$$\ddot{y} + 3\,\dot{y} + 2\,y = u\,(t) \quad \text{where } \dot{y} = \frac{d\,y}{d\,t}$$

The transfer function of the above system is given by

$$G\,(s) = \frac{Y(s)}{U(s)} = \frac{1}{s^2 + 3\,s + 2}$$

Let us introduce the following variables: $x_1 = y$; $x_2 = \dot{y}$. Using the original differential equation and the above definitions we get

$$\dot{x}_1 = x_2$$

$$\dot{x}_2 = -2x_1 - 3x_2 + u$$

Now, defining the vector x with components x_1 and x_2, we can write the above two equations in vector matrix form:

$$\dot{x} = \begin{bmatrix} 0 & 1 \\ -2 & -3 \end{bmatrix} x + \begin{bmatrix} 0 \\ 1 \end{bmatrix} u$$

$$y = [\, 1 \quad 0 \,]\, x + [\, 0 \,]\, u$$

In general, any linear differential equation can always be put into the above form. If we denote the above matrix and vectors as

$$A = \begin{bmatrix} 0 & 1 \\ -2 & -3 \end{bmatrix}; \quad B = \begin{bmatrix} 0 \\ 1 \end{bmatrix}; \quad C = [\, 1 \quad 0 \,]; \quad D = 0$$

we get the general state space realization

$$\dot{x} = A\,x + B\,u$$

$$y = C\,x + D\,u$$

The vector x is the *state vector,* and its components are called *state variables*; u and y are input and output vectors, respectively. State space representation applies equally to systems that have multiple inputs and outputs. In this case, u and y will be column vectors, and B, C, and D will be matrices. In general, if the system is nth order with m outputs and p inputs, the dimensions of the matrices become

$$A = n \times n, \quad B = n \times p, \quad C = m \times n, \quad D = m \times p$$

Note that the state space form is not unique. If we relabel the state variables, we get different matrices. For example, if we denote

$$x_2 = y \; ; \; x_1 = \dot{y}$$

we obtain another realization:

$$\dot{x} = \begin{bmatrix} -3 & -2 \\ 1 & 0 \end{bmatrix} x + \begin{bmatrix} 1 \\ 0 \end{bmatrix} u$$

$$y = [\, 0 \quad 1 \,] \; x + [\, 0 \,] \, u$$

We can also derive two other forms as follows. Let

$$x_1 = y \quad \text{and} \quad x_2 = \dot{y} + \alpha \, y$$

then $\quad \dot{x}_1 = x_2 - \alpha x_1$, and $\quad \dot{x}_2 = \ddot{y} + \alpha \dot{y} = -3\dot{y} - 2y + u + \alpha\dot{y}$

To eliminate $\dot{y}$ from the equation, set $\alpha = 3$. We get

$$\dot{x} = \begin{bmatrix} -3 & 1 \\ -2 & 0 \end{bmatrix} x + \begin{bmatrix} 0 \\ 1 \end{bmatrix} u$$

$$y = [\, 1 \quad 0 \,] \; x + [\, 0 \,] \, u$$

Note that we can again exchange the labels of x_1 and x_2 to get a fourth realization

$$\dot{x} = \begin{bmatrix} 0 & -2 \\ 1 & -3 \end{bmatrix} x + \begin{bmatrix} 1 \\ 0 \end{bmatrix} u$$

$$y = [\, 0 \quad 1 \,] \; x + [\, 0 \,] \, u$$

The above four forms are called *canonical realizations*. The first two are *controllable forms I* and *II*, and the last two are *observable forms I* and *II*. Note, however, that these names are not standard.

Now, suppose a system with transfer function $G(s)$ has distinct real poles. We can perform partial fraction expansion and write it as a sum of first order transfer functions. If the expanded system is converted to state space form, the A matrix will be in diagonal form.

The diagonal elements of A will be the poles of $G(s)$, which are also eigenvalues of A, and are referred to as system *modes*, hence the name *modal form*. We also recall that the system will be stable if and only if the poles have negative real parts; i.e., modes are in the LHP. This form is quite useful for analysis because the system is effectively decoupled. Let us obtain the modal form of our example:

$$G(s) = \frac{Y(s)}{U(s)} = \frac{1}{s^2 + 3s + 2} = \frac{1}{s+1} - \frac{1}{s+2} = G_1(s) - G_2(s)$$

Hence, $Y(s) = G_1(s)\, U(s) - G_2(s)\, U(s) = X_1(s) - X_2(s)$

where $U(s) = (s+1)\, X_1(s)$ and $U(s) = (s+2)\, X_2(s)$

This leads directly to

$$\dot{x}_1 = -x_1 + u, \quad \dot{x}_2 = -2x_2 + u, \quad \text{and} \quad y = x_1 - x_2, \quad \text{or}$$

$$\dot{x} = \begin{bmatrix} -1 & 0 \\ 0 & -2 \end{bmatrix} x + \begin{bmatrix} 1 \\ 1 \end{bmatrix} u$$

$$y = \begin{bmatrix} 1 & -1 \end{bmatrix} x + \begin{bmatrix} 0 \end{bmatrix} u$$

Note that even though the matrices of the various realizations above *look* different, they are similar in a mathematical sense, and they all represent the same system with the unique transfer function, $G(s)$, given by

$$G(s) = \frac{1}{s^2 + 3s + 2}$$

To transform one realization to another, we have to find a similarity transformation matrix, T, which is nonsingular, and then proceed as shown below.

Let $x = T\,z$, where z represents the states in the new coordinate system. The state equations in the new coordinate system are

$$\dot{z} = T^{-1}\dot{x} = (T^{-1}A)\,x + (T^{-1}B)\,u = (T^{-1}AT)\,z + (T^{-1}B)\,u$$

$$y = C\,x + D\,u = (CT)\,z + D\,u$$

Hence, the new realization becomes $\{\,\overline{A}, \overline{B}, \overline{C}, \overline{D}\,\}$, where

$$\overline{A} = T^{-1}AT, \quad \overline{B} = T^{-1}B, \quad \overline{C} = CT, \quad \overline{D} = D$$

Note that $\bar{A}$ and A have the same eigenvalues.

The canonical forms discussed above can be generalized. Consider the transfer function

$$G(s) = \frac{b_1 s^{n-1} + \dots + b_{n-1} s + b_n}{s^n + a_1 s^{n-1} + \dots + a_n}$$

The observable form II is given by

$$A = \begin{bmatrix} 0 & . & . & 0 & | & -a_n \\ - & - & - & - & | & . \\ . & . & . & . & | & . \\ . & I_{n-1} & . & & | & . \\ . & . & . & & | & -a_1 \end{bmatrix} \quad , \quad B = \begin{bmatrix} b_n \\ . \\ . \\ . \\ b_1 \end{bmatrix} \quad , \quad C = [\, 0 \ \dots \ 0 \ 1\,] \quad , \quad D = [\, 0\,]$$

The controllable form I is given by

$$A = \begin{bmatrix} 0 & | & . & . & . & . \\ 0 & | & I_{n-1} & . & . & . \\ . & | & & . & . & . \\ - & & - & . & - & - \\ -a_n. & -a_{n-1} & . & . & -a_1 \end{bmatrix} \quad , \quad B = \begin{bmatrix} 0 \\ . \\ . \\ 0 \\ 1 \end{bmatrix} \quad , \quad C = [\, b_n \ b_{n-1} \dots \ b_1\,] \quad , \quad D = [\, 0\,]$$

The other two forms can likewise be obtained (see problem 5.9). We can obtain the transfer function directly by Laplace transforming the state equations

$$s\,X(s) = A\,X(s) + B\,U(s) \ \rightarrow \ X(s) = (s\,I - A\,)^{-1} B\,U(s)$$

$$Y(s) = C\,X(s) + D\,U(s) = [\,C\,(s\,I - A\,)^{-1} B + D\,]\,U(s) = G(s)\,U(s)$$

Hence , $G(s) = C\,\Phi(s)\,B + D$ where $\Phi(s) = (s\,I - A\,)^{-1}$

The solution of the linear time invariant state equations can be shown to be

$$x(t) = e^{A\,t}\,x_0 + \int_0^t e^{A\,(t-\sigma)}\,B\,u(\sigma)\,d\sigma , \quad e^{A\,t} = L^{-1}\{\,\Phi(s)\,\} = \phi(t)$$

where $\phi(t)$ is called the *state transition matrix*, and $\Phi(s)$ is called the *resolvent matrix*. Needless to say, analytical solution of state equations can be very cumbersome; therefore, we use computer programs to solve them numerically.

5.3 Asymptotic Stability

An important property of systems is the notion of stability. Consider the unforced equation

$$\dot{x} = A\,x\,, \qquad\qquad x(0) = x_o$$

We say the system is *asymptotically stable* if the states asymptotically approach zero with time; i.e., $x(t) \rightarrow 0 \quad as \quad t \rightarrow \infty$.

It can be shown that this happens when all eigenvalues of the matrix A have negative real parts; i.e., they are strictly in the LHP. It can also be shown that in the absence of pole-zero cancellations in the transfer function, system eigenvalues and transfer function poles are identical. This can be seen from the following:

$$G(s) = \frac{n(s)}{d(s)} = C\,(sI - A)^{-1}B = \frac{C\,Adj\,(s\,I - A)\,B}{\det\,(s\,I - A)}$$

The poles of $G(s)$ are the roots of $d(s)$, and the eigenvalues of A are the roots of the characteristic polynomial of A [i.e., $\det\,(s\,I - A)$].

5.4 State Space Analysis Using MATLAB

State space representation requires specifying four matrices $\{A, B, C, D\}$. We can easily convert from transfer function to state space form and vice versa using *tf2ss*, *zp2ss*, *ss2tf*, and *ss2zp* commands.

```
>> [a,b,c,d]=tf2ss(num,den)
>> [a,b,c,d]=zp2ss(z,p,k)
>> [num,den]=ss2tf(a,b,c,d,ui)
>> [z,p,k]=ss2zp(a,b,c,d,ui)
```

The input arguments for *tf2ss*, in the SISO case, are the numerator and denominator (entered as row vectors); for *zp2ss* they are the poles and zeros (entered as column vectors), and the gain. If the system has no finite zeros (all zeros at infinity), enter either an empty matrix [ ] or inf for the zeros in the *zp2ss* command. The state space form obtained using the *tf2tss* (or *zp2ss*) command is in Controllable form II. The argument, ui, in the *ss2tf* and *ss2zp* commands is the input channel number for multi-input systems.

The Control Systems Toolbox commands do not handle MIMO systems directly, but instead deal with MISO (multi-input–single output) and SIMO (single input–multi output) systems. The commands *ss2tf* and *ss2zp* find transfer functions of MISO or SIMO systems. For MISO systems, you specify a particular input and the transfer function from that input to the output is returned. For SIMO, the transfer function is a column vector; the denominator is returned as a row vector; the numerator is returned as a matrix with each row corresponding to each numerator. The command, *tf2ss*, is the inverse of *ss2tf*. For SIMO systems, enter the numerator as a matrix, one row per numerator. Recapitulating,

$$ss2tf = \begin{cases} \text{SIMO} & \text{enter den and MATLAB returns den and num=} \begin{bmatrix} num_1 \\ num_2 \end{bmatrix}. \\ \\ \text{MISO} & \text{enter [a,b,c,d,ui], and MATLAB returns individual transfer functions.} \end{cases}$$

$$tf2ss = \begin{cases} \text{SIMO} & \text{enter den and num} = \begin{bmatrix} num_1 \\ num_2 \end{bmatrix}, \text{and MATLAB returns a,b,c,d.} \\ \\ \text{MISO} & \textit{not available.} \end{cases}$$

The following example demonstrates the use of these commands. Consider the 2-output 1-input system transfer function

$$G(s) = \frac{1}{s^2 + 5s + 6} \begin{bmatrix} 1 \\ s + 1 \end{bmatrix}$$

The numerator coefficients can be written as a matrix, one row per numerator:

```
>> n1=[0 1]; n2=[1  1]; num=[n1;n2]; den=[1 5 6];
>> [a,b,c,d]=tf2ss(num,den)

a =
  -5  -6
   1   0
b =
   1
   0
c =
   0   1
   1   1
d =
   0
   0
```

Now let us use the above matrices to define a new 2-input 1-output system. The transfer functions from the individual inputs to the output is given by

```
>> [num1,den1]=ss2tf(a,c',b',d',1)

num1 =
   0   0  -6
den1 =
   1   5   6
>> [num2,den2]=ss2tf(a,c',b',d',2)
```

```
num2 =
    0   1  -6
den2 =
    1   5   6
```

Therefore, the overall transfer function for the above system is

$$G_2(s) = \frac{1}{s^2 + 5s + 6} [-6 \quad s - 6]$$

Now, let us obtain the transfer function of the original 2-output 1-input system

```
>> [num3,den3]=ss2tf(a,b,c,d)

num3 =
    0   0   1
    0   1   1
den3 =
    1   5   6
```

This is the same transfer function we started with. Similarly, we can also use the *ss2zp* command. For instance, in the SIMO case, the zeros are returned in a matrix, one column per output. For our example, we get

```
>> [z,p,k]=ss2zp(a,b,c,d)

z =
    ∞   -1.0000
p =
   -3
   -2
k =
    1.0000
    1.0000
```

The modal (or diagonal) form of a system can be obtained using the *canon* command. Its syntax is

```
>> [am,bm,cm,dm,T]=canon(a,b,c,d, 'modal')
```

The entry '*modal*' is an option. If you type '*companion*' instead, the A matrix will have its characteristic equation coefficients placed in the last column (the matrix is said to be in *companion form*). For the modal form, it is assumed that system is diagonalizable, which is guaranteed if the A matrix has distinct eigenvalues. The optional output, T, returns the similarity transformation matrix. Note that the algorithm uses the transformation $z = M x$. Comparing this with our presentation (where we used T), it is clear that $T = M^{-1}$

We can check for asymptotic stability by finding the eigenvalues of *A* using the *eig* command:

```
>> evalues=eig(a)
```

The eigenvalues can be sorted in descending order by real part using the *esort* command. Alternately, the *damp* command will return a table containing the eigenvalues, their damping ratios (ζ) , and natural frequencies (ω_n). In the following example, we will use the *zp2ss* command to create a matrix with known eigenvalues to demonstrate these commands. Note that the transfer function numerator is 1, which means it has unity gain with zeros at infinity; hence, we enter *inf* for the zeros.

```
>> a=zp2ss(inf,[-5,-2+j*2 -2-j*2 3],1); eig(a)
```

ans =
 -2.0000 + 2.0000i
 -2.0000 - 2.0000i
  3.0000
 -5.0000

```
>> esort(ans)
```

ans =
  3.0000
 -2.0000 + 2.0000i
 -2.0000 - 2.0000i
 -5.0000

```
>>  damp(a)
```

Eigenvalue	Damping	Freq. (rad/sec)
3.0000	-1.0000	3.0000
-2.0000 + 2.0000i	0.7071	2.8284
-2.0000 - 2.0000i	0.7071	2.8284
-5.0000	1.0000	5.0000

The *damp* command interprets its input in three ways. If the input is a matrix, it is interpreted as the state space *A* matrix; if the input is a row vector, it is treated as the denominator of a transfer function; if the input is a column vector, it is treated as pole locations.

If a system has pole-zero cancellations, we can obtain the *minimal realization* (i.e., cancel the common poles and zeros) using the *minreal* command:

```
>> [ar,br,cr,dr]=minreal(a,b,c,d,Tol)
>> [numr,denr]=minreal(num,den,Tol)
```

```
>> [zr,pr]=minreal(z,p,Tol)
```

The last input argument `Tol` is optional. It is the tolerance level that allows you to control how close the poles and zeros are before they are canceled. The main power of this command is in the state space form, because pole-zero cancellations are not apparent in state space. You should especially use this when you combine systems using the interconnection commands (discussed in the next section) to ensure that the overall system is of minimal order. This is important because minimality of the system realization is often one of the requirements of modern design techniques.

All of the simulation commands like *step, bode, lsim*, etc., have equivalent state space forms. Some commands, however, have special features available only in their state space form; for example, *lsim* with nonzero initial conditions. Some commands only have state space forms; for example, the *initial* command. Most commands internally use state space operations, so it is more efficient to use the state space representations in most commands. Also, for numerical reasons such as round-off error and conditioning, it is strongly advised that you use the state space forms of the commands as much as possible. The state space syntaxes for the commands will be briefly discussed next.

Frequency response commands such as *bode, nyquist*, and *nichols* share the following state space syntax:

```
>> command name(a,b,c,d,ui,w)
```

The only additional feature available in the state space form is the allowance for MIMO systems. For instance, if a system has two inputs and three outputs, the following command returns two three-column matrices for the magnitude and phase. The first column is the frequency response between the first input and the first output; the second column corresponds to the first input and the second output, etc. Without left-hand arguments, the magnitude (and phase) plots are drawn with three curves each.

```
>> [mag,phase]=bode(a,b,c,d,1,w)
```

Time response commands such as *step* and *impulse* share thr following state space syntax:

```
>> [y,x]=command name(a,b,c,d,ui,t)
>> command name(a,b,c,d)
```

For each input, all outputs, y, and states, x, are returned as matrices. In the auto-plot mode, all of the outputs will be plotted. This is very convenient for MIMO systems. Note that although we did not specify this in Chapter 4, these commands can also return the states in the transfer function mode.

The *lsim* command can be used to obtain the response of a MIMO system to arbitrary inputs. The additional state space feature is the allowance for nonzero initial conditions.

```
>> [y,x]=lsim(a,b,c,d,u,t,xo)
```

The output y (input u) has as many columns as the number of outputs (inputs). The number of rows of u equals that of t.

The zero-input response (i.e., response to initial conditions) of systems can be obtained by the *initial* command. It has the following syntax (not available in transfer function form):

```
>> [y,x]=initial(a,b,c,d,xo,t)
```

The *rlocus* and *rlocfind* commands apply to SISO systems only. In the state space form, replace the (num,den) inputs by (a,b,c,d).

The DC gain of a stable system (gain or transfer function at zero frequency) is equal to the steady state forced step response of the system. In state space, it is given by

$$\text{DC gain} = G(s) \mid_{s=0} = [C(sI - A)^{-1} B + D] \mid_{s=0} = -CA^{-1}B + D$$

The command, *dcgain*, can be used to compute this quantity. It is also available for transfer functions.

```
>> gain=dcgain(a,b,c,d)
```

A final state space utility command is the *printsys* command. It enables you to display the state space matrices with labels. It has the following syntax:

```
>> printsys(a,b,c,d,ulabels,ylabels,xlabels)
```

The labels are vectors of string variables. For example, we will use the *rmodel* command (introduced informally in this example) to generate a stable random model with two states, one output, and two inputs. Suppose the states are voltage and current, the output is load voltage, and the inputs are source and noise.

```
>> [a,b,c,d]=rmodel(2,1,2);
>> xlabel=['voltage current']; ulabel=['source noise'];
>> ylabel=['load_voltage'];
>> printsys(a,b,c,d,ulabel,ylabel,xlabel)
```

a =

	voltage	current
voltage	-0.02889	-0.37838
current	-0.37838	-4.95650

b =

	source	noise
voltage	0	-0.33671
current	-0.55709	0

c =

	voltage	current
load_voltage	1.55781	-2.44430

d =

	source	noise
load_voltage	0	1.12265

5.5 System Interconnections

MATLAB has several interconnection commands that make it possible to connect systems in various configurations directly in state space. It is also possible to connect systems using SIMULINK (formerly called SIMULAB and discussed in Chapter 6), but for LTI systems, it is much easier and faster to use state space commands. We use SIMULINK for nonlinear systems and more complicated block diagrams. We will explain these interconnection commands and demonstrate their features via examples.

5.5.1 Series (Cascade) Connection

Suppose systems S_1 and S_2 are given:

$$S_1 = \begin{bmatrix} A_1, B_1 ; C_1, D_1 \end{bmatrix} \quad \text{and} \quad S_2 = \begin{bmatrix} A_2, B_2 ; C_2, D_2 \end{bmatrix}$$

At this point, we will introduce a notation that is rapidly becoming popular for representing transfer functions with state space matrices. This notation is called the *packed-matrix* notation. Advanced robust control techniques use this notation, and the Robust Control Toolbox for MATLAB supports this representation. Recall that the transfer function of a system with state space matrices $\{A, B, C, D\}$ is given by

$$G(s) = C(sI - A)^{-1} B + D$$

This transfer function is written in packed matrix notation as

$$G(s) = \begin{bmatrix} A & B \\ C & D \end{bmatrix}$$

Now, we want to find the state space realization, $S = \{A, B; C, D\}$, of the series connection of S_1 and S_2 (see Figure 5-1).

$$\dot{x}_1 = A_1 x_1 + B_1 u_1, \quad y_1 = C_1 x_1 + D_1 u_1$$

$$\dot{x}_2 = A_2 x_2 + B_2 u_2, \quad y_2 = C_2 x_2 + D_2 u_2$$

Note from the block diagram that $u_2 = y_1$, $y = y_2$, and $u = u_1$, substituting y_1 in the state and output equations for S_2, we get

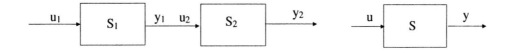

Figure 5-1 Series connection.

$$\dot{x}_2 = A_2\,x_2 + B_2\,y_1 = A_2\,x_2 + B_2\,(C_1\,x_1 + D_1\,u_1) = B_2\,C_1\,x_1 + A_2\,x_2 + B_2\,D_1\,u_1$$

$$y_2 = C_2\,x_2 + D_2\,y_1 = C_2\,x_2 + D_2\,(C_1\,x_1 + D_1\,u_1) = D_2\,C_1\,x_1 + C_2\,x_2 + D_2\,D_1\,u_1$$

Define the combined state x for the S system with components x_1 and x_2, and write the two state equations together:

$$\begin{bmatrix} \dot{x}_1 \\ \dot{x}_2 \end{bmatrix} = \begin{bmatrix} A_1 & 0 \\ B_2\,C_1 & A_2 \end{bmatrix} \begin{bmatrix} x_1 \\ x_2 \end{bmatrix} + \begin{bmatrix} B_1 \\ B_2\,D_1 \end{bmatrix} u_1$$

$$y_2 = [\,D_2\,C_1 \quad C_2\,] \begin{bmatrix} x_1 \\ x_2 \end{bmatrix} + [D_2\,D_1]\,u_1$$

Note that the order of the series system is the sum of the orders of S_1 and S_2; S is given by

$$G(s) = \text{series}\,(S_2,\,S_1) = \begin{bmatrix} A_2 & \vert & B_2 \\ - & - & \\ C_2 & \vert & D_2 \end{bmatrix} \cdot \begin{bmatrix} A_1 & \vert & B_1 \\ - & - & \\ C_1 & \vert & D_1 \end{bmatrix} = \begin{bmatrix} A_1 & 0 & \vert & B_1 \\ B_2\,C_1 & A_2 & \vert & B_2\,D_1 \\ - & - & & \\ D_2\,C_1 & C_2 & \vert & D_2\,D_1 \end{bmatrix}$$

The above result is shown in packed matrix notation and requires further clarification. By a series connection of two systems, we actually mean the product of their transfer functions; i.e.,

$$G(s) = G_2(s)\,G_1(s) \qquad \text{is represented by} \quad S = \text{series}\,(\,S_2,\,S_1\,)$$

where the S matrix is the state space representation of $G(s)$.

The command to find the series connection of two systems is the *series* command. It has the following syntaxes:

```
>> [as,bs,cs,ds]=series(a1,b1,c1,d1,a2,b2,c2,d2)
>> [as,bs,cs,ds]=series(a1,b1,c1,d1,a2,b2,c2,d2,OUTPUTS1,INPUTS2)
```

The second form is more general. It allows connection of selective outputs of system 1 to selected inputs of system 2. The input arguments, OUTPUTS1 and INPUTS2, are the indices of these selected outputs and inputs. For instance, suppose the first system has 4 outputs and the second system has 3 inputs. If outputs 1 and 4 of the first system are connected to inputs 2 and 3 of the second system, we enter

```
>> OUTPUTS1=[1,4]; INPUTS2=[2,3]
>> [as,bs,cs,ds]=series(a1,b1,c1,d1,a2,b2,c2,d2,OUTPUTS1,INPUTS2}
```

We will demonstrate the *series* and subsequent interconnection commands using the following systems:

$$G_1(s) = \frac{s-3}{s^2-5s+4}, \qquad G_2(s) = \frac{5s-8}{s+2}$$

```
>> ng1=[1 -3];dg1=[1 -5 4];ng2=[5 -8];dg2=[1 2];
>> [a1,b1,c1,d1]=tf2ss(ng1,dg1)
```

```
a1 =
    5  -4
    1   0
b1 =
    1
    0
c1 =
    1  -3
d1 =
    0
```

```
>> [a2,b2,c2,d2]=tf2ss(ng2,dg2)
```

```
a2 =
   -2
b2 =
    1
c2 =
  -18
d2 =
    5
```

```
>> [as,bs,cs,ds]=series(a1,b1,c1,d1,a2,b2,c2,d2)
```

```
as =
    5  -4   0
    1   0   0
    1  -3  -2
bs =
    1
    0
    0
```

```
cs =
    5  -15  -18
ds =
    0


>>   [ngs,dgs]=ss2tf(as,bs,cs,ds)


ngs =
    0   5.0000  -23.0000   24.0000
dgs =
    1   -3   -6   8
```

In summary, we have

$$G_s(s) = \begin{bmatrix} 5 & -4 & 0 & 1 \\ 1 & 0 & 0 & 0 \\ 1 & -3 & -2 & 0 \\ 5 & 15 & -18 & 0 \end{bmatrix} \rightarrow G_s(s) = \frac{5\,s^2 - 23s + 24}{s^3 - 3s^2 - 6s + 8}$$

where the transfer function is also given in packed matrix notation.

5.5.2 Parallel Connection

In the parallel connection, the output of two systems are added as shown in Figure 5-2. The derivation of the state space matrices is left as an exercise. The syntaxes are given by

```
>>   [ap,bp,cp,dp]=parallel(a1,b1,c1,d1,a2,b2,c2,d2)
>>   [ap,bp,cp,dp]=parallel(a1,b1,c1,d1,a2,b2,c2,d2,IN1,IN2,OUT1,OUT2)
```

The first syntax assumes that the systems have common inputs and all their outputs are added together. The second syntax allows the systems to have inputs that are not common, and outputs that are not summed. Input argument IN1 specifies the input indices of system 1 that are to be connected to input indices of system 2, specified by IN2. Likewise OUT1 and OUT2 indicate which outputs are connected. Continuing with our example, using the example systems, we get

```
>>   [ap,bp,cp,dp]=parallel(a1,b1,c1,d1,a2,b2,c2,d2)


ap =
    5  -4   0
    1   0   0
    0   0  -2
bp =
    1
    0
    1
```

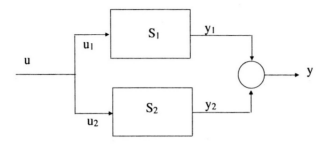

Figure 5-2 Parallel connection.

```
cp =
   1  -3  -18
dp =
   5

>>  [ngp,dgp]=ss2tf(ap,bp,cp,dp)

ngp =
   5.0000 -32.0000  59.0000 -38.0000
dgp =
   1  -3  -6  8
```

In summary, we have

$$G_p(s) = \begin{bmatrix} 5 & -4 & 0 & 1 \\ 1 & 0 & 0 & 0 \\ 0 & 0 & -2 & 1 \\ 1 & -3 & -18 & 5 \end{bmatrix} \rightarrow G_p(s) = \frac{5\,s^3 - 32\,s^2 + 59\,s - 38}{s^3 - 3\,s^2 - 6\,s + 8} = G_1(s) + G_2(s)$$

5.5.3 Feedback Connection

The feedback configuration appears frequently as shown in Figure 5-3A. We will obtain the system matrix for the feedback configuration. The key to this derivation is to note that the input to S_2 is y_1, and the input to S_1 is (u_1 - y_2). We then make these substitutions in the state space equations. For simplicity, we will assume that D_1 is equal to zero (i.e., $y_1 = C_1 x$).

$$\dot{x}_2 = A_2\,x_2 + B_2\,u_2 = A_2\,x_2 + B_2\,y_1 = B_2\,C_1\,x_1 + A_2\,x_2$$

$$y_2 = C_2\,x_2 + D_2\,u_2 = C_2\,x_2 + D_2\,y_1 = C_2\,x_2 + D_2\,C_1\,x_1$$

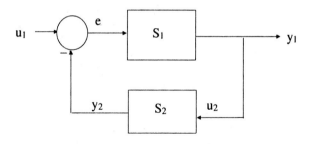

Figure 5-3A Feedback connection.

$$\dot{x}_1 = A_1 x_1 + B_1 (u_1 - y_2) = A_1 x_1 + B_1 u_1 - B_1 C_2 x_2 - B_1 D_2 C_1 x_1$$
$$= (A_1 - B_1 D_2 C_1) x_1 - B_1 C_2 x_2 + B_1 u_1$$

Therefore, the system matrix becomes

$$G(s) = \begin{bmatrix} A_1 - B_1 D_2 C_1 & -B_1 C_2 & B_1 \\ B_2 C_1 & A_2 & 0 \\ C_1 & 0 & 0 \end{bmatrix}$$

The following are the syntaxes for feedback configurations:

```
>> [af,bf,cf,df]=feedback(a1,b1,c1,d1,a2,b2,c2,d2,SIGN)
>> [af,bf,cf,df]=feedback(a1,b1,c1,d1,a2,b2,c2,d2,IN1,OUT1)
```

In the first syntax, the input argument, SIGN, is ±1. If not specified, negative feedback is assumed. The second syntax allows selected outputs of system 1, OUT1, to be fed into all inputs of system 2, and all outputs of system 2 to be fed back to selected inputs, IN1, of system 1. The block diagram, shown in Figure 5-3B, demonstrates this case. There is no default sign convention in this case (for negative feedback, use -IN1).

The *cloop* command discussed in Chapter 4, is similar to the *feedback* command except it assumes unity feedback ($G_2(s) = 1$).

Going back to our example systems, we get

```
>> [af,bf,cf,df]=feedback(a1,b1,c1,d1,a2,b2,c2,d2)
```

```
af =
    0  11  18
    1   0   0
    1  -3  -2
bf =
    1
    0
    0
```

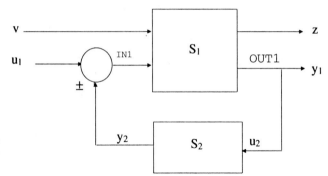

Figure 5-3B Feedback connection with selective inputs and outputs.

```
cf =
   1  -3   0
df =
   0


>>  [ngf,dgf]=ss2tf(af,bf,cf,df)


ngf =
     0   1.0000  -1.0000  -6.0000
dgf =
   1.0000   2.0000  -29.0000   32.0000
```

$$G_f(s) = \begin{bmatrix} 0 & 11 & 18 & 1 \\ 1 & 0 & 0 & 0 \\ 1 & -3 & -2 & 0 \\ 1 & -3 & 0 & 0 \end{bmatrix} \rightarrow G_f(s) = \frac{s^2 - s - 6}{s^3 + 2 s^2 - 29 s + 32} = \frac{G_1(s)}{1 + G_1(s)\, G_2(s)}$$

5.5.4 Append, Blkbuild, and Connect

These commands are usually used together to create very general interconnections. The *append* command simply puts two systems together in a decoupled form. Let S_1 and S_2 be represented by (see Figure 5-4)

$$\dot{x}_1 = A_1 x_1 + B_1 u_1 \quad , \quad y_1 = C_1 x_1 + D_1 u_1$$
$$\dot{x}_2 = A_2 x_2 + B_2 u_2 \quad , \quad y_2 = C_2 x_2 + D_2 u_2$$

Then, *append* will combine the two systems into one decoupled system as

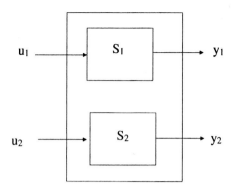

Figure 5-4 Append connection.

$$\begin{bmatrix} \dot{x}_1 \\ \dot{x}_2 \end{bmatrix} = \begin{bmatrix} A_1 & 0 \\ 0 & A_2 \end{bmatrix} \begin{bmatrix} x_1 \\ x_2 \end{bmatrix} + \begin{bmatrix} B_1 & 0 \\ 0 & B_2 \end{bmatrix} \begin{bmatrix} u_1 \\ u_2 \end{bmatrix}$$

$$\begin{bmatrix} y_1 \\ y_2 \end{bmatrix} = \begin{bmatrix} C_1 & 0 \\ 0 & C_2 \end{bmatrix} \begin{bmatrix} x_1 \\ x_2 \end{bmatrix} + \begin{bmatrix} D_1 & 0 \\ 0 & D_2 \end{bmatrix} \begin{bmatrix} u_1 \\ u_2 \end{bmatrix}$$

The system matrix is clearly given by

$$S = \begin{bmatrix} A_1 & 0 & B_1 & 0 \\ 0 & A_2 & 0 & B_2 \\ C_1 & 0 & D_1 & 0 \\ 0 & C_2 & 0 & D_2 \end{bmatrix}$$

The syntax for the *append* command is given by (there is no transfer function version)

```
>> [aa,ba,ca,da]=append(a1,b1,c1,d1,a2,b2,c2,d2)
```

Blkbuild is a script file that automatically converts systems to state space form and appends all specified systems. To use it, define all the systems and specify the number of blocks (enter nblocks = number of blocks, and type blkbuild). Finally, use the *connect* command to put the system together. The syntax for the *connect* command is given by

```
>> [ac,bc,cc,dc]=connect(a,b,c,d,Q,INPUTS,OUTPUTS)
```

The input argument, Q, is the interconnection matrix. The vectors, INPUTS and OUTPUTS, are the selected external inputs and outputs of the final connected system. Setting up the interconnection matrix correctly is the most important and error-prone step. The following is a systematic procedure for modeling a block diagram.

1. Number and label all blocks (transfer functions, state space matrices, or gain blocks). Number the inputs and outputs of all blocks. This is needed because the order of blocks is important.

2. Enter the transfer functions as (n1,d1), (n2,d2), etc. Enter the state space matrices as (a1,b1,c1,d1), (a2,b2,c2,d2), etc. The numbering must be consistent with the block numbers you chose. The naming is important for using the *blkbuild* command. The names must be (n1,d1) and not (num1,den1) or any other names. Gain blocks can be defined as transfer functions with numerator equal to the gain and the denominator equal to 1 (in state space form, a scalar gain can be represented as a=b=c=0 and d=gain).

3. Enter nblocks = number of blocks.

4. Enter blkbuild.

5. Define the interconnection matrix, Q. This matrix has a row for every block input. The first element of every row is the input number of a block. The remaining elements are the output numbers of all blocks connected to this block. Use positive numbers for positive connections and negative numbers for negative connections.

6. Define the INPUTS and OUTPUTS row vectors. The elements of these vectors are the input and output numbers of selected inputs and outputs respectively.

We will use this procedure to model the block diagram shown in Figure 5-5, where

$$G_1(s) = \frac{1}{s+1} \quad \text{and} \quad G_2(s) = \frac{1}{s-1}.$$

The first step is to number the blocks. Transfer functions G_1 and G_2 are blocks 1 and 2 respectively. The gain blocks 3 and 2 are block 3 and 4, respectively. Next, we define the blocks:

```
>> n1=1; d1=[1,1]; n2=1; d2=[1,-1]; n3=3; d3=1; n4=2; d4=1;
```

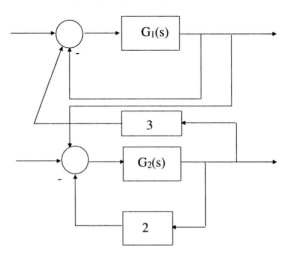

Figure 5-5 Block diagram to be modeled using *blkbuild* and *connect* commands.

We now use *blkbuild* to prepare the system for connection. The *blkbuild* command returns the system in state space form as (a,b,c,d):

```
>> nblocks=4; blkbuild
```

The interconnection matrix and inputs and outputs are defined next. Block 1 inputs come from output 1 with negative sign and output 3 with positive sign. Block 2 inputs come from output 1 (positive sign) and output 4 (negative sign). Block 3 receives its input from output 2 (0 is added to the row to make its number of columns compatible with the previous rows). Finally, block 4 gets one input from output 2. The inputs and outputs of the transfer function blocks are selected as the external inputs and outputs.

```
>> q=[1 -1 3;2 1 -4;3 2 0;4 2 0]; in=[1 2]; out=[1 2];
```

We are now ready to connect the blocks:

```
>> [ac,bc,cc,dc]=connect(a,b,c,d,q,in,out)

ac =
   -2   3
    1  -1
bc =
    1   0
    0   1
cc =
    1   0
    0   1
dc =
    0   0
    0   0
```

One can easily verify that the state equations of the connected system are given by

$$\dot{x}_1 = -2x_1 + 3x_2 + u_1 , \quad y_1 = x_1$$
$$\dot{x}_2 = x_1 - x_2 + u_2 , \quad y_2 = x_2$$

The transfer function of the system is given by

```
>> [ngc1,dgc1]=ss2tf(ac,bc,cc,dc,1)
>> [ngc2,dgc2]=ss2tf(ac,bc,cc,dc,2)

ngc1 =
        0   1.0000   1.0000
        0        0   1.0000
dgc1 =
   1.0000   3.0000  -1.0000
```

```
ngc2 =
    0   0   3
    0   1   2
dgc2 =
    1.0000   3.0000  -1.0000
```

This is equal to

$$G(s) = \begin{bmatrix} s+1 & 3 \\ 1 & s+2 \end{bmatrix} \frac{1}{s^2 + 3s - 1}$$

The next example shows that sometimes you may have to add fictitious blocks of gain 1 to model a system. Consider the block diagram in Figure 5-6A, with the closed loop transfer function given by

$$T(s) = \frac{-s}{s+2} \quad \text{where} \quad G(s) = \frac{1}{s+1}$$

For this system, there is a feedback signal from the output, and a feedforward signal from the input. For connection purposes, signals must be output of blocks; therefore, we will add dummy blocks of gain 1 to the diagram as shown in Figure 5-6B.
The following is the MATLAB session:

```
>> n1=1; d1=1; n2=1; d2=[1,1]; n3=1; d3=1;
>> nblocks=3;blkbuild
>> q=[2 -3 1;3 -1 2];in=1;out=3;
>> [ac,bc,cc,dc]=connect(a,b,c,d,q,in,out);
>> [nt,dt]=ss2tf(ac,bc,cc,dc)
nt =
   -1   0
dt =
    1   2
```

There are two other commands, *ssdelete* and *ssselect*, that are used to delete or select states, inputs and outputs of a system. The syntaxes for these commands are

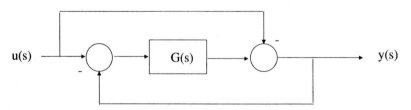

u(s)   G(s)   y(s)

Figure 5-6A   Block diagram for the second connection example.

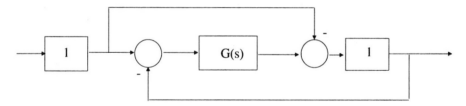

Figure 5-6B Block diagram for the second connection example with dummy blocks.

```
>> [ad,bd,cd,dd]=ssdelete(a,b,c,d,IN,OUT,STATES)
>> [ae,be,ce,de]=ssselect(a,b,c,d,IN,OUT,STATES)
```

Input arguments, IN, OUT, and STATES (optional) are the indices of the corresponding inputs, outputs, and states that are to be deleted (selected). These commands are mainly useful for large-scale or MIMO systems.

5.6 Feedback and Sensitivity Measures

The following transfer functions (matrices in the MIMO case) were introduced in Chapter 1 and are used to measure feedback properties, such as disturbance rejection, noise suppression, and effects of parameter variations. The system matrices of these transfer functions can be obtained using the connection commands as presented below. The derivations are left as exercises.

Return Difference is defined by : $J(s) = I + L(s)$

The system matrix for J is given below (assuming that $L(s)$ is square; i.e., it has the same number of inputs and outputs). Note that $L(s)$ is the loop transfer function matrix (also called the loop gain, or open loop transfer function in classical control, and is shown in Figure 5-7).

$$L(s) = \begin{bmatrix} A & B \\ C & D \end{bmatrix}, \ J(s) = \begin{bmatrix} A & B \\ C & D+I \end{bmatrix}$$

L(s) is also used to define the inverse return difference

$$R(s) = I + L^{-1}$$

Note that this is not the " inverse " of the return difference matrix. Its system matrix is given by (assuming that L is invertible, i.e., square and biproper, which ensures D has an inverse).

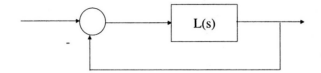

Figure 5-7 Feedback diagram showing the loop transfer function.

$$R = \begin{bmatrix} A - B D^{-1} C & B D^{-1} \\ - D^{-1} C & D^{-1} + I \end{bmatrix}$$

Sensitivity transfer function (matrix) is defined by

$$S(s) = (I + L)^{-1}$$

Its system matrix is given by (assuming square L)

$$S(s) = \begin{bmatrix} A - B V C & - B V \\ V C & V \end{bmatrix} \quad \text{where} \quad V = (I + D)^{-1}$$

Complementary sensitivity transfer function (matrix) is defined by

$$T(s) = L (I + L)^{-1}$$

Note that $S + T = I$, or $T = I - S$. Therefore, its system matrix is given by

$$T = \begin{bmatrix} A - B V C & - B V \\ V C & V - I \end{bmatrix}$$

5.7 Problems

5.1 Consider the following system:

$$\ddot{y}_1 + \dot{y}_1 + 2 y_1 + 3 \dot{y}_2 + 4 y_2 = u_1$$
$$\ddot{y}_2 + \dot{y}_2 + 2 y_2 + 3 \dot{y}_1 + 4 y_1 = u_2$$

a. Find a state space representation for the above system. (Let $x_1 = y_1$, $x_2 = \dot{y}_1$, etc.).
b. Find the system transfer function, poles and zeros.
c. Determine the stability of the system.

5.2 Consider the following system:

$$G(s) = \frac{2\,(s+4)}{s\,(s+1)\,(s+2)}$$

a. Obtain the four canonical form realizations for $G(s)$.
b. Obtain a diagonal realization for $G(s)$.
c. Discuss stability of the system.

5.3 Consider the following transfer function matrix:

$$G(s) = \begin{bmatrix} \dfrac{1}{(s+1)^3\,(s+10)} & \dfrac{1}{s+10} \\[2ex] \dfrac{1}{s+1} & 0 \end{bmatrix}$$

a. Obtain a state space realization for the system.
b. Determine its poles, zeros, and stability.

5.4 Show that the system matrix for the parallel representation (or sum) of two systems is given by

$$S = \begin{bmatrix} A_1 & 0 & B_1 & 0 \\ 0 & A_2 & 0 & B_2 \\ C_1 & C_2 & D_1 & D_2 \end{bmatrix}$$

5.5 Show that the system matrix for the feedback connection in the general case in which D_1 is nonzero is given by

$$S = \begin{bmatrix} A_1 - B_1\,V\,D_2\,C_1 & -B_1\,V\,C_2 & B_1 - B_1\,V\,D_2\,D_1 \\ B_2\,W\,C_1 & A_2 - B_2\,D_1\,V\,C_2 & B_2\,W\,D_1 \\ W\,C_1 & -D_1\,V\,C_2 & W\,D_1 \end{bmatrix}$$

where $V = (I + D_2\,D_1)^{-1}$ and $W = (I + D_1\,D_2)^{-1}$

5.6 The Inverse of a system is defined as follows: If $y = G\,u$, then $u = G^{-1}\,y$. If the system matrix of G is given by the quadruplet $\{A, B, C, D\}$, and assuming that G is square and D is invertible, show that the system matrix for G^{-1} is given by

$$G^{-1} = \begin{bmatrix} A - B\,D^{-1}\,C & -B\,D^{-1} \\ D^{-1}\,C & D^{-1} \end{bmatrix}$$

5.7 Derive the system matrices for the return difference, inverse return difference, sensitivity, and complementary sensitivity transfer function matrices defined in Section 5.6. In addition, show how the above system matrices can be computed using standard system connection commands.

5.8 The loop transfer function, $L(s)$, of a *full order observer* (defined in Chapter 8) or a *Kalman-Bucy filter* (defined in Chapter 12) is given by

$$L (s) = C \, \Phi (s) \, L = C (s I - A)^{-1} L$$

Compute the return difference, sensitivity, and complementary sensitivity transfer function matrices for this system.

5.9 Obtain the general form of the state space matrices, {A, B, C, D} for the observable form I and controllable form II.

Notes and References

According to the survey [F91], the most frequently used books in linear systems/state variable analysis are: [B91], [C84], [F86], [K80], and [De89]. Other books mentioned for graduate level linear systems courses are [FPE91], [DH88], [Do89], and [L79].

6

Introduction to SIMULINK

SIMULINK (formerly SIMULAB) is an extension of MATLAB that is used to simulate dynamic systems. SIMULINK differs from MATLAB in that it has a window-based (using block diagrams) graphical user interface. It also adds many functionalities to MATLAB. Because SIMULINK is such an extensive and powerful program, it would take much more than a brief chapter to fully describe its features. Therefore, this chapter is written as a hands-on guided tour of SIMULINK. We will describe the basic concepts and some of the commands you will be using to simulate dynamic systems. We will take you step by step through a simple example and show you how to build a model. After working through Example 6.1, you should try the other examples on your own; we have included the block diagrams and results of simulations in the body of these examples. The examples serve two purposes for us; first, they are used to provide some practice in building simple models; second, we use SIMULINK as a tool to discuss some system concepts (effects of saturation, effects of unstable pole-zero cancellation, and a view of chaotic systems).

How you physically interact with the program depends on the particular hardware, Macintosh, Microsoft Windows (we will refer to it as PC), Workstation or Mainframe, you are using. The look of the screen, interface, and a few of the available utilities and menu items also vary with the hardware platform. To keep the chapter brief, we will assume that you are familiar with the windowing environment of your computer. Therefore, you know how to work with a mouse, and you know what is meant by clicking, double clicking, dragging, and holding while dragging a mouse (a recent magazine advertisement for a computer training school depicted a person holding the mouse in midair. We assume you are not a graduate of such schools!). Our presentation and the corresponding graphics are based on the Macintosh version of SIMULINK. In cases where there are some differences in the steps or the commands between the Macintosh and the PC version, the PC equivalent commands will also be shown. One simple difference is that the PC mouse has two or three buttons, while the standard Macintosh mouse has one button. We frequently have to click or double click the mouse for many of the operations. With the PC mouse, this refers to the left button (if you have a three-button PC mouse, the middle button is not used). Because of the way SIMULINK works, it is important that you use your computer when you study this chapter.

6.1 Basic Steps in Model Building

First, you need to access SIMULINK. This is done by typing its name at the MATLAB prompt (you must first be in MATLAB). After the program has been invoked, the main block library of SIMULINK will be displayed in a new window. Most of the block types that you need to build a block diagram are already available in this library. All you need to do is to pick the blocks you need, connect them together, set their parameters; you are then almost done. It is that simple. The main block library is divided into appropriate categories, shown in Figure 6-1. To see the contents of each category, double click on that category and a new window opens. In Figure 6-1, we have opened five windows displaying most of the contents of each category.

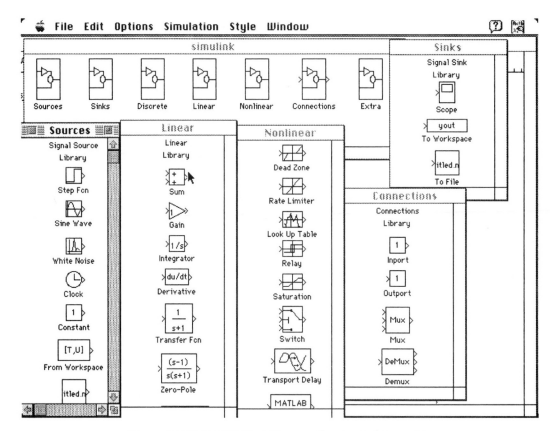

Figure 6-1 SIMULINK block library and contents of some of them.

Note that when you open SIMULINK, your menu title bar also changes. The File, Edit, and Style menus are the usual menu items in window environments. The Options and Simulation menus are related specifically to SIMULINK. They will be described shortly. Before building a model you need to create a working area. This is accomplished by going to the File menu and selecting New, which will open a new window with the title "Untitled 1". You will construct your model within this window (we will refer to this as your *working window*). Let us begin our first example.

Example 6.1

Consider the double integrator system *G(s)*, which is open loop unstable. To stabilize this plant, we use a lead compensator, *K(s)*, as shown in Figure 6-2.

$$G(s) = \frac{1}{s^2}, \quad K(s) = 10\frac{(s+1)}{(s+5)}$$

Our goal is to obtain the step response of this system. We will use six objects in this diagram: two transfer functions, one summing junction, one input source (step), and two objects for viewing the output.

Input source elements are located in the *Sources* library. Double click this library to open its window and note its contents. We are interested in the *Step Fcn* source. To select this block, put the mouse cursor on it, click and hold the mouse while you drag the object into your working window (we will refer to this procedure as *dragging*).

Note that this will only place a copy of the object into your window. The *Step Fcn* itself will remain in the library. Because we do not need this library any more, close the *Sources* library. During a SIMULINK session you will open many windows; close the windows you no longer need to reduce the clutter on the screen.

The transfer function and summing junction blocks are located in the *Linear* library. Open the *Linear* library (by double clicking on it). Drag the *Transfer Fcn* block into your working window. Repeat this step for the second transfer function; also drag the *Sum*. Close the *Linear* library.

The simulation outputs are obtained using the *Sinks* library. Open this library and you will see that there are three objects available. The *Scope* acts like an oscilloscope and

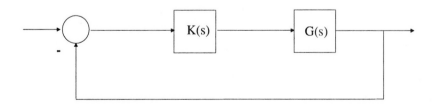

Figure 6-2 Block diagram for Example 6.1.

gives you a live display of any signal during simulation. The *To Workspace* block passes the output vectors to the MATLAB workspace as matrices. This allows you to analyze and plot your data using MATLAB. The *To File* block passes the data to a file and saves them under a given name. Drag the *Scope* and the *To Workspace* blocks to your working window. Close the *Sinks* window.

You should now have six blocks in your working window. The next step after block selection is setting the block parameters. If you double click on any block (we refer to this as *opening a block*), a window opens to show the parameters of that block. The window displays brief information on that block; a Help option is also available for more detailed information. Most blocks have default parameters that can be changed.

Open one of the transfer function blocks (double click on it). There are two fill-in boxes for the *Numerator* and *Denominator*. Enter [10 10] and [1 5] in these boxes, respectively. This, of course, is the usual way of entering vectors in MATLAB. Select OK when done. Open the second transfer function block; enter [1] and [1 0 0], and select OK.

Open the *Sum* block and enter +- for the *List of signs*. If the summing element has more than two inputs, simply enter all their signs. The block will expand to accommodate all the inputs.

Open the *Step Fcn* block. There are three fill-in boxes. The *Step time* is the initial starting time for the step function (enter 0). Enter the *Initial value* and *Final value* (0 and 1, respectively).

Open the *To Workspace* block. Enter *y* for the *Variable name* (the step response will appear under this name in the MATLAB workspace after simulation). Enter 100 for the *Maximum number of rows*. Each row corresponds to a time step. We plan to generate 100 points and simulate the system from time 0 to 9.9 in steps of 0.1.

The final step in model building is connecting the blocks. All blocks, with the exception of *Sources* and *Sinks* blocks, have at least one angle bracket (>) pointing out of them. This is their *output port*. They also have an angle bracket pointing toward them, which is their *input port*. The *Sources* blocks have no inputs, so they only have output ports. Similarly, the *Sinks* blocks only have input ports. Multiple input blocks (e.g., *Sum* block) have more than one input port.

To connect two blocks, click on the output port of one block, drag the mouse to the input port of the other block, and release the mouse button. The angle brackets will disappear, and a line (with an arrowhead) will be drawn making the connection. As you move the mouse up or down, the line will be drawn in multiples of 45 degrees. To draw a line at any angle, hold the Shift button down while you drag the mouse (PC users: Hold the right and left buttons together while you drag the mouse).

Use the above procedure to connect the step input to the positive port of the summing block. Note that as you get close to the input port, the line automatically snaps to the port. If it snaps to the wrong port, click on the connection line; go to the Edit Menu and select Cut (shortcut: Click on the line, hold the Command key down while you press X. PC users: Use Shift Delete). This will delete the connection. Repeat this procedure to connect the summing block to the first transfer function; the first transfer function to the second transfer function; the second transfer function to the output (*To Workspace*).

The final connection to be made is the feedback loop; i.e., from the plant to the negative port of the summing junction. Note that the plant block ($1/s^2$) is already connected to the output block (*To Workspace*), so it does not have an output angle bracket any more. It is possible to pick several outputs from a single block. Click on the output port of the block (plant transfer function), and drag the mouse. Release the mouse before you reach another block; this creates an angle bracket at the place where you released the mouse. Click on this bracket (we refer to it as an *extended port*) and drag it, this draws another line. Releasing the mouse button while drawing a line allows you to draw multiple line segments. Using this technique, you can go around blocks and draw nice-looking block diagrams. Use this procedure to finish drawing your block diagram.

Before we get to simulation, let us mention a few drawing tricks that you should try. Suppose there are two line segments meeting at a corner (e.g., the feedback loop). You can move this corner around by clicking on the corner and dragging it (note that a circle will appear temporarily at the corner in this case). You can move a line segment by clicking in the middle of it and dragging it. Finally, you can add a new vertex in the middle of a line. Click in the middle of a line, hold the Shift key down (PC users: Hold down both mouse buttons) while you drag the line; this creates a new vertex at that location.

The block diagram is complete now. You can embellish it by going to the Style menu and change the screen color, background color, fonts, drop shadows around blocks, etc. If you click the title of a block, it will be highlighted and you can type in a new name. From the Options menu, you can also flip and rotate the blocks.

The final step is simulation. This is done from the Simulation menu. There are normally two items to choose from. You can either select Start (shortcut: Command T; PC users: Ctrl T) to start the simulation, or you can set the simulation parameters. To open the Parameters dialog box, select Parameters from the Simulation menu. You have a choice of seven integration algorithms. For linear systems, choose *Linsim*. Enter 0 for the *Start Time*, 9.9 for the *Stop Time*, 0.001 for *Relative Error* (relative error of integration at each step), 0.1 for the *Minimum Step Size*, and 0.1 for the *Maximum Step Size*. You can also obtain the time variable of integration by filling in the *Return variables* box. Enter *t* in that box. After simulation, two variables will be returned to the MATLAB workspace; namely, *t* and *y*. Select OK to leave the dialog box.

Now, select Start from the Simulation menu. You will hear a beep (or whatever sound your computer makes) when the simulation is finished.

To view the output, we can use the scope. Note that we did not connect the scope to any particular block. What we have here is called a *floating scope*. If you click on any line, the signal on that line will be displayed in the scope. Make sure you resize your windows so that the scope graph is clearly visible. If you start the simulation again, you should see the output shown in Figure 6-3. You can change the vertical and horizontal ranges for the scope by entering a desired number in the text boxes (PC users: Move the sliders or change the values in the text boxes). In Figure 6-3, our *Vertical Range* is 1.6, and the *Horizontal Range* is 10.

You can now save your block diagram by using Save in the File Menu; save the diagram and call it "example1". This will create a MATLAB M-file that describes your

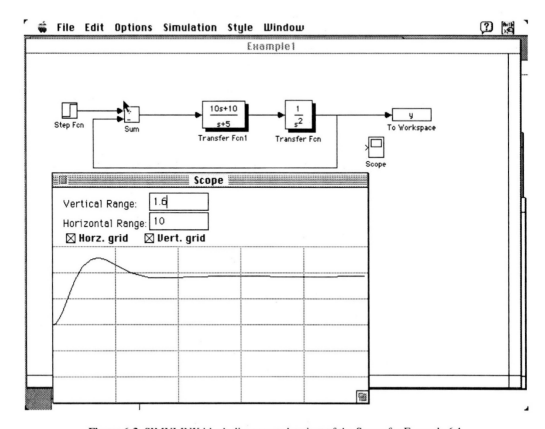

Figure 6-3 SIMULINK block diagram and a view of the Scope for Example 6.1.

block diagram model. You can always recall your diagram from the MATLAB prompt (in the Command window) by simply typing the name of the file (the same way you execute any script file).

Return to the MATLAB Command window by clicking on its window. If you type *whos*, you should see the two variables *t* and *y*. If you plot the output versus time, you get the result in Figure 6-4.

6.2 SIMULINK Commands

6.2.1 Simulation from the Command Line

Using the name of the simulation algorithms, it is possible to perform simulations directly from MATLAB. The syntax for all algorithms is the same and is given below:

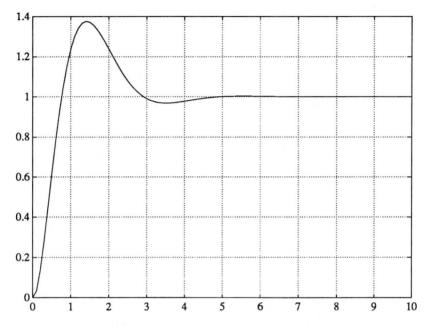

Figure 6-4 Step response of Example 6.1.

```
>> [t,x,y]=linsim('model',tf,xo,options,u)
```

The input arguments are as follows: The name of the SIMULINK generated model is entered first (within single quotes); the second input argument is the final time of simulation (you can enter a two-element row vector to simulate from a nonzero initial time to the final time). The rest of the input arguments are optional. The third argument is the vector of initial conditions; these values will override any initial conditions set in the block diagram. Moreover, you can simulate transfer function models with initial conditions from the Command line (the transfer function dialog box in SIMULINK does not have any box entries for initial conditions). The fourth argument is a vector of options for controlling the integration features, such as step size and error tolerance.

The last input argument allows external inputs for simulation. You can either set the input from the Sources block library within SIMULINK, or directly from the Command line. From the Command line you have two choices; the input can either be a string or a table of values. As a string, any valid MATLAB function or expression is allowed. For example, if you enter 'sin', the MATLAB function *sin* will be evaluated as a function of the time vector *t* and will be used as an external input. If the input is a table of values, the first column must be a vector of time values in increasing order; other columns can be input vectors. For example, if the system has three inputs, the vector *u* will have four columns.

The output arguments are the time vector, states, and outputs. Without left-hand arguments, the states will be plotted automatically. If the model has outputs, the outputs will be plotted. For example, the following two command lines will simulate and plot the states for Example 1:

```
>> linsim('example1',10)
>> euler('example1',10,[1 2 3])
```

The first command, uses the *linsim* algorithm; the second command uses the *euler* algorithm with specified initial conditions.

6.2.2 Choice of Integration Algorithms

There are six integration algorithms to choose from; the choice depends primarily on the problem. Some guidelines are given in the following:

- **linsim**
  is used primarily for linear systems, or systems containing few nonlinear elements. It is the desired algorithm for *stiff systems* (systems with both slow and fast dynamics; e.g., a system with a pole at 0.01 and another at 1000).
- **rk45, rk23**
  are Runge-Kutta fifth order and third order, respectively. They are well suited for highly nonlinear and discontinuous systems, also suitable for mixed continuous and discrete time systems. The *rk45* method is faster and more accurate than the *rk23* method, but uses fewer points that leads to nonsmooth plots. They are not recommended for stiff systems.
- **gear**
  stands for the Gear's predictor-corrector method. It is recommended for smooth nonlinear systems. Gear's method is particularly designed for stiff systems. It is not recommended for discontinuous systems.
- **adams**
  is the Adams predictor-corrector method. It is recommended for smooth, nonlinear, and nonstiff systems.
- **euler**
  is the Euler's method. It is the simplest and most widely known technique. It is also the fastest method, but suffers from accuracy and stability problems. For example, given a stable system, it is possible to obtain an unstable response for a poorly chosen step size. You may use it to quickly verify results of other simulation methods.

6.2.3 Linearization

Consider the following nonlinear system:

$$\dot{x} = f(x,u,t)$$
$$y = g(x,u,t)$$

The above nonlinear system can be linearized about an equilibrium point (x^*,u^*). Let us define the perturbed states and control inputs by

$$\delta x = x - x^* \quad \text{and} \quad \delta u = u - u^*$$

Then to a first order approximation, using Taylor's series expansion, the linearized equations are given by

$$\delta \dot{x} = \left[\frac{\partial f}{\partial x} \right] \delta x + \left[\frac{\partial f}{\partial u} \right] \delta u$$

$$y = \left[\frac{\partial g}{\partial x} \right] \delta x + \left[\frac{\partial g}{\partial u} \right] \delta u$$

where $\frac{\partial f}{\partial x}$ stands for the *Jacobian* of the vector function f with respect to the state vector x. The Jacobians are all evaluated at the specified equilibrium point (x^*,u^*). If the system is not explicitly a function of time (time invariant system), the Jacobian matrices will be constant matrices.

The *linmod* command is used to obtain the state space representation of linearized systems. Its syntax is given by

```
>> [a,b,c,d]=linmod('model')
>> [a,b,c,d]=linmod('model',x,u)
```

The '*model*' is the name of the SIMULINK-generated block diagram model. In the second syntax form, the equilibrium points for the states and control inputs can be specified. There are also additional syntax forms that allow you to control the perturbation levels for states, controls, etc. The discrete form of the command is *dlinmod* that works for mixed continuous and discrete time systems. For linear systems, the commands give the state space equations.

For example, we will obtain the closed loop transfer function of the system in Example 6.1. Before we do that, we need to add two more blocks to our diagram. These are the blocks, *inport* and *outport*, located in the *Connections* library. These blocks provide access to external inputs and outputs. Without these blocks, the *linmod* command would give us zero vectors for the input and output connection matrices. The modified block diagram is shown in Figure 6-5. Make sure you save your diagram after you make the changes under the same name.

```
>> [a,b,c,d]=linmod('example1'); [nt,dt]=ss2tf(a,b,c,d)
```

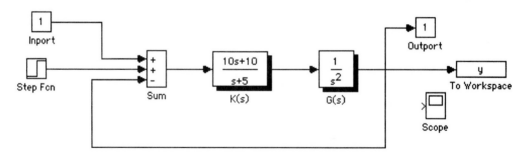

Figure 6-5 SIMULINK block diagram for Example 6.1.

```
nt =
    0      0   10.0000   10.0000
dt =
    1.0000   5.0000   10.0000   10.0000
```

A related command that computes equilibrium points is the *trim* command:

```
>> [x,u,y,dx]=trim('model')
>> [x,u,y,dx]=trim('model',xo,uo,yo,ix,iu,iy)
```

This command tries to find values for the states and inputs such that the derivatives of the states are zero (i.e., the system reaches steady state). The second syntax form has two additional sets of arguments (set of three elements). The first set contains the initial starting guesses or desired values. The second set contains the indices for elements that you may wish to fix. For instance, consider the following system:

$$\dot{x}_1 = -x_1 - x_2 + u$$
$$\dot{x}_2 = x_1 - 2x_2 + u$$
$$y = x_1 + 3x_2$$

The problem is to find the steady state values for the control input and the states such that the output will be equal to 1.

To use the *trim* command, you need to define the system in SIMULINK. Invoke SIMULINK; open a new file; open the *Linear* library and drag the *State-space* block into your new workspace; open this block to set its parameters; open the *Connections* library and drag the *inport* and *outport* blocks; connect all the blocks and save it under a given name; e.g., "*trimtest*". Return to MATLAB and issue the following command:

```
>> [x,u,y,dx]=trim('trimtest',[],[],1,[],[],1)
```

```
x =
    0.1429
    0.2857
```

```
u =
   0.4286
y =
   1.0000
dx =
  1.0e-016 *
   0.2776
  -0.2776
```

6.2.4 Data Interpolation

The integration algorithms in SIMULINK use variable step sizes that result in simulation outputs with unevenly spaced points. This makes it difficult to compare simulations that are run under different conditions (e.g., comparing responses under different initial conditions). In such cases, the data have to be interpolated to produce results with equal number of points. MATLAB commands such as *spline, table1*, and *interp2* are available for interpolation.

Suppose the vector *y* has been evaluated as a function of the vector *x*. If another abscissa vector *x1* is given, the command *interp2* can find the corresponding ordinate vector *y2* by interpolation. Its syntax is given by

```
>> y1=interp2(x,y,x1)
```

A more concrete example of data interpolation appears in the next example.

6.3 Examples

Example 6.2 Effects of Saturation

We will investigate the effects of saturation in the previous example. Saturation is a nonlinear phenomenon that is very common in control systems. For instance, electronic amplifiers have almost linear gain up to a certain range, beyond which the output saturates. It occurs in electric motors due to saturation of magnetic fields, and it is present in almost every real physical system. Although saturation effects can be analyzed using "describing functions" and other approximate nonlinear methods, we will examine their effects using simulation. The input-output characteristic of a nonlinear saturation element is shown in Figure 6-6.

The gain of the nonlinear element is M/E for input signals with a magnitude less than E, and has a fixed gain of M for input magnitudes greater than E. The overall result is that the "effective gain" of the amplifier decreases as the amplitude of the external input increases. This gain reduction generally has stabilizing effects and makes the system more sluggish. Of course, for conditionally stable systems that become unstable for lower gains, saturation can be destabilizing. It is worth noting that during saturation, the system temporarily becomes open loop; the system must tolerate this mode. The bottom line is that for real systems, simulation incorporating all nonlinear effects must be performed to ensure proper performance.

After generating the block diagram (saved under the name "*ex2*") of the system shown in Figure 6-7, we are ready for simulation. We will vary the input level from one to six where

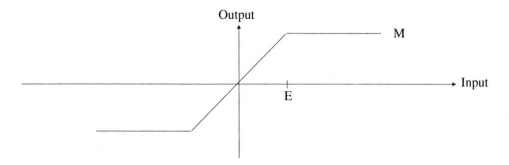

Figure 6-6 Input-Output characteristic of a saturation element.

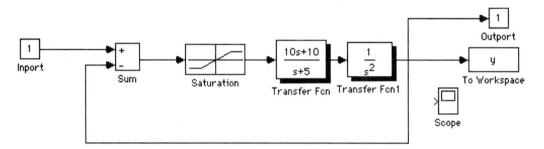

Figure 6-7 SIMULINK block diagram for Example 6.2.

the saturation limits are set to ±1; we will also simulate the system and compute the overshoot for all cases. Finally, we will plot the step responses together for comparison.

The simulation will be performed from the Command line using the *for* command. Because the simulations will produce different number of points, all outputs are interpolated using the 100-point time axis defined by the vector t. The following is the code:

```
t=[0:.1:9.9]';
for i=1:6
        ut=[t , i*ones(t)];
        [tt,xx,yy]=linsim('ex2',10,[],[],ut);
        yint=interp2(tt,yy,t); y(:,i)=yint;
        i=i+1;
end
sy=size(y); yss=y(sy(1),:); pos=100*(max(y)-yss)./yss;


pos =
   37.6548  34.6111  31.4223  29.5730  29.7324  30.7281  30.7281
```

The simulation result is shown in Figure 6-8. From the plot, we observe that the settling time increases with larger inputs. Notice that in linear systems, when the input level changes, the output level changes accordingly—system dynamic behavior, however, does not change. With saturation, dynamic characteristics, such as settling time and overshoot, are dependent on input levels. This is strictly a nonlinear phenomenon. The root locus of the system, shown in Figure 6-9, will shed some light on the above results. To obtain the open loop transfer function, we need to disconnect the feedback loop; save the diagram, and use the *linmod* command to get the state space equations of the open loop system.

Because the effective gain decreases, the real part of the complex root decreases; settling time is inversely proportional to this real part; we expect, therefore, longer settling time for larger input values. Also note that the damping ratio (ζ) initially increases but then decreases. This explains the initial reduction in POS and the final slight increase.

Example 6.3 Pole-Zero Cancellation Effects

We will investigate the effects of pole-zero cancellation. Stable pole-zero cancellation is a very common and effective design strategy. It is also referred to as "pole shifting", in which stable poles are canceled with zeros and replaced with poles in more desirable locations. It is also the idea behind notch filter design. Although it has to be noted that exact pole-zero cancellation is not possible in practice, due to component tolerances in continuous systems and finite word length effects in digital systems, it is still a very popular and effective strategy. The main point of this example is to demonstrate, through analysis and simulation, the effects of *unstable* pole-zero cancellation, and explain why it must not be done.

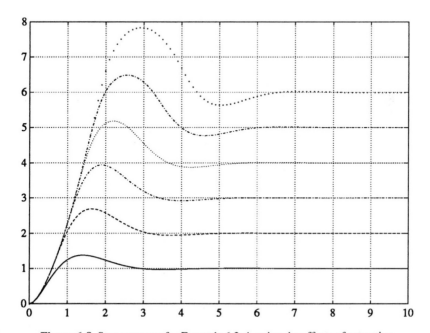

Figure 6-8 Step response for Example 6.2 showing the effects of saturation.

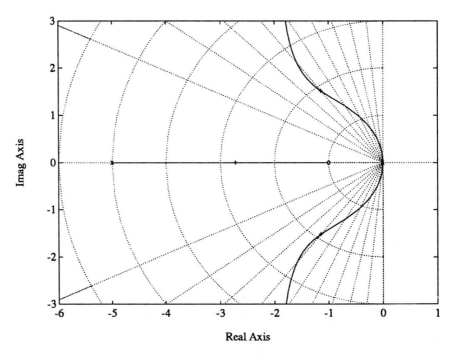

Figure 6-9 Root locus for Example 6.2.

We will consider the following example adapted from [K80]:

$$G(s) = \frac{1}{s-1} \quad \text{and} \quad K(s) = \frac{s-1}{s+1}$$

where $G(s)$ is the plant, and $K(s)$ is the cancellation compensator. The product $G(s)K(s)$ is, of course, stable in the bounded input–bounded output sense (i.e., BIBO stable). Because the system is now second order, we can represent it as a set of two first order differential equations and solve for the step response (the details are left as an exercise):

$$\dot{x}_1 = x_1 + u$$
$$\dot{x}_2 = 2\,x_1 - x_2$$
$$y = x_1 + x_2$$

The SIMULINK block diagram corresponding to these equations is shown in Figure 6-10. Solving for the states and the output, we get

$$x_1(t) = (\alpha + 1)\,e^t - 1 \qquad \text{where } x_1(0) = \alpha$$
$$x_2(t) = 2 + (\alpha + \beta - 1)\,e^{-t} - (\alpha + 1)\,e^t \qquad \text{where } x_2(0) = \beta$$
$$y(t) = x_1 + x_2 = 1 + (\alpha + \beta - 1)\,e^{-t}$$

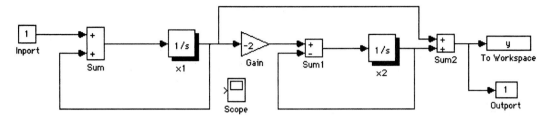

Figure 6-10 SIMULINK block diagram for $G(s)K(s)$.

Now, note that as $t \rightarrow \infty$; $x_1 \rightarrow \infty$, $x_2 \rightarrow -\infty$, and $y \rightarrow 1$

Therefore, even though the internal variables within the system are unbounded, the output somehow masks this information and, in fact, converges to 1 for any initial condition. We define a system to be *internally stable* if all possible transfer functions between all inputs and outputs are stable. Hence, the above system, although BIBO stable, is not internally stable. Also, note that the system has two "modes," e^t and e^{-t}, and the unstable mode gets canceled. The canceled mode is called a *hidden mode* and corresponds to the pole at $s = 1$, which is precisely the pole that was canceled.

In summary, when a pole is canceled by a zero, it creates hidden modes within the system; if the pole is unstable, it leads to a system that is not internally stable, which is unacceptable. For those familiar with state space concepts, we say that the system becomes unobservable (or undetectable if the mode is unstable). It is worth noting, however, that when the initial condition $\alpha = -1$, all variables remain bounded. For all other initial conditions, we get the previous result. The plots for initial conditions of $(-1,1)$ and $(1,1)$ are shown in Figures 6-11 and 6-12.

We will now analyze the case where the compensator precedes the plant; i.e., $K(s)G(s)$. In a transfer function sense, there should not be any difference, because the closed loop transfer function is the same in both cases (GK and KG are the same). In the time domain, however, we will see some differences due to the effects of initial conditions. It can be shown that the following set of differential equations represents the system (this is left as an exercise). The SIMULINK block diagram is shown in Figure 6-13.

The equations and the step response calculation results are shown below:

$$\dot{x}_1 = -x_1 - 2u$$
$$\dot{x}_2 = x_1 + x_2 + u$$
$$y = x_2$$
$$x_1(t) = -2 + (\alpha + 2)e^{-t}$$
$$y(t) = x_2(t) = 1 + \left(\frac{\alpha + 2\beta}{2}\right)e^t - \left(\frac{\alpha + 2}{2}\right)e^{-t}$$

We note, again, that for initial conditions of $\alpha = 2\beta$, the unstable mode is canceled, and

$$x_1 \rightarrow -2 \quad \text{and} \quad y = x_2 \rightarrow 1$$

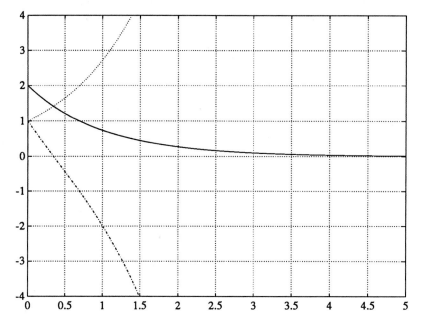

Figure 6-11 Step response of $G(s)K(s)$ for (1,1) initial conditions.

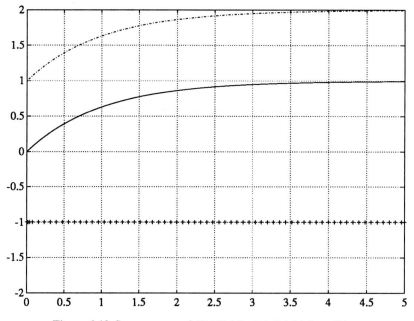

Figure 6-12 Step response of $G(s)K(s)$ for (−1,1) initial conditions.

For all other initial conditions, the output is unbounded. From the state space point of view, the present realization is uncontrollable, or rather not stabilizable, because the hidden mode is unstable. For the particular choice of initial conditions $(-2,1)$ we have $x_1(t)=-2$ and $x_2(t)=y(t)$ $= 1$ as shown in Figure 6-14. The plot for initial conditions of $(1,1)$ is shown in Figure 6-15.

Example 6.4 Simulation of a Chaotic System: The Lorenz System

The Lorenz system is a set of three first order nonlinear differential equations. They were first presented in 1963 by E. N. Lorenz, whose motivation for the problem was weather forecasting.

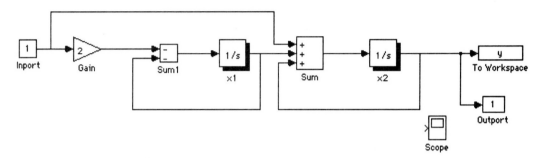

Figure 6-13 SIMULINK block diagram for $K(s)G(s)$.

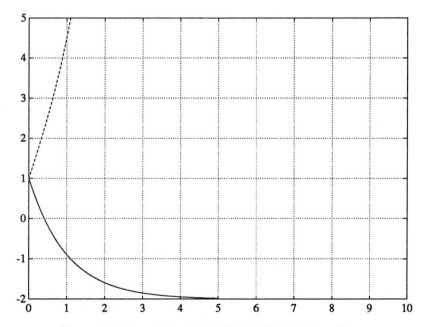

Figure 6-14 Step response of $K(s)G(s)$ for $(1,1)$ initial conditions.

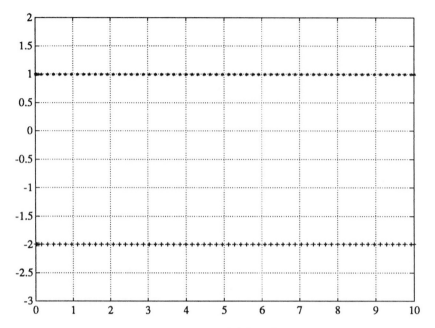

Figure 6-15 Step response of $K(s)G(s)$ for $(-2,1)$ initial conditions.

For more details, see Thompson and Stewart [TS86]. The equations are given below:

$$\dot{x} = a\,(\,y - x\,)$$
$$\dot{y} = x\,(\,b - z\,) - y$$
$$\dot{z} = c\,z + x\,y$$

Lorenz realized the exponential divergence of nearby initial conditions and concluded that the fundamental problem of long-term weather forecasting is imprecise knowledge of initial conditions. The strong dependence of solutions of nonlinear dynamic systems on their initial conditions has been long recognized. The term *chaos* commonly refers to the fact that it is impossible to exactly predict the behavior of nonlinear systems in the long run, even though the underlying phenomenon is deterministic and represented by a simple set of differential equations.

Before using SIMULINK, you must have a plan. You must first draw a draft version of the diagram on paper and determine how many of each block you need. The simulation parameters are $\{a = 10, b = 28, c = 2.67, x(0) = y(0) = z(0) = 5\}$.

The SIMULINK block diagram for the system is shown in Figure 6-16. This third order system can be thought of as an interconnection of three first order subsystems. When you are dealing with diagrams that contain many blocks (resulting in a cluttered and confusing diagram), it is recommended that the overall system be broken up into appropriate subsystems. The Options menu contains an option called *Group* that will group selected blocks in a subsystem.

To form a subsystem block, hold down and drag the mouse over the desired area; release the mouse; all blocks within the area will be highlighted; choose the Options menu and select *Group*; the highlighted blocks will be replaced by a single subsystem block. Figure 6-17 on

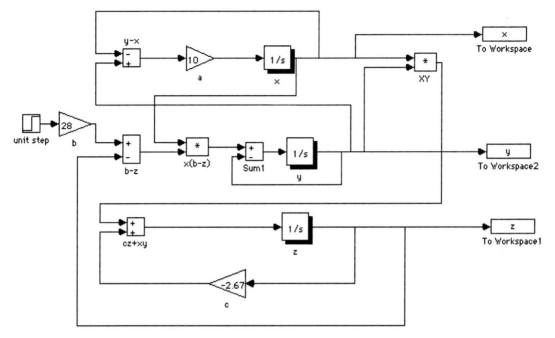

Figure 6-16 SIMULINK block diagram for the Lorenz system.

page 162 shows the Lorenz system broken up into three subsystems (X, Y, and Z). You can open a subsystem block by double clicking on it. The results of simulation are shown in Figure 6-18 on page 162. The *Linsim* algorithm (stop time=100, min step size=0.01, max step size=10) was used for simulation.

Example 6.5 Demonstration of Other Blocks

This example introduces four additional blocks: *From Workspace* (*Sources* library), *DeMux* and *Mux* (*Connections* library), and *Switch* (*Nonlinear* library). The example is simple and is used mainly to demonstrate these useful blocks.

The *From Workspace* block allows you to use data from MATLAB workspace as inputs in your block diagram. The first column of data must be an ascending vector (time axis); the other columns are data vectors.

The *Mux* block takes vectors as inputs and packs them into a matrix. For example, if you wish to view several vectors simultaneously on the *Scope*, you may multiplex them first using this block. The *DeMux* vector performs the opposite task (demultiplexer); it takes a matrix input and breaks it into column vectors.

The *Switch* block is a conditional block. It has three inputs; it uses its second input as a condition checker. The output of the switch is equal to the first input if the second input is greater or equal to zero; otherwise, the output is equal to the third input.

To demonstrate these blocks, we will generate three input vectors (plus the time axis vector) in MATLAB. The first input is a sine wave; the third input is the negative of the first

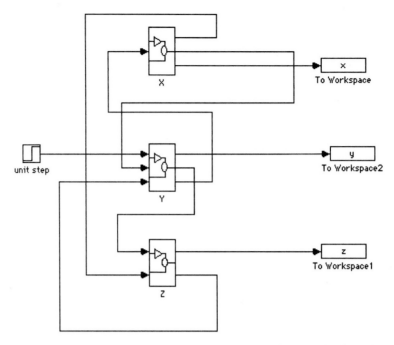

Figure 6-17 SIMULINK block diagram for the Lorenz system using grouping into subsystems.

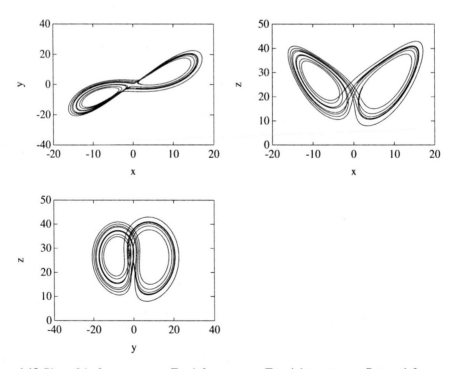

Figure 6-18 Plots of the Lorenz system. Top left: y versus x. Top right: z versus x. Bottom left: z versus y.

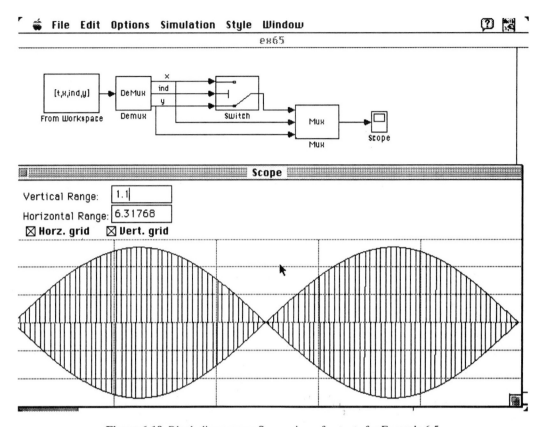

Figure 6-19 Block diagram ans Scope view of outputs for Example 6.5

input; the second input (condition checker) is a vector of alternating 1s and –1s. The output, therefore, is an alternating sample of +sin(t) and –sin(t). The block diagram is shown in Figure 6-19 above. The following input vectors are created first in MATLAB:

```
>> t=[0:pi/50:2*pi]'; x=sin(t); y=-sin(t);
>> ind=(-1).^[0:100]';    % second input
```

Enter SIMULINK and create the block diagram. The first block loads the input vectors from the MATLAB workspace. Its output is a matrix with three columns. The *DeMux* block splits this matrix into three columns that are fed into the *Switch*. The output of the *Switch* and the x and y vectors from the *DeMux* are then multiplexed together for viewing on the *Scope*. If you now simulate the system, you should see the plot shown in Figure 6-19. Note that there are actually three plots; the x and y vectors form the envelope of the *Switch* output.

The labels you see at the outputs of the *DeMux* block were added using the Text block. This block (unlike all other blocks) has no icons anywhere. If you click anywhere in your workspace within SIMULINK, you can type any text. You can then select this text and move it anywhere you want.

6.4 Advanced Features

SIMULINK has several other advanced features that we will briefly mention but not pursue any further here. When you create a block diagram, SIMULINK creates an M-file (a function) for that model. These functions are called *S-functions*, and like any other MATLAB function are open files that can be accessed and edited by the user. The name of the command that is used to create an S-function is *sfun*. This means that you can write your own customized programs to simulate a system without going through the graphical interface. An S-function can also be converted to a block from within SIMULINK. You can also create and add new block types to SIMULINK using the *Mask* option in the Options menu. You can take any existing block or S-function and change its characteristics using the Mask option. A collection of mask blocks are available in the Extra block library. The S-function and Mask features of SIMULINK follow the MATLAB philosophy of open M-files allowing the user to add functionalities to the program. Because these features are quite involved and are beyond our intention of giving you a quick introduction, we refer you to the SIMULINK User's Guide.

6.5 Problems

6.1 The purpose of this problem is to investigate the behavior of two famous nonlinear systems that exhibit chaotic behavior. Simulate the systems for the given parameters and initial states. Plot the states versus time, and also plot all combinations of one state versus another (e.g., see Example 6.4). You may vary the parameters or the initial states to see vastly different behavior.

a. The *Rossler* system

$$\dot{x} = -y - z \qquad\qquad x(0) = 5$$

$$\dot{y} = x + \frac{1}{5}\,y \qquad\qquad y(0) = 5$$

$$\dot{z} = \frac{1}{5} + z\,x - 5.7\,z \qquad z(0) = 5$$

b. The *Duffing* system

$$\dot{x} = y \qquad\qquad\qquad x(0) = 5$$

$$\dot{y} = -(x^3 + x + y) + \cos\theta \qquad y(0) = 5$$

$$\dot{\theta} = \omega \qquad\qquad\qquad \theta(0) = 3$$

6.2 The purpose of this problem is to illustrate the effects of computational errors in a nonlinear system. Repeat the simulations in Example 6.4 and problem 6.1, but use a different integration algorithm (e.g., Euler). Plot the responses and plot the difference between the states obtained using different algorithms. Observe that the errors build up and the systems are very sensitive to computational errors.

6.3 The purpose of this problem is to demonstrate that systems with identical gain, or phase, margin can have step responses with vastly different qualities. Hence, good margins do not necessarily imply good time responses [AH84].

a. For each transfer function given, obtain the Nyquist or Bode plot, and compute and compare gain and phase margins.

$$G_1(s) = \frac{1.4 \, (1 + 0.5s) \, e^{-0.4s}}{s^2}, \quad G_2(s) = \frac{0.072 \, e^{5s}}{s \, (1 + 5s)^2}, \quad G_3(s) = \frac{1.65 \, e^{-12s}}{1 + 20s}$$

$$G_4(s) = \frac{1.25 \, e^{-15s}}{(1 + 5s)^2}, \quad G_5(s) = \frac{0.1}{s \, (1 + 5s)^2}, \quad G_6(s) = \frac{1.4 \, (1 + 1.2s) \, e^{-0.2s}}{s^2}$$

b. Assuming unity feedback, obtain closed loop step response and compute POS and T_s, also obtain closed loop Bode magnitude plot and compute peak resonance, M_r.

c. Tabulate your responses and draw conclusions about the relationships between stability margins and time response. Determine which one of the frequency response measures (GM, PM, M_r) is the most reliable indicator of the quality of the step response as measured by POS.

6.4 Consider the systems in Example 6.3. Analytically solve for the states and the outputs in both cases, and verify that the stated results and conclusions are correct.

6.5 [Problem suggested by B. Torby] A standard problem in mechanical vibrations is the two-degree-of-freedom problem. There are two masses; the first mass is connected to a fixed wall via springs and dashpots, there is also a spring and a dashpot between the masses, as shown in Figure 6-20. A sinusoidal input force is applied to the second mass. The problem is to find the resulting positions and velocities of the masses. The equations of motion and the parameters are

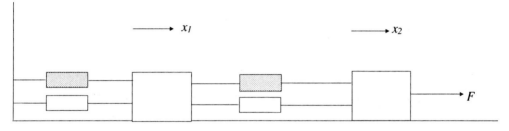

Figure 6-20 Two-degree-of-freedom problem. The filled (hollow) boxes represent dashpots (springs).

$$M_1 \ddot{x}_1 + (k_1 + k_2) x_1 + (c_1 + c_2) \dot{x}_1 - k_2 x_2 - c_2 \dot{x}_2 = 0$$

$$M_2 \ddot{x}_2 + k_2 x_2 + c_2 \dot{x}_2 - c_2 \dot{x}_1 - k_2 x_1 = F \sin (20\, t)$$

$$M_1 = 10 \, kg, \quad M_2 = 20 \, kg, \quad k_1 = 1000 \, N/m, \quad k_2 = 200 \, N/m, \quad c_1 = c_2 = 120 \, N.s/m, \quad F = 100$$

Build the above system and simulate it for 4 sec. Plot the four states (positions and velocities) versus time. Plot x_1 versus x_2, $\dot{x}_1$ versus x_1, $\dot{x}_2$ versus x_2 .

7

Classical Design

7.1 Introduction

Classical control system design is usually performed using transfer function descriptions; the two most popular techniques are root locus and Bode plot design. Closed loop specifications are most often given in terms of steady state error and such desired system step response parameters as rise time, peak time, settling time, peak overshoot, etc. Steady state error, system type, and step response parameters are discussed in Chapter 1. The step response parameters are used to derive the desired open loop frequency domain characteristics of gain and phase margin. Remember that these relationships are derived assuming the system can be described with a pair of dominant poles. Zeros and additional poles close to the dominant poles affect the step response of the system. These effects were described and simulated in Chapter 1.

An advantage of using the computer to aid in control system design is that the complete closed loop system can be modeled and analyzed. Always treat the techniques we describe here as the initial design procedure. Close the loop and perform a time domain and frequency domain analysis and adjust your design as needed. Before discussing specific design strategies, we will review how the root locus and Bode plots can be used to predict closed loop behavior.

7.1.1 Root Locus

The root locus plot shows the location of the closed loop poles as a particular transfer function parameter, usually its gain, is varied. The root locus is an excellent technique for determining closed loop stability and relative stability. Even if the Bode plots are used in the design process, the root locus can be used for stability analysis.

Constant contours in the s-plane for settling time (T_s), damped frequency (ω_d), damping ratio (ζ), and (undamped) natural frequency (ω_n) can be determined for a second order system. The roots of the second order characteristic equation are given by

$$s = -\zeta \omega_n \pm j \sqrt{1 - \zeta^2} \quad \omega_n = -\sigma \pm j \omega_d$$

The standard zero-state step response is described mathematically below:

$$y(t) = 1 - \frac{1}{\sqrt{1 - \zeta^2}} e^{-\zeta \omega_n t} \cos(\omega_d t - \sin^{-1} \zeta)$$

Settling time is usually taken to be between four and five time constants, so

$$4\tau < T_s < 5\tau, \quad \text{where} \quad \tau = \frac{1}{\sigma} \quad \text{and} \quad \sigma = \zeta \omega_n$$

Although there are no exact relationships for rise time, T_r, and delay time, T_d, they both are inversely proportional to ω_n. Peak overshoot (POS) as a percentage is given by

$$POS = 100 \, e^{\frac{-\pi \zeta}{\sqrt{1 - \zeta^2}}} \quad 0 \le \zeta < 1$$

Consider, for example, the specifications:

    overshoot < 25%
    settling time < 5 sec

From these specifications we determine that

$$\zeta > 0.4 \rightarrow \theta < 66°$$

$$T_s < 5 \rightarrow \sigma < -1$$

The allowable region in the s-plane for the given specification is shaded dark in Figure 7-1.

   Again, all of the foregoing assumes that we are dealing with a system that is adequately described with a single pair of complex conjugate poles. If the actual system has poles or zeros close to these complex poles, then the closed loop response will not be as predicted.

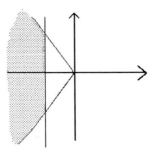

Figure 7-1 Region of allowable pole locations.

7.1.2 Bode Plots

The Bode plots can be used to determine closed loop steady state error, damping ratio, natural frequency (for a dominant pole system), and stability margins. The use of Bode plots to determine the stability of nonminimum phase systems (i.e., poles or zeros in the RHP) is not recommended; instead, use Nyquist stability criterion.

Let us assume that the plant in a unity feedback configuration is described by

$$KG(s) = \frac{K \omega_n^2}{s^2 + 2\zeta\omega_n s + \omega_n^2}$$

We can determine immediately from the Bode plot of the open loop system what the system Type is. In this case, the initial slope is zero, so $KG(0)$ is finite. This implies that the system is Type 0 with $K_p = KG(0) = K$, the low frequency gain. An initial slope of $-20n$ dB/dec indicates a Type n system.

The closed loop transfer function for this system is

$$T(s) = \frac{K \omega_n^2}{s^2 + 2 \zeta \omega_n s + (K+1) \omega_n^2} = \frac{K \omega_n^2}{s^2 + 2 \zeta_{CL} \omega_{n_{CL}} s + \omega_{n_{CL}}^2}$$

where $\quad \omega_{n_{CL}} = \omega_n\sqrt{K+1} \quad$ and $\quad \zeta_{CL} = \dfrac{\zeta}{\sqrt{K+1}}$

For large K, the gain crossover frequency ($\omega_{gc} \approx \omega_n\sqrt{K}$) gives an accurate measure of the closed loop natural frequency. The closed loop bandwidth is also approximated by ω_{gc}; however, the actual closed loop bandwidth may vary by as much as 100% of this value.

The damping ratio of the closed loop system is approximately $1/\sqrt{K}$ of the open loop damping ratio. The closed loop system will therefore be faster and have greater overshoot than the open loop system. Can the closed loop damping ratio (ζ_{CL}) be predicted from the open loop Bode plots? From the definition of phase margin (PM) in Nyquist plots and using simple geometry, we obtain

$$PM = 2 \sin^{-1} \frac{1}{2 \, | \, T(j \omega_{gc}) \, |}$$

Because $\omega_{gc} \approx \omega_n \sqrt{K}$, then

$$PM \approx 2 \sin^{-1}(\zeta_{CL}) \quad \text{or} \quad \zeta_{CL} \approx \sin\left(\frac{PM}{2}\right)$$

Some authors [FPE91] use the following approximation:

$$\zeta_{CL} \approx .01 \, PM \text{ (degrees)}$$

Relative stability can be determined from both the phase margin and the gain margin (GM), which is defined as

$$\text{GM} = - \mid G(\, j \, \omega_{pc}\,) \mid_{dB}\,, \quad \text{where} \quad \angle G(\, j\omega_{pc}\,) = - \, 180\,°$$

Either the root locus or the Bode plots can be used to predict closed loop behavior. The root locus gives a very accurate picture of the closed loop poles, whereas the Bode plots can be used to determine closed loop steady state error, bandwidth, and stability margins.

7.2 Compensation

There are various configurations that can be used for compensation. Among them are series (cascade), feedback, and combination of both. In series compensation, the compensator is placed in cascade with the plant. In the feedback configuration, the compensator is placed within the feedback path. In both cases the open loop transfer function and the closed loop poles are identical. Therefore, they have the same root locus and Bode plots, so the stability properties are similar. The closed loop zeros are different, however, so the steady state errors are different. Because feedback reduces the effects of parameter variations with respect to elements in the forward path, the series configuration has better sensitivity properties. It is also easier to control the error constants in the unity feedback case. As a result, the cascade configuration has traditionally been more popular.

It is also possible to place filters outside of the loop to filter out extraneous signals. Notch filters that damp out specific known frequencies are commonly used. Because these filters are placed outside of the loop, they do not benefit from feedback properties. Hence, their use is recommended only when the frequencies they are supposed to attenuate are accurately known.

A compensation technique that is often used in the classroom is pole-zero cancellation. The dominant poles (zeros) of the plant are canceled with a compensator that has zeros (poles) at the same locations. The desired system loop gain poles are then added to the denominator of the compensator.

Although this technique may be feasible for canceling LHP plant poles and zeros, it should never be used to cancel plant poles or zeros in the RHP. One problem with pole-zero cancellation is that we never really know where the plant poles and zeros are. Our plant transfer function is only a model for plant behavior. It is never absolutely accurate. Another problem with pole-zero cancellation is that even though the canceled poles disappear in the command input to output transfer function, they may still be present in other transfer functions (e.g., in the disturbance to output transfer function). Hence, we have good command following, but poor disturbance rejection. If pole-zero cancellation is used, the designer must be sure to examine how sensitive closed loop response is to variations in plant pole and zero locations.

Two commonly used controllers are *proportional-integral-derivative (PID)* and *lead-lag*. The transfer functions of these controllers are

$$PID \qquad K_p + K_d s + \frac{K_i}{s}$$

$$Lead\ (or\ Lag) \qquad K\,\frac{s+a}{s+b}$$

7.3 Proportional-Integral-Derivative Control

The proportional-integral-derivative (or PID) controller can take several forms: *proportional* only, $K_d = K_i = 0$; *proportional plus derivative (PD)*, $K_i = 0$; *proportional plus integral (PI)*, $K_d = 0$; full PID. Proportional only control is the simplest control scheme. It allows the designer, however, to satisfy only one closed loop specification; e.g., GM, PM, steady state error, etc. The addition of derivative control increases the damping in the closed loop system while integral control increases the system type and, hence, decreases steady state error. PID is usually effective in meeting most specifications. It is by far the most widely used controller in the process industry. It is also widely available in various forms (analog, digital, and adaptive).

7.3.1 Ziegler–Nichols Method

Because three parameters must be adjusted in the design of PID controllers, root locus and Bode design techniques are usually not used directly. Ziegler and Nichols [ZN42] developed a method for tuning a PID controller, which is based on a simple stability analysis. First, set $K_d = K_i = 0$, and then increase the proportional gain until the system just oscillates (i.e., closed loop poles on the $j\omega$ axis). The proportional gain is then multiplied by 0.6, and the other two gains are calculated as

$$K_p = 0.6\,K_m \qquad K_d = \frac{K_p\,\pi}{4\,\omega_m} \qquad K_i = \frac{K_p\,\omega_m}{\pi}$$

where K_m is gain at which the proportional system oscillates, and ω_m is the oscillation frequency. Note that this technique does not design to any specifications. Rather, Ziegler and Nichols found that this design procedure provided "good" behavior for process controllers. Years of experience by process control engineers have indicated that it is indeed a good technique.

Either the root locus or the Bode plots can be used to determine K_m and ω_m. For example, a root locus is obtained for the given plant transfer function. The gain at which the root locus crosses the $j\omega$ axis is K_m, and the frequency on the $j\omega$ axis gives us ω_m. Alternatively, Bode plots are plotted for the given plant transfer function. The GM is determined at the frequency ω_{pc}: $K_m = 10^{(GM/20)}$ and $\omega_m = \omega_{pc}$. Be aware that the Bode technique gives approximate answers only.

Example 7.1 PID Control—Ziegler–Nichols Method

Given the plant

$$G(s) = \frac{400}{s\,(s^2 + 30s + 200)}$$

The above transfer function will be used in all subsequent examples for PID, PD, and lead design. It has the following characteristics:

Closed loop poles = {- 4.2 ± j0.93, -21.59}
Gain crossover frequency = 1.95 rad/sec
GM = 23 dB
PM = 73 degrees

The closed loop step response has no overshoot, and the steady state error to a unit ramp input is 0.5. The root locus for this plant is shown in Figure 7-2. The *rlocus* and *rlocfind* commands can be used to find the crossover gain of $K_m = 14$ and crossover frequency (phase crossover frequency) of $\omega_m = 14$ rad/sec. We can now use Ziegler–Nichols equations to find the gain parameters

$$K_p = 9 \qquad K_d = 0.5 \qquad K_i = 40$$

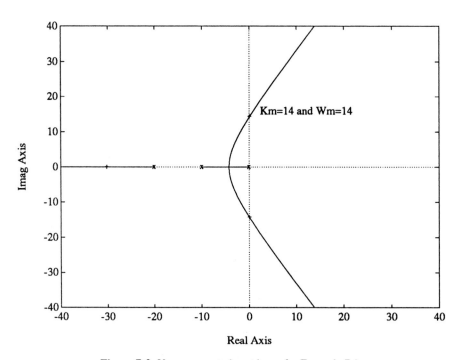

Figure 7-2 Uncompensated root locus for Example 7.1.

The open loop Bode plots and the closed loop step response of the system before and after compensation are shown in Figure 7-3. The compensated step response shows a 60% overshoot with a settling time of approximately 1.2 sec. The gain crossover frequency is 11 rad/sec with a phase margin of 25 degrees. The Ziegler–Nichols program in the Appendix can be used to obtain the compensator.

7.3.2 Analytical Method

As stated previously, the Ziegler–Nichols technique does not allow us to design a PID controller to achieve specific closed loop behavior. An analytical technique can be developed to determine the PID parameters given steady state error and performance specifications. The loop gain of a PID controlled system is given by

$$(K_p + K_d\,s + \frac{K_i}{s})\,G(s)$$

If $G(s)$ is a type n plant, the compensated system will be type $n + 1$. The error constant is equal to the inverse of the steady state error and is given by

$$K_{n+1} = s^n\,K_i\,G(s)\,|_{s=0} = \frac{1}{e_{ss}}$$

For a given steady state error specification, we find K_i from the preceding equation. From time domain specifications such as overshoot and settling time, we determine the required closed loop damping ratio and natural frequency. We know from the first section of this chapter that the closed loop natural frequency corresponds to the open loop gain crossover frequency (ω_{gc}) and that the desired PM can be found from the closed loop damping ratio. Therefore, at $\omega = \omega_{gc}$, the compensated system should have a gain of 1 and phase of $\theta(\omega_{gc}) = -180° + \text{PM}$.

With this information, remembering that K_i is now known, we can write

$$(K_p + j\omega_{gc}K_d + \frac{K_i}{j\omega_{gc}})\,G(j\omega_{gc}) = 1\,e^{\,j\theta(\omega_{gc})}$$

which leads to

$$K_p + j\omega_{gc}K_d = \frac{1}{G(j\omega_{gc})}\,e^{j\theta(\omega_{gc})} + \frac{j\,K_i}{\omega_{gc}} = R + j\,X$$

Hence, we see that $K_p = R$ and $K_d = X/\omega_{gc}$.

The above procedure can easily be programmed. Program 2 (Analytic PID) in the Appendix was used to solve the following example.

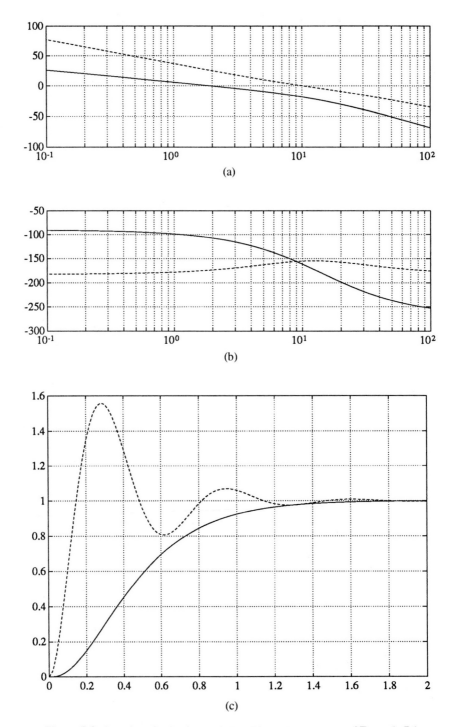

Figure 7-3 Open loop Bode plots and closed loop step response of Example 7.1.

Example 7.2 PID Control—Analytical Technique

Consider the plant given in Example 7.1 and repeated here:

$$G(s) = \frac{400}{s\,(s^2 + 30s + 200)}$$

The following specifications are given:

> steady state error to unit ramp input = 0.1
> overshoot = 10%
> settling time = 2 sec

Because the plant is Type 1, we find the steady state error constant for the PID-plant combination to be

$$K_2 = s\,K_i\,G(s)\,|_{s=0} = 2\,K_i = 1/0.1 = 10 \;\rightarrow\; K_i = 5$$

From the overshoot and settling time specifications, we determine that the desired closed loop damping ratio and natural frequency are $\zeta = 0.6$ and $\omega_n = 4$ rad/sec. Therefore, we will specify that $\omega_{gc} = 4$ rad/sec and $PM = 2\sin^{-1}(0.6) = 80$ degrees.

Using the Analytical PID program in the Appendix, we get: $K_p = 2.02$, $K_d = 0.52$.

The Bode plots in Figure 7-4 indicate that PM is 80 degrees and the gain crossover frequency is 4 rad/sec, as expected. The step response of the closed loop system is shown in Figure 7-5. We see from the step response that we have approximated the required settling time of 2 sec. The overshoot of 22% is larger than the specification, however. This is due to the zeros that the PID controller introduces into the system. It is often the case that a PID controller cannot meet all system specifications, and some trial and error is required.

7.3.3 PD Control

Because the PD controller is very common, we will discuss it here. Integral control is only used if we want to increase the system type and, thus, reduce steady state errors. The drawback of integral control is that the additional pole at the origin tends to destabilize the system. Conversely, the additional zero added by derivative control usually increases system stability. Therefore, derivative control is often added to feedback systems, especially if increased damping is desired. We will discuss root locus and Bode techniques for PD control in the next section. Here, we will show you the application of an analytical technique to PD design.

Example 7.3 PD Control

Given the plant used in the first two examples, design a PD controller to meet the following specifications:

$PM = 45°$ at $\omega_{gc} = 13.5$ rad/sec.

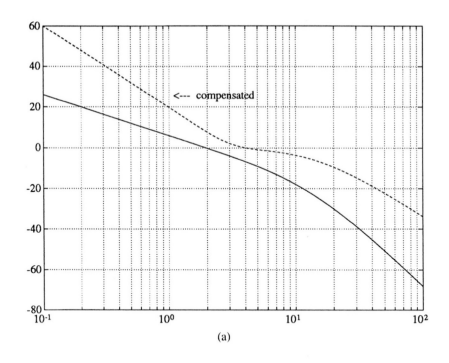

(a)

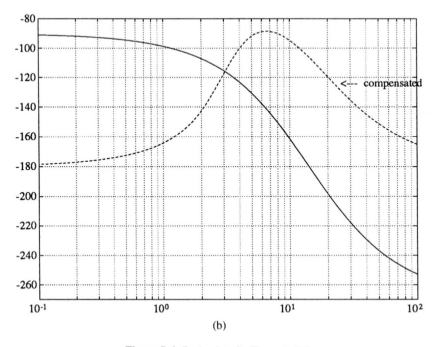

(b)

Figure 7-4 Bode plots for Example 7.2.

176

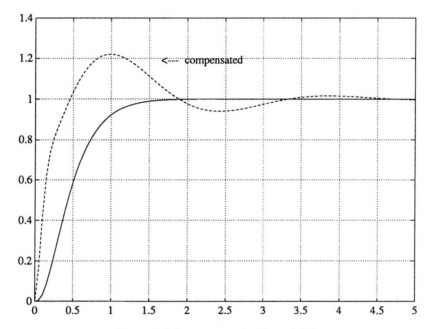

Figure 7-5 Step response for Example 7.2.

Note that the PD controller has only two parameters, so we cannot meet the same number of specifications as we can with the PID controller. The PID program with $K_i = 0$ can be used for design. The PD coefficients are $K_p = 10$ and $K_d = 0.68$. Figure 7-6 shows that the step response for this PD controlled system has an overshoot of 24% and a settling time of 0.8 sec. The error constant for the compensated system is 20.

Note that we never actually build a pure differentiator ($K_d s$) because of the noise problems inherent in such a device. Rather, the derivative term always has a pole associated with it. In this case, we can treat the PD controller as a lead compensator, as discussed in the next section. PD control is often achieved with a sensor that can directly measure the velocity of the output; e.g., a tachometer. In this case the derivative term is usually placed in a minor feedback loop around the plant as shown in Figure 7-7.

With this configuration, the step response for Example 7.3 is shown in Figure 7-8. We see that the overshoot is now only 11%. The reason for this is that the derivative term in a feedback loop does not create an additional system zero.

7.4 Lead Compensation

The simplest and most common form of compensation is a filter with one zero and one pole. The general transfer function for this compensator is

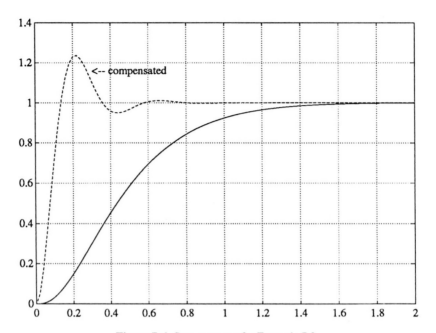

Figure 7-6 Step response for Example 7.3.

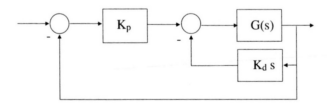

Figure 7-7 PD with tachometer feedback.

$$K(s) = K_c \frac{s+a}{s+b}$$

If the zero occurs before the pole ($0 < a < b$), $K(s)$ is known as a *lead* compensator. If the pole occurs before the zero ($a > b > 0$), $K(s)$ is a *lag* compensator. The maximum phase contribution, lead or lag, occurs at $\omega = \sqrt{ab}$.

How does the designer know whether to use a lead or a lag compensator? The answer, of course, is in the system specifications. For example, if the only requirement is to stabilize the closed loop system, then either type of compensation can usually be used (assuming that the plant is stable—for unstable plants, lead compensation must be used). Additional

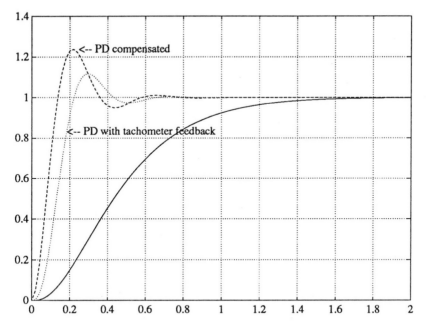

Figure 7-8 Step responses for Example 7.3: uncompensated, using PD, and with the D term in minor feedback loop.

specifications, however, will often lead to a choice of one type of compensation over the other. For example, if a certain ω_{gc} is desired, an examination of the plant Bode plot will immediately determine the compensator type. If the desired ω_{gc} is larger than the plant ω_{gc}, then a lead compensator is needed; if smaller, a lag compensator is needed.

For the lead and the lag compensator, we will describe root locus, Bode and analytical techniques for design. Remember, all of these design procedures assume the plant can be adequately described with a pair of dominant poles. The actual closed loop response will vary somewhat from that predicted from these designs. Always close the loop and simulate the total system; make adjustments as necessary.

All compensators affect the stability, steady state error, and bandwidth of closed loop systems. Lead compensation, in general, increases relative stability by increasing phase margin. For a given system gain, K_c, lead compensators increase steady state error. This is because $a < b$, which means that $K_c\,a/b < K_c$. To decrease steady state error, a large compensator gain must be used. Lead compensators also increase the gain crossover frequency, ω_{gc}. This has the effect of decreasing step response settling time (i.e., increasing system damping). Although this is often desirable, the increase in ω_{gc} also leads to an increase in closed loop bandwidth. This increased bandwidth can result in undesirable signals or noise in the system or instability in systems with time delays (transportation lags).

The following design procedures are to be used as a starting point in a design cycle. They are merely *guidelines* rather than laws or methods that will always work. Not every system can be adequately compensated using simple lead-lag compensators. After all, we are limiting the choice of compensator poles and zeros to the negative real axis, which ensures the compensator itself is always stable. This leaves out compensators with complex poles and zeros or unstable compensators. Although stable compensators are desirable, it is also known that some systems require unstable compensators for closed loop stability. Systems that can be stabilized using stable compensators are called *strongly stable* systems. For systems that cannot adequately be stabilized using classical methods discussed in this chapter, state space or optimal control methods can be used. These more advanced methods are discussed in later chapters. Classical methods, where they are applicable, usually result in low order stable compensators that are adequately designed after a few iterations. It is recommended that you start with these simple compensators before applying more advanced methods that usually result in more complex compensators.

7.4.1 Root Locus Design

Root locus design is based on reshaping the root locus of the system—by adding poles and zeros to the plant—to force the loci to pass through a desired point in the complex plane. The following steps are common to root locus design techniques:

- Determine the desired complex pole location, s_1, from the specifications.
- Locate the compensator zero.
- Determine the compensator pole location using the property that for an s-plane point s_1 to lie on the root locus, the angle of $K(s_1) G(s_1)$ must be 180°.
- Does the system gain at s_1 satisfy steady state error requirement? If not, change s_1 and repeat the design.
- Close the loop and determine if the specifications are met.

There are several procedures in the literature for determining the zero location. Of course, the designer can use his or her experience and intuition to locate the zero. Dorf [Do89] recommends that the zero be located directly under the desired s-plane point s_1. Ogata [O90], and D'Azzo and Houpis [DH88] describe a more involved geometric procedure that determines both the zero and pole locations.

Select the desired point in the s-plane, s_1, and find $\varphi_c = 180° - \angle G(s_1)$; the angle that must be contributed by the lead compensator. If φ_c is negative, a lead compensator cannot be designed—go to the lag compensator design. A lead compensator can contribute an angle of approximately 50 to 60 degrees. If more phase lead is required, more than one compensator section can be used. The rest of the procedure is described in Figure 7-9.

Draw a line from the origin to s_1 and a horizontal line from s_1. Find the angle φ formed by these two lines. Bisect this angle. The lines from the desired zero and pole locations are constructed so that each line forms an angle of $\varphi_c/2$ with the bisector. This procedure minimizes the distance between the zero and pole locations. By keeping this ratio close to 1, we minimize the required compensator gain K_c.

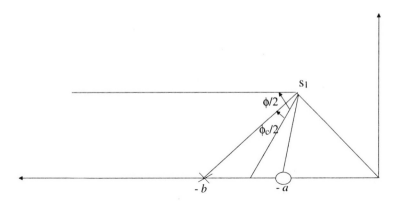

Figure 7-9 Geometric procedure.

7.4.2 Root Locus—Geometric Method

A purely analytical technique can be derived for the geometric procedure that can easily be programmed. The program (No. 3) appears in the Appendix.

- Select desired s-plane location s_1.
- Define $\varphi = \angle(s_1)$ and $\varphi_c = 180\,° - \angle G(s_1)$.
- Define $\theta_p = \dfrac{\varphi - \varphi_c}{2}$ and $\theta_z = \dfrac{\varphi + \varphi_c}{2}$.
- Find the pole location from: $p_c = -b = Re(s_1) - \dfrac{Im(s_1)}{\tan \theta_p}$.
- Find the zero location from: $z_c = -a = Re(s_1) - \dfrac{Im(s_1)}{\tan \theta_z}$.
- Find K_c so that $|\,K(s_1)\,G(s_1)\,| = 1$.
- If K_c is too small for steady state error requirements, choose a new s_1 and repeat the procedure.

Example 7.4   Lead Compensation: Geometric Method

As an example of this design procedure, we reexamine the plant used in the previous sections. That is,

$$G(s) = \frac{400}{s\,(s^2 + 30s + 200)}$$

The specifications require

$\zeta = 0.5$ and $\omega_n = 13.5$ rad/sec

These parameters result in a desired s-plane location of $s_1 = -6.75 \pm j\,11.69$. The *ord2* command can be used at this step. This command returns a second order transfer function with a specified ζ and ω_n. The design procedure described above leads to

$$\varphi = \angle(-6.75 + j\,11.69) = 120^\circ$$

$$\varphi_c = -180 - \angle G(-6.75 + j\,11.69) = 55.8^\circ$$

$$\theta_p = \frac{\varphi - \varphi_c}{2} = 32^\circ$$

$$\theta_z = \frac{\varphi + \varphi_c}{2} = 87.9^\circ$$

$$p_c = -b = Re(s_1) - \frac{Im(s_1)}{\tan\theta_p} = -25.41$$

$$p_z = -a = Re(s_1) - \frac{Im(s_1)}{\tan\theta_z} = -7.16$$

$$K_c = \frac{1}{|G(s_1)\,K(s_1)|} = 13.62$$

The final compensator design for this problem is

$$K(s) = 13.62\,\frac{s + 7.16}{s + 25.41}$$

The step and frequency response are shown in Figure 7-10. It can be seen that the overshoot is now 8% and the settling time is 0.8 sec. The Bode plots show a GM of 15 dB and PM of 60° with the gain crossover frequency at 8. This compares very favorably with the PD design,

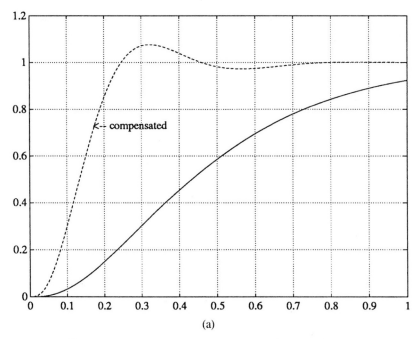

(a)

Figure 7-10 Step and frequency responses for Example 7.4.

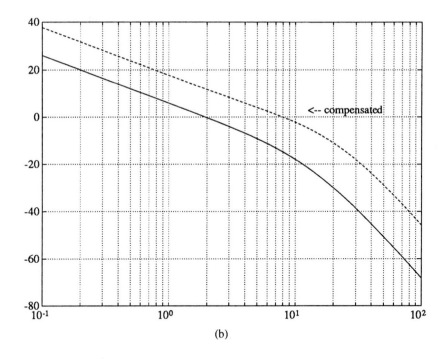

(b)

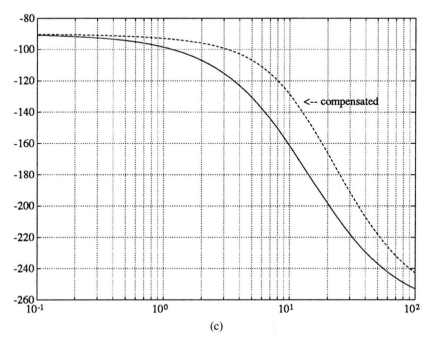

(c)

Figure 7-10 Frequency responses for Example 7.4.

which resulted in an overshoot of 24% and a PM of 45°. A major difference, however, is that the error constant in the lead compensator design is only 7.68, which is lower than the error constant of 20 obtained with the PD design. Also the higher gain crossover frequency of 13.5 rad/sec results in a faster PD response.

Again, designing to a specific error constant with the root locus techniques is not straightforward. If the error constant of 7.68 that we just obtained is not large enough, we would need to pick a new s-plane point for the design and keep iterating until an acceptable error constant is achieved. There are, however, some analytical methods that may allow the designer to use the root locus technique to design to a specific steady state error requirement.

7.4.3 Root Locus—Analytical Method

We present here an analytical method, modified from [PH88], that can be used to design either lead or lag compensators. For this design, we use the following alternative representation for the compensator:

$$K(s) = K_c \frac{s\,\tau_z + 1}{s\,\tau_p + 1}$$

We first choose K_c and the desired s-plane location, s_1, from steady state error and transient specifications. For the compensated system to lie on the root locus

$$K(s_1)\,G(s_1) = K_c \frac{s_1\,\tau_z + 1}{s_1\,\tau_p + 1}\,M_G\,e^{j\theta_G} = 1\,e^{j\pi}$$

where $G(s_1) = M_G\,e^{j\theta_G}$. Because K_c is known, we need to solve the above equation for τ_z and τ_p. If s_1 is represented by $s_1 = M_s\,e^{j\theta_s}$, then we have

$$M_s\,e^{j\theta_s}\,\tau_z + 1 = \left(\frac{1\,e^{j\pi}}{M_G\,e^{j\theta_G}\,K_c}\right)\!\left(M_s\,e^{j\theta_s}\,\tau_p + 1\right)$$

This equation can be separated into its real and imaginary parts, resulting in two equations and two unknowns. The solutions of these equations are

$$\tau_z = \frac{\sin\theta_s - K_c\,M_G\,\sin(\theta_G - \theta_s)}{K_c\,M_G\,M_s\,\sin\theta_G}$$

and

$$\tau_p = -\frac{K_c\,M_G\,\sin\theta_s + \sin(\theta_G + \theta_s)}{M_s\,\sin\theta_G}$$

This technique only works if both τ_z and τ_p are positive. Of course, to design a lead compensator we also need $\tau_p < \tau_z$. In practice, we would usually perform this design for several values of K_c and choose the compensator that gives the best overall performance. A program (No. 4) for this procedure appears in the Appendix.

Example 7.5   Analytical Design

We repeat the previous example, with an additional steady state error requirement. That is,

$$G(s) = \frac{400}{s\,(s^2 + 30s + 200)}$$

The specifications are

$\zeta = 0.5$, $\omega_n = 13.5$ rad/sec, and velocity error constant of 10.

We will design for $K_c = 5$ and $s_1 = -6.75 \pm j11.69$
We first determine that

$s_1 = -6.75 + j11.69 = 13.49\,e^{j120} = M_s\,e^{j\theta_s}$
$G(s_1) = 0.13\,e^{\,j124.1} = M_G\,e^{\,j\,\theta_G}$

Using the desired K_c and the values above, we solve for τ_z and τ_p .
The compensator for this design is

$$K(s) = 5\,\frac{0.1s + 1}{0.027s + 1}$$

Figure 7-11 shows the step and frequency responses for this compensated system. The compensated system has an overshoot of 14% and a settling time of 0.9 sec. We have achieved similar performance as in Example 7.4, but we have a larger error constant here. Note that in Figure 7-11, we have plotted the uncompensated system with the gain of 5 for comparison. The Bode plots show that with the compensator, we have been able to increase both stability margins and speed of response, and reduce the overshoot.

We mention in passing that if this design were repeated with the requirement that $K_c = 10$, a negative τ_p would result. In general, to obtain a final compensator design, we would run the program iteratively for several values of K_c .

7.4.4 Lead Compensation—Bode Design

The basic idea in Bode design is to shape the open loop transfer function so that it will have desirable low frequency gain (for steady state error or disturbance rejection properties), desirable gain crossover frequency (for speed of response), and adequate stability margins. It is common to parameterize the compensator as shown below for Bode design.

$$K(s) = K_c\,\frac{\alpha\,T\,s + 1}{T\,s + 1}$$

In the Bode design method, we first choose the gain to satisfy steady state error requirements. This is one advantage of designs using Bode plots where steady state error specifications can easily be met. Then we satisfy PM requirements and attempt to achieve

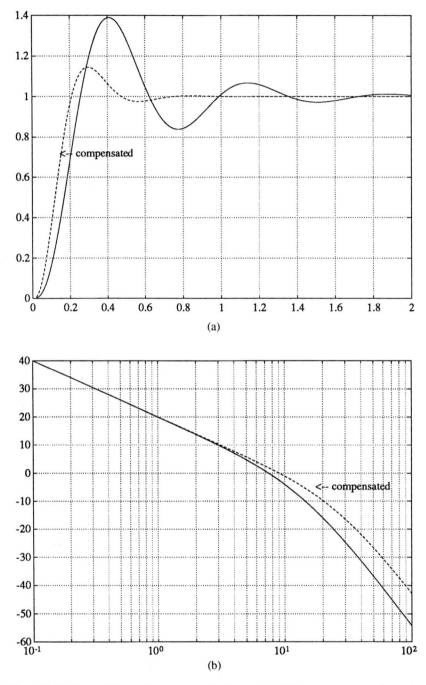

Figure 7-11 Step and frequency responses for Example 7.5. The uncompensated transfer function has been multiplied by K_c

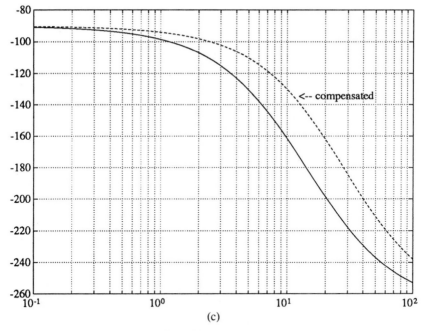

Figure 7-11 continued.

the desired gain crossover frequency. To use this procedure properly, it is necessary to understand the derivation of the formulas involved. To that end, we will quickly derive the appropriate relationships by considering the phase and magnitude contributions of the compensator:

$$K_1(s) = \frac{\alpha T s + 1}{T s + 1}$$

where $K(s) = K_c K_1(s)$.

Because we would have already chosen K_c to satisfy steady state error criterion, we can exclude it from this discussion. We are only concerned with the additional phase and magnitude that $K_1(s)$ contributes. The phase of this lead compensator is

$$\angle K_1(j\omega) = \tan^{-1} \alpha T\omega - \tan^{-1} T\omega$$

Because we are using this method to achieve the desired *PM*, we are concerned with the amount of phase lead added by the compensator at the compensated ω_{gc}. For ease of design, we usually try to add the maximum phase lead possible at $\omega = \omega_{gc}$. The frequency at which maximum phase lead occurs can be found by taking the derivative of the above equation and is

$$\omega_{max} = \frac{1}{\sqrt{\alpha}\,T}$$

The maximum phase lead that can be achieved is therefore

$$\angle K_1(j\omega_{max}) = \angle K_1(j\omega_{gc}) = \Phi = \tan^{-1}\sqrt{\alpha} - \tan^{-1}\frac{1}{\sqrt{\alpha}}$$

Finally, a little trigonometry shows that the relationship between α and Φ can be written as

$$\sin\Phi = \frac{\alpha - 1}{\alpha + 1} \quad\text{and}\quad \alpha = \frac{1 + \sin\Phi}{1 - \sin\Phi} \quad\text{at}\quad \omega_{max} = \frac{1}{\sqrt{\alpha}\,T}$$

Remember, for this design, we set $\omega_{gc} = \omega_{max}$. The additional magnitude, in dB, contributed by $K_1(s)$ at $\omega = \omega_{max} = \omega_{gc}$, is

$$M = |K_1(j\omega_{max})|_{dB} = |K_1(j\omega_{gc})|_{dB} = 10\log\alpha$$

We are now ready to describe the procedure.

First, draw the Bode plot using the new gain K_c to satisfy the steady state error requirement. Determine additional phase lead (Φ) needed to satisfy PM requirements. Compute α. Now, knowing that the lead compensator will raise the magnitude by M dB, find the frequency where the uncompensated magnitude is $-M$ dB. This forces the compensated magnitude to have 0 dB gain at this frequency. This is the new gain crossover frequency, which is used to compute T. A listing of this procedure is shown below:

*   Select K_c to achieve the required error constant.
*   Draw Bode plots for $K_cG(j\omega)$, and determine PM for $K_c\,G(j\omega)$.
*   Determine additional phase lead required; this is the initial Φ.
*   Add a few degrees to the phase just determined to find the working Φ (see below).
*   Compute α from $\alpha = \dfrac{1 + \sin\Phi}{1 - \sin\Phi}$.
*   Find the frequency at which the gain of $K_cG(j\omega) = -10\log\alpha$; this frequency will be the compensated ω_{gc}.
*   Compute T from $T = \dfrac{1}{\sqrt{\alpha}\,\omega_{gc}}$.
*   Draw Bode plots of $K(j\omega)G(j\omega)$ to confirm design.
*   Close the loop, and determine appropriate closed loop responses.

The reason that we must add a few (e.g., 5) degrees to the phase lead needed to obtain the desired PM (fourth bullet) is that the addition of the compensator zero will cause the compensated crossover frequency to increase. This increase in ω_{gc} will result in a smaller PM than calculated per the third bullet. A program (No. 5) for this procedure is available in the Appendix.

It is important to note that with this design procedure, we cannot predetermine the compensated ω_{gc}. We may have to adjust the PM or steady state error requirements if the resultant ω_{gc} is unacceptable.

Example 7.6 Bode Method

As an example of this procedure, we again consider the plant

$$G(s) = \frac{400}{s\,(s^2 + 30s + 200)}$$

The specifications are:

velocity error constant = 10

PM = 45°

The steady state error constant requires $K_c = 5$. The Bode plot for $K_cG(j\omega)$, shown in Figure 7-12 on page 190, indicates that PM = 32°. Because we want a PM of 45°, the initial $\Phi = 13°$. We add 5° for safety and calculate α as described above to be $\alpha = 1.89$. We now calculate $-10 \log \alpha = -2.77$ dB. Examination of Figure 7-12 shows that this gain occurs at what will become the compensated gain crossover frequency $\omega_{gc} \approx 9$ rad/sec. We now find T as

$$T = \frac{1}{\sqrt{\alpha}\,\omega_{gc}} = 0.08$$

The compensator is

$$K(s) = 5\,\frac{0.15s + 1}{0.08s + 1}$$

The compensated PM now is 41°, which is close to the requirement. The step response for the closed loop system is shown in Figure 7-13 on page 191. The overshoot is 28%, and the settling time is 1.4 sec.

7.4.5 Bode Design—Analytical Method

The analytical method described previously for root locus design can be modified and applied to Bode design. In this case, we want the compensated system $K(s)G(s)$ to have a gain of 1.0 and a phase of $-180°+$PM at $s = j\omega_{gc}$. Assuming the time constant formulation of the compensator, we get

$$K(j\omega_{gc})\,G(j\omega_{gc}) = K_c\,\frac{j\,\omega_{gc}\,\tau_z + 1}{j\,\omega_{gc}\,\tau_p + 1}\,M_G\,e^{j\theta_G} = 1\,e^{\,j(-180+PM)}$$

where M_G and θ_G are the gain (not in dB) and phase of $G(j\omega)$ at $\omega = \omega_{gc}$. This equation can be separated into its real and imaginary parts, resulting in two equations in two unknowns. These equations can then be solved to find

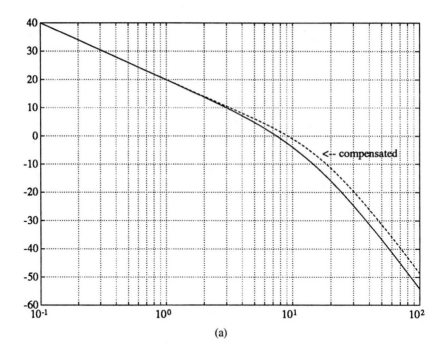

(a)

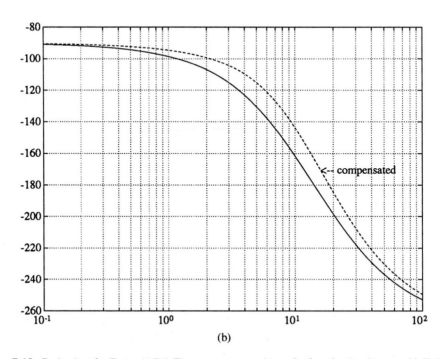

(b)

Figure 7-12 Bode plots for Example 7.6. The uncompensated transfer function has been multiplied by K_c.

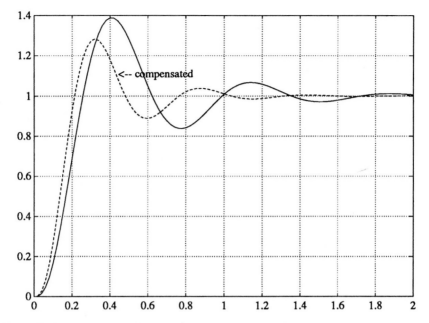

Figure 7-13 Step responses for Example 7.6. The uncompensated transfer function has been multiplied by K_c.

$$\tau_z = \frac{1 + K_c M_G \cos{(PM - \theta_G)}}{-\omega_{gc} K_c M_G \sin{(PM - \theta_G)}} \quad \text{and} \quad \tau_p = \frac{\cos{(PM - \theta_G)} + K_c M_G}{\omega_{gc} \sin{(PM - \theta_G)}}$$

To use these equations, we first determine K_c and draw the Bode plots for $K_c G(j\omega)$. We then examine these plots at $\omega = \omega_{gc}$ to find K_c, M_G, and θ_G. Remember that $K_c M_G$ is the actual magnitude and not the magnitude in dB. Program No. 6 in the Appendix implements this procedure.

Example 7.7 Bode Analytical Method

Consider our plant

$$G(s) = \frac{400}{s\,(s^2 + 30s + 200)}$$

with the following specifications:

> Steady state error to unit ramp input less than 10%
> $\omega_{gc} = 14$ rad/sec
> PM = 45°

To satisfy the steady state error requirement, we set $K_c = 5$. We examine the Bode plots of $K_c G(j\omega)$, already shown in Figure 7-12. At $\omega = \omega_{gc} = 14$ rad/sec, we find that

$K_c M_G = 0.34$ and $\theta_G = -180^\circ$

Using these values, and the desired ω_{gc} and PM, we get $\tau_z = 0.227$, $\tau_p = 0.038$.

The compensator, therefore, is $K(s) = 5 \dfrac{0.227\, s + 1}{0.038\, s + 1}$.

The Bode plots for the compensated system are shown in Figure 7-14. We see that the required ω_{gc} and PM have been met. The closed loop step response is shown in Figure 7-15. The overshoot and settling time are 19% and 0.9 sec, respectively. This response is similar to that obtained from the first method.

7.4.6 Comparison of PD Controller and Lead Compensator

The PD controller discussed in Section 7.3.3 is never actually constructed. Differentiation severely decreases signal to noise ratio and is, therefore, avoided. Rather, the derivative term usually contains a pole to filter out high frequency noise. A more realistic PD controller would be

$$PD(s) = K_p + \frac{K_d s}{s T_d + 1}$$

Combining into a single fraction gives us

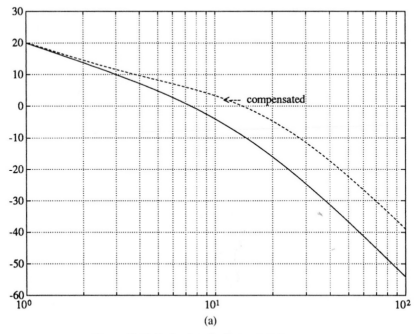

(a)

Figure 7-14 Bode plots for Example 7.7.

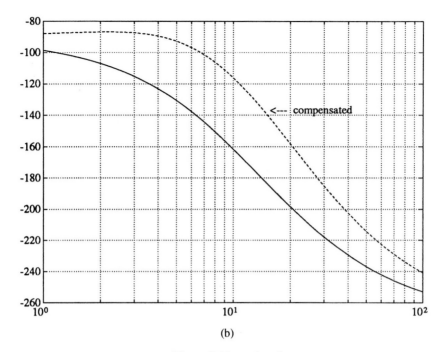

(b)

Figure 7-14 continued.

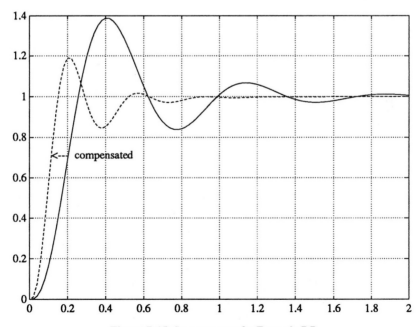

Figure 7-15 Step response for Example 7.7.

$$PD(s) = \frac{K_p T_d s + K_p + K_d s}{T_d s + 1} = K_p \frac{(T_d + K_d/K_p) s + 1}{T_d s + 1}$$

which is the equation for a lead compensator. Hence, PD control is similar to lead compensation where, in the ideal case, the lead compensator pole has been extended to infinity.

7.5 Lag Compensation

In a lag compensator, the pole is smaller than the zero. Because lag compensation adds phase lag to a system, it tends to be destabilizing. For this reason, it is never used if the plant itself is already unstable or has small relative stability margins. However, lag compensation can sometimes be used to increase relative stability by decreasing the system gain. This will be explained in greater detail when we describe Bode plot techniques.

One of the primary uses for lag compensation is to decrease steady state error. This is clearly demonstrated by considering the extreme case of letting the pole in the lag compensator go to zero. In this case, the lag compensator adds an integrator to the system, which increases the system type and, therefore, decreases steady state error. For the general lag compensator, $a > b$, so $K_c a/b > K_c$, which leads to a decrease in steady state error.

Lag compensation decreases the gain crossover frequency, ω_{gc}. This leads to systems with slower step responses. Conversely, we often want to limit the closed loop bandwidth to keep extraneous signals out of the control loop. The decreased bandwidth created by the lag compensator would, in this case, be a desirable characteristic.

7.5.1 Root Locus Design

For convenience, we repeat the compensator transfer function:

$$K(s) = K_c \frac{s + a}{s + b}$$

The root locus technique is most often used with systems that already satisfy stability and dynamic performance requirements but do not have the necessary steady state error. In this case, the following procedure can be used:

- Determine the desired s-plane location, s_1, from the given specifications.
- Draw the root locus of the plant, $G(s)$.
- Determine the value of K_c that places the root locus at, or near, the desired s-plane location.
- If K_c is too small to meet steady state error requirements, proceed to the next step.

- Choose the ratio of a/b that will yield the desired steady state error.
- Maintaining this ratio, place the pole-zero combination to achieve the desired root locus.
- Check closed loop response.

The next to last step is, of course, the tricky one. There are no formal rules that guarantee success. The following idea, however, is in widespread use: Choose a and b close to each other and yet maintain the required ratio. How can two numbers be very close and yet maintain a ratio such as 10? The answer is to choose them between 0 and 1. For instance, if $b = 0.01$ and $a = 0.1$, they have a ratio of 10, but their total contribution to the time response may be negligible because they almost cancel each other. The main negative effect on time response is that the small compensator zero will attract one of the poles; hence, the system will have a closed loop pole near the origin. This will dominate the settling time of the system. The smaller the pole, the longer the settling time.

Example 7.8 Lag Compensation—Root Locus

Consider the following Type 1 plant:

$$G(s) = \frac{10}{s(s+5)}$$

The specifications are:

damping ratio of 0.707
steady state error to unit ramp less than 5%

The point on the root locus that satisfies the damping ratio requirement is $s_1 = -2.5 + 2.5j$. The value of K_c that places the root locus at this point is 1.25. For this value, the error constant is 2.5, which yields a steady state error of 40%.

To reduce the steady state error, we use a lag compensator with the ratio $a/b = 8$. We set the compensator zero (rather arbitrarily) at $a = 0.1$ and compute $b = 0.0125$. The compensator becomes

$$K(s) = 1.25 \frac{s+0.1}{s+0.0125}$$

The closed loop poles and zero are at $\{-0.1037, -2.45 \pm j\,2.45\}$ and $\{-0.1\}$, respectively. Note that the closed loop zero almost cancels the real closed loop pole; hence, the complex poles are almost dominant and meet the damping ratio requirement. The real closed loop pole causes a larger settling time, however. The closed loop step responses of the system before and after compensation are shown in Figure 7-16. The uncompensated step response was plotted with the gain 1.25 included. This response meets the damping ratio requirement but has a larger steady state error. The compensated response has a slightly larger overshoot and longer settling time, but meets the steady state error specification.

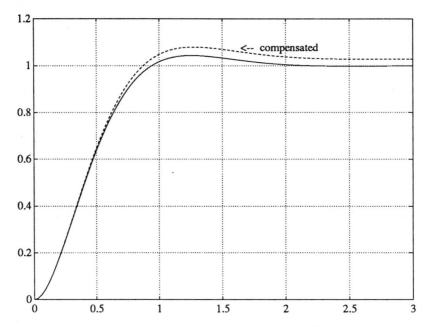

Figure 7-16 Step responses for Example 7.8.

7.5.2 Root Locus—Analytical Method

In Section 7.4.3, we showed you an analytical technique for using root locus data to design a lead compensator. Theoretically, this method should also work for lag compensator design. We simply plug the relevant data into the equations. In this case, we should find that $\tau_p > \tau_z$. The problem is the typical lag compensator design philosophy that we discussed above and demonstrated in Example 7.8. In this procedure, the original root locus is acceptable and we merely use the lag compensator to increase the steady state error constant. Therefore, at the s-plane point of interest, $\theta_G \approx 180\,°$. With this phase, the equations for τ_p and τ_z blow up.

However, if our intent is to use the lag compensator to change ζ and/or ω_n, then we can proceed as follows. Using the time constant form for the compensator

- Choose K_c to meet steady state error requirements.
- Draw root locus for $K_cG(s)$.
- Locate point on s-plane, s_1, that satisfies performance requirements.
- Find M_s and θ_s, where $s_1 = M_s\,e^{j\theta_s}$.
- Find $K_c\,M_G$ and θ_G from $K_c\,G(s_1) = K_c\,M_G\,e^{j\theta_G}$, then compute

$$\tau_z = \frac{\sin \theta_s - K_c M_G \sin (\theta_G - \theta_s)}{K_c M_G M_s \sin \theta_G} \quad \text{and} \quad \tau_p = -\frac{K_c \, M_G \sin \theta_s + \sin (\theta_G + \theta_s)}{M_s \sin \theta_G}$$

- Draw root locus of $K(s)G(s)$ to confirm design.
- Close the loop, and determine time domain response.

Example 7.9 Lag Compensator—Analytical Root Locus

Consider the following plant and specifications:

$$G(s) = \frac{10}{s(s + 5)}$$

Steady state error to unit ramp is less than 5%
Closed loop $\zeta = 0.707$, and $\omega_n = 1.5$ rad/sec

The desired steady state error requires $K_c = 10$. The s-plane point that corresponds to the given ζ and ω_n is $s_1 = -1.06 + j1.06$. The relevant magnitudes and angles are

$$M_s = 1.5 \qquad \theta_s = 135\,^\circ \qquad M_G = 1.63 \qquad \theta_G = -150\,^\circ$$

Finally we get $\tau_z = 1.232$, and $\tau_p = 15.091$. Therefore, the compensator is

$$K(s) = 10\,\frac{1.232\,s + 1}{15.091\,s + 1}$$

The closed loop system has poles at $\{ -1.06 \pm j\,1.06, -2.94 \}$ and a zero at $\{-0.81 \}$.

The step response and Bode plots of the system before and after compensation are shown in Figures 7-17 and 7-18 on pages 198 and 199. In the previous example, we showed the uncompensated response that satisfies the time response requirements. In this example, we have shown the uncompensated system with the additional gain of 10, so it satisfies the steady state error specifications. We note, however, that the system is now lightly damped with an overshoot of almost 43% compared with the compensated system, which has an overshoot of 30%. From the Bode plots, we observe that the PM has also increased from 28 to 48 degrees, whereas the gain crossover frequency has decreased from 9.4 to 1.7 rad/sec.

Note that even though the damping ratio is 0.707, the percent overshoot is higher than expected. This is due to the closed loop zero (resulting from the compensator zero) that is to the right of the complex poles, which are not dominant anymore. If this much overshoot cannot be tolerated, the compensator zero should be moved to the left until it almost cancels the real closed loop pole. The problem is that the location of this pole cannot be determined ahead of time. Hence, some trial and error or another method should be tried.

7.5.3 Lag Compensation—Bode Design

As can be seen from the Bode plots in the previous example, the lag compensator reduces the gain of the system and adds phase lag. Lag compensation is usually used when we wish to reduce the plant gain. This is done either to increase the PM or to lower the closed loop bandwidth. As with the lead compensation technique, the most common Bode method allows the engineer to design to a given steady state error requirement and a desired PM.

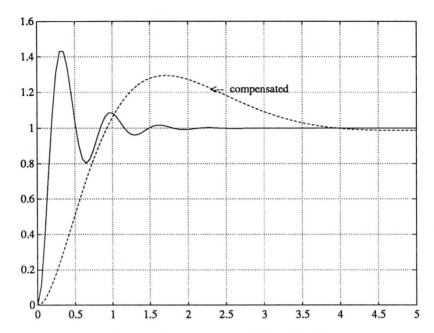

Figure 7-17 Step responses for Example 7.9.

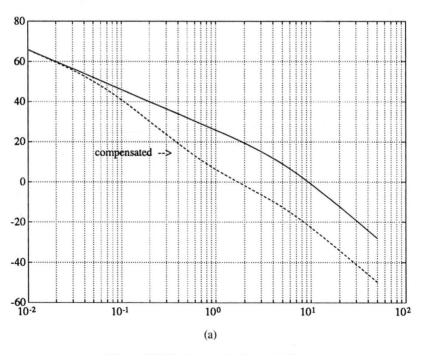

(a)

Figure 7-18 Bode plots for Example 7.9.

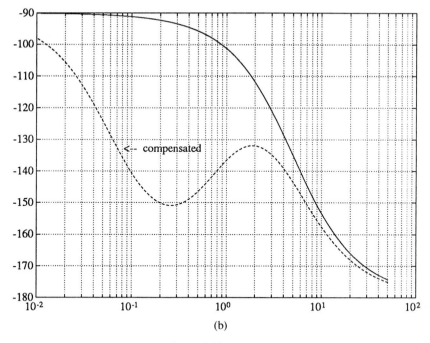

(b)

Figure 7-18 continued.

In this section, we present a method based on Bode plots. A purely analytical technique appears in the next section.

For this method, the most useful form for the lag compensator is

$$K(s) = K_c \frac{1 + \alpha Ts}{1 + Ts} \qquad \alpha < 1$$

As with lead compensation, we first chose K_c to satisfy the steady state error requirement. The parameters α and T are then found to meet the required PM. Before proceeding, let us determine how these parameters affect the gain and phase of the compensator. Evaluating the compensator gain at infinity shows that the maximum reduction in gain is

$$\text{gain reduction in dB} = (GR) = 20 \log \alpha$$

We can also see that at the frequency $\omega = 10/\alpha T$, there is minimal phase contribution from the lag compensator. These facts lead to the following design methodology:

- Determine K_c to satisfy steady state error requirement.
- Draw Bode plots of $K_c G(j\omega)$.

- If the PM is insufficient, find the frequency at which the PM is satisfied (add $5°$ for safety). This frequency will be the compensated ω_{gc}.
- Find the gain of $K_c G(j\omega)$ at $\omega = \omega_{gc}$. This is the amount of gain that needs to be reduced by the compensator; i.e.,

$$GR = -\mid K_c G(j\omega_{gc}) \mid_{dB} \quad \rightarrow \quad \alpha = 10^{GR/20}$$

- To minimize the phase contribution of the compensator, let $T = \dfrac{10}{\alpha \, \omega_{gc}}$.
- Draw Bode plots of $K(j\omega) \, G(j\omega)$ and confirm the design.
- Simulate the closed loop system.

The program Bode Lag (No. 7) in the Appendix was used to solve the following example.

Example 7.10 Lag Compensator—Bode Method

Consider the system and specifications in Example 7.9.

We start by choosing $K_c = 10$ to satisfy the steady state error criterion. We now draw the Bode plots of $K_c G(j\omega)$, as shown in Figure 7-19.

A closed loop damping ratio of 0.707 requires a PM of $70°$, where we have used the approximation $PM \approx 100 \, \zeta$. We add 5 degrees for safety and examine the Bode plots to determine the frequency at which the PM requirement would be satisfied. This gives the compensated $\omega_{gc} \approx 1.34$ rad/sec. Because the gain of $K_c G(j\omega_{gc}) = 23$ dB, we find α and T as $\alpha = 0.069$ and $T = 106.7$.

The lag compensator, therefore, is

$$K(s) = 10 \, \frac{7.46s + 1}{106.7s + 1}$$

The closed loop poles and zero are $\{-0.148, -2.43 \pm 0.64\}$ and $\{-0.134\}$, respectively. The Bode plots and step response are shown in Figures 7-19 and 7-20. We see that the overshoot has decreased from 43% to 7%. The gain crossover frequency is at 1.35 rad/sec with 70 degrees of PM.

Note the phase lag contribution of the compensator and the fact that it occurs at low frequencies. Most of this lag effect is gone when we approach the gain crossover frequency. By the way, this explains why you want to choose small numbers for the compensator pole and zero in the root locus approach. You want to ensure the phase lag occurs at low enough frequencies so it would not adversely affect the PM.

In comparing the root locus and Bode design methods of the previous two examples, we see there is no clear-cut choice of techniques. For this plant and specifications, the root locus design gave us a faster response, but the Bode design gave us less overshoot. For any given problem, we recommend that you use both techniques and choose the compensator that most closely produces the *closed loop* response that you want.

A disadvantage to the preceding technique is that we cannot arbitrarily choose a desired gain crossover frequency. Thus, lag compensation is usually used for adjustments

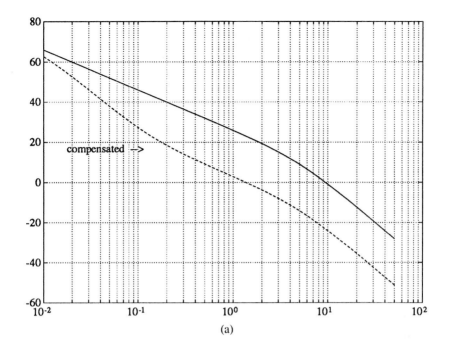

(a)

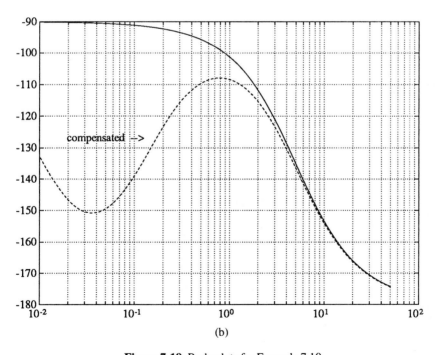

(b)

Figure 7-19 Bode plots for Example 7.10.

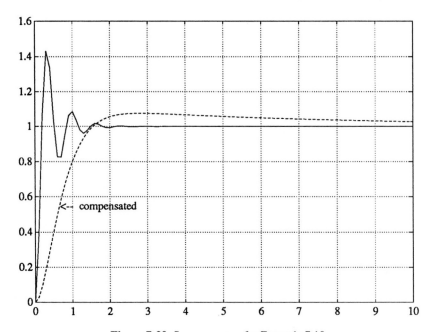

Figure 7-20 Step responses for Example 7.10.

to the steady state error. Lead compensation can then be added to satisfy other performance criteria. Under the right circumstances, however, we can achieve both steady state and transient specifications with a lag design.

7.5.4 Bode Design—Analytical Method

The analytical method previously presented in Section 7.4.5 for Bode lead compensator design can be used, with some restrictions, for lag compensator design. We first repeat the design rules, show an example, and then discuss the limitations of the method.

- Choose K_c to meet steady state error requirements.
- Draw Bode plots of $K_c G(j\omega)$ and determine K_c, M_G, and θ_G at the desired $\omega = \omega_{gc}$.
- For the desired PM, find the pole and zero time constants from

$$\tau_z = \frac{1 + K_c M_G \cos (PM - \theta_G)}{- \omega_{gc} K_c M_G \sin (PM - \theta_G)} \quad \text{and} \quad \tau_p = \frac{\cos (PM - \theta_G) + K_c M_G}{\omega_{gc} \sin (PM - \theta_G)}$$

- Draw compensated Bode plots to check design.
- Simulate closed loop response.

Example 7.11 Lag Compensator—Bode Analytical Method

Consider the following plant and specifications:

$$G(s) = \frac{10}{s(s+5)}$$

Steady state error to unit ramp input of less than 5%

$\omega_{gc} = 2$ rad/sec, and PM $= 40°$

We first set $K_c = 10$ and draw the Bode plots for $K_c\, G(j\omega)$; using program No. 6 in the Appendix, we get

$M_G = 0.92$ and $\theta_G = -111.8°$; the compensator parameters are $\tau_z = 0.81$ and $\tau_p = 8.89$. The compensator is

$$K(s) = 10\,\frac{0.81\, s + 1}{8.89\, s + 1}$$

The closed loop poles and zero are $\{-0.98 \pm j1.61, -3.1430\}$ and $\{-1.22\}$, respectively. From the step responses and Bode plots in Figures 7-21 and 7-22, we see that the specifications have been met. The large overshoot is due to the low damping ratio of the complex poles.

In the analytical technique, because we find the time constants by dividing by the term $\sin(\text{PM} - \theta_G)$, this method blows up if the angle in the sin approaches 180 degrees. There will be instances, therefore, when an arbitrary selection of error constant, ω_{gc}, and PM cannot be achieved. In these cases, you must consider one of these parameters as a variable and iterate the design procedure until an acceptable compensator is found.

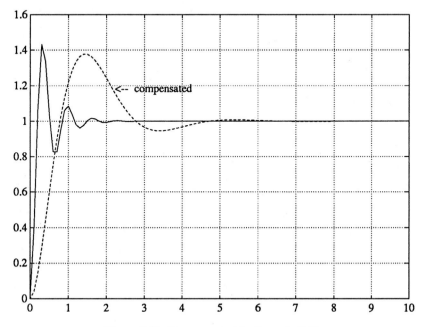

Figure 7-21 Step responses for Example 7.11.

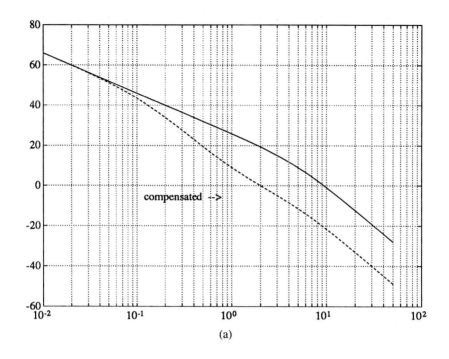

(a)

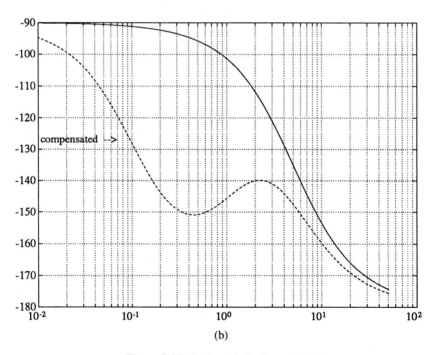

(b)

Figure 7-22 Bode plots for Example 7.11.

We can also modify our programs to compute a set of compensators by using loops and conditional structures, compute all step responses, and choose the one that best meets the criteria. Alternatively, we can use more sophisticated optimization algorithms available in the Optimization Toolbox of MATLAB to do an optimal design.

7.5.5 Comparison of Lag Compensator and PI Controller

The proportional–integral (PI) controller described in Sections 7.2 and 7.3 can be written as

$$K_p + \frac{K_i}{s} = \frac{K_p s + K_i}{s} = K_p \frac{s + K_i / K_p}{s}$$

We see that a PI controller is a special case of a lag compensator where the compensator pole has been shifted to the origin; i.e., PI approximates lag compensation in the limit.

7.6 General Compensation

For many systems, desired stability and performance specification cannot be accomplished with the PID, lead, or lag compensators we have discussed in the previous sections. In some of these cases, a combination of two or more of these controllers can be used. In other cases, an ad hoc approach is often adopted by the designer. That is, the designer uses her or his experience and insight to choose compensator pole and zero locations, uses the computer to simulate the design, and iterates the design process until an acceptable solution is found. This is where classical design becomes an art, and experience and insight are the best guidelines.

As a final example in this chapter, we will examine a helicopter problem, given in Franklin et al. [FPE91].

Example 7.12 Ad Hoc Design

Problem 6.17, in Franklin et al. [FPE91], gives a state space model for longitudinal motions of a helicopter near hover. The model is

$$\begin{bmatrix} \dot{q} \\ \dot{\theta} \\ \dot{u} \end{bmatrix} = \begin{bmatrix} -0.4 & 0 & -0.01 \\ 1 & 0 & 0 \\ -1.4 & 9.8 & -0.02 \end{bmatrix} \begin{bmatrix} q \\ \theta \\ u \end{bmatrix} + \begin{bmatrix} 6.3 \\ 0 \\ 9.8 \end{bmatrix} \delta$$

$$y = \begin{bmatrix} 0 & 0 & 1 \end{bmatrix} \begin{bmatrix} q \\ \theta \\ u \end{bmatrix}$$

where

q = pitch rate
θ = pitch angle of fuselage
u = horizontal velocity
δ = rotor tilt angle

We will use the *ss2tf* and *printsys* commands to convert to transfer function form and display the system.

```
>> [ng,dg]=ss2yf(a,b,c,d);
>> printsys(ng,dg)
```

num/den =
     9.8 s^2 - 4.9 s + 61.74
     _____

   s^3 + 0.42 s^2 - 0.006 s + 0.098

This gives us the helicopter transfer function between rotor tilt angle and horizontal velocity:

$$G(s) = \frac{9.8s^2 - 4.9s + 61.74}{s^3 + 0.42s^2 - 0.006s + 0.098}$$

The system has both zeros and poles in the RHP, obtained by the *ss2zp* command:

```
>> [open_zer,open_pol,gain]=ss2zp(a,b,c,d)
```

open_zer =
  0.2500 + 2.4975i
  0.2500 - 2.4975i

open_pol =
  -0.6565
  0.1183 + 0.3678i
  0.1183 - 0.3678i
gain =
  9.8000

The system is clearly unstable for all gains. We cannot stabilize this system with any of the methods presented earlier in the chapter. Rather, we adopt an ad hoc approach.

We first cancel the pole at –0.65 with the pole-zero combination $K_1(s) = \dfrac{s + 0.65}{s + 10}$.

The pole is necessary for realizability so we add it approximately a decade away. We next add a zero at the origin to pull the RHP poles into the LHP. Again we need a pole, so we try the following total compensator:

$$K(s) = K_c \; \frac{s + 0.65}{s + 10} \; \frac{s}{s + 10}$$

The transfer functions are multiplied using the *series* command; the *minreal* command is used to cancel the common pole-zero combination; the root locus is then obtained. The root locus (zoomed in the vicinity of the origin) for the compensated is shown in Figure 7-23. The system is conditionally stable; i.e., it becomes destabilized for excessively low or high gains. We achieve maximum stability when $K_c = 2$ (found using the *rlocfind* command). Our ad hoc approach here has resulted in the cascading of two lead compensators.

Finally, we close the loop (using the *cloop* command) and obtain the step response shown in Figure 7-24.

The output goes to zero because of the compensator zero at the origin. If the step input is considered a disturbance, then this is exactly the response we would want.

In this case, however, we want the rotor tilt angle to control longitudinal speed. We can accomplish this by splitting the compensator into two parts. We use

$$K_1(s) = \hat{K}_1 \, \frac{s + 0.65}{s + 10}$$

in the forward path and

$$K_2(s) = \hat{K}_2 \, \frac{s}{s + 10}$$

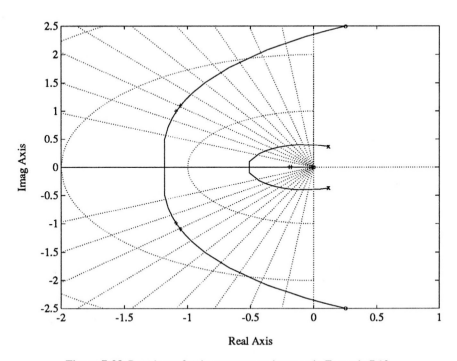

Figure 7-23 Root locus for the compensated system in Example 7.12.

in the feedback path; note that $K_c = 2 = \hat{K}_1 \hat{K}_2$. We will now select these gains to achieve zero steady state error to a unit step input. This implies that the closed loop transfer function must be 1 at zero frequency; i.e., $T(0) = 1$, where

$$ T(s) \;=\; \frac{\hat{K}_1 \, G(s) \, K_1(s)}{1 + \hat{K}_1 \, \hat{K}_2 \, K_1(s) \, K_2(s) \, G(s)} $$

Solving for the gains, we get, $\hat{K}_1 = 0.0242$ and $\hat{K}_2 = 82.7206$ as shown below:

```
>> k1_=dk1(2)*dg(4)/(ng(4)*nk1(2))
```

```
k1_ =
   0.0242
```

```
>> k2_=2/k1_
```

```
k2_ =
  82.7206
```

The open loop Bode plots and closed loop step response for the modified design are shown in Figures 7-25 and 7-26. You can see that we have achieved a steady state input–output ratio of 1.0 with this design. Any particular steady state ratio between helicopter speed and rotor tilt angle can be achieved with the appropriate selection of the gains as long as their product is 2.

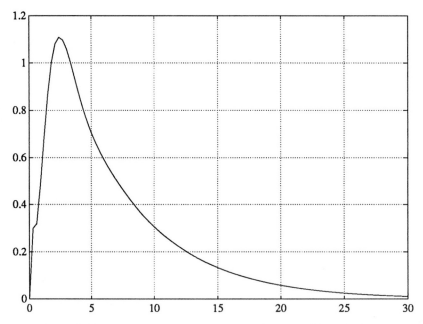

Figure 7-24 Step response for the compensated system in Example 7.12.

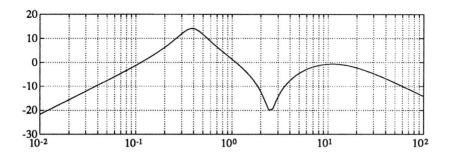

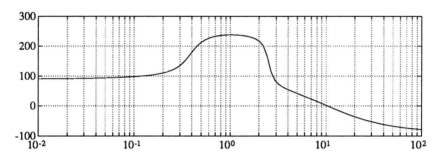

Figure 7-25 Bode plots for the compensated system in Example 7.12.

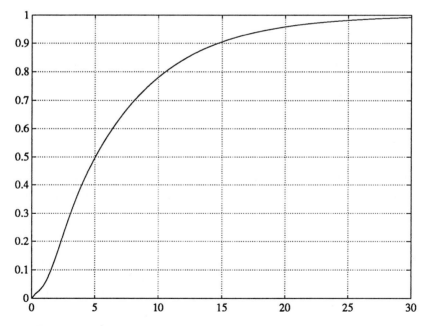

Figure 7-26 Step response for the compensated system with modified gains.

Note that $K_2(s)$ is an approximate differentiator. It can be constructed either from electronic devices such as an op-amps or through the use of an accelerometer mounted to measure longitudinal movement of the helicopter.

We then use the *series* and *feedback* commands to close the loop; use *minreal* to cancel common pole-zero pairs, and use *tf2zp* to find the closed loop poles and zeros:

```
clzero =
-10.0000
  0.2500 + 2.4975i
  0.2500 - 2.4975i

clpole =
-37.1320
 -1.0325 + 1.1611i
 -1.0325 - 1.1611i
 -0.1665
gain =
  0.2369
```

Measures of relative stability, GM and PM, obtained from the *margin* command are shown below:

```
>> margin=[20*log10(gm) pm wgc wpc]

margin =

 -13.9762  57.4381  1.0986  0.4002
```

Because we have met our objective of stabilizing the system while achieving zero steady state error to step command input, our design is finished. We will end this chapter by careful analysis of the stability margins of this system.

7.7 Stability Margins of Nonminimum Phase Systems

Correct determination and interpretation of stability margins of nonminimum phase systems (systems with RHP open loop poles/zeros) is a confusing and tricky task. Most control textbooks define gain and phase margins for minimum phase systems (as we did in Chapter 1); margins for nonminimum phase systems are either not discussed or simply given lip service. We will use the compensated helicopter system to show how these margins can be found and interpreted.

The root locus of the system indicated that there are both upper and lower limits on the gain of the system. Hence, the system has two gain margins, an upper gain margin (the usually defined GM) and a lower gain margin (or gain reduction margin, GRM). The Bode plots verify this as there are two phase crossover frequencies. Because there are also two gain crossover frequencies, there are two phase margins. The MATLAB *margin* command has apparently found only one of each. It seems to imply that the system has a GM of -14

dB and a PM of 57 degrees. There are a few odd features in the Bode plot of this system that need attention.

1. There are multiple crossover frequencies.
2. At the phase crossover frequencies, the gain is above 0 dB at one frequency and below 0 dB at another. The same phenomenon occurs at the gain crossover frequencies.
3. The GM is negative even though the system is closed loop stable.

We usually read in textbooks that in a closed loop stable system, the GM must be positive (i.e., the gain must be below 0 dB at the phase crossover frequency). But this statement is true only for open loop transfer functions that are minimum phase. To clarify these issues, we need to define these margins more carefully.

A system (such as the one in our example) may be destabilized by gain *changes*; i.e., either an increase or decrease in gain can destabilize the system. The traditional GM is the factor by which the gain can be increased before the onset of instability (it measures the upper limit of gain). The lower limit (i.e., the factor by which the gain can be *decreased* before instability) is measured by the GRM. Because the lower limit is less than the nominal gain, and we take logarithms, GRM is negative. The *margin* command has actually found the GRM.

A partial listing of the frequency response of the system is shown next.

	Freq	dB	Phase
	0.1000	−1.1833	98.0366
wgc1	0.1293	1.3661	100.9193
wpc1	0.3929	14.1172	176.8220
	0.4222	13.7436	189.3819
wgc2	1.0960	0.0415	237.5135
	1.1253	−0.3476	237.3798
	2.3263	−18.4412	185.2157
wpc2	2.3556	−18.9708	180.1352
	2.3848	−19.4528	174.5451

From the data, we draw the following conclusions about the gain margins:

1. At the frequency 0.39 rad/sec, GRM = −14 dB. This is also clear from the Bode plot. Note that if at this frequency the gain is reduced by 14 dB (with no phase change, i.e., pure gain), the magnitude plot will move down and cross the 0 dB line at a point where the phase is 180 degrees.
2. At the frequency 2.35 rad/sec, GM = 18.9 dB. If the gain is increased by this amount (with no phase change), the magnitude plot will move up and cross the 0 dB line when the phase is 180 degrees.

These observations can be formally confirmed using the Nyquist plot shown in Figure 7-27a. The open loop transfer function has 2 RHP poles. According to the Nyquist stability criterion, our system is stable because it encircles the (−1,0) point twice in the counterclockwise direction. Note that the Bode plot cannot be used to determine closed loop stability of nonminimum phase systems. Also observe that if the gain is reduced, the Nyquist plot will move to the right, and we will lose the encirclements and hence the stability. The encirclements are also lost if the gain is increased.

The system may also be destabilized by phase *changes*. Hence, negative phase (or phase lag, produced by time delays or poles) added to the system, can destabilize the system. This is measured by PM; in our example it is (237 − 180) 57 degrees at the frequency 1.096. The *margin* command has determined this quantity. The system, however, can also be destabilized by positive phase (i.e., phase lead). This is quite surprising because phase lead is usually used to stabilize systems. The data indicate that at the frequency 0.129 there is a phase margin of −79 degrees. This is clear from the Bode and Nyquist plots. In the Bode plot, if a transfer function with unity gain and +79 phase is added to the loop, the phase plot would move upward and cross the 180-degree line at a point where the gain is unity. In the Nyquist plot, the same change will rotate the plot and cause it to cross the (−1,0) point. Both phase margins are shown in Figure 7-27b.

For completeness, the margins are also indicated in the Nichols plot of Figure 7-28. We conclude by pointing out that stability margins (which are really measures of how much model uncertainty the designed system can tolerate) must be carefully computed from frequency response data, and confirmed and verified by root locus and Nyquist plots.

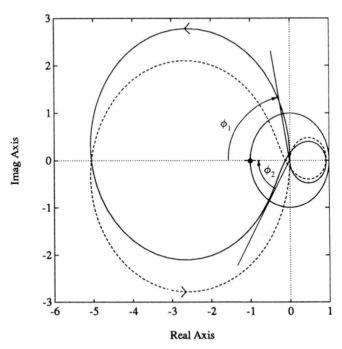

Figure 7-27 Nyquist plot of the compensated helicopter example with the unit circle.
(a) The gain margins are shown. (b) The phase margins are shown.

ϕ_1 = phase (lead) margin = -80°
ϕ_2 = phase (lag) margin = 57°

(a)

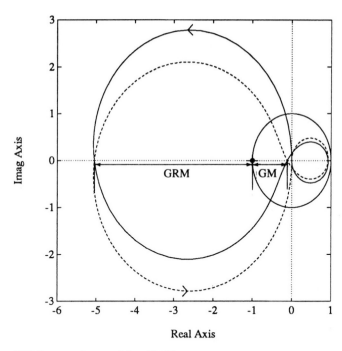

GM (upper gain margin) = 19 dB
GRM (lower gain margin) = -14 dB

(b)   **Figure 7-27** continued.

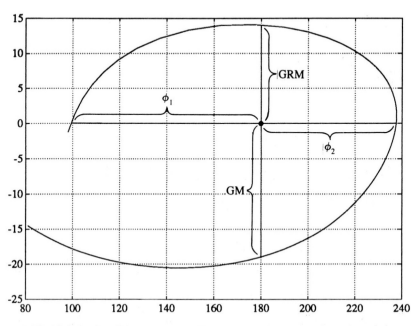

Figure 7-28 Nichols plot of the compensated helicopter example showing gain and phase margins.

7.8 Appendix: Design Programs

In the following programs, the plant *G(s)* is denoted by ng, dg; the compensator *K(s)* by nk, dk. The desired phase margin and gain crossover frequency are denoted by dpm and wgc. Other symbols are defined at the beginning of each program.

1. Ziegler–Nichols Program

This program requires ng and dg; The *keyboard* command stops the program so that you can use the *rlocfind* command to find and define Km and Wm. Type RETURN when done.

```
clg, rlocus(ng,dg)
[km,pole]=rlocfind(ng,dg)
keyboard
wm=imag(pole);
kp=0.6*km; kd=kp*pi/(4*wm); ki=kp*wm/pi;
nk=[kd kp ki]; dk=[1 0];
```

2. Analytical PID/PD Program

This program requires ng, dg, wgc, dpm, and ki.

```
function [kp,kd,nk,dk]=pid(ng,dg,ki,dpm,wgc)
ngv=polyval(ng,j*wgc); dgv=polyval(dg,j*wgc); g=ngv/dgv;
thetar=(dpm-180)*pi/180;
ejtheta=cos(thetar)+j*sin(thetar);
eqn=(ejtheta/g)+j*(ki/wgc)
x=imag(eqn);
r=real(eqn);
kp=r
kd=x/wgc
if ki~=0,
    dk=[1 0]; nk=[kd kp ki];
    else dk=1; nk=[kd  kp];
end;
```

3. Root Locus Lead: Geometric Design Program

```
function [nk,dk,kc]=rllead(ng,dg,s_1)
ngv=polyval(ng,s_1);dgv=polyval(dg,s_1);g=ngv/dgv;
theta=angle(g);
if theta > 0; phi_c=pi-theta; end;
if theta < 0; phi_c= -theta; end;
phi=angle(s_1);
theta_z=(phi+phi_c)/2;
theta_p=(phi-phi_c)/2;
z_c=real(s_1)-imag(s_1)/tan(theta_z)
```

```
p_c=real(s_1)-imag(s_1)/tan(theta_p);
nk=[1 -z_c];
dk=[1 -p_c];
nkv=polyval(nk,s_1); dkv=polyval(dk,s_1); kv=nkv/dkv;
kc=abs(1/(g*kv));
if theta < 0; k= -k; end;
```

4. Root Locus Lead: Analytical Design Program

```
function [nk,dk]=anrllead(ng,dg,s_1,kc)
ngv=polyval(ng,s_1); dgv=polyval(dg,s_1);g=ngv/dgv;
thetag=angle(g); thetag_d=thetag*180/pi;
mg=abs(g); ms=abs(s_1);
thetas=angle(s_1); thetas_d=thetas*180/pi;
tz=(sin(thetas)-kc*mg*sin(thetag-thetas))/(kc*mg*ms*sin(thetag));
tp=-(kc*mg*sin(thetas)+sin(thetag+thetas))/(ms*sin(thetag));
nk=[tz , 1];
dk=[tp , 1];
```

5. Bode Lead Design Program

The input argument, w (frequency vector), must be a column. The *spline* command is used to find the frequency where the gain of $K_cG = -10 \log a$.

```
function [nk,dk]=bodelead(ng,dg,kc,w,dpm)
[mu,pu]=bode(kc*ng,dg,w);
smo=length(mu);
phi=dpm*pi/180;
a=(1+sin(phi))/(1-sin(phi));
mu_db=20*log10(mu);   mm=-10*log10(a);
wgc=spline(mu_db,w,mm);
T=1/(wgc*sqrt(a));
z=a*T; p=T;
nk=[z , 1];
dk=[p , 1];
```

6. Bode Lead/Lag: Analytical Design Program

```
function [nk,dk]=anbdlead(ng,dg,kc,wgc,dpm)
ngv=polyval(ng,j*wgc); dgv=polyval(dg,j*wgc); g=ngv/dgv;
thetag=angle(g); thetag_d=thetag*180/pi
mg=abs(g)
dpm_rad=dpm*pi/180;
t_z=(1+kc*mg*cos(dpm_rad-thetag))/(-wgc*kc*mg*sin(dpm_rad-thetag))
t_p=(cos(dpm_rad-thetag)+kc*mg)/(wgc*sin(dpm_rad-thetag))
nk=[t_z , 1]
dk=[t_p , 1]
```

7. Bode Lag Design Program

The input argument, `w` (frequency vector), must be a column.

```
function [nk,dk]=bodelag(ng,dg,w,kc,dpm)
wgc=spline(pu,w,dpm-180)
mu_db=20*log10(mu);
ind=find(w=wgc); ind=ind(1);
gr=-mu_db(ind)
alpha=10^(gr/20)
T=10/(alpha*wgc);
nk=[alpha*T   , 1]
dk=[T , 1]
```

7.9 Problems

7.1 Derive the formulas for the pole and zero location in the root locus geometric method given in Section 7.4.2.

7.2 Derive the formulas for τ_z and τ_p for the root locus analytical method given in Section 7.4.3.

7.3 Derive the formulas for ω_{max}, sin Φ, and M given in Section 7.4.4.

7.4 Derive the formulas for τ_z and τ_p for the Bode analytical method given in Section 7.4.5.

7.5 For each of the following plants, a set of specifications are given. You are to design a cascade compensator to satisfy the specs in each case. You are to use either lead, lag, PID, or combinations of these basic types. If you cannot meet the specs using the cascade configuration, try others.

In each case, document your design by providing the following information regarding the compensated system: the compensator transfer function, closed loop transfer function, closed loop poles and zeros, root locus, open loop Bode magnitude and phase plots, closed loop Bode magnitude plot, closed loop step response, POS, T_r, T_s, M_r, BW, PM, and GM.

For practical reasons, the compensators must be proper (if you use PD or PID, either add a high frequency pole to the compensator to make it proper or implement the derivative term in feedback). If you use lead or lag, keep the ratio of the compensator pole and zero to less than 20. If the ratio has to be bigger, split the compensator into stages. The reason for this is that larger ratios might lead to impractical component values when we implement the compensator electronically.

Note: In the following problems, we use the symbol e_{ss} __/ to represent steady state error to a unit ramp input, and the symbol e_{ss} __| for unit step inputs.

a. $G(s) = \dfrac{10\,(s+5)}{(s+15)\,(s^2+8s+20)}$ specs: $e_{ss}\underline{\quad}| \leq 10\%$, $\zeta \geq 0.707$

b. $G(s) = \dfrac{1}{s\,(s+1)\,(s+5)}$ specs: $\zeta \geq 0.707$, $T_s \leq 4$, $T_r \leq 3\;sec$

c. $G(s) = \dfrac{1}{s\,(s+8)^2}$ specs: $e_{ss}\diagup \leq 5\%$, $\zeta \geq 0.707$

d. $G(s) = \dfrac{1}{(s+1)\,(s+3)}$ specs: $e_{ss}\underline{\quad}| \leq 1\%$, $POS \leq 10\%$, $T_s \leq 5\;sec$

e. $G(s) = \dfrac{1}{s\,(s+2)}$ specs: $e_{ss}\diagup \leq 1\%$, $POS \leq 10\%$, $T_s \leq 6\;sec$

f. $G(s) = \dfrac{100}{s^2\,(s+10)}$ specs: $POS \leq 10\%$, $T_s \leq 2\;sec$, $PM \approx 40\;deg$

g. $G(s) = \dfrac{1}{s\,(s+1)\,(s+5)}$ specs: $e_{ss}\diagup \leq 0.1\%$, $PM \approx 45\;deg$

h. $G(s) = \dfrac{10}{s^2\,(s+40)}$ specs: $POS \leq 15\%$, $PM \approx 45\;deg$

i. $G(s) = \dfrac{10\,(s+2)}{s\,(s+0.1)\,(s+10)}$ specs: $POS \leq 10\%$, $T_s \leq 1\;sec$

j. $G(s) = \dfrac{1}{s\,(s+0.5)}$ specs: $e_{ss}\underline{\quad}| \leq 1\%$, $\zeta \approx 0.707$, $\omega_n \approx 5$

k. $G(s) = \dfrac{80}{s\,(s+4)}$ specs: $\zeta \approx 0.707$, $\omega_n \approx 10$

l. $G(s) = \dfrac{1600}{s\,(s+4)\,(s+16)}$ specs: $e_{ss}\diagup \leq 4\%$, $PM \approx 30\;deg$

m. $G(s) = \dfrac{60990}{(s+58)\,(s+50)\,(s-50)}$

Specs: $POS < 5\%$, fastest possible response with as much gain and phase margin as you can get.

n. $G(s) = \dfrac{1}{s^2}$ specs: $T_s \leq 4\;sec$, $POS \leq 30\%$

o. $G(s) = \dfrac{10}{s^2}$ specs: $T_s \leq 4\;sec$, $POS \leq 20\%$

p. $G(s) = \dfrac{25}{s\,(s+25)}$ specs: $e_{ss}\diagup \leq 1\%$, $PM \approx 45\;deg$

q. $G(s) = \dfrac{1}{s\,(s+1)\,(s+2)}$ specs: $e_{ss}\diagup \leq 20\%$, $PM \approx 45\;deg$

7.6 The inverted pendulum problem is common in control theory. The inverted pendulum is a rod connected via a hinge on its bottom end to a movable cart. We want the pendulum to remain upright. As you will show, however, this system is unstable. The pendulum, therefore, will tend to fall. We wish to control the motion of the cart so that we can keep the pendulum upright. The equations that describe the behavior of this system are nonlinear and are given by

$$\ddot{y} = \frac{1}{(M/m) + \sin^2 \theta} \left(\frac{u}{m} + \dot{\theta}\ ^2l \sin \theta - g \sin \theta \cos \theta \right)$$

$$\ddot{\theta} = \frac{1}{l\,(M/m) + \sin^2 \theta} \left(-\frac{u}{m} \cos \theta - \dot{\theta}\ ^2l \cos \theta \sin \theta + \frac{m+M}{m} g \sin \theta \right)$$

where M is cart mass, m is pendulum mass, l is pendulum length, g is acceleration due to gravity, y is cart position, θ is the angle the pendulum makes to the vertical, and u is the control input force acting on the cart.

Because we want to keep the pendulum upright, we are interested in linearizing this model about $\theta = 0$. The linearized state space model for this system is

$$\dot{x} = \begin{pmatrix} 0 & 1 & 0 & 0 \\ 0 & 0 & -mg/M & 0 \\ 0 & 0 & 0 & 1 \\ 0 & 0 & (M+m)g/Ml & 0 \end{pmatrix} x + \begin{pmatrix} 0 \\ 1/M \\ 0 \\ -1/Ml \end{pmatrix} u$$

where the state vector is $x = [y \quad \dot{y} \quad \theta \quad \dot{\theta}\,]'$.

Because all of the states can be directly measured, there are a number of possible output vectors, z

$$z = \begin{pmatrix} \alpha_1 & 0 & 0 & 0 \\ 0 & \alpha_2 & 0 & 0 \\ 0 & 0 & \alpha_3 & 0 \\ 0 & 0 & 0 & \alpha_4 \end{pmatrix} x$$

where α_i is 1 if its corresponding state is being measured and 0 if otherwise.

a. Given the following values: $l = 1\ m$, $M = 1\ kg$, $m = 0.1\ kg$, $g = 9.8\ m/sec^2$, and the fact that we can stabilize this system by measuring only the position of the cart (i.e., $z = [1 \quad 0 \quad 0 \quad 0]\,x$), find the transfer function between the input u and the output y.

b. Show the system is unstable.

c. Design a compensator that will stabilize the system. Find the GM and PM for your design.

d. Find and plot the impulse response of the closed loop system.

e. Design a new compensator that will reduce the settling time, while improving the stability margins of the system if possible.

7.7 Redo the preceding problem with a new pendulum mass, m, of 1 kg. Explain any differences in the results of the two problems.

*7.8 In problem 7.6, we can also easily measure the pendulum rod position. In this case, we have two outputs, so $z = \begin{pmatrix} 1 & 0 & 0 & 0 \\ 0 & 0 & 1 & 0 \end{pmatrix} x$. This is now a one-input two-output system.

a. Find the transfer functions between the input and each output.

b. Find a suitable configuration and design compensator(s) that will stabilize both system outputs. For example, you might consider feeding back the pendulum angle in an inner loop, and feeding back the cart position in an outer loop.

c. Find and plot the impulse responses for your design.

8

State Space Design
of Regulator Systems

8.1 Introduction

Control systems can be divided into two broad categories: regulation and tracking. Regulators attempt to maintain a constant system output in the face of internal or external disturbances, plant parameter variation, etc. The thermal control system in your house or apartment attempts to maintain the constant temperature set at the thermostat. Satellite attitude control systems are often designed to maintain a constant angle between transmitting and earth-based receiving antennas. Voltage regulators try to maintain a constant voltage across a load as line voltage or load resistance changes. The primary design criterion for regulators is the desired transient response.

In a tracking system, the output must follow, with minimal error, a prescribed course represented as a time-varying input. For example, an autopilot might be designed to steer an airplane or ship on a predetermined path. In tracking systems, both the transient response and the steady state response must fall within certain error bounds.

Because this chapter is concerned only with the design of regulator systems, we will limit our discussion to the control of the transient response. Because a system's transient response is primarily determined by its pole locations, regulator design involves moving the open loop (plant) poles to desired locations by the use of feedback.

You are already familiar with the classical design techniques that use the root locus and Bode plot. In this chapter, we will discuss the use of state space techniques that allow us to place the closed loop poles at desired locations; these methods are known as *pole placement* techniques.

8.2 Pole Placement (State Feedback)

Consider the simple first order system described by

$$\dot{x} = x + u \qquad x(0) = x_0$$
$$y = x$$

where u is the input to the plant actuator. Note that in regulator systems, the external control input is usually set to zero unless it represents a disturbance input. The pole of this open loop system is 1, indicating that the open loop system is unstable. In state space systems, we usually achieve feedback control by setting the actuator input equal to a gain times the state vector; i.e.,

$$u = -k\, x$$

Therefore,

$$\dot{x} = x - k\, x = (1 - k)\, x$$

The closed loop pole is $1 - k$, which results in an asymptotically stable system for $k > 1$. In fact, by a suitable choice of k, we can place the closed loop pole anywhere on the real axis.

Let us now consider the second order open loop system:

$$\dot{x} = \begin{bmatrix} 3 & -2 \\ 1 & 0 \end{bmatrix} x + \begin{bmatrix} 1 \\ 0 \end{bmatrix} u$$

This system has poles at $s = 1, 2$ and is, therefore, unstable. Can we use state feedback to place the closed loop poles in the left half plane and stabilize the system? A second order system with the desired closed loop poles located at p_1 and p_2 will have the characteristic equation

$$\Delta_d(s) = s^2 + (p_1 + p_2)\, s + p_1\, p_2 = s^2 + \alpha\, s + \beta$$

If we use state feedback, i.e.,

$$u = -k_1\, x_1 - k_2\, x_2$$

in our unstable system, we obtain the closed loop system

$$\dot{x} = \begin{bmatrix} 3 - k_1 & -2 - k_2 \\ 1 & 0 \end{bmatrix} x$$

which has the characteristic equation

$$\Delta_c(s) = s^2 + (k_1 - 3)s + (2 + k_2)$$

By setting the actual characteristic equation to the desired characteristic equation, we get

$$k_1 = \alpha + 3 \quad \text{and} \quad k_2 = \beta - 2$$

Therefore, we can realize any pole locations we desire.

Now, several questions arise. How and why does this kind of feedback control work? Does it work for all systems, and, if not, what are the conditions? Can we derive a general formula for the feedback coefficients? Is the method practical? We will briefly discuss answers to these questions.

Among the many definitions of the concept of "state" we have:

> "The state of a system is the minimum amount of information necessary to fully describe the system. That is to say, if the initial state $x(\tau)$ and inputs of the system are known for $t > \tau$, we can predict all future states of the system."

According to this definition, it is not surprising that state feedback is so effective. After all, the system is using all the necessary information; i.e., the state, to correct itself. This is in contrast to classical compensation where usually only the output is fed back. Of course, this is just an intuitive argument, and we will make it more rigorous later.

Whether state feedback works for all systems can be seen by noticing that when we set coefficients of the two characteristic equations equal to each other, we get several equations in several unknowns. These equations do not always have (unique) solutions. Also, the practicality of state feedback is a more subtle and involved issue that will be discussed in more detail later in this chapter.

Consider the nth order system

$$\dot{x} = Ax + Bu$$
$$y = Cx + Du$$
$$G(s) = C(sI - A)^{-1}B + D = \begin{bmatrix} A & B \\ C & D \end{bmatrix}$$

We say the system is *controllable* if, using appropriate control inputs, the states can be moved in any direction in the state space. If the system is in modal form, this is equivalent to the ability to move the system modes or poles arbitrarily in the complex plane. Controllability is a property of the pair (A, B) and can be checked as follows.

The pair (A, B) is *controllable* if and only if the rank of the *controllability matrix*, C, is n (n is the system order, i.e., dimension of A). The controllability matrix, C, is given by

$$C = [B \ \ AB \ \ A^2B \ \dots \ A^{n-1}B \ ]$$

In the preceding, by appropriate control input we mean state feedback; i.e., $u = -k \ x$. Therefore, if the system is controllable, one can use state feedback to place the poles anywhere in the complex plane. Also we assume that $y = x$, which means that all states are available for measurement and feedback.

It turns out in practice that a weaker notion than controllability is sufficient for most purposes. This notion is called *stabilizability*. It refers to the ability to move only the unstable modes of the system. Therefore, we say a system is *stabilizable* if the unstable modes are controllable, or equivalently, if the uncontrollable modes are stable. The easiest way to check this is to convert the system to modal form and check each eigenvalue and the corresponding row in the input distribution (B) matrix. The next simple example illustrates the concept. Consider the following systems:

$$\dot{x} = \begin{bmatrix} 3 & 0 \\ 0 & -1 \end{bmatrix} x + \begin{bmatrix} 1 \\ 0 \end{bmatrix} u \ , \qquad \dot{z} = \begin{bmatrix} 3 & 0 \\ 0 & 1 \end{bmatrix} z + \begin{bmatrix} 1 \\ 0 \end{bmatrix} u$$

Neither of the above systems are controllable, because the C matrix has rank one. In the first system, the stable mode $\{-1\}$ is not controllable, whereas the unstable mode $\{3\}$ is controllable. Hence, the system is stabilizable. That is, by using state feedback control, $u = -k \ x_1$, with $k > 3$, the system is stabilized. In the second system, observe that the unstable mode $\{1\}$ is not controllable; therefore, the system is not stabilizable. Note that either stability or controllability implies that the system is stabilizable.

Another fact that is important to mention is obtained from a transfer function analysis of systems that have controllability problems. It can be proven that in the SISO case, lack of controllability will result in pole-zero cancellation in the corresponding transfer function. Therefore, the transfer function of an uncontrollable system is not coprime. The converse of this statement is not true though; i.e., pole-zero cancellation in the transfer function does not necessarily imply uncontrollability. For further details, see [C84], [K80].

Several formulas exist for computation of the state feedback gain (see [K80]). *Ackermann's formula* is one example (for SISO systems). Given the desired characteristic equation

$$\Delta_d (s) = s^n + \alpha_1 s^{n-1} + \ \dots \ + \alpha_n$$

$$k = [\ 0 \ , 0 \ , \ \dots \ , 1 \ ] \ C^{-1} \Delta_d (A) \qquad \text{where} \qquad \Delta_d (A) = A^n + \alpha_1 A^{n-1} + \dots + \alpha_{n-1} A + \alpha_n I$$

The above formula is not directly suitable for numerical implementation, but various reliable numerical algorithms exist for computation of k. The choice of the pole locations is arbitrary. Although there are various "optimal" choices, for our purposes now, we select a complex pair to satisfy transient response specifications and place the rest of the poles "far" into the LHP. This is the only choice the designer has to make, and the rest of the design process can be fully automated.

8.2.1 Transfer Function Analysis

It is instructive to apply the classical techniques of root locus and frequency response analysis to our state space compensator design. This is needed for two reasons:

1. Frequently, some of the problem specifications are in the frequency domain, such as, gain and phase margins, bandwidth, etc.; these tests are performed to verify these specifications.
2. To obtain the resulting compensator transfer function in order to gain more insight into the solution, and to compare with an equivalent classical design.

To make this comparison, we first find the open loop transfer function of the state feedback system. The plant is represented by

$$\dot{x} = A\,x + B\,u \quad \rightarrow \quad X\,(s) = \Phi(s)\,B\,U(s)\,, \quad \text{where} \quad \Phi(s) = (sI - A)^{-1}$$
$$y = C\,x + D\,u \quad \rightarrow \quad Y(s) = (C\,\Phi(s)\,B + D)\,U(s) = G(s)\,U(s)$$

$$U(s) = -k\,X(s) = -k\,\Phi(s)\,B$$

Figure 8-1 shows a block diagram of the zero-input state feedback system. To compute the open loop transfer function, we break the loop at the point indicated ($\approx$), inject a signal at $U(s)$, and measure the response at $U_1(s)$. Therefore, the open loop transfer function is $-k\,\Phi(s)\,B$. The equivalent classical open loop transfer function is $G(s)\,K(s)$, *where $G(s)$ is the plant and $K(s)$ is the compensator transfer function.* For these loop transfer functions to be equal

$$- G(s)\,K(s) \; = \; -\,k\,\Phi(s)\,B$$

and because $\;G(s) \;=\; C\Phi(s)B + D\,, \quad K(s) \;=\; \dfrac{k\,\Phi(s)\,B}{C\,\Phi(s)\,B + D}$

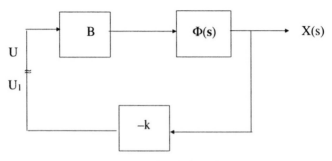

Figure 8-1 State feedback block diagram.

That is, if we build $K(s)$, the classically designed and state space systems will have the same transient behavior. Also, we can apply root locus, Bode, and Nyquist analysis to $k \, \Phi(s) \, B$ to determine stability margins, bandwidth, etc.

The closed loop transfer function of the state feedback system can be obtained by introducing a reference input v ; *i.e.*,

$$u = -k\,x + \overline{N}\,v$$

$$\dot{x} = (A - B\,k)\,x + B\,\overline{N}\,v \quad \rightarrow \quad X(s) = (sI - A + B\,k)^{-1}B\,\overline{N}V(s)$$

$$Y(s) \;=\; C(sI - A + B\,k)^{-1}B\overline{N}V(s) \quad \rightarrow \quad T(s) \;=\; C(sI - A + B\,k)^{-1}B\overline{N}$$

In the above, $\underline{D}$ is assumed zero (strictly proper plant) to avoid messy formulas. The constant gain $\overline{N}$ can be easily computed to produce zero steady state error for constant reference inputs. Using packed matrix notation (introduced in Chapter 5), we have the open and closed loop transfer functions represented by

$$KG(s) = \begin{bmatrix} A & B \\ k & 0 \end{bmatrix} \quad \text{and} \quad T(s) = \begin{bmatrix} A - B\,k & B\,\overline{N} \\ C & 0 \end{bmatrix}$$

8.2.2 MATLAB Commands

The commands related to the topics discussed in this chapter are *ctrb*, *obsv*, *place*, and *augstate*. The command *ctrb*, uses A and B as inputs and returns the controllability matrix; *obsv* uses A and C and returns the observability matrix (refer to Section 8.3 for the definition of observability). The *place* command finds the state feedback gain. It has the following syntax:

```
>> k=place(a,b,CP)
```

The input argument, CP, is the vector of desired closed loop poles. The *augstate* command will augment the state equations to prepare it for state feedback. This is necessary because in the system definition, the C matrix picks out certain states as outputs. For state feedback, we need all of the states; *augstate* will send the states as additional outputs.

The combinations of *augstate*, *series*, and *feedback* commands can be used to obtain open and closed loop system matrices for further analysis. As an example, consider a SISO third order system given by (a,b,c,d). The desired closed loop poles are [−1,−2]. The following commands determine the closed loop (*T*) and open loop (*KG*) transfer functions:

```
>> cp=[-1,-2]; k=place(a,b,cp)
>> [aa,ba,ca,da]=augstate(a,b,c,d);
>> [ac,bc,cc,dc]=feedback(aa,ba,ca,da,[],[],[],-k,1,[2:4]);
>> [ao,bo,co,do]=series(aa,ba,ca,da,[],[],[],k,[2:4],[1:3]);
```

The ca matrix (second line) has 4 rows; row 1 is the output and rows 2 through 4 are the states. These outputs are selected as inputs to the feedback system to form the closed loop system. The feedback system is a gain, so its A, B, and C matrices are entered as null (or zero) matrices. Because we use the form of the *feedback* command that has input-output selection, the negative feedback sign must be enforced. That is why we use $-k$. The *series* command is used to find the open loop transfer function.

Example 8.1 State Feedback Design

The following is the model for the longitudinal motion of a helicopter near hover [FPE91]. The state variables are pitch rate, pitch angle of fuselage, and horizontal velocity. The control input is the rotor tilt angle. The state equations are

$$\dot{x} = \begin{bmatrix} -0.4 & 0 & -0.01 \\ 1 & 0 & 0 \\ -1.4 & 9.8 & -0.02 \end{bmatrix} x + \begin{bmatrix} 6.3 \\ 0 \\ 9.8 \end{bmatrix} u$$

$$y = [\, 0 \ \ 0 \ \ 1 \,]\, x$$

For your convenience, the programs used to perform the designs in this chapter are included in the Appendix. Partial inputs and outputs will be shown here. The open loop system zeros (olz), poles (olp), and DC gain (olg) are found using the *ss2zp* command:

```
olz =
  0.2500 + 2.4975i
  0.2500 - 2.4975i
olp =
 -0.6565
  0.1183 + 0.3678i
  0.1183 - 0.3678i
olg =
  9.8000
```

Therefore, the system is unstable with a pair of complex poles in the RHP. It is desired to place the system poles at $\{ -1 \pm j , -2 \}$. The control gain vector is obtained from

```
>> cp=[-2,-1+j, -1-j]; k=place(a,b,cp)

k =
  0.4706   1.0000   0.0627
```

The compensated open loop transfer function is obtained and used for root locus and Bode analysis; it is given by (you can use the *augstate* and *series* as shown earlier, but since we know the formula for the open loop system, we will use it):

```
>> agk=a; bgk=b; cgk=k; dgk=0;
>> rlocus(agk,bgk,cgk,dgk)
>> [mc,pc]=bode(agk,bgk,cgk,dgk,1,w);
```

The root locus and Bode plots are shown in Figures 8-2 and 8-3.
The GM and PM are given by

gm =
    0.1083
pm =
    69.8397

The GM is –19.3 dB. You have to be careful interpreting these answers. From the root locus, the system is always stable for high gain; hence, the GM is infinite. Gain reduction margin (GRM), however, is –19 dB; i.e., the gain can be reduced by a factor of 10 before instability occurs. It is this margin that the command has produced. The PM is 69 degrees.

Now, we find the compensator transfer function $K(s)$. This requires the inversion of $G(s)$. If $G(s)$ is strictly proper, its inverse will be improper and will not have a state space representation; therefore, we will indirectly use transfer functions. If we denote $G(s)$ by ng/dg and $G(s)K(s)$ by ngk/dgk, we have

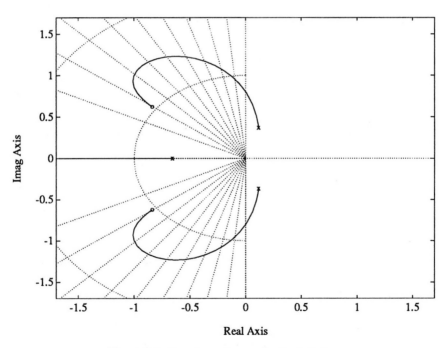

Figure 8-2 Root locus for state feedback design.

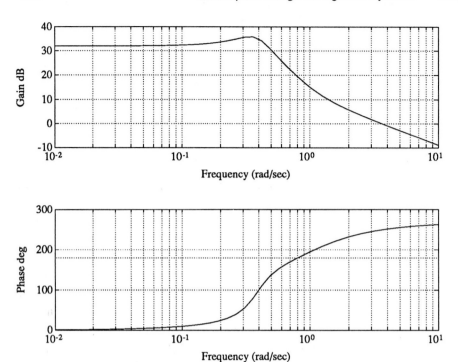

Figure 8-3 Bode plots for state feedback design.

$$K(s) \; = \; \frac{G(s)\,K(s)}{G(s)} \; = \; \frac{ngk/dgk}{ng/dg} \; = \; \frac{(ngk)\,(dg)}{(ng)\,(dgk)}$$

We will try to use the *convolve* and *minreal* commands to perform the necessary polynomial multiplication and pole zero cancellations to find $K(s)$. If $K(s)$ is improper (which it usually is for state feedback), the above will not work and has to be done partially manually (the corresponding commands are commented out in the State Feedback Exec File in the Appendix to prevent error messages).

```
>> [ng,dg]=ss2tf(a,b,c,d); [ngk,dgk]=ss2tf(agk,bgk,cgk,dgk)
>> nk=conv(ngk,dg); dk=conv(dgk,ng)
>> dk=dk(2:length(dk));nk=nk(2:length(nk));
>> [nk,dk]=minreal(nk,dk); [zK,pK,gainK]=tf2zp(nk,dk)
```

zK =
  -0.8388 + 0.6215i
  -0.8388 - 0.6215i

pK =
  0.2500 + 2.4975i
  0.2500 - 2.4975i

gainK =
  0.3653

Hence, $K(s) = \dfrac{0.36\,(s + 0.83 \pm j\,0.62)}{s - 0.25 \pm j\,2.49}$ and $G(s) = \dfrac{9.8\,(s - 0.25 \pm j\,2.49)}{(s + 0.65)\,(s - 0.11 \pm j\,0.36)}$

We notice that $G(s)$ has two RHP zeros, and $K(s)$ effectively cancels these and places two zeros in the LHP to pull the RHP poles into the LHP. The result of this is an unstable compensator that is undesirable, because any disturbance or noise at the input of $K(s)$ gets greatly amplified and may create saturation problems.

Systems with unstable compensators are only *conditionally stable*. Of course, an unstable compensator is not surprising, because, after all, stability of the compensator was not ever used as a constraint on design. Note that we do not build $K(s)$. We implement the design with the state feedback gain k. Finally, notice that $K(s)$ has no classical counterpart. The closed loop transfer function and its poles and zeros are found by

```
>> at=a-b*k;bt=b;ct=c;dt=d;
>> [zT,pT,gainT]=ss2zp(at,bt,ct,dt)
```

zT =
  0.2500 + 2.4975i
  0.2500 - 2.4975i
pT =
  -2.0000
  -1.0000 + 1.0000i
  -1.0000 - 1.0000i
gainT =
  9.8000

The closed loop poles are indeed in their specified locations. Note that the zeros are unchanged. State feedback is able to shift only the poles and not the zeros. Finally, the step response is found and appears in Figure 8-4. Note, we have normalized the output to eliminate steady state error to step inputs (we used the *dcgain* command to find $\overline{N}$):

```
>> dcg=dcgain(at,bt,ct,dt)
>> yc=step(at,bt,ct,dt,1,t); yc1=yc/dcg;
```

The design has resulted in a system that is very stable; GM = ∞, GRM = –19 dB, and PM= 70 degrees; has little overshoot, and a settling time of about 4 sec. If the states are available for measurement and feedback, this design would be acceptable.

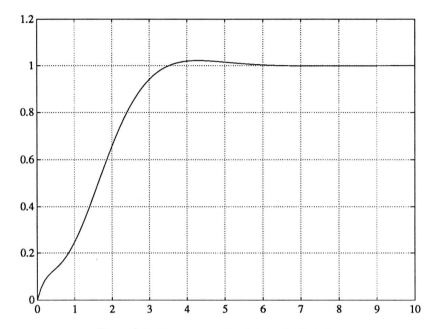

Figure 8-4   Step response for state feedback design.

8.3 Observer Design

The major problem with state feedback is that it is not usually practical. That is, in a typical system with many states, it is simply not possible or practical to sense all the states and feed them back. Constant state feedback requires ideal sensors (infinite bandwidth) for all states, whereas real sensors have limited bandwidth. Sometimes the states are not actual physical variables of the system and as such may not be measurable. Even if the states are actual physical variables, it may not be technologically possible, or economically feasible, to measure all the states. Besides the measurement problem, each feedback loop requires actual hardware (or additional software in computer control), adding to the complexity and cost, and reducing overall reliability of the system. If one sensor fails, the whole system may become unstable. In reality, only certain states or combinations of them are measurable as outputs. Consequently, any practical compensator must rely only on measured system outputs and inputs for compensation; this is called output feedback.

  The concept of the observer is both ingenious and simple. If we do not have the states, is it possible to use system inputs and outputs to estimate the states? The answer is yes. This state estimator is called an "observer" by D. Luenberger, who originally proposed and developed its theory [L64]. The idea is that if we know all system parameters, we can always simulate the model on an analog or digital computer. Even though we do not have access to system states, we have full access to the states of our simulation. Letting $\hat{x}$ denote the state estimates, we have

$$\dot{x} = Ax + Bu, \quad x(0) = x_o \quad \text{and} \quad \dot{\hat{x}} = A\hat{x} + Bu, \quad \hat{x}(0) = \hat{x}_o$$

$$\text{let} \quad \tilde{x} = x - \hat{x}, \quad \text{then} \quad \dot{\tilde{x}} = A\tilde{x}, \quad \tilde{x}(0) = \tilde{x}_o = x_o - \hat{x}_o \;\rightarrow\; \tilde{x}(t) = e^{At}\tilde{x}_o$$

Hence, the observer error, $\tilde{x}$, defined above, approaches zero as long as the original system is stable, or the initial conditions of the observer and the system are the same. We do not know the initial conditions of the system, however. If we did, we could have just solved the system equations and computed the states for all time. Therefore, the main problem is estimating the initial conditions of the system. Now, note that the above proposed observer is open loop; i.e., it does not use the information provided by the system outputs. It seems reasonable that if we compare the system output with the output of the observer and use it as a correction mechanism, we could stabilize the error dynamics. After all, we know that feedback can stabilize unstable systems. So we propose a closed loop observer

$$\boxed{\dot{\hat{x}} = A\hat{x} + Bu + L(y - C\hat{x}), \qquad \hat{x}(0) = \hat{x}_o}$$

Then the state equations for the error system become

$$\dot{\tilde{x}} = (A - LC)\tilde{x}, \qquad \tilde{x}(0) = \tilde{x}_o$$

Now, if we can choose L such that the eigenvalues of $(A - LC)$ can be arbitrarily placed in the complex plane, our problem is solved. We can guarantee the observer errors to converge to zero for any initial conditions. The above property is the dual of the controllability property and is called *observability*. It is loosely defined as the ability to estimate the system states from a record of output measurements. In the context of our discussion, observability is the ability to place the eigenvalues of $(A - LC)$ arbitrarily by using some gain L. Observability can be mathematically tested by checking the rank of the observability matrix O. If the rank is equal to n (dimension of the A matrix), the system is observable. The *observability matrix* is defined by

$$O = \begin{bmatrix} C \\ CA \\ CA^2 \\ \cdot \\ \cdot \\ \cdot \\ CA^{n-1} \end{bmatrix}$$

We say that controllability and observability are *dual* notions. By this, we mean that if we transpose the controllability matrix $\mathbf{C}$ (rank remains the same), and replace A' with

A and B' with C, we get O. The dual notion of *stabilizability* is called *detectability*. We say a system is *detectable* if the unstable modes are observable or equivalently the unobservable modes are stable.

A consequence of duality is that the same algorithm can be used to solve both problems. For instance, to solve for L, the observer gain, we use the *place* command as shown below:

```
>> L=place(a',c',OP)
```

where OP is the vector of desired observer poles. The observer gain L will be given as a row vector and has to be transposed. The same comments made about the choice of controller poles apply to observer poles, with the modification that observer poles must be several times faster than controller poles to ensure fast convergence of the estimation process. If the poles are too far in the LHP, values of k and L will be large and may cause saturation problems and even instability; also, the observer bandwidth increases, which causes noise problems. Hence, proper judgment has to be used by the designer.

Now that we know how to estimate the states, let us go back to the control problem. The idea is that we can use the estimated states in lieu of the actual states for state feedback. This renders state feedback practical. How can we guarantee closed loop stability of the overall system, however? After all, we are not using the states, but only their estimates. The answer is that there is a separation between the control problem and the observer problem. That is, we can find the controller gain assuming the states are available, and then design an observer to estimate these states and use the estimates in place of the states. The closed loop poles of the system will be the union of the controller poles and observer poles. This result is commonly known as the *Separation Property* and is a cornerstone result of modern control theory. The separation property can be shown by combining the plant, controller, and observer error systems; we get

$$\begin{bmatrix} \dot{x} \\ \dot{\tilde{x}} \end{bmatrix} = \begin{bmatrix} A - Bk & -Bk \\ 0 & A - LC \end{bmatrix} \begin{bmatrix} x \\ \tilde{x} \end{bmatrix}$$

We recall from matrix theory that eigenvalues of a block triangular matrix are the union of the eigenvalues of the diagonal blocks, hence, the separation property.

8.3.1 Transfer Function Analysis

The compensator (combination of state feedback and observer) equation is

$$\dot{\hat{x}} = A\hat{x} + Bu + L(y - C\hat{x})$$

$$u = -k\hat{x}$$

Substituting for u in the observer, taking Laplace transforms and solving for $K(s)$, we get

$$K(s) = k \, (\, sI - A + Bk + LC \,)^{-1} \, L \quad \rightarrow \quad K(s) = \begin{bmatrix} A - Bk - LC & L \\ k & 0 \end{bmatrix}$$

Note that even though $(A - Bk)$ and $(A - LC)$ are stable, the compensator matrix $(A - Bk - LC)$ may be unstable. This will result in a conditionally stable system, as can be seen from the root locus plot in the following example. Other problems with observer based controllers are poor robustness (i.e., sensitivity to parameter uncertainty and variations [DS79]), reduced stability margins compared with state feedback, and compensator complexity. Essentially, for an nth order system, we obtain an nth order compensator that may be too complex and expensive. It should be mentioned that some of the above shortcomings can be corrected using modified and more advanced design methods.

The loop transfer function can be obtained by cascading $G(s)$ and $K(s)$ using the *series* command. The closed loop transfer function is obtained by introducing an external reference input with a gain adjusted to produce zero steady state error to step inputs. (*Note*: the *feedback* command can be used to find the closed loop transfer function.)

$$u = -K\hat{x} + \overline{N} v$$

$$\begin{bmatrix} \dot{x} \\ \dot{\hat{x}} \end{bmatrix} = \begin{bmatrix} A & -Bk \\ LC & A - Bk - LC \end{bmatrix} \begin{bmatrix} x \\ \hat{x} \end{bmatrix} + \begin{bmatrix} B\overline{N} \\ B\overline{N} \end{bmatrix} v \quad \rightarrow \quad T(s) = \begin{bmatrix} A & -Bk & B\overline{N} \\ LC & A - Bk - LC & B\overline{N} \\ C & 0 & 0 \end{bmatrix}$$

Example 8.2 Observer-Based Design

We will design an observer-based controller for Example 8.1. The observer poles are selected to be at $\{-3 \pm 3j, -4\}$, three times faster than the controller poles.

```
>> op=[-3+3*j, -3-3*j  -4];
>> l=place(a',c',op);   l=l';           % L must be a column vector
```

l =
    5.4664
    4.6762
    9.5800

The compensator transfer function is obtained from

```
>> ak=a-b*k-l*c-l*d*k; bk=l; ck=k;
```

The next step is needed in case d is a scalar 0 (in that case *zeros (d)* would give an error message):

```
>> [tmp1,tmp2]=size(d);  dk=zeros(tmp1,tmp2);
>> [zK,pK,gainK]=ss2zp(ak,bk,ck,dk,1);
```

pK =
-14.3751
  0.3975 + 4.0793i
  0.3975 - 4.0793i
zK =
-6.4156e-001+ 3.6576e-001i
-6.4156e-001- 3.6576e-001i

$$\text{so} \qquad K_2(s) = \frac{7.85\ (s + 0.64 \pm j\,0.36\ )}{(s + 14.37\ )\ (s - 0.39 \pm j\,4.07\ )}$$

Comparing $K_2(s)$ with classical lag-lead type compensators, we note that in classical design, compensator poles and zeros are restricted to be on the negative real axis, whereas in state space design, compensator poles and zeros are not restricted and fall anywhere on the complex plane. This extra freedom leads to arbitrary closed loop pole placement, although the compensator may turn out to be unstable.

Now, we find the open loop transfer function to obtain root locus, Bode plots, and margins:

```
>> [agk,bgk,cgk,dgk]=series(a,b,c,dk,ak,bk,ck,dk);
>> [mc,pc]=bode(agk,bgk,cgk,dgk,1,w);
>> rlocus(agk,bgk,cgk,dgk)
>> [gm,pm,wpc,wgc]=margin(mc,pc,w)
```

gm =
  3.8034
pm =
  44.2624

The root locus and Bode plots are shown in Figures 8-5 and 8-6. Note that the root locus shows the conditional stability of the system; i.e., the system becomes unstable for low and high gains. Using the *rlocfind* command we find the lower and upper limits of gain to be 0.24 (there is also a lower limit of 0.16, but 0.24 dominates this) and 3.8, resulting in GM of 11.6 dB and GRM of –12.3 dB. The PMs obtained from the Bode plot are 44, –74, and 52 degrees. Note that Bode plots for systems with RHP poles and zeros give multiple positive and negative GMs and PMs and, as such, have to be interpreted carefully (see Section 7.7).

We will use the *feedback* command to find the closed loop transfer function, $T(s)$:

```
>> [at,bt,ct,dt]=feedback(a,b,c,d,ak,bk,ck,dk);
>> [zT,pT,gainT]=ss2zp(at,bt,ct,dt,1);
```

pT =
-3.0000 + 3.0000i
-3.0000 - 3.0000i
-4.0000
-2.0000
-1.0000 + 1.0000i
-1.0000 - 1.0000i

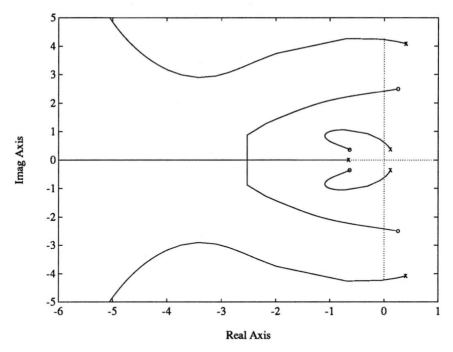

Figure 8-5 Root locus for observer-based design.

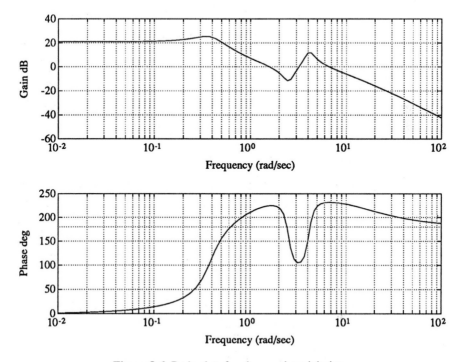

Figure 8-6 Bode plots for observer-based design.

zT =
3.9754e-001+ 4.0793e+000i
3.9754e-001- 4.0793e+000i
-1.4375e+001
2.5000e-001+ 2.4975e+000i
2.5000e-001- 2.4975e+000i

Note that closed loop zeros are the combination of open loop zeros and compensator poles, as expected. The closed loop poles are the union of controller and observer poles, as expected from the separation property. The normalized step response is given by

```
>> yc=step(at,bt,ct,dt,1,t); dcg=dcgain(at,bt,ct,dt);yc=yc/dcg;
```

The step response of the state feedback and observer based controller are shown in Figure 8-7. We note from the margins that the addition of the observer has reduced the stability margins of the system. The settling time, peak time, and overshoot (2%) are slightly higher in the observer-based design.

To see how well the observer estimates track the actual states, we will plot the states and estimates together in Figure 8-8. The *augstate* command is used to pick the states of the closed loop system (i.e., the states and their estimates). The initial conditions for the system and observer are chosen as [1, 2, 3] and [−1, −2, −3], respectively. Note, because the real parts of the observer eigenvalues are −3, we expect the observer to converge in about 1.5 sec, which is indeed the case.

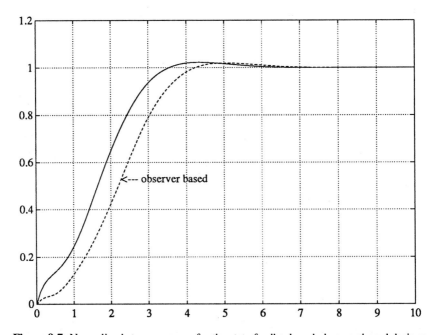

Figure 8-7 Normalized step responses for the state feedback and observer-based designs.

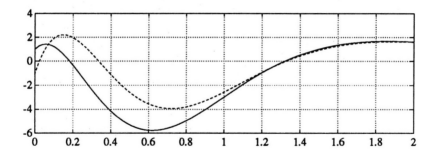

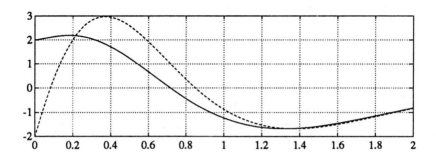

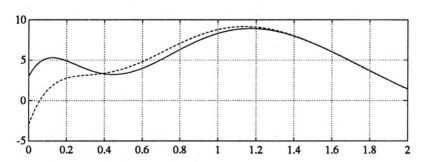

Figure 8-8 Plots of states and observer estimates (solid lines are states; dashed lines are estimates).

```
>> t2=[0:.02:2]';
>> [ata,bta,cta,dta]=augstate(at,bt,ct,dt);
>> x_xh=initial(ata,bta,cta,dta,[1 2 3 -1 -2 -3],t2);
>> x=x_xh(:,2:4); xh=x_xh(:,5:7);
>> plot(t2,[x(:,1) xh(:,1)]); plot(t2,[x(:,2) xh(:,2)]);
>> plot(t2,[x(:,3) xh(:,3)])
```

8.4 Reduced-Order Observer Design

The observer introduced in the previous section has the same order as the system and is referred to as the *full-order observer*. If the system has n states and m measurement outputs, it seems redundant to estimate the known states. For instance, if $y = x_1$, a full-order observer estimates x_1, even though it is clearly unnecessary. Theoretically, all we need is to estimate the unknown states. This results in an $(n - m)$ dimensional observer, first introduced by D. Luenberger [L64], and referred to as a *reduced-order* (or *Luenberger*) *observer*. This reduction in order leads to simpler and more economical compensators. If the number of measurements, m, is large, the benefits are substantial.

The derivation of the reduced order observer starts by defining a linear transformation of the states

$$z = T x , \quad \text{where } \dim(T) = (n - m) \times n , \quad \text{and } \dim(z) = (n - m) \times 1$$

where T is any matrix such that $E = \begin{bmatrix} C \\ T \end{bmatrix}$ is nonsingular and we define $E^{-1} = [P \mid M]$, which exists if rank $(C) = m$. Combining y and z, we get

$$\begin{bmatrix} y \\ z \end{bmatrix} = \begin{bmatrix} C \\ T \end{bmatrix} x \quad \rightarrow \quad x = \begin{bmatrix} C \\ T \end{bmatrix}^{-1} \begin{bmatrix} y \\ z \end{bmatrix} = [P \mid M] \begin{bmatrix} y \\ z \end{bmatrix} = P y + M z$$

Now, suppose we build a full-order observer to estimate z (the observer dimension = dimension of $z = n - m$), then we can generate estimates of x from

$$\hat{x} = P y + M \hat{z}, \quad \text{where } \hat{z} \text{ is the estimate of } z$$

Therefore, to estimate x, all we have to do is design an observer to estimate z. To do this, we need to know its dynamics; i.e., a differential equation governing the behavior of z. We obtain a differential equation for z by premultiplying the original state equations by E. This simply corresponds to a change of basis and, hence, a new realization for the system.

$$E \dot{x} = EA x + EB u$$

Substituting for x and E, we get

$$E \dot{x} = \begin{bmatrix} C \\ T \end{bmatrix} \dot{x} = \begin{bmatrix} \dot{y} \\ \dot{z} \end{bmatrix} = \begin{bmatrix} C \\ T \end{bmatrix} A x + \begin{bmatrix} C \\ T \end{bmatrix} B u = \begin{bmatrix} C \\ T \end{bmatrix} A [P \mid M] \begin{bmatrix} y \\ z \end{bmatrix} + \begin{bmatrix} C \\ T \end{bmatrix} B u$$

Therefore, we get

$$\begin{bmatrix} \dot{y} \\ \dot{z} \end{bmatrix} = \begin{bmatrix} CAP & CAM \\ TAP & TAM \end{bmatrix} \begin{bmatrix} y \\ z \end{bmatrix} + \begin{bmatrix} CB \\ TB \end{bmatrix} u \overset{\Delta}{=} \begin{bmatrix} A_{11} & A_{12} \\ A_{21} & A_{22} \end{bmatrix} \begin{bmatrix} y \\ z \end{bmatrix} + \begin{bmatrix} B_1 \\ B_2 \end{bmatrix} u$$

The differential equation for z is then given by

$$\dot{z} = A_{22}\, z + (\, A_{21}\, y + B_2\, u\,)$$

Now, a full-order observer for z is designed following the approach in the previous section. Namely, we copy the differential equation for z, replace z by $\hat{z}$, and add an error term for correction.

$$\dot{\hat{z}} = A_{22}\, \hat{z} + (\, A_{21}\, y + B_2\, u\,) + L\,(y - C\,\hat{x}\,)$$

The first term within parentheses is a known quantity and is considered as an input to the observer; the second term is the correction term to stabilize the observer error system. Note that because $[P \mid M\,]$ is the inverse of E, we have $CP = I$ and $CM = 0$, hence,

$$y - C\,\hat{x} = y - C\,(P\,y + M\,\hat{z}\,) = y - CP\,y - CM\,\hat{z} = y - y\ - 0 = 0$$

So, the correction term provides no correction after all. We recall from classical control that sometimes when output feedback alone is not effective, feeding back the output and its derivative (i.e., rate feedback) may help. Theoretically, if y is available, we can assume that its derivatives are also available. Hence, we will instead use the derivative of the measurements as the correction term. The differential equation for y is available from the transformed system equations given previously:

$$\dot{y} = A_{11}\, y + A_{12}\, z + B_1\, u$$

Collecting all the known quantities on one side and using them as the "observer output" for the correction term, we get the sought-after reduced-order observer (dim $= n - m$):

$$\dot{\hat{z}} = A_{22}\, \hat{z} + (\, A_{21}\, y + B_2\, u\,) + L\,(\,\dot{y} - A_{11}\, y - B_1\, u - A_{12}\,\hat{z}\,)$$

To show that this observer works, we need to demonstrate that the estimation errors approach zero asymptotically with time. This is verified by showing that the error system is asymptotically stable. By subtracting the differential equation for z from $\hat{z}$, we get the error system dynamics:

$$\dot{\tilde{z}} = (A_{22} - L\,A_{12})\,\tilde{z}$$

The error system contains an undetermined vector L (or matrix in the multi-output case). The question is whether L can be chosen to place the observer eigenvalues arbitrarily (or at least stabilize the error system). Luenberger has shown that observability of the pair

(C, A) is equivalent to observability of (A_{12}, A_{22}). Therefore, by duality, L can be chosen to place eigenvalues of the error system anywhere in the complex plane. The *place* command can be used to obtain L by substituting A_{22} for A and A_{12} for C:

```
>> L=place( A22',A12',OP)
```

The $\dot{y}$ term in the above observer equation can be eliminated by a simple change of variable. Define w as

$$w \overset{\Delta}{=} \hat{z} - L y$$

A bit of algebra results in the final form of the reduced-order observer

$$
\boxed{
\begin{aligned}
\dot{w} &= F w + D y + G u \\
\hat{x} &= M w + N y
\end{aligned}
}
$$

where $F \overset{\Delta}{=} A_{22} - L A_{12}$, $D \overset{\Delta}{=} F L + A_{21} - L A_{11}$, $G \overset{\Delta}{=} B_2 - L B_1$, $N \overset{\Delta}{=} P + M L$

Note: In the special case in which C has the following form, T can be selected as

$$C = [\, I_m \mid 0_{m,n-m}\,] \quad \rightarrow \quad T = [\, 0_{n-m,m} \mid I_{n-m}\,] \quad \rightarrow \quad E = I_n$$

In this case, no transformation is needed, and A and B can be directly partitioned to get A_{11}, A_{12}, and other required matrices. Also observe that the measurements appear directly in the output of the observer; hence, measurement noise can pass through the observer. We conclude that the choice of a reduced-order observer has to be made carefully in cases where noise may be a problem.

The separation property also holds in the reduced-order case. It can be derived by combining the closed loop system and error system equations

$$u = -k \hat{x}, \quad \dot{x} = A x - B k \hat{x}, \quad \text{it can be shown that} \quad \hat{x} = x - M \tilde{z}$$

$$
\begin{bmatrix} \dot{x} \\ \dot{\tilde{z}} \end{bmatrix} = \begin{bmatrix} A - Bk & BkM \\ 0 & A_{22} - L A_{12} \end{bmatrix} \begin{bmatrix} x \\ \tilde{z} \end{bmatrix}
$$

Therefore, the closed loop eigenvalues are the union of the controller and observer eigenvalues.

8.4.1 Transfer Function Analysis

The compensator transfer function is derived by substituting for u in the observer equation

$$u = -k\hat{x} = -kMw - kNy$$

$$\begin{aligned}\dot{w} &= (F - GkM)w + (D - GkN)y \\ u &= -k\hat{x} - kNy\end{aligned} \quad \rightarrow \quad K(s) = \begin{bmatrix} F - GkM & D - GkN \\ -kM & -kN \end{bmatrix}$$

The *series* and *feedback* commands can be used to obtain open loop and closed loop transfer functions. The closed loop transfer function can be obtained directly by combining the closed loop system and observer equations using an external reference input v:

$$u = -k\hat{x} + \overline{N}v$$

$$\begin{bmatrix} \dot{x} \\ \dot{w} \end{bmatrix} = \begin{bmatrix} A - BkNC & -BkM \\ DC - GkNC & F - GkM \end{bmatrix} \begin{bmatrix} x \\ w \end{bmatrix} + \begin{bmatrix} B\overline{N} \\ G\overline{N} \end{bmatrix} v \quad \rightarrow \quad T(s) = \begin{bmatrix} A - BkNC & -BkM & B\overline{N} \\ DC - GkNC & F - GkM & G\overline{N} \\ C & 0 & 0 \end{bmatrix}$$

Example 8.3 Reduced-Order Observer-Based Compensator Design

The helicopter example is redesigned using a reduced-order observer. It is assumed that the third state variable (i.e., the horizontal velocity) is being measured; hence, we build a second order observer yielding a second order compensator. The observer poles are placed at $\{-3\pm j3\}$. The first step is to choose T. Almost any random matrix will do (as long as E is nonsingular). Then E is inverted, and P and M are peeled off from the inverse of E. Finally, the new realization partitions (A_{11}, A_{12}, etc.) are computed:

```
>> T=[0 1 0;1 0 0];  % T is capitalized to reserve t for time
>> e=[c;T]; ei=inv(e);
>> [mm,nn]=size(c);  % dimensions of c are needed to split E⁻¹
>> p=ei(:,1:mm);m=ei(:,mm+1:nn);
>> a11=c*a*p; a12=c*a*m; a21=T*a*p; a22=T*a*m; b1=c*b; b2=T*b;
>> lr=place(a22',a12',opr); lr=lr';
```

We are now ready to find observer gain, parameters, and compensator transfer function:

```
>> f=a22-lr*a12; g=b2-lr*b1; D=f*lr+(a21-lr*a11); n=p+m*lr;
>> ak=f-g*k*m ; bk=D-g*k*n; ck=k*m; dk=k*n;
>> [zK,pK,gK]=ss2zp(ak,bk,ck,dk,1)
```

pK =
  2.8907 + 5.2744i
  2.8907 - 5.2744i

zK =
  -0.7141 + 0.4443i
  -0.7141 - 0.4443i

After computing the poles and zeros of the compensator, we get

$$K_3(s) = \frac{1.56\,(s + 0.714 \pm j\,0.44)}{(s - 2.89 \pm j\,5.27)}$$

We now find the open loop transfer function and obtain root locus, Bode plots, and stability margins:

```
>> [agk,bgk,cgk,dgk]=series(a,b,c,d,ak,bk,ck,dk);
>> rlocus(agk,bgk,cgk,dgk)
>> w=logspace(-2,2,100)'; [mc,pc]=bode(agk,bgk,cgk,dgk,1,w);
```

The root locus and Bode plots are shown in Figures 8-9 and 8-10.

```
>>[gm,pm,wpc,wgc]=margin(mc,pc,w)

gm =
    0.4472
pm =
   -48.3129
```

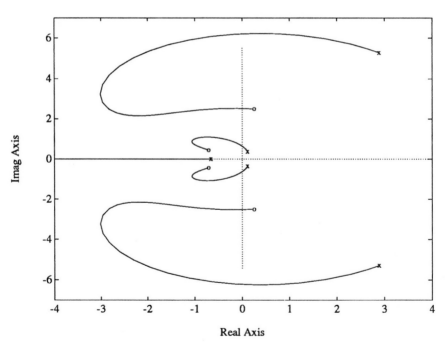

Figure 8-9 Root locus for reduced-order observer design.

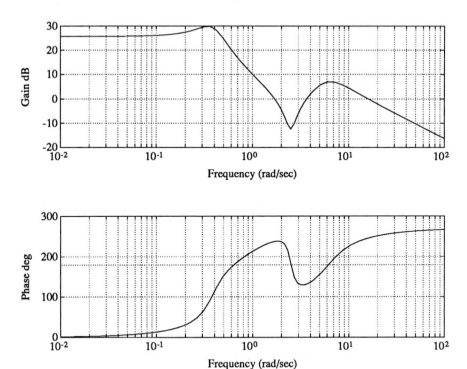

Figure 8-10 Bode plots for reduced-order observer design.

The root locus and the Bode plots verify that the GM is 12.2 dB, and the GRM is –7 dB; so the system is conditionally stable for $0.44 < k < 4.14$. The PMs are –48 and +57 degrees. Compared with the full order case, PM and GM have increased, but the GRM is better in the full-order case. We next obtain the closed loop transfer function, its poles and zeros, and the normalized step response, which is shown in Figure 8-11.

```
>> [at,bt,ct,dt]=feedback(a,b,c,d,ak,bk,ck,dk);
>> t=[0:.1:9.9]'; yc=step(at,bt,ct,dt,1,t);
>> dcg=dcgain(at,bt,ct,dt);yc=yc/dcg;
>> [zT,pT,gT]=ss2zp(at,bt,ct,dt,1)
```

```
pT =
 -3.0000 + 3.0000i
 -3.0000 - 3.0000i
 -2.0000
 -1.0000 + 1.0000i
 -1.0000 - 1.0000i
```

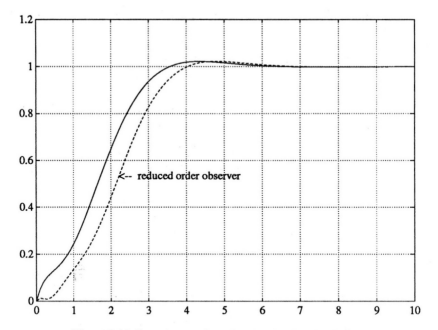

Figure 8-11 Step response for reduced-order observer design.

zT =
    2.8907 + 5.2744i
    2.8907 - 5.2744i
    0.2500 + 2.4975i
    0.2500 - 2.4975i

The presence of the observer results in performance degradation because of incorrect observer initial conditions. To see this, we will use the *lsim* command to find the step response with nonzero initial conditions [1,2,3,1,2].

```
>> xor=[1,2,3,1,2];
>> ycc=lsim(at,bt,ct,dt,ones(100,1),t,xor); ycc=ycc/dcg;
```

The normalized step response is shown in Figure 8-12. Finally, we plot the states and estimates together. Recall that the closed loop system equations are (with no reference input)

$$
\begin{bmatrix} \dot{x} \\ \dot{w} \end{bmatrix} = \begin{bmatrix} A - BkNC & -BkM \\ DC - GkNC & F - GkM \end{bmatrix} \begin{bmatrix} x \\ w \end{bmatrix}
$$

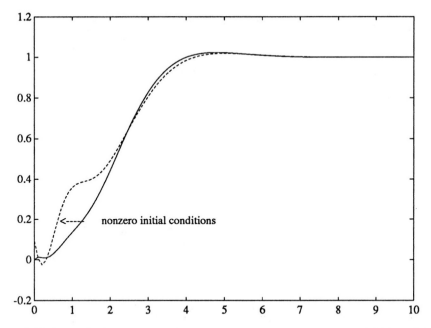

Figure 8-12 Normalized step response for reduced-order observer with nonzero initial conditions.

Because, $\hat{x} = N\,y + M\,w = N\,C\,x + M\,w$, we can peel off the states and estimates by computing the simulation output matrix from

$$\begin{bmatrix} x \\ \hat{x} \end{bmatrix} = \begin{bmatrix} I & 0 \\ N\,C & M \end{bmatrix} \begin{bmatrix} x \\ w \end{bmatrix}$$

```
>> ct_=[eye(3) zeros(3,2);n*c m]; dt_=zeros(6,1);
```

We now choose the system initial state as $x(0) = x_o = [1, 2, 3]$, and the initial state estimates as $[-1, -2, -3]$. Because the states of the closed loop system are x and w, we need to convert the initial conditions of $\hat{x}$ to w. The initial conditions of w are computed from

$$w = \hat{z} - L\,y = T\hat{x} - L\,C\,x \quad \rightarrow \quad w(0) = T\hat{x}(0) - L\,C\,x(0)$$

```
>> t2=[0:.02:2]'; xo=[1;2;3]; xho=-xo; wo=-T*xho-lr*c*xo;
>> x_xh=initial(at,bt,ct_,dt_,[xo;wo],t2);
>> plot(t2,[x_xh(:,1) x_xh(:,4)]); plot(t2,[x_xh(:,2) x_xh(:,5)])
>> plot(t2,[x_xh(:,3) x_xh(:,6)])
```

The plots are shown in Figure 8-13. The observer converges in about 1.6 sec. Note, the third state is exact, because it is not estimated.

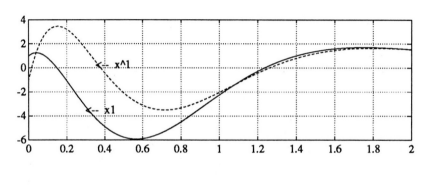

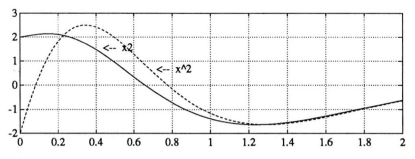

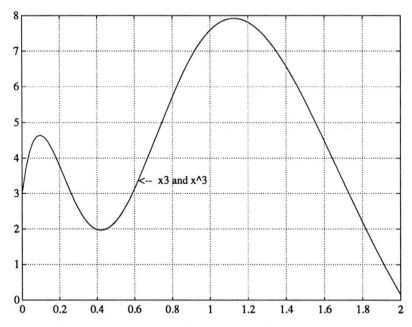

Figure 8-13 Plots of states and estimates using a reduced-order observer (solid lines are states).

8.5 Comments Regarding State Space Design

The techniques discussed in this chapter are very powerful and have expanded the range of problems that can be solved. We would like to discuss briefly some of the advantages and limitations of pole placement here.

The main advantage, as the name implies, is arbitrary pole placement. No matter where the open loop poles and zeros are, we can arbitrarily place the closed loop poles. This gives us a good deal of control over the time response of systems. If all the states can be sensed and fed back economically, state feedback can usually provide an easy and adequate design. Otherwise, observers can be implemented to estimate the states. Observers increase the complexity of the system, and they add to the overall cost. More components, more connections, or more lines of code in the digital case translate into less reliability and increased maintenance costs. From a control design viewpoint, observers generally reduce the stability margins. They may also introduce RHP poles or zeros, resulting in conditionally stable systems that may not be desirable. Reduced order observers also generally have a higher bandwidth, making the system more susceptible to high-frequency noise. Therefore the choice between full or reduced order observers has to be made carefully. In general, several designs must be performed and time response, stability margins, conditional stability, bandwidth, compensator order, component counts, reliability, sensitivity, etc., have to be compared.

Time response depends not only on closed loop poles but also on closed loop zeros; as you may have noticed, we have no control over the zeros. It is possible to modify our techniques to achieve zero placement, but the procedures become somewhat involved in state space [FPE91]. Transfer function based algebraic techniques are also available that allow simultaneous pole and zero placement. These methods are discussed in Chapter 10. Another disadvantage is that the compensator has the same dimension as the system. This may not be necessary. For example, a large order system may be compensated adequately using low order lead-lag type classical compensators. Therefore, classical techniques should be tried at the first stage. If the results are not satisfactory, try state space methods.

Two other important issues that were not discussed in this chapter are selection of poles and MIMO (multivariable) systems. The issue of pole selection is discussed in Chapter 10. Regarding multivariable systems, although techniques discussed in the present chapter apply theoretically, the issues are more complex. The control and observer gains are matrices in this case. If the system has n states, and p inputs, the control gain matrix k will have $p*m$ elements. Selecting n eigenvalues gives n constraints, so we have $p*n$ equations in n unknowns with an infinite number of solutions. Control gain k is no longer unique; similar situation exists for the observer problem. The *place* command uses the extra degrees of freedom to minimize the sensitivity of the closed loop poles to perturbations in the closed loop system matrix. Other possibilities exist. One solution is to use the extra degrees of freedom to place both closed loop system eigenvalues and eigenvectors. This is usually called *eigen-structure assignment* and has found some applications in aerospace control problems [DH88]. Another solution is to find the optimal control gain.

A special case of this approach, which is very popular and has found many applications in multivariable systems, is the *LQR/LQG* approach. MATLAB has several commands relating to *LQR/LQG*, which are available in the Control System and the Robust Control Toolbox.

Finally, it must be noted that because state space methods are time domain design techniques, frequency domain specifications such as stability margins cannot usually be met as specified. In fact, an observer-based compensated system can be dangerously close to instability or very sensitive to model uncertainties [DS79]. The lack of robustness of these techniques must be taken seriously because models are rarely perfect. A recent solution to this problem is to apply state-space-based algorithms and methods that improve system robustness. These methods are generally called *robust control*. Refer to [M89], [F87], [BPDGS91], and [CS91] for these more advanced methods.

8.6 Appendix: Design Programs

1. State Feedback Design Program

```
% The program requires: a,b,c,d, cp,t,w,
[olp,olz,olg]=ss2zp(a,b,c,d)
k=place(a,b,cp)
[mc,pc]=bode(a,b,k,0,1,w);
rlocus(a,b,k,0)
agk=a;bgk=b;cgk=k;dgk=0;
% The following commands are used to find the compensator transfer
% function, K(s). They are commented out to avoid error messages.
% [ng,dg]=ss2tf(a,b,c,d);
% [ngk,dgk]=ss2tf(agk,bgk,cgk,dgk)
% nk=conv(ngk,dg);dk=conv(dgk,ng)
% we remove the first coefficient because it is zero
% dk=dk(2:length(dk)); nk=nk(2:length(nk));
% [nk,dk]=minreal(nk,dk)
% disp(' the compensator pole and zeros are')
% [zK,pK,gainK]=tf2zp(nk,dk)
at=a-b*k; bt=b; ct=c; dt=d;
disp(' The closed loop zeros and poles are')
[zT,pT,gainT]=ss2zp(at,bt,ct,dt)
dcg=dcgain(at,bt,ct,dt); yc=step(at,bt,ct,dt,1,t);yc=yc/dcg;
[gm,pm,wpc,wgc]=margin(mc,pc,w)
```

2. Full-Order Observer-Based Design Program

```
%The program requires: a,b,c,d, cp (controller poles), op (observer
% poles), xo, xho (observer initial conditions), w, t
k=place(a,b,cp);
l=place(a',c',op); l=l'
ak=a-b*k-l*c-l*d*k; bk=l; ck=k;
```

```
% If d is a scalar and 0, zeros(d) will give an error. The Next
% line is needed to prevent this.
[tmp1,tmp2]=size(d); dk=zeros(tmp1,tmp2);
[zK,pK,gainK]=ss2zp(ak,bk,ck,dk,1);
disp(' the compensator poles are');pK
disp(' the compensator zeros are '); zK
[agk,bgk,cgk,dgk]=series(a,b,c,d,ak,bk,ck,dk);
[mc,pc]=bode(agk,bgk,cgk,dgk,1,w);
[gm,pm,wpc,wgc]=margin(mc,pc,w)
rlocus(agk,bgk,cgk,dgk)
[at,bt,ct,dt]=feedback(a,b,c,d,ak,bk,ck,dk);
[zT,pT,gainT]=ss2zp(at,bt,ct,dt,1);
disp('the closed loop poles are'); pT
disp(' the closed loop zeros are '); zT
yc=step(at,bt,ct,dt,1,t); dcg=dcgain(at,bt,ct,dt); yc=yc/dcg;
% plot states and state estimates together
[ata,bta,cta,dta]=augstate(at,bt,ct,dt); t2=[0:.02:2]';
x_xh=initial(ata,bta,cta,dta,[xo xho],t2);
x=x_xh(:,2:4);xh=x_xh(:,5:7);
plot(t2,[x(:,1) xh(:,1)]); plot(t2,[x(:,2) xh(:,2)])
plot(t2,[x(:,3) xh(:,3)])
```

3. Reduced-Order Observer-Based Design Program

```
%The program requires: a,b,c,d, cp (controller poles), opr (reduced
% order observer poles), xo, xho (observer initial conditions), w, t
k=place(a,b,cp);
T=input (' enter T such that [C ; T] is nonsingular')
e=[c;T];  %note that T is capitalized to reserve t for time
ei=inv(e);  [mm, nn]=size(c);
p=ei(:,1:mm); m=ei(:,mm+1:nn);
a11=c*a*p; a12=c*a*m; a21=T*a*p; a22=T*a*m; b1=c*b; b2=T*b;
lr=place(a22',a12',opr); lr=lr';
f=a22-lr*a12; g=b2-lr*b1; D=f*lr+(a21-lr*a11); n=p+m*lr;
ak=f-g*k*m ; bk=D-g*k*n; ck=k*m; dk=k*n;
[zK,pK,gK]=ss2zp(ak,bk,ck,dk,1);
disp (' the compensator poles are '), pK
disp (' the compensator zeros are '), zK
[agk,bgk,cgk,dgk]=series(a,b,c,d,ak,bk,ck,dk);
rlocus(agk,bgk,cgk,dgk)
[mc,pc]=bode(agk,bgk,cgk,dgk,1,w);
[gm,pm,wpc,wgc]=margin(mc,pc,w)
[at,bt,ct,dt]=feedback(a,b,c,d,ak,bk,ck,dk);
yc=step(at,bt,ct,dt,1,t); dcg=dcgain(at,bt,ct,dt);yc=yc/dcg;
ycc=lsim(at,bt,ct,dt,ones(100,1),t,[xo xho(1:2)]); ycc=ycc/dcg;
[zT,pT,gT]=ss2zp(at,bt,ct,dt,1);
disp('the closed loop poles are '), pT
```

```
disp(' the closed loop zeros are '); zT
ct_=[eye(nn) zeros(nn,nn-mm);n*c m]; dt_=zeros(2*nn,1);
wo=T*xho-lr*c*xo;t2=[0:.02:2]';
x_xh=initial(at,bt,ct_,dt_,[xo;wo],t2);
plot(t2,[x_xh(:,1) x_xh(:,4)]); plot(t2,[x_xh(:,2) x_xh(:,5)])
plot(t2,[x_xh(:,3) x_xh(:,6)])
```

8.7 Problems

8.1 Consider the system represented in state space form by $\{A, B, C, D\}$:

$$A = \begin{bmatrix} 0 & 1 & -1 \\ -2 & -3 & 0 \\ \beta & 1 & 1 \end{bmatrix} \quad, \quad B = \begin{bmatrix} 1 \\ 0 \\ 0 \end{bmatrix} \quad, \quad C = [0 \; 0 \; 1] \quad, \quad D = 0$$

a. For what values of β is the system controllable?

b. For what values of β is the system observable?

c. Find the transfer function of the system.

d. For what values of β is the system stabilizable?

e. For what values of β is the system detectable?

8.2 Consider the following plant:

$$A = \begin{bmatrix} 0 & 1 & 0 \\ 0 & 0 & 1 \\ 2 & 0 & -1 \end{bmatrix} \quad, \quad B = \begin{bmatrix} 1 \\ 2 \\ 0 \end{bmatrix} \quad, \quad C = [1 \; 0 \; 0] \quad, \quad D = 0$$

a. We want to place the closed loop poles at $\{-10, -1+j, -1-j\}$. Find the state feedback gain vector.

b. Obtain the equivalent transfer function of the compensator, root locus, Bode plots and closed loop step response. Tabulate the step response features (POS, T_p, T_s), phase and gain margins.

c. Design a full order observer. Choose observer poles at $\{-40, -4+j4, -4-j4\}$. Repeat part *b*.

d. Design a reduced order observer. Choose observer poles at $\{-4+j4, -4-j4\}$. Repeat part *b*.

e. Repeat part *c* with the observer poles at $\{-40, -1, -2\}$.

f. Repeat part *d* with the observer poles at $-1, -2$.

Note: In parts *e* and *f*, the observer poles are chosen at the plant zeros. It is known that such a choice increases the robustness of the system. Because PM and GM are classical measures of robustness (protection against uncertainty), compare the margins in all cases. Does the choice of observer poles in parts *e* and *f* really improve the margins?

8.3 Consider the inverted pendulum described in Problem 7.5.

a. Find the eigenvalues of the linearized system. Is the system stable?

b. Determine the controllability of the system.

c. Determine the observability of the system if only the cart position is measured.

d. Determine the observability of the system if only the pendulum angle is measured.

e. Given the following values: $l = 1\ m$, $M = 1\ kg$, $m = 0.1\ kg$, $g = 9.8\ m/s^2$, use the *place* command to find the controller gain that will place the closed loop poles at $-1, -3, -2+2j, -2-2j$. Obtain the root locus and Bode plots of the compensated system. Find the stability margins, GM and PM.

f. If we use full state feedback ($z = x$), find and plot $y(t)$ and $\theta(t)$ for the closed loop system if the pendulum is displaced by 0.01 radians; i.e., $\theta(0) = 0.01$.

8.4 Suppose in the preceding problem we can only measure the cart position.

a. Design a full order observer to estimate the states. Select the observer poles at $\{-6+6j, -6-6j, -10, -20\}$.

b. Obtain the root locus and Bode plots of the compensated system. Find the stability margins, GM and PM.

c. Find and plot $y(t)$ and $\theta(t)$ for the closed loop system if the pendulum is displaced by 0.01 radians; i.e., $\theta(0) = 0.01$.

8.5 Repeat Problem 8.4 using a reduced order observer with poles at $\{-6+6j, -6-6j, -10\}$. Compare the results of the three designs: full-state feedback, observer, reduced-order observer.

8.6 A problem that is similar to the pendulum problem is the attempt to balance a wedge in the inverted position. Hsu and Wendlandt [HW91] examined this problem by constructing a wedge with an internal balancing mechanism. In their final design choice, the internal balancing mechanism was provided by controlling the position of a mass sliding along the wedge sides. We reproduce here their final set of equations, which include the actuator and sensor dynamics (we do not include the A/D and D/A conversion constants). The nonlinear equations are

$$[5.53 + 14.38\,(0.25 + x^2)]\,\ddot{\theta}\ + 28.76\,x\,\dot{x}\,\dot{\theta}\ -\ 141.7 \sin\theta\ +\ 99.61\,x\cos\theta\ =\ 0$$

$$18.79\ddot{x}\ +\ 305.17\dot{x}\ -\ 14.38x\,\dot{\theta}^{\,2}\ +\ 99.61 \sin\theta\ =\ 2.22\,u$$

where θ is the angle the wedge makes with the vertical axis, x is the position of the sliding mass, and u is the voltage control input. The linearized equations are

$$
\dot{q} = \begin{pmatrix} 0 & 0 & 1 & 0 \\ 0 & 0 & 0 & 1 \\ 15.54 & -10.93 & 0 & 0 \\ -5.31 & 0 & 0 & -16.24 \end{pmatrix} q + \begin{pmatrix} 0 \\ 0 \\ 0 \\ 1.96 \end{pmatrix} u
$$

$$
y = \begin{pmatrix} 57.29 & 0 & 0 & 0 \\ 0 & 29.9 & 0 & 0 \end{pmatrix} q
$$

where the state vector is given by $q = [\theta, x, \dot{\theta}, \dot{x}]'$.

a. Discuss the controllability and observability of the system.

b. Find a state feedback controller to place the closed loop eigenvalues at $\{-0.7 + 1.8j, -0.7 - 1.8j, -5, -20\}$. Obtain the root locus and Bode plots of the compensated system, and determine its stability margins.

c. Assuming full-state feedback, find the response of the system to an initial angular displacement of 0.1 rad in the wedge angle.

9

Digital Control

9.1 Introduction

Many of today's control systems use digital computers to provide the compensation that was discussed in the previous two chapters. A typical digital control system is shown in Figure 9-1. Usually, a continuous error signal is digitized by an analog-to-digital converter (ADC). The on-board computer processes this signal to provide a control signal to the plant. Because most plants are continuous, the computer's output is passed through a digital-to-analog converter (DAC).

As in continuous control systems, the control engineer must design compensators for digital control systems. The compensator is then realized as a set of difference equations programmed into the computer. Design techniques for digital systems parallel those developed for continuous systems. Compensators for single input–single output systems can be designed with transform techniques that use the root locus or Bode plot. As we shall see, however, design of digital systems is more complicated than the corresponding continuous system design. We will first review some basics of discrete-time systems analysis.

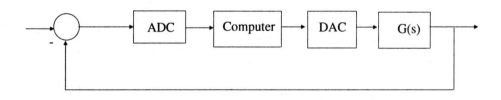

Figure 9-1 Digital control system.

9.2 Difference Equations

Dynamic behavior in a continuous system is described with differential equations. Dynamic behavior in a digital system is described with difference equations. For example, a second order difference equation might be

$$y\,[(k+2)T] - 0.7y\,[(k+1)T] + 0.1y\,[kT] \;=\; 10\,x\,[(k+2)T]$$

Difference equations are very easy to program. We can rewrite the above as

$$y\,[(k+2)T] \;=\; 0.7y\,[(k+1)T] - 0.1y\,[kT] + 10\,x\,[(k+2)T]$$

To solve this equation, we only need two registers. We initialize these registers with $y(0)$ and $y(1)$ and then write a generic program that is similar to

```
STORE Y(0) IN REGISTER A
STORE Y(1) IN REGISTER B
1  Y = 10 X - 0.1A + 0.7B
2  STORE B IN A
3  STORE Y IN B
4  RETURN TO 1
```

where each pass through this code provides the latest value of y.

The relationship between a difference equation and a differential equation can be seen by considering

$$\frac{dy}{dt} + 5y \;=\; x(t)$$

where the derivative term represents the velocity of the continuous system. Now, how could we measure velocity if we only observed the system's position every T seconds? The simplest method is to assume that velocity is constant between measurements, so that

$$\frac{dy}{dt} \approx \frac{y\,[(k+1)T] - y\,[kT]}{T}$$

If the present measurement is taken at $[(k+1)T]$, then the differential equation can be approximated by

$$\frac{y\,[(k+1)T] - y\,[kT]}{T} + 5\,y\,[(k+1)T] \;=\; x\,[(k+1)T]$$

The difference term in this equation is readily apparent. After some rearrangement of terms, we get

$$y\,[(k+1)T] \;-\; \frac{1}{1+5T}\; y\,[kT] \;=\; \frac{T}{1+5T}\; x\,[(k+1)T]$$

which has the typical appearance of a difference equation.

It is clear that the final form of the difference equation depends on the approximation we use for velocity. Later in this chapter we will discuss some other approximations and their advantages and disadvantages.

There are several ways to solve difference equations. We have seen an example of the simplest approach; write a program that determines each successive value of the output by combining past values of the output with the appropriate present and past values of the input. The problem with this method is that closed form solutions are not obtained. This makes it difficult to predict the behavior and stability of the system.

The other methods that can be used to solve difference equations parallel those for differential equations. The solution can be found in the time domain as a sum of natural and forced solutions. Frequency transform techniques can be used. Finally, the system can be modeled with the state space approach and solutions found by convolving the input with the impulse response. We finish this section by finding the natural solutions to first and second order difference equations. This will give us some insight into the stability of digital systems.

Consider the homogeneous first order difference equation with the given initial condition

$$y_{k+1} - a y_k = 0 \qquad y_0 = 1$$

where the notation y_{k+1} is shorthand for $y\,[(k+1)T]$. The characteristic equation for a difference equation is formed by replacing y_{k+n} with r^n. The characteristic equation for this first order difference equation, therefore, is

$$r - a = 0 \quad \text{so} \quad r = a$$

The natural solution for real roots of the characteristic equation is r^k. The solution for this homogeneous first order difference equation with $y_0 = 1$ is

$$y_k = a^k \quad k = 0, 1, 2, \ldots$$

It can be seen that if the magnitude of a is less than 1, the natural solution returns to 0 and the system is stable. If the magnitude of a is greater than 1, the system is unstable. Note also the interesting behavior for a negative. The system response oscillates (flip-flops between positive and negative values) even though we are dealing with a first order system. This is different from continuous systems, where no oscillations exist in a first order system.

A typical homogeneous second order difference equation is

$$y_{k+2} - a\, y_{k+1} + b\, y_k = 0$$

We have not given any initial conditions here because we are only interested in the form of the natural solution. The characteristic equation for this system is

$$r^2 - ar + b = 0$$

The two solutions to the second order characteristic equation can be real and distinct (overdamped), identical (critically damped), or complex (underdamped). The natural solution for these various cases is

$$\text{overdamped:} \quad r = r_1, r_2 \quad \rightarrow \quad y_k = C r_1{}^k + C_2 r_2{}^k$$

$$\text{critically damped:} \quad r = r_1, r_1 \quad \rightarrow \quad y_k = (C_1 + C_2 k) r_1{}^k$$

$$\text{underdamped:} \quad r = \alpha \pm j\beta = R e^{j \pm \theta} \quad \rightarrow \quad y_k = R^k (C_1 \cos \theta k + C_2 \sin \theta k)$$

It is clear from the above, that for a stable system, the magnitude of r must be less than 1.

9.3 Spectrum of Sampled Signal

A discrete signal can be constructed by sampling a continuous signal. That is, every T seconds, a switch closes for an infinitesimally short time. This results in the signals shown in Figure 9-2, where the discrete signal is given by

$$f^*(t) = f(kT) \quad \text{for } k = \dots -3, -2, -1, 0, 1, 2, 3, \dots$$

We can also mathematically model a discrete signal as the product of an impulse train and the original continuous signal (*impulse modulation*). That is,

$$f^*(t) = f(t) \sum_{k=-\infty}^{\infty} \delta(t - kT)$$

Because the impulse train is a periodic function, we can represent it with a Fourier series:

$$\sum_{k=-\infty}^{\infty} \delta(t - kT) = \frac{1}{T} \sum_{n=-\infty}^{\infty} e^{j(2\pi n/T)t}$$

We can now find the Fourier transform of the sampled signal as

$$F^*(\omega) = \int_{-\infty}^{\infty} (f(t) \frac{1}{T} \sum_{n=-\infty}^{\infty} e^{j(2\pi n/T)t}) e^{-j\omega t} dt$$

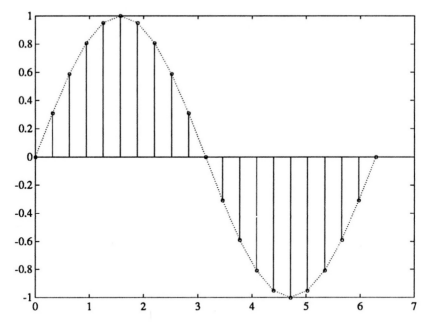

Figure 9-2 A signal and its sampled version.

After some rearranging, we get

$$F^*(\omega) = \frac{1}{T} \sum_{n=-\infty}^{\infty} \int_{-\infty}^{\infty} f(t)\, e^{-j(\omega - 2\pi n/T)t}\, dt$$

Because the Fourier transform of the original continuous signal is

$$F(\omega) = \int_{-\infty}^{\infty} f(t)\, e^{-j\omega t}\, dt$$

We find the Fourier transform of the sampled signal as

$$F^*(\omega) = \frac{1}{T} \sum_{n=-\infty}^{\infty} F(\omega - 2\pi n/T)$$

Figure 9-3 shows the relationship between the frequency content of the continuous and the sampled signals. You can see that the spectrum of the sampled signal is a periodic (in ω) replication of the continuous spectrum. This can lead to several problems in sampled systems.

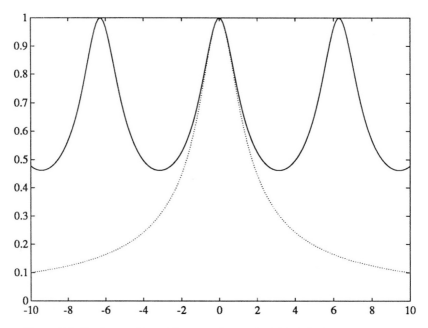

Figure 9-3 Continuous (dotted line) and discrete (solid line) frequency responses.

9.3.1 Sampling Theorem

A continuous signal can, in theory, be recovered from the sampled signal by filtering the sampled signal. The output of a low pass filter with appropriate bandwidth is the original continuous spectrum. As the sample rate decreases (sample period increases), however, the separation between succeeding cycles of the sampled spectrum decreases. If $2\pi/T < 2\omega_0$, then we get the picture shown in Figure 9-5. In this case, we cannot reconstruct the original signal with the low pass filter. This leads to the following limit on sample rate:

$$\frac{2\pi}{T} > 2\omega_0$$

where ω_0 is the highest frequency of interest in the original signal. This relationship is known as the *Nyquist*, or *Shannon*, *sampling theorem*.

9.3.2 Aliasing

In practice, of course, we cannot build ideal filters. Also, the spectrum of any real signal never ends abruptly at a given frequency. Unlike the band limited spectrum shown in Figure 9-4, all real spectra extend to plus and minus infinity. This situation is shown in Figure 9-5. There will

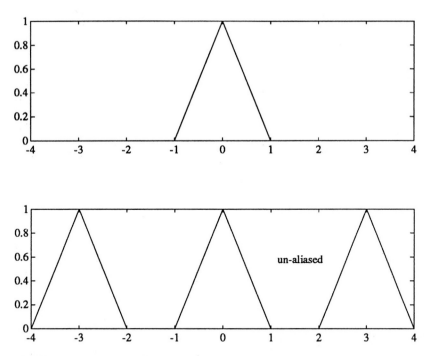

Figure 9-4 Frequency response of a band limited signal and its discrete unaliased frequeny response.

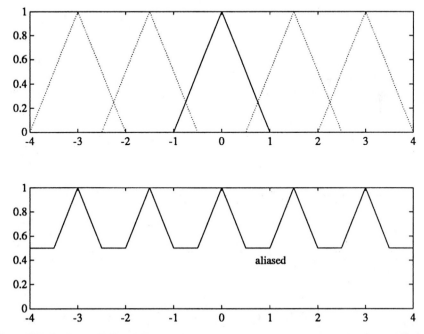

Figure 9-5 Analog and aliased discrete frequency responses of a signal that is not band-limited.

always be some overlapping between the central lobe and the sidebands of the sampled spectrum. The distortion caused by this overlap is known as *aliasing*. Because we can reduce the amount of overlap by increasing the distance between sidebands, we can reduce aliasing by sampling at a faster rate than the Nyquist rate.

Aliasing causes another problem that cannot be corrected with faster sampling. Noise in a system is often high frequency. In a continuous system, if this noise is outside the control bandwidth, it will not affect the response. When we sample a noisy signal, however, the spectrum of the noise is repeated up and down the frequency axis. That is, if the noise is centered at a frequency ω_D, then the sampled signal will contain the frequencies $\omega_D - 2\pi n/T$. No matter what you choose for the sample period, you will get noise within the control bandwidth.

To avoid the problems associated with side band overlap and high frequency noise, we often precede the sampler with an analog low pass filter. This filter, known as an *anti-aliasing filter*, reduces the high-frequency content of a signal, which minimizes the problems we have discussed. If your control system design uses an anti-aliasing filter, you want to be sure to include it in your final simulation.

9.4 The z-Transform

To apply transform techniques, we need to know the Laplace transform of the discrete signal. To find the transform, we define again the sampled signal as the product of the continuous signal and the impulse train. Now, however, we assume that the signal starts at $t = 0$. We find the Laplace transform of the sampled signal as follows:

$$F^*(s) = \int_0^\infty f^*(t)\, e^{-st} dt = \int_0^\infty \left(\sum_{k=0}^\infty f(kT)\, \delta(t - kT) \right) e^{-st} dt$$

We move the summation outside the integral to get

$$F^*(s) = \sum_{k=0}^\infty \int_0^\infty f(kT)\, e^{-st}\, \delta(t - kT)\ dt = \sum_{k=0}^\infty f(kT)\, e^{-skT}$$

We see that the Laplace transform of a sampled signal is not a rational function of s. We can define a new variable z, however, as

$$z = e^{sT}$$

Using this definition will give us $F^*(s)$ as a function of z. For ease of notation we replace $F^*(s)$ with $F(z)$. We have now defined the z-transform for a sampled signal:

$$F(z) = \sum_{k=0}^{\infty} f(kT) \, z^{-k}$$

Digital control or signal processing textbooks give extended tables of sampled signal, z-transform pairs. Some of the most basic transform pairs are given in Table 9-1 in the Appendix at the end of this chapter. More important for us is the property of the z-transform that allows us to transform a difference equation into a frequency domain (algebraic) equation

$$f[(k+1)T] \rightarrow z \, F(z) - z f(0)$$

$$f[(k+2)T] \rightarrow z^2 F(z) - z^2 f(0) - z f(1)$$

$$\cdot$$
$$\cdot$$

$$f[(k+n)T] \rightarrow z^n F(z) - z^n f(0) - \dots - z f(n-1)$$

As an example, we can transform the following zero state difference equation

$$y_{k+3} + 0.3y_{k+2} - y_{k+1} - 0.05y_k = 5x_{k+1} + x_k$$

into the frequency domain equation

$$(z^3 + 0.3z^2 - z - 0.05) \, Y(z) = (5z + 1)X(z)$$

Solving for $Y(z)$ gives us

$$Y(z) = \frac{5z + 1}{z^3 + 0.3z^2 - z - 0.05} X(z)$$

Given the z-transform of the input, we can find the output y_k by any number of inverse z-transform methods. For instance, we can use *Partial Fraction Expansion*. It is common practice to first divide $Y(z)$ by z and then perform the expansion. After the expansion coefficients are found, we multiply the result by z. The purpose of this procedure is to get factors of the form $z / (z - a)$ that are shown in Table 9-1.

Control engineers, of course, are more interested in system behavior than in specific outputs. System behavior is determined by examining the transfer function, which for this example is

$$H(z) = \frac{Y(z)}{X(z)} = \frac{5z + 1}{z^3 + 0.3z^2 - z - 0.05}$$

A control system composed of blocks of z-domain transfer functions obeys the same principles of cascade parallel and feedback combinations as continuous systems. Mason's rule, likewise, can be applied to sampled systems.

9.5 Discrete State Space Model

As with continuous systems, we can represent discrete systems with a state space model:

$$x_{k+1} = Ax_k + Bu_k$$

$$y_k = Cx_k + Du_k$$

The z-transform model can be derived from the state space model as follows. First z-transform the state space equations (assuming zero initial conditions).

$$zX(z) = A\,X(z) + B\,U(z)$$

$$Y(z) = C\,X(z) + D\,U(z)$$

Solve for $X(z)$ from the first of these equations:

$$(z\,I - A)\,X(z) = B\,U(z) \quad \rightarrow \quad X(z) = (z\,I - A)^{-1}\,B\,U(z)$$

Substitute for $X(z)$ in the output equation:

$$Y(z) = C\,(z\,I - A)^{-1}\,B\,U(z) + D\,U(z)$$

The transfer function is then given by

$$G(z) = C\,\Phi(z)\,B + D \quad \text{where} \quad \Phi(z) = (z\,I - A)^{-1}$$

Many of the useful commands in MATLAB are based on state space models. Therefore, we will often convert between transfer function models and state space models. The relevant commands are *tf2ss*, *ss2zp*, and *ss2tf*, as discussed in Chapter 5.

9.6 Mapping the s-Plane to the z-Plane

Before we start designing digital compensators, we should examine how digital poles and zeros affect stability and the step response. Because we are already familiar with how pole and zero locations in the s-plane determine stability and step response, we will examine how points in the s-plane map into the z-plane. This mapping is determined by the defining relationship between s and z:

$$z = e^{sT}$$

We first look at the s-plane $j\omega$ axis, where $s = j\omega$:

$$z = e^{j\omega T}$$

This function has a magnitude of 1.0 for all ω and an angle of ωT. As ω varies from 0 to $2\pi/T$, a circle with a radius of 1.0 is swept out in the z-plane. As ω is varied from $2\pi/T$ to $4\pi/T$, we go around the circle again. In fact, the entire infinitely long jω axis in the s-plane is mapped onto the unit circle in the z-plane.

We know that the stability region in the s-plane is the entire left half of the plane. Because $Re(s)$ in the left-hand plane is negative, the mapping is

$$z = e^{(-\alpha + j\omega)T} = e^{-\alpha T} e^{j\omega T}$$

where $Re(s) = -\alpha$. Because $e^{-\alpha T}$ is the magnitude of z, and because $e^{-\alpha T} < 1.0$, the left half of the s-plane maps into the inside of the unit circle. Therefore, we can state: "A sampled system is BIBO stable if and only if all poles of $G(z)$ lie inside the unit circle." Clearly, poles outside or on the unit circle produce unstable responses. Nonrepeated poles on the unit circle, although not BIBO stable, correspond to marginally stable systems. As with continuous systems, real poles in the z-plane produce overdamped responses, whereas complex poles produce underdamped responses. It is interesting to note the negative real axis in the s-plane maps into the real axis from 0 to 1 in the z-plane. A digital system with a pole at –0.5 in the z-plane has no corresponding continuous system.

For design purposes, the most important mappings involve the contours for constant T_s, ζ, and ω_n. An example of an s-plane and z-plane region satisfying settling time less than or equal to a given amount is shown in Figure 9-6.

In the s-plane, points on the settling time contour have a fixed negative real value; i.e.,

$$s = -\sigma + j\omega, \quad \text{where} \quad T_s \approx 5/\sigma$$

which corresponds to

$$z = e^{-\sigma T} e^{j\omega T} = R e^{j\omega T}$$

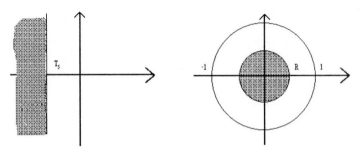

Figure 9-6 Shaded areas represent a region satisfying settling time requirement.

This contour is a circle of radius R. As R decreases, the settling time decreases.

Figure 9-7 shows the s-plane and z-plane regions satisfying damping ratio larger than a given amount. Although there is no simple way to formulate the equations for these contours, we can point out the following. Because an s-plane root of the second order characteristic equation is given by $s = -\zeta\omega_n + j\sqrt{1-\zeta^2}\,\omega_n$, the corresponding z-plane root is

$$z = e^{-\zeta\omega_n T}\, e^{\,j\sqrt{1-\zeta^2}\,\omega_n T}$$

so

$$|z| = e^{-\zeta\omega_n T} \quad \text{and} \quad \theta_z = \sqrt{1-\zeta^2}\,\omega_n T$$

If we fix ζ and let ω_n vary from 0 to π/T, the magnitude of z decreases exponentially while the phase increases linearly. This creates the logarithmic spiral for constant ζ we see in Figure 9-7.

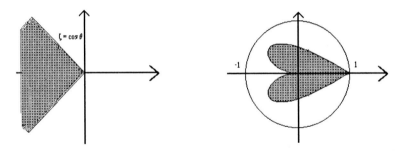

Figure 9-7 Region satisfying damping ratio requirement.

The contour for constant ω_n is more complicated. Although the magnitude of z will still decrease exponentially, the phase is not linearly dependent on ζ. The only easily determined points in the z-plane for this contour occur at $\zeta = 0$ and $\zeta = 1$. The constant contour for ω_n starts on the unit circle at an angle of $\omega_n T$ and ends on the real axis with a magnitude of $e^{-\omega_n T}$. It may help to note that this contour is always perpendicular to the constant ζ contours that it intersects. The region satisfying a constraint for ω_n less than a given amount is shown in Figure 9-8.

A region satisfying settling time and ω_n constraints simultaneously is shown in Figure 9-9.

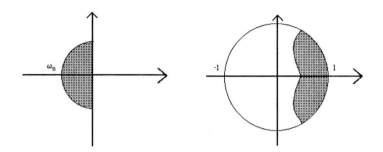

Figure 9-8 Region satisfying natural frequency constraint.

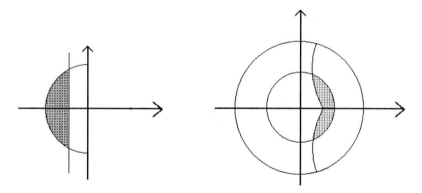

Figure 9-9 Region satisfying settling time and natural frequency constraints.

9.7 System Type and Steady State Error

A z-transform property that is very useful is the final value theorem:

$$\text{Final Value Theorem:}\quad \lim_{k \to \infty} f(kT) = \lim_{z \to 1} (z - 1)\, F(z)$$

We can use the final value theorem to find the steady state error constants for a unity feedback digital control system. The error for such a system is

$$E(z) = \frac{1}{1 + G(z)}\, R(z)$$

where $G(z)$ is the forward path gain, and $R(z)$ is the input to the system. We begin with a discrete step input:

$$E(z) = \frac{1}{1 + G(z)} \frac{z}{z - 1}$$

The steady state error is

$$e(\infty) = \frac{1}{1 + G(1)}$$

If $G(1)$ is finite, then this system can track a step with constant error. This is a Type 0 system and we define the error constant K_p so that

$$\text{Type 0:} \quad e(\infty) = \frac{1}{1 + K_p} \qquad K_p = G(1)$$

For a ramp input, $r(t) = kT$, the error is

$$E(z) = \frac{1}{1 + G(z)} \frac{zT}{(z - 1)^2}$$

The final error is

$$e(\infty) = \lim_{z \to 1} \frac{1}{1 + G(z)} \frac{zT}{z - 1}$$

If $G(z)$ has no poles at $z = 1$, then the steady state error will be infinite. If $G(z)$ has one pole at $z = 1$, then the steady state error will be finite and equal to

$$e(\infty) = \frac{T}{(z - 1) G(z)} \bigg|_{z = 1}$$

This is a Type 1 system, and we define the steady state error constant K_v so that

$$\text{Type 1:} \quad e(\infty) = \frac{1}{K_v} \qquad K_v = \frac{(z - 1)}{T} G(z)\big|_{z = 1}$$

For a digital unity feedback system, the system type is equal to the number of poles at $z = 1$. We can extend the above procedure to find the error constants for all system types:

$$K_n = \frac{(z - 1)^n}{T^n} G(z)\big|_{z = 1}$$

where the system input is $r(k) = \dfrac{(kT)^n}{n!}$, and n is the system type.

An important and simplifying note: If $G(s)$ is digitized using the zero order hold (ZOH) equivalence (to be discussed shortly), then $G(s)$ and $G(z)$ have the same error constant. Because this is the usual technique for digitizing a plant model, we can find the plant error constant from the s-plane model.

9.8 Simulation of Digital Control Systems

Digital control systems usually contain both digital and continuous elements. In the frequency domain, digital elements are modeled with the z-transform and continuous elements with the Laplace transform. We must, therefore, make some compromises to combine these elements into a single systems analysis. Because of these compromises, frequency domain design techniques in digital systems must be verified by a complete time domain simulation of the system. Simulink (Chapter 6) allows the user to model the continuous and digital components, including such parameters as finite word length, as they are actually used in the system.

When we model digital systems, we convert continuous transfer functions represented by $G(s)$ into an "equivalent" discrete transfer function $G(z)$. We enclose the word equivalent in quotation marks because it is not possible for a $G(z)$ to match exactly the behavior of the $G(s)$ from whence it was derived. If the digital model produces the same impulse response as the continuous model, it will not match the step response. If it matches the step response, it will not match the impulse response. The frequency response of the digital model never exactly matches the frequency response of the continuous model.

Several techniques exist for discretizing continuous systems. Among them are time response matching (impulse and step), and numerical integration methods such as Euler backward, forward, and trapezoidal. Each one has its advantages and pitfalls. As mentioned earlier, some preserve the time response, whereas others better preserve the frequency response. From a control view point, stability preservation is very important; some techniques preserve stability, whereas others do not. Techniques that do not preserve the system stability have to be used very cautiously, or misleading simulations will result.

9.8.1 Impulse Invariant Transformation

Impulse invariant transformation converts a continuous system to a discrete one by matching their impulse responses. Consider the continuous transfer function and its impulse response:

$$H(s) = \frac{10}{s+5}, \qquad h(t) = 10\, e^{-5t} u(t)$$

The sampled version of this impulse response and its z-transform is

$$h(nT) = 10 \, e^{-5nT} u(nT) , \qquad H(z) = \frac{10 \, z}{z - e^{-5T}}$$

The procedure we use to preserve the impulse response when we represent a continuous plant with a digital model is the following:

> Find the impulse response from $H(s)$; let $t = nT$ to convert the continuous response to the discrete response; transform the discrete impulse response into $H(z)$.

The conversion can also be done in state space form. The impulse response of a continuous system and the pulse response of a discrete system are given by

$$h(t) = C \, e^{At} B + D \, \delta(t) , \quad h(nT) = C_d \, A_d^{n-1} B_d + (D_d - C_d A \, \bar{}_d^1 B_d) \, \delta(nT)$$

Now, sample $h(t)$ (by letting $t = nT$) to convert the continuous response to the discrete response. Comparing the two responses, we conclude that

$$\boxed{A_d = e^{AT}, \quad B_d = e^{AT} B, \quad C_d = C, \quad D_d = D + C B}$$

You can write a function to perform this conversion.

9.8.2 Zero Order Hold Equivalence

In practice, a discrete signal never directly drives a continuous filter or plant. The discrete signal is first passed through a digital-to-analog converter (DAC). The DAC produces a continuous output that reflects its discrete input. The simplest and most commonly used DACs are devices that convert the binary computer output to a voltage level and then hold that level until the computer outputs the next data word T seconds later. This device is known as a zero order hold (ZOH). The output of the ZOH reconstruction of the signal shown in Figure 9-2 is shown in Figure 9-10.

The zero order hold creates an output pulse for each input impulse. Because a step is derived from an impulse by integration, we get the ZOH transfer function (Laplace transform of a unit pulse of duration T):

$$\text{ZOH:} \quad \frac{1 - e^{-sT}}{s}$$

The delay term resets the integrator before the next impulse comes in. The total transfer function between the switch output and the plant output, therefore, is

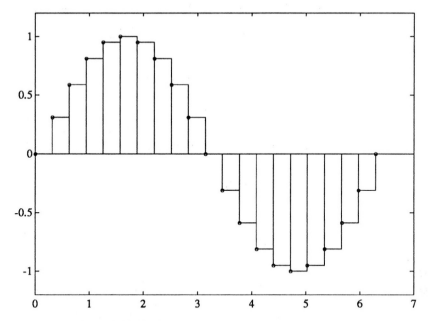

Figure 9-10 ZOH reconstruction of the signal in Figure 9-2.

$$\frac{1 - e^{-sT}}{s} \, G(s)$$

Whenever there is a ZOH preceding a plant, we take the z-transform of the above as follows. First note that

$$\mathbf{Z} \left\{ \frac{1 - e^{-sT}}{s} G(s) \right\} = \mathbf{Z} \left\{ \frac{G(s)}{s} \right\} - \mathbf{Z} \left\{ \frac{e^{-sT} G(s)}{s} \right\}$$

The second term in preceding expression is the delayed version of the first term. Because the z-transform of a unit delay is z^{-1}, we get

$$\boxed{G(z)_{ZOH} = (1 - z^{-1}) \, \mathbf{Z} \left\{ \frac{G(s)}{s} \right\}}$$

To find the z-transform of an s-domain transfer function $G(s)$, we perform the following operations: Find $g(t)$ from $G(s)$, replace t by nT; take the z-transform to obtain $G(z)$.

We will use this procedure on $G(s)/s$ to find ZOH equivalent transfer function. Consider the following simple example :

$$G(s) = \frac{1}{s+1}$$

$$G(z)_{ZOH} = (1 - z^{-1}) \; Z \left\{ \frac{1}{s\,(s+1)} \right\}$$

$$L^{-1} \left\{ \frac{1}{s\,(s+1)} \right\} = (1 - e^{-t})\,u(t) \;\;\Rightarrow\;\; Z \left\{ (1 - e^{-nT})\,u(nT) \right\} = \frac{z\,(1 - e^{-T})}{(z-1)\,(z - e^{-T})}$$

$$G(z)_{ZOH} = (1 - z^{-1}) \; \frac{z\,(1 - e^{-T})}{(z-1)\,(z - e^{-T})} = \frac{1 - e^{-T}}{z - e^{-T}}$$

The zero order hold equivalent is also known as the *step invariant* transformation, because it matches the step response of a discrete system to a continuous one. It is, by far, the most common technique used by control engineers. Table 9-2 in the Appendix at the end of this chapter shows some simple ZOH equivalents. This discretization can also be obtained in state space (see the exercises). The ZOH state space matrices are given by

$$A_d = e^{AT}, \quad B_d = \int_0^T e^{A\sigma} B\,d\sigma, \quad C_d = C, \quad D_d = D$$

If we use the series expansion of the matrix exponential, perform the integration, and use some matrix algebra, we can show that the discrete B matrix can be computed from

$$B_d = A^{-1}\,[\,A_d - I\,]\,B = e^{\left[\begin{smallmatrix} A & B \\ 0 & 0 \end{smallmatrix}\right] T}$$

The final form requires only matrix operations. The ZOH is the default discretization technique used by the Control System Toolbox of MATLAB.

9.8.3 Numerical Integration Methods

To convert analog filters to equivalent digital filters, we are most interested in maintaining the frequency response of the original transfer function. The most common techniques that attempt to maintain the frequency response of the digitized transfer function can be derived from approximations of the integral or derivative; they are *forward Euler*, *backward Euler*, and *trapezoidal*. With these techniques we replace s everywhere in $H(s)$ with a function of z.

Consider the following situation. We want to know our present position, $y(kT)$, given that we knew where we were T seconds ago and we know the velocity, V, has been constant over this interval. We can then write

$$V = \frac{y\,[kT] - y\,[(k-1)T]}{T}$$

We have several choices for V. We can use the velocity at kT seconds, the velocity at $(k-1)T$ seconds, or the average of the two. The first of these yields the approximation known as backward Euler:

$$v\,[kT] = \frac{y\,[kT] - y\,[(k-1)T]}{T}$$

Taking the z-transform of the above:

$$V(z) = \frac{z-1}{Tz}\,Y(z)$$

In the continuous domain, velocity is represented by $sY(s)$. By comparison, we can derive a relationship between s and z.

Backward Euler:	$s \approx \dfrac{z-1}{Tz}$

Using the velocity at $(k-1)T$ seconds gives us

$$v\,[(k-1)T] = \frac{y\,[kT] - y\,[(k-1)T]}{T} \qquad \rightarrow \qquad z^{-1}\,V(z) = \frac{1-z^{-1}}{T}\,Y(z)$$

and we get

Forward Euler:	$s \approx \dfrac{z-1}{T}$

Using the average value of the beginning and ending velocity, we get

Trapezoidal:	$s \approx \dfrac{2}{T}\dfrac{z-1}{z+1}$

The trapezoidal transformation is known as the *bilinear* or *Tustin's* transformation. Tustin's transformation is the most commonly used technique for converting an analog filter to a digital one.

These transforms can also be done using matrix operations in state space. For example, consider the backward Euler's method. The continuous state space equation in the s-domain is

$$s\, X(s) = A\, X(s) + B\, U(s)$$

$$Y(s) = CX(s) + DU(s)$$

Now, replace s by $(z - 1)/Tz$, and apply inverse z-transform to get the approximating difference equation:

$$\frac{z-1}{Tz} X(z) = A\, X(z) + B\, U(z) \quad \rightarrow \quad x\, [(k+1)T] = \Psi\, x(kT) + \Psi\, T\, B\, u\, [(k+1)T]$$

where $\Psi = (I - TA)^{-1}$.

To obtain a state space representation, we define

$$\eta\, (kT) = x\, (kT) - \Psi\, T\, B\, u\, (kT)$$

Now, rewrite the state equations in terms of the new state, $\eta\, (kT)$:

$$\eta\, [(k+1)\, T] = \Psi\, \eta\, (kT) + \Psi^2\, T\, B\, u\, (kT)$$

$$y\, (kT) = C\, \eta\, (kT) + (\, C\, \Psi\, T\, B + D\,)\, u\, (kT)$$

Hence, the discrete state space matrices are

$$\boxed{A_d = \Psi\, , \quad B_d = \Psi^2\, T\, B\, , \quad C_d = C\, , \quad D_d = C\, \Psi\, T\, B + D\, , \quad \Psi = (I - TA)^{-1}}$$

Matrices for Tustin and forward Euler can also be derived (see the exercises).

There are some additional points to consider when comparing these three techniques. The first point is that the forward Euler technique does not always preserve stability. For example, consider the stable continuous filter:

$$H(s) = \frac{1}{s+1} \quad \rightarrow \quad \text{pole} = -1$$

The forward Euler transformation is

$$H(z) = \frac{T}{z - 1 + T} \quad \rightarrow \quad \text{pole} = 1 - T$$

If T is greater than 2, the discrete pole lies outside the unit circle, and the filter response will be unstable. Forward Euler can produce a numerically unstable system from a stable continuous system. This is only a problem for slow sample rates.

It is instructive to solve for z from each of the transformation techniques:

$$\text{forward Euler:} \quad z = 1 + sT$$

$$\text{backward Euler:} \quad z = \frac{1}{1 - sT}$$

$$\text{Tustin:} \quad z = \frac{1 + sT/2}{1 - sT/2}$$

The forward Euler is actually the first two terms in the Taylor series expansion of the exponential (remember $z = e^{sT}$). The Tustin transformation is the *Pade* approximation to the exponential.

We know that the $j\omega$ axis in the s-plane maps into the unit circle in the z-plane. Neither of the Euler techniques preserves this mapping. The Tustin technique does, however. To see this, let $s = j\omega$ in the Tustin approximation:

$$z = \frac{1 + j\omega T/2}{1 - j\omega T/2}$$

From this equation we find the magnitude and phase as

$$|z| = 1 \quad \text{and} \quad \theta_z = 2 \tan \omega T/2$$

As ω increases, the phase increases while the magnitude stays constant at 1.0. Thus, a unit circle is swept out. Tustin's suffers from another problem, however, known as *warping*, which will be discussed in Section 9.10.

9.9 MATLAB Discrete Commands

Most control system commands in MATLAB have equivalent discrete versions. The discrete version of these commands usually starts with the letter d, such as *dstep, dnyquist, dbode*, and others. The syntax and usage of the discrete commands is almost identical to their continuous counterparts. When they are different, we will discuss them in more detail. The most important commands are *c2d* and *c2dm*. Their syntaxes are given by

```
>> [ad,db]=c2d(a,b,ts)
>> [ad,bd,cd,dd]=c2dm(a,b,c,d,ts, 'method')
>> [numz,denz]=c2dm(num,den,ts, 'method')
```

The *c2d* command uses the ZOH technique for discretization. It is only available in state space form. The *c2dm* command (available in both transfer function and state space forms) will convert a continuous system to a discrete one using one of five methods. The parameter `ts` is the sampling period. The `method` option allows the user to choose one of five techniques: *zoh, foh, matched, tustin,* and *prewarp*. We have already discussed *zoh* and *tustin*; *foh* (first-order hold) is a generalization of zero order hold. We assume the control inputs are piecewise linear (rather than constant) over the sampling period. The *prewarp* method is discussed in the next section; the *matched* technique is discussed in Problem 9.15. If no method is specified, then *zoh* method is assumed.

The discrete step response (*dstep*) command has the following syntax:

```
>> [y,x]=dstep(a,b,c,d,ui,n)
>> [y,x]=dstep(num,den,n)
```

The input arguments u i (input channel specified for multi-input systems) and n (number of samples) are both optional. Without left-hand arguments plots are generated automatically. All comments made about the *step* command also apply here. Other time response commands are *dimpulse, dinitial,* and *dlsim*.

Time responses for discrete systems are typically plotted using the *stairs* command. This command produces staircase plots similar to Figure 9-10. It has the following syntax forms:

```
>> stairs(y)    or    stairs(x,y)
>> [xs,ys]=stairs(y)    or    stairs(x,y)
```

Without left-hand arguments, plots are generated. With two input arguments, y will be plotted at points specified in the vector x. If left-hand arguments are specified, data will be returned; you can then use the *plot* command to customize your staircase plots.

Frequency response of discrete systems can be obtained using the *dbode* command (*dnyquist* and *dnichols* are also available). It has the following syntax forms:

```
>> [mag,phase]=dbode(a,b,c,d,ts,ui,w)
>> [mag,phase]=dbode(num,den,ts,w)
```

All comments made about the *bode* command apply here. The only additional input is t s, the sampling period.

Root locus of discrete and continuous systems are similar. The only difference is the coordinate system. The rectangular coordinate system is used for continuous systems, whereas polar coordinates are used for discrete systems. The following command, *zgrid*, sets up the damping ratio and natural frequency lines within the unit circle; it sets *hold* on to overlay the root locus:

```
>> zgrid('new')
```

Other appropriate commands are *ddcgain* (for computing DC gain), *drmodel* (create a random and stable model), *dsort* (sort complex eigenvalues in a vector by magnitude), and *ddamp*. The *ddamp* command with the following syntax:

```
>> ddamp(a,ts)
```

returns the eigenvalues of the matrix a (or roots of the polynomial if a is a vector), their magnitudes, and their *s*-plane equivalent damping ratios and natural frequencies.

The following example compares the step response of an original continuous model and its digital ZOH model.

Example 9.1 Response of Impulse Matched and ZOH Transfer Function

Use ZOH to convert $G(s)$ to $G(z)$ with $T = 0.1$ sec. Compare the step responses of $G(s)$ and $G(z)$:

$$G(s) = \frac{10}{(s+2)(s+5)}$$

We first find the continuous and discrete step responses:

$$g(t) = (1 - \frac{5}{3} e^{-2t} + \frac{2}{3} e^{-5t}) u(t)$$

$$g(nt) = (1 - \frac{5}{3} e^{-0.2n} + \frac{2}{3} e^{-0.5n}) u(nT)$$

You can verify the following ZOH transform analytically:

```
>> nc=10; dc=[1 7 10]; ts=0.1;
>> [n_zoh,d_zoh]=c2dm(nc,dc,ts)

n_zoh =
      0   0.0398   0.0315
d_zoh =
  1.0000  -1.4253   0.4966
```

Before we find the step response for $G(z)$, we will determine the response for the continuous $G(s)$. We will use the *step* command and also generate the continuous responses by programming the actual step response, $g(t)$:

```
>> i=[0:35]'; gc=1-(5/3)*exp(-0.2*i)+(2/3)*exp(-0.5*i);
>> yc=step(nc,dc,i*ts); time=i*ts;
>> g_zoh=dstep(n_zoh,d_zoh,36);
>> stairs(time,g_zoh), hold, plot(time,[gc y])
```

Figure 9-11 shows that the continuous and ZOH equivalent step responses are identical. This digitization technique always produces the same step response as the continuous system.

The next example compares the frequency response of the ZOH equivalent and the continuous system. As we shall see, the fidelity of the frequency response depends very much on the sample rate.

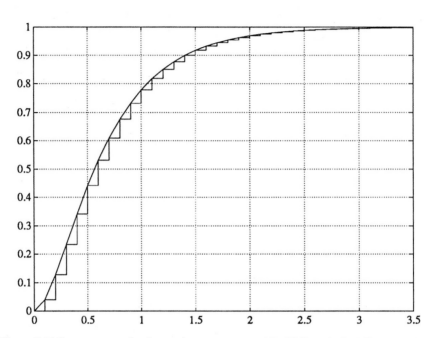

Figure 9-11 Step responses for the continuous system and its ZOH equivalent discrete system.

Example 9.2   Frequency Response of the ZOH Equivalent

Use the ZOH equivalent to digitize $H(s) = \dfrac{10}{s+1}$ for the sample periods $T = 1, 0.5,$ and 0.1 sec. Compare the Bode plots for the continuous and three discrete transfer functions.

Because the code is simple, we only show a few lines:

```
>> w=linspace(0,10); mc=bode(nc,dc,w);
>> [nz1,dz1]=c2dm(nc,dc,1); mz1=dbode(nz1,dz1,1,w);
```

Figure 9-12 shows the result. Several interesting properties can be seen in the figure. First, the frequency response of the ZOH equivalent depends very much on the sample period. As the sample period decreases, the ZOH equivalent approaches the continuous frequency response. At larger sample periods, the frequency response appears to be cyclical.

We have discussed earlier the importance of sampling at a rate greater than the Nyquist rate. For this transfer function, the bandwidth is 1.0 rad/ sec. Therefore, we should sample at least at 2 rad/sec. In other words, the maximum sample period should be

$$T_{\max} = \frac{2\pi}{2} \approx 3.14 \text{ sec}$$

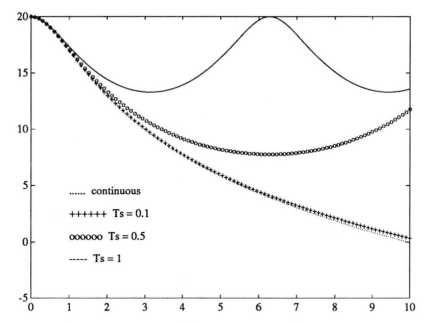

Figure 9-12 Frequency responses of ZOH for T = 1, 0.5, 0.1, and the continuous system.

Even at our slowest sample rate ($T = 1$ sec), we are still sampling at 3 times the Nyquist rate. To achieve a good frequency fit, however, we need to sample at 30 times the sample rate! Clearly, the ZOH equivalence is not good at maintaining the frequency response of the original continuous transfer function.

The cyclical nature of the frequency response of the discrete transfer function is not due to the digitization technique used. It is inherent in all z-transform transfer functions. To see this, consider the simple transfer function

$$H(z) = \frac{1}{z - 0.5}$$

Because $z = e^{sT}$ and $s = j\omega$, we find the frequency response of the discrete transfer function from

$$H_z(\omega) = \frac{1}{e^{j\omega T} - 0.5}$$

The function $e^{j\omega T}$ repeats itself, however, whenever $\omega T = 0,\ 2\pi,\ 4\pi,\ \ldots$. Therefore, the transfer function will repeat itself at the frequency intervals

$$\omega = \frac{2\pi}{T}, \frac{4\pi}{T}, \cdots$$

That is, all discrete Bode plots are periodic and repeat at the sample rate ($2\pi/T$). There is no such thing as a true low-pass digital filter. At best, a digital filter will exhibit its expected behavior only for frequency values significantly less than the sampling rate.

When do we use the ZOH equivalence? We usually use this technique only to model a continuous plant. This is because we are most often interested in the time response of the plant. We rarely use the ZOH equivalence to convert a continuous filter to a digital filter, because we have seen that this technique does not faithfully reproduce frequency response and we design filters for their frequency response characteristics.

9.10 The Warping Problem

Consider the following continuous filter with a bandwidth of a:

$$H(s) = \frac{1}{s/a + 1}$$

The Tustin's transformation of this filter yields

$$H(z) = \frac{1}{\dfrac{2}{T}\dfrac{z-1}{z+1}\dfrac{1}{a} + 1}$$

To find the frequency response of the digital filter, we let $z = e^{j\omega T}$. Before we return to $H(z)$, let us examine

$$\frac{z-1}{z+1} \quad \rightarrow \quad \frac{e^{j\omega T} - 1}{e^{j\omega T} + 1}$$

If we factor out $e^{j\omega/2}$ from the numerator and denominator, we get

$$\frac{z-1}{z+1} \quad \rightarrow \quad \frac{2j\sin \omega T/2}{2\cos \omega T/2} = j\tan \frac{\omega T}{2}$$

For $s = j\omega$, our discrete filter becomes

$$H_z(\omega) = \frac{1}{j\left(\dfrac{2}{T}\tan \omega \dfrac{T}{2}\right)\dfrac{1}{a} + 1}$$

Because the bandwidth of a first order filter is the frequency at which the imaginary term equals the real term, we get the bandwidth of the discrete filter as

$$\omega_{BW} = \frac{2}{T} \tan^{-1}\left(\frac{aT}{2}\right)$$

This formula gives us the relationship between the continuous and discrete equivalent bandwidths. It is also known as the *warping formula*, and shows how the frequency scale is distorted (or warped) by the Tustin transformation. As we sample faster and faster, T gets smaller and smaller. Because the arctan of a small number is equal to that number, we conclude that at a high sample rate, the discrete filter has the same bandwidth as the continuous filter. For the lower sample rates we often use in control systems, however, the digitized filter can have a significantly different bandwidth from the original continuous filter.

9.10.1 Prewarping

The warping problem has been addressed by *prewarping* the continuous filter before we digitize. This is done by replacing a in $H(s)$ with $\bar{a}$, where $\bar{a}$ is defined as

$$prewarping: \quad \bar{a} = \frac{2}{T} \tan \frac{aT}{2}$$

If we replace the original continuous filter with

$$H_{pw}(s) = \frac{1}{s/\bar{a} + 1}$$

and then apply Tustin's transformation to this filter, the resulting discrete filter will have the same bandwidth as the original $H(s)$.

Note that if we apply prewarping to a filter $H(s)$ to get $H_{pw}(s)$

$$H(s) = \frac{K}{s + a} \quad \Rightarrow \quad H_{pw}(s) = \frac{K}{s + \bar{a}}$$

and then use Tustin's, we will get the correct bandwidth. We have changed the low frequency gain, however. To avoid this, we first divide through by a and then apply prewarping to

$$H(s) = \frac{K/a}{s/a + 1} \quad \Rightarrow \quad H_{pw}(s) = \frac{K/\bar{a}}{s/\bar{a} + 1}$$

Example 9.3   Tustin's with Prewarping

Use Tustin's with prewarping to digitize $H(s)$ for sample periods of 0.5 and 1.0 sec:

$$H(s) = \frac{10}{s+2}$$

We first divide through by 2 to get

$$H(s) = \frac{5}{s/2 + 1}$$

For $T = 0.5$ sec, we get, $\bar{a}_1 = \frac{2}{0.5} \tan \frac{2 \times 0.5}{2} = 2.1852$. Hence, using *c2dm* with *tustin* we get

$$H_1(s) = \frac{5}{s/2.1852 + 1} \qquad \rightarrow \qquad H_1(z) = 1.7665 \frac{z+1}{z-0.2934}$$

The above steps have been shown for demonstration only. The *c2dm* command using the *prewarp* method simplifies the process as shown next:

```
>> ts1=0.5; ts2=1.0; nc=10; dc=[1 2];
>> [nz1,dz1]=c2dm(nc,dc,ts1,'p',2); [nz2,dz2]=c2dm(nc,dc,ts2,'p',2);
>> printsys(nz1,dz1,'z')
```

num/den =
  1.766 z + 1.766
  ----
   z - 0.293

```
>> printsys(nz2,dz2,'z')
```

num/den =
  3.045 z + 3.045
  ----
   z + 0.218

Note the use of the *printsys* command with the '*z*' option for displaying discrete transfer functions. Also, the first letter of the method (e.g., '*p*' for '*prewarp*') is sufficient. Figure 9-13 shows the Bode plots for the continuous $H(s)$ and the digitized versions of the two prewarped transfer functions. As predicted, all three plots have the same bandwidth. It is clear, however, that the complete frequency responses for the three transfer functions are quite different.

The procedure we have just derived for prewarping is not so easily applied when digitizing higher order transfer functions. Do we prewarp each pole and zero? Do we try to maintain the center frequency of a band-pass filter, or the bandwidth, or both? The bottom line is that we can force a digitized version of a continuous transfer function to

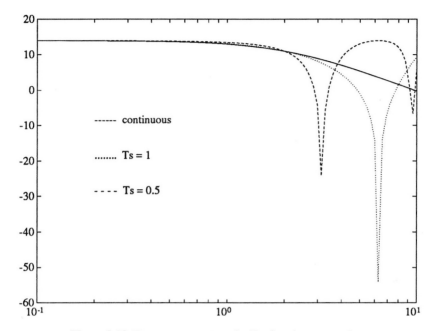

Figure 9-13 Frequency responses for Tustin using prewarping.

match the original transfer function at a single frequency only. We either have to live with the rest of the digitized frequency response, play with the parameters of the continuous transfer function before digitizing, or design the filter directly in the z-plane.

The best solution is to design the filter, or compensator, directly in the z-plane. This we will do in the next section. However, control engineers are still often faced with the task of replacing an analog compensator with its digital equivalent. The following modification, known as *critical frequency prewarping*, provides a reasonable method for doing this.

9.10.2 Critical Frequency Prewarping

Let us revisit the Tustin approximation for s:

$$s \approx K \frac{z-1}{z+1}$$

where $K = 2/T$ in the standard approximation. We state the problem as follows: Can we find a K so that that at a specific frequency the above approximation becomes exact? The frequency we choose is one that we determine is critical to our filter design; i.e., $\omega = \omega_c$. Letting $s = j\,\omega_c$

$$j\,\omega_c \;=\; j\,K\,\tan\frac{\omega_c T}{2}$$

Clearly, if we choose

$$K \;=\; \frac{\omega_c}{\tan\,\omega_c T/2}$$

$H(s)$ and $H(z)$ will be identical at $\omega = \omega_c$. The critical frequency prewarping technique, therefore, is

$$\boxed{\;Critical\ Frequency\ Prewarping:\ s \;\rightarrow\; \frac{\omega_c}{\tan\,\omega_c T/2}\;\frac{z-1}{z+1}\;}$$

Note that as T gets small, this transformation approaches the regular Tustin's approximation. The *c2dm* command using the *prewarp* method accomplishes this. The next example will show the use of critical frequency warping in digitizing a notch filter.

Example 9.4 Critical Frequency Prewarping

For the sample period $T = 0.1$ sec, digitize the notch filter

$$H(s) = \frac{s^2 + 0.2s + 100}{s^2 + 10s + 100}$$

We note the notch occurs at 10 rad/sec, which becomes our critical frequency. We will obtain Bode magnitude plots of the continuous filter, the unwarped digital notch filter at $T = 0.1$ sec and the prewarped filter.

Prewarping at the critical frequency results in the following filter:

```
>> nc=[1 0.2 100]; dc=[1 10 100]; [nz1,dz1]=c2dm(nc,dc,0.1,'p',10)

nz1 =
   0.7098  -0.7606   0.6979
dz1 =
   1.0000  -0.7606   0.4077
```

The digital (not prewarped) filter for T = 0.1 is given by

```
>> [nz2,dz2]=c2dm(nc,dc,0.1,'t')

nz2 =
   0.7200  -0.8571   0.7086
dz2 =
   1.0000  -0.8571   0.4286
```

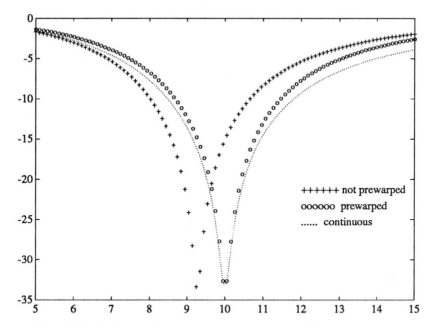

Figure 9-14 Analog and digital notch filters showing the effects of prewarping.

Figure 9-14 shows the plots of the original and digitized magnitudes. Only with critical frequency prewarping have we achieved the goal of maintaining the notch frequency. Note, however, that we cannot control the bandwidth or other parameters with this (or any) digitization technique.

9.11 Digital Compensators

There are several methods for designing digital compensators:

1. Conversion of a classically designed continuous compensator into an equivalent digital compensator.
2. Direct design of a digital compensator using frequency transform techniques.
3. Direct design of a digital compensator using state-space techniques.

As we have seen in the previous sections, great care must be taken with the first method. Conversion of a continuous compensator to a digital compensator is most often accomplished with Tustin's, with or without prewarping. At very high sample rates, these techniques have proved very effective. At lower sample rates, however, this conversion usually creates unexpected problems. This happens because the digital compensator has significantly different response characteristics from the original continuous compensator.

Design in the z-plane more often allows the designer to incorporate the effects of the sample period. The most useful technique here is the root locus. We have already seen that frequency response plots of z-domain transfer functions are not as well behaved as their continuous counterparts. Later, however, we will introduce another transformation, the w-transform, which will allow us to use Bode plots for digital design.

9.11.1 Proportional-Integral-Derivative Control

The proportional-integral-derivative (PID) controller, introduced in Chapter 7, is as effective in digital systems as it is in continuous systems. In fact, it is the most popular and commercially available controller used in the process industry. The integral controller increases the system type, which reduces steady state error. The derivative controller increases the damping and, hence, the stability of the system. The most common discrete PID controller has the following form:

$$PID \qquad K_p + K_D \frac{(z-1)}{zT} + K_I \frac{zT}{z-1}$$

In this formulation, velocity is found as the difference between present and past value divided by the sample period, $(1 - z^{-1})/T$. The integral term assumes that we are finding the area under a constant value over the period T.

The Ziegler–Nichols method, described in Chapter 7, can also be used here. Do not forget to include the sample period in the controller formulation.

First, set $K_d = K_I = 0$ and then increase the proportional gain until the system just oscillates (i.e., closed loop poles on the unit circle in the z-plane). The proportional gain is then multiplied by 0.6, and the other two gains are calculated as

$$\boxed{K_p = 0.6\, K_m \qquad K_D = \frac{K_p \pi}{4\, \omega_m} \qquad K_I = \frac{K_p\, \omega_m}{\pi}}$$

where K_m is the gain at which the proportional system oscillates and ω_m is the oscillation frequency. The oscillation frequency can be found from the angle of the pole that crosses the unit circle; i.e., $\omega_m = \theta/T$. The oscillation frequency can also be found by running a closed loop step response with $K_p = K_m$.

Note that this technique does not design to any specifications. Rather, Ziegler and Nichols found that this design procedure provided "good" behavior for process controllers.

Example 9.5 PID Design with Ziegler–Nichols

Design a digital PID controller for $G(s)$ with a sample period of $T = 0.25$ sec:

$$G(s) = \frac{10}{s(s+2)}$$

Remember always to use the ZOH equivalent to digitize a plant. We then run a root locus on $G(z)$ to determine K_m and ω_m. Finally, we calculate the PID controller parameters and run a step response. Using *rlocus* and *rlocfind* we find

```
>> ts=0.25; ng=10; dg=[1 2 0]; [ng_z,dg_z]=c2dm(ng,dg,ts)
>> axis('square'), zgrid('new'), rlocus(ng_z,dg_z)
>> [km,pole]=rlocfind(ng_z,dg_z)
```

```
km =
  1.7046
pole =
  0.5763 + 0.8117i
  0.5763 - 0.8117i
```

Therefore, the system starts oscillating at a gain of 1.7. The oscillation frequency is given by

```
>> wm=angle(pole(1))/ts
```

```
wm =
  3.8137
```

The root locus is shown in Figure 9-15. Then km and wm are used to find the PID parameters.

```
kp =
  1.0228
kd =
  0.2106
ki =
  1.2416
```

We then form the compensator and use the *series* and *cloop* commands to find the open and closed loop transfer functions. The *ddamp* command shows all the pertinent information about the behavior of the compensated system:

```
>> ddamp(dt,ts)
```

Eigenvalue	Magnitude	Equiv. Damping	Equiv. Freq. (rad/sec)
0.4796 + 0.6693i	0.8234	0.2006	3.8747
0.4796 −0.6693i	0.8234	0.2006	3.8747
0.6034	0.6034	1.0000	2.0210
0.4645	0.4645	1.0000	3.0673

The compensated root locus and the step response are shown in Figures 9-16 and 9-17. The small damping ratio explains the 90% overshoot in the step response. The response appears

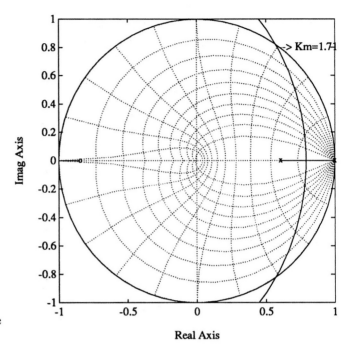

Figure 9-15 The uncompensated root locus for the Ziegler–Nichols design.

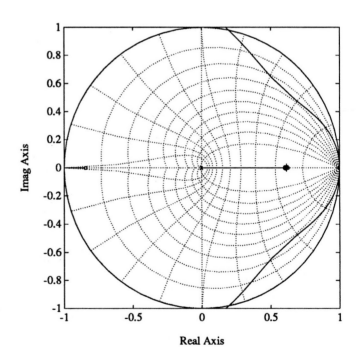

Figure 9-16 The compensated root locus for the Ziegler–Nichols design.

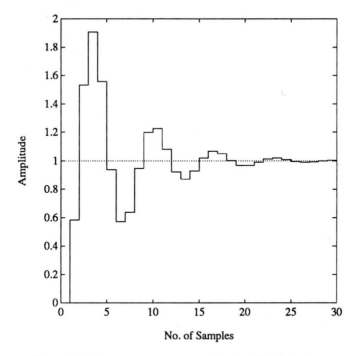

Figure 9-17 The step response of the Ziegler–Nichols design.

to have settled after 20 samples; i.e. the settling time is about 5 sec (settling time = number of samples $\times$ sampling period). Using the *rlocfind* command on the compensated root locus, we find that the system becomes unstable for a gain of 3.4, resulting in a gain margin of 10 dB.

9.11.2 PID—Analytical Technique

The analytical technique we discussed in Chapter 7 was based on phase margin calculations. This procedure will not work easily here. We can derive a new analytical procedure, however, that is based on the root locus technique.

We first determine K_I from the steady state error requirement. Next we determine the desired z-plane point, z_1, from the time domain specifications. If z_1 is to be on the root locus, then

$$(K_p + K_D \frac{z_1 - 1}{z_1 T} + K_I \frac{z_1 T}{z_1 - 1}) G(z_1) = -1$$

Because K_I and z_1 are known,

$$K_p + K_D \frac{z_1 - 1}{z_1 T} = -\frac{1}{G(z_1)} - K_I \frac{z_1 T}{z_1 - 1}$$

The preceding is a complex equation. Equating the real and imaginary parts of the equation results in two equations in two unknowns. Let R and X denote the real and imaginary parts of the right-hand side of the preceding equation and define

$$\alpha + j\beta = \frac{z_1 - 1}{z_1 T}$$

We find that $K_p + K_D (\alpha + j\beta) = R + jX$
Hence,

$$K_D = X/\beta \quad , \quad K_p = R - \alpha K_D$$

Example 9.6 PID Analytical Design

Given $G(s)$, design a PID controller satisfying the following requirements:

$T = 0.25$ sec, $\zeta = 0.707$, and $\omega_n = 1.414$ rad/sec.

Track a unit ramp input with zero steady state error:

$$G(s) = \frac{10}{s(s + 2)}$$

The desired s-plane point is $s_1 = -1 + j$. The z-plane location for the pole is given by $z_1 = e^{s_1 T} = 0.7546 + j\,0.1927$.

Because the plant is Type 1, the PID controller will increase the system to Type 2. Therefore, we have satisfied immediately the only steady state error requirement. This gives us some freedom in choosing K_I. We start with $K_I = 4$ and use program 1 in the Appendix to find K_p and K_D.

When we check the closed loop poles, we find that the largest poles have a magnitude of 1.5 and hence are unstable. Has the program failed to place the poles at the desired location? The answer is that the program has not failed; the design has. This is obvious if we compare the closed loop poles to the desired pole location. We have achieved the desired pole location.

This is the problem with analytical techniques. We can guarantee that one of the system poles will be where we want it to be. We have no control over where the other poles go.

If we rerun the simulation with $K_I = 1$, we do achieve a stable design, as shown in Figure 9-19. The root locus of the compensated system is also shown in Figure 9-18. The various parameters are $R = 0.55$, $X = 0.51$, $\alpha = -0.97$, and $\beta = 1.27$. The PID parameters for this

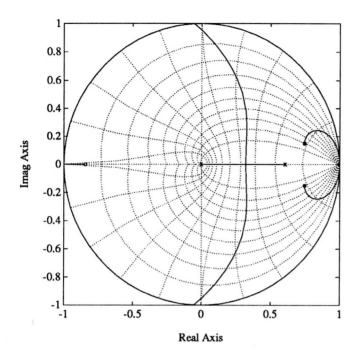

Figure 9-18 Root locus of the system using analytical PID design.

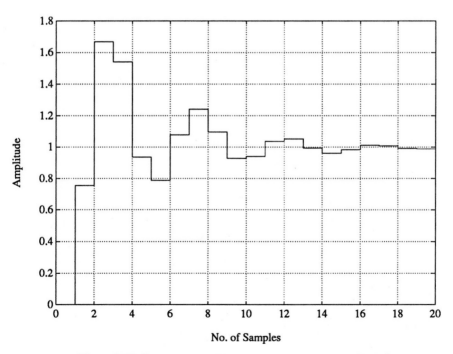

Figure 9-19 Step response of the system using analytical PID design.

design are $K_p = 0.95$, $K_D = 0.40$, and $K_I = 1.0$. The *ddamp* command provides the following information regarding the compensated system:

Eigenvalue	Magnitude	Equiv. Damping	Equiv. Freq. (rad/sec)
0.7546 + 0.1927i	0.7788	0.7071	1.4142
0.7546 - 0.1927i	0.7788	0.7071	1.4142
0.1714 + 0.7593i	0.7784	0.1826	5.4871
0.1714 - 0.7593i	0.7784	0.1826	5.4871

The magnitudes of the poles are 0.7784 and 0.7788, verifying a stable design. Note that the design specifications on the damping ratio and natural frequency are met. Also note from the step response the large overshoot. This is due to our lack of control over poles and zeros using this technique.

9.11.3 Lead-Lag Compensation

A discrete lead or lag compensator can be designed with the root locus technique. Because a discrete root locus follows the same mathematics as the continuous root locus, all of the graphical techniques discussed in Chapter 7 should work here. The exception is that the focus is now on the inside of the unit circle in the z-plane rather than on the LHP in the s-plane.

Being limited to working within the unit circle creates some problems. A digital system will go unstable at lower gains than the equivalent continuous system. Also, discrete transfer functions often have more zeros than continuous transfer functions. This makes for a complicated root locus, all of which is squeezed inside a small working area.

To aid in lead (or lag) discrete compensator design, we have developed an analytical technique. Always consider such techniques as starting points in the design. Remember the problem with the PID analytical design. We can guarantee that the root locus will go through the desired z-plane locations, but we cannot guarantee that these will be the dominant poles. The final discrete compensator has the form

$$K(z) = K_c \frac{z+a}{z+b}$$

Because we find steady state error constants for $z = 1$, we will reformulate the compensator transfer function as

$$K(z) = \overline{K} \; \frac{\dfrac{z-1}{v} + 1}{\dfrac{z-1}{w} + 1} = \overline{K} \; \frac{\dfrac{\overline{z}}{v} + 1}{\dfrac{\overline{z}}{w} + 1}$$

where $\overline{z} = z - 1$, $a = v - 1$, $b = w - 1$, $K_c = \overline{K} w/v$. Now, when $z = 1$, $\overline{z} = 0$, so $\overline{K}$ is the compensator's contribution to the steady state error.

From the transient requirements for the system, we determine s_1, the desired s-plane location. We then use $z_1 = e^{sT}$ to find first the z-plane location z_1 and then $\bar{z}_1$. The derivation of this analytical technique follows. For z_1 to be on the root locus:

$$K(z_1)\, G(z_1) = \bar{K}\, \frac{\dfrac{\bar{z}_1}{v} + 1}{\dfrac{z_1}{w} + 1}\, G(z_1) = -1 \quad \Rightarrow \quad \frac{\dfrac{\bar{z}_1}{v} + 1}{\dfrac{z_1}{w} + 1} = \frac{-1}{\bar{K}\, G(z_1)}$$

If we solve for $1/v$

$$v^{-1} = -\frac{w^{-1}}{\bar{K}\, G(z_1)} - \frac{1}{\bar{z}_1}\left(1 + \frac{1}{\bar{K}\, G(z_1)}\right)$$

Now, because both the compensator pole and zero must be real, v^{-1} and w^{-1} must be real. Therefore, the imaginary terms on both sides of this equation must be 0. Setting the imaginary term of the right side of the equation to 0 and factoring out the real w^{-1} gives us

$$w^{-1} = \frac{-\,\mathrm{Im}\left(\dfrac{1}{\bar{z}_1} + \dfrac{1}{\bar{z}_1\, \bar{K}\, G(z_1)}\right)}{\mathrm{Im}\left(\dfrac{1}{\bar{z}_1\, \bar{K}\, G(z_1)}\right)} \quad \text{and} \quad v^{-1} = -\frac{w^{-1}}{\bar{K}\, G(z_1)} - \frac{1}{\bar{z}_1\, \bar{K}\, G(z_1)} - \frac{1}{\bar{z}_1}$$

This design procedure is given as program 2 in Appendix A-1.

Example 9.7 Digital Lead Compensator Design

Consider the plant $G(s)$, where the sampling period is 0.05 sec. The specifications are steady state error of 20%, $\zeta = 0.5$, and $\omega_n = 14$ rad/sec .

$$G(s) = \frac{400}{s\,(s^2 + 30s + 200)}$$

The steady state error specification requires an error constant of 5. Because the plant has an error constant of 2, the compensator must contribute 2.5; i.e., $\bar{K} = 2.5$.

The transient specifications require the s-plane root of $-7 + j12.12$ and predict a settling time of 0.7 sec. The desired z-plane poles are at $0.5792 + j\,0.4014$. Using program 2 in the Appendix, we find the compensator as

$$K(z) = 9.9935\, \frac{z - 0.7609}{z - 0.0441}$$

The *ddamp* command provides the following information:

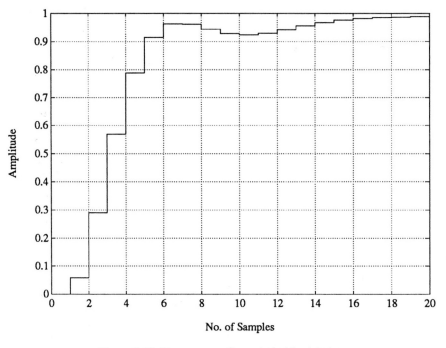

Figure 9-20 Step response for analytical lead design.

Eigenvalue	Magnitude	Equiv. Damping	Equiv. Freq. (rad/sec)
0.8289	0.8289	1.0000	3.7543
0.5792 + 0.4014i	0.7047	0.5001	13.9962
0.5792 −0.4014i	0.7047	0.5001	13.9962
−0.0270	0.0270	0.7547	95.7655

The closed loop zeros are at

−2.6170
0.7609
−0.1806

The compensated root locus is shown in Figure 9-21 on page 293. All closed loop poles are inside the unit circle, but the system has a zero outside the circle. Figure 9-20 (above)shows the step response. We have achieved our desired complex poles and a settling time of 1.0 sec. The step response looks quite different from a second order system with dominant poles. As you can see from the pole-zero structure of the system, the complex poles are not dominant in this case.

9.11.4 The *w*-Transform

To this point, we have discussed two methods for designing digital compensators: conversion of a continuous compensator using various transformations; and design in the

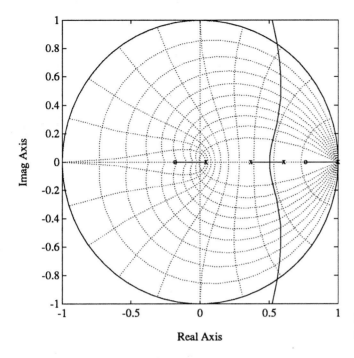

Figure 9-21 Root locus for analytical lead design.

z-domain. Conversion of a continuous compensator works well when the sample rate is high. The *z*-domain techniques are preferable at lower sample rates.

The *z*-domain technique has some disadvantages. For one, all of the design must take place within the limited confines of the unit circle. For another, Bode design techniques that correlate gain crossover frequency and phase margin with closed loop behavior do not apply to the *z*-transform. These techniques apply to transfer functions whose stability region is the left-hand plane.

The *w-transform* is a technique that allows us to apply all *s*-domain design methods to digital systems. In this technique, we transform $H(z)$ into $H(w)$ using the following variable substitution:

$$ w = \frac{2}{T} \frac{z-1}{z+1} $$

If this equation looks familiar, it is because it has the same form as Tustin's approximation for *s*. We already know that the Tustin approximation preserves the mapping of the $j\omega$ axis into the unit circle. We can conclude that the *w*-transform also preserves this mapping. That is, the interior of the unit circle in the *z*-plane maps into the left side of the *w*-plane.

All design techniques that we describe in Chapter 7 for $G(s)$ can be applied to $G(w)$. In this procedure, we first use the ZOH approximation to convert the continuous plant $G(s)$ to the discrete plant $G(z)$. We then use the following to convert to $G(w)$:

$$z = \frac{1 + wT/2}{1 - wT/2}$$

We now design the compensator using the Bode or root locus techniques discussed in Chapter 7. Finally, we convert the compensator design back to the z-plane. The last step is necessary because we implement digital compensators as difference equations.

As an example of converting a continuous plant to the w-plane, consider

$$H(s) = \frac{1}{s + 1}$$

Digitizing with ZOH approximation for $T = 0.5$ sec (using the $c2dm$ command),

$$H(z) = \frac{0.393}{z - 0.607}$$

Continuing with the process, we replace z to get

$$H(w) = \frac{1}{\dfrac{1 + 0.25w}{1 - 0.25w} + 1} = \frac{1 - 0.25w}{1 + 1.023w}$$

We see that the poles of $H(w)$ and the original $H(s)$ are very close. As we shall see in the next example, this is a function of the sample period. We also note that $H(w)$ has a RHP zero that does not exist in the original $H(s)$. This zero, introduced by the sampling process, is also a function of the sampling period and is common in w-transforms. You must be careful, therefore, when using Bode plots to determine stability of w-plane transfer functions.

We can use the $d2cm$ command with the *tustin* method to convert from the z to the w domain and use $c2dm$ (*tustin* method) to transform back.

Example 9.8 The w-Transform

Given $H(s)$, convert to the w-domain using three sample periods, T = 0.5, 0.1, and 0.05 sec. Draw the Bode magnitude plots for the continuous and the three different w-transformed transfer functions:

$$H(s) = \frac{10}{s + 5}$$

We first use the $c2dm$ command with the default ZOH method to convert to the z-domain and then use $d2cm$ with the tustin method to convert to the w-domain. Here is a partial listing:

```
>> ng=10; dg=[1 5]; [ngz1,dgz1]=c2dm(ng,dg,0.5);
>> [ngw1,dgw1]=d2cm(ngz1,dgz1,0.5,'t')
>> w=logspace(-1,2,50); mc=bode(ng,dg,w); mw1=bode(ngw1,dgw1,w);
```

$$T = 0.5, \quad H_1(w) = 1.69 \frac{-w + 4}{w + 3.393}$$

$$T = 0.1, \quad H_2(w) = 0.49 \frac{-w + 20}{w + 4.898}$$

$$T = 0.05, \quad H_3(w) = 0.24 \frac{-w + 40}{w + 4.974}$$

We see that as T gets smaller, the w-plane pole approaches the s-plane pole. Also note that all three w-plane transfer functions have the same low frequency gain of 2 as the continuous transfer function. The w-transform always preserves the low frequency gain of $H(s)$.

A big difference in the three transformed functions is the right half plane zero location. As the sample rate gets smaller, the zero moves further and further away from frequencies of interest and will have less effect on the design process.

Figure 9-22 shows the Bode plots for the three w-transformed transfer functions along with the Bode plot for the continuous plant. The fact that there are differences between these plots does not invalidate the use of the w-transform. The w-transform accurately reflects the effect of driving a continuous plant with a sampled signal.

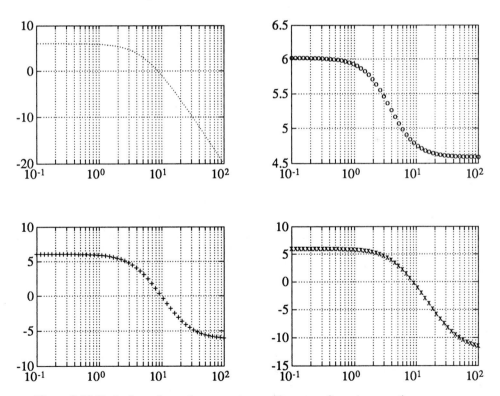

Figure 9-22 Bode plots of a continuous system and its w-transform. (...... continuous; ooooo T = 0.5; +++++ T = 0.1; xxxxx T = 0.05)

Before we use the w-transform for compensator design, we must examine the relationship between s and w in more detail. Remember that transient specifications lead to requirements on the gain crossover frequency when $s = j\omega$. How do we use this information in the w-plane? If we return to the defining relationship for w and let $z = e^{sT}$, we get

$$w = \frac{2}{T} \frac{e^{sT} - 1}{e^{sT} + 1}$$

where both w and s are complex variables. For frequency plots of continuous systems we let $s = j\omega$. In this case, w will be imaginary, and we can let $w = jv$. So

$$jv = \frac{2}{T} \frac{e^{j\omega T} - 1}{e^{j\omega T} + 1} = j\frac{2}{T} \tan\frac{\omega T}{2}$$

After we determine the gain crossover frequency ω_{gc} from the transient specifications for the plant, we determine the w-plane crossover frequency from

$$v_{gc} = \frac{2}{T} \tan\frac{T\omega_{gc}}{2}$$

We then use the standard Bode design techniques to determine the compensator.

Example 9.9 w-Transform Design

Use the w-Transform to perform the compensator design for the plant and specification given in Example 9.7.

We will use the analytical Bode design technique described in Chapter 7 (see the Appendix in Chapter 7 for the program). We first discretize the plant with $T = 0.05$. We then use the w-transform to get the w-plane model for the plant:

$$G(w) = \frac{0.0018w^3 - 0.1261w^2 - 6.8186w + 362.176}{w(w^2 + 28.2814w + 181.0898)}$$

The steady state error requirement of 20% requires a compensator gain of 2.5. We also require $\zeta = 0.5$ and $\omega_n = 14$ rad/sec. Translating these to the frequency domain implies a PM of 50 degrees and gain crossover frequency of 14 rad/sec. Before proceeding with the design, we must convert the s-plane frequency to the w-plane:

$$v_{gc} = \frac{2}{T} \tan\frac{\omega_n T}{2} = 14.6$$

Using the analytical Bode lead program in Chapter 7 gives the following w-plane lead compensator:

$$K(w) = \frac{0.4132w + 1}{0.0134w + 1}$$

We now use Tustin transform to convert this back to the z-plane:

$$K(z) = \frac{28.5602z - 25.3015}{z + 0.3035}$$

The system closed loop information is

Eigenvalue	Magnitude	Equiv. Damping	Equiv. Freq. (rad/sec)
0.9134	0.9134	1.0000	1.8124
0.4228 + 0.6424i	0.7690	0.2567	20.4602
0.4228 −0.6424i	0.7690	0.2567	20.4602
−0.2543	0.2543	0.3995	68.5397

The closed loop zeros are at

−2.6170
 0.8859
−0.1806

The step responses for the uncompensated and compensated feedback system are shown in Figure 9-23. We have achieved an overshoot of 10% and a settling time of 2 sec. Note that the complex poles are not dominant.

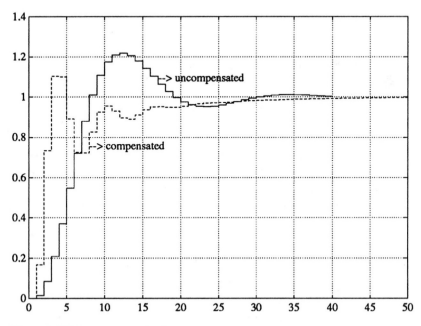

Figure 9-23 Step responses for the w-transform design, before and after compensation.

9.11.5 Compensator Delay

To this point, we have assumed that there is no delay between the compensator input and output. This is, in fact, never the case. We implement a digital compensator as a difference equation in the computer controller. There will always be some processing delay in the controller. System delays tend to destabilize. Also, we can expect that delays will effect the transient response. Therefore, it is wise to include known delays in the design process. The easiest way to do this is to include the delay in the plant model; i.e., multiply $G(z)$ by $1 / z^n$ for a delay of nT periods, and then proceed with the design.

9.12 Discrete State Space Design

The state space model for a discrete plant is given by

$$x_{k+1} = A x_k + B u_k$$

$$y_k = C x_k + D u_k$$

where the plant poles are the eigenvalues of A. As with continuous systems, we can design compensators for discrete systems using the pole placement techniques discussed in Chapter 8, the linear quadratic regulator algorithms discussed in Chapter 12, or the algebraic design techniques described in Chapter 10. The control input is then given by

$$u_k = - K x_k$$

The *place* command applies in the discrete case without any modifications. The plant is discretized, and the desired poles are chosen within the unit circle (or in the LHP and transformed via the exponential map). Observers are designed similarly, with the exception that the observer equations are difference equations rather than differential equations.

9.13 Appendix

9.13.1 Programs

1. Analytical PID Design Program
This program requires the following parameters to be defined on the workspace:

$G(s) = ng/dg$, s1, T = ts, Ki = ki

```
[a,b,c,d]=tf2ss(ng,dg);
[ad,bd]=c2d(a,b,ts);
z1=exp(s1*ts)
kz1=c*inv(z1*eye(ad)-ad)*bd+d
R=-real(1/kz1+(ki*z1*ts)/(z1-1))
X=-imag(1/kz1+(ki*z1*ts)/(z1-1))
alpha=real((z1-1)/(z1*ts))
beta=imag((z1-1)/(z1*ts))
kd=real(X/beta)
kp=real(R-kd*alpha)
nk_PID=[kp*ts+kd+ki*ts*ts -kp*ts-2*kd kd]
dk_PID=[ts -ts 0]
[ngz,dgz]=ss2tf(ad,bd,c,d);
[ngk,dgk]=series(nk_PID,dk_PID,ngz,dgz);
[nt,dt]=cloop(ngk,dgk);
[mag,wn,zeta]=ddamp(dt,ts)
dstep(nt,dt)
axis('square'), zgrid('new'), rlocus(ngk,dgk)
```

2. Digital Lead Design Program

This program requires the following parameters to be defined on the workspace:

$G(S)=ng/dg$; T=ts; K = kbar; s1

```
z1=exp(s1*ts);
zbar1=z1-1;
[ngz,dgz]=c2dm(ng,dg,ts);
ngz_z1=polyval(ngz,z1);dgz_z1=polyval(dgz,z1);
g_z1=ngz_z1/dgz_z1
w_inv = -imag((1+1/(kbar*g_z1))/zbar1)/imag(1/(kbar*g_z1));
v_inv=-w_inv/(kbar*g_z1) - (1 + 1/(kbar*g_z1))/zbar1;
w=1/w_inv, v=1/v_inv
a=v-1; b=w-1; kc=kbar*w/v;
[ngk,dgk]=series(ngz,dgz,nk,dk);
[nt,dt]=cloop(ngk,dgk);
ddamp(dt,ts)
dstep(nt,dt)
axis('square'), zgrid('new'), rlocus(ngk,dgk)
```

9.13.2 Tables of z-Transform and ZOH Equivalents

Table 9-1 Table of z-Transform Pairs and Properties

f(t)	f(kT)	F(z)
$\delta(t)$	δ_k	1
$u(t)$	$u(kT)$	$\dfrac{z}{z-1}$
e^{-at}	e^{-aTk}	$\dfrac{z}{z-e^{-aT}}$
t	kT	$\dfrac{Tz}{(z-1)^2}$
$\cos \omega T$	$\cos \omega Tk$	$\dfrac{z(z-\cos \omega T)}{z^2-(2\cos \omega T)z+1}$
$\sin \omega T$	$\sin \omega Tk$	$\dfrac{z \sin \omega T}{z^2-(2\cos \omega T)z+1}$
$e^{-at}f(t)$	$e^{-aTk}f(kT)$	$F(e^{aT}z)$
$f(t-nT)$	$f((k-n)T)$	$z^{-n}F(z)$
$f(t+nT)$	$f((k+n)T)$	$z^n F(z)-z^n f(0)-\ldots-zf(n-1)$
	$f(\infty)$	$\lim_{z\to 1}(z-1)F(z)$

Table 9-2 Table of Transfer Functions, Their z-transform, and ZOH Equivalents

G(s)	G(z)	G(z)$_{ZOH}$
$\dfrac{1}{s}$	$\dfrac{z}{z-1}$	$\dfrac{T}{z-1}$
$\dfrac{a}{s+a}$	$\dfrac{az}{z-e^{-aT}}$	$\dfrac{1-e^{-aT}}{z-e^{-aT}}$

Table 9-2 Table of Transfer Functions, Their *z*-transform, and ZOH Equivalents (cont.)		
$G(s)$	$G(z)$	$G(z)_{ZOH}$
$\dfrac{a^2}{(s+a)^2}$	$\dfrac{a^2 T z e^{-aT}}{(z - e^{-aT})^2}$	$\dfrac{Az + B}{(z - e^{-at})^2}$ where $A = 1 - e^{-aT} - aTe^{-aT}$ and $B = (aT - 1)e^{-aT} + e^{-2aT}$
$\dfrac{\omega_n^2}{s^2 + 2\zeta\omega_n s + \omega_n^2}$	$K \dfrac{ze^{-aT}\sin bT}{z^2 - 2e^{-aT}(\cos bT)z + e^{-2aT}}$ where $a = 2\zeta\omega_n$ $b = \omega_n\sqrt{1 - \zeta^2}$ and $K = \omega_n^2/b$	$\dfrac{Az + B}{z^2 - 2e^{-aT}(\cos bT)z + e^{-2aT}}$ where $A = 1 - e^{-aT}\cos bT - (a/b)e^{-aT}\sin bT$ and $B = e^{-2aT} + (a/b)e^{-aT} - e^{-aT}\cos bT$

9.14 Problems

9.1 Solve the following difference equations.

a. $y_{n+1} + y_n = -\cos(n\pi)$, $y_0 = 0$

b. $y_{n+1} - y_n = x_{n+1} - x_n$, $x_n =$ unit step

c. $y_{n+2} + y_n = 0$, $y(-1) = 0$, $y(-2) = -2$

9.2 Consider the following relaxed system:

$$y_n = x_n + 0.5\,(x_{n-1} + y_{n-1})$$

a. Find the impulse response, h_n.

b. Find the unit step response, y_n.

9.3 Suppose you borrow money from the bank at the rate, β, and make monthly payments of P dollars. Let the initial loan be for L dollars.

a. Find a general formula for your debt, d_n, at start of month n.

b. Find your monthly payments, P, to pay off the loan in N years.

c. Write a program that will compute and tabulate the debt and monthly payments.

d. Find monthly mortgage payments for a $125,000, 30-year loan at the rate of 9.125%.

9.4 Let y_n denote the step response, h_n the impulse response, and recall that by definition of the transfer function, $H(z)$ is the z-transform of h_n.

a. If the input is a step, find a difference equation relating y_n to h_n. (*Note:* this gives you a way to find the impulse response directly in the time domain from the step response.)

b. Show that $y_n = \sum_{m=0}^{n} h_m$ satisfies the above equation.

c. Use z-transform to find impulse and step responses for the system $H(z) = \dfrac{z+1}{z-1}$.

d. Use the step response in part c and the equation obtained in part a to find the impulse response directly in the time domain.

e. Note that part b gives a direct time domain formula to find the step response from the impulse response. Now use the impulse response in part c to find the step response using the formula given in part b.

9.5 Let y_n and h_n denote unit step and impulse response of an LTI system.

a. Use z-transform to obtain a difference equation relation between h_n and y_n .

b. Using z-transform, find step response of a digital filter satisfying:
$$y_n - y_{n-1} = x_n , \qquad y(-1) = 0$$
c. Find the impulse response of the above filter using the relation in part a.

d. Based on the above input–output pairs, what do you think the filter does?

9.6 Find the inverse z-transform of $H(z) = \dfrac{4(z-3)}{(z-2)(z-1)}$.

9.7 Consider the following so-called running sum:

$$y_n = \sum_{i=0}^{n} h_i$$

a. Write a first order difference equation involving y_n, y_{n-1}, and h_n.

b. Use the equation in part a to find $Y(z)$ in terms of $H(z)$.

c. Use the result in part b to find a general formula for the sum of first n integers.

9.8 Find $F(z)$ if $f(n)$ is given by

$$f(n) = \begin{cases} 1 & n \text{ even} \\ 0 & n \text{ odd} \end{cases}$$

9.9 Derive a general formula for the sum of n squared integers as follows.

a. Find $Z\{k^2\}$

b. Note that y_n satisfies

$y_n - y_{n-1} = n^2 \quad , \quad y(-1) = 0$

Solving this difference equation will provide the general formula.

9.10 Consider the following finite impulse response (FIR) filter:

$$y_{k+3} = \frac{1}{4} \sum_{i=0}^{3} u_{k+i}$$

a. Obtain a state space representation $\{A,b,c,d\}$.

b. The impulse response of this filter is equal to 0 for values of $k > N$. Find N (this is why it is called FIR).

9.11 Consider the following system:

$$x(k+1) = A\,x(k) + B\,u(k) \quad \text{where} \quad A = \begin{bmatrix} 3 & -4 \\ 2 & -3 \end{bmatrix}, \quad B = \begin{bmatrix} 1 \\ 0 \end{bmatrix}$$

$$y(k) = C\,x(k) \qquad\qquad C = \begin{bmatrix} 1 & 0 \end{bmatrix}$$

a. Find the transfer function $H(z)$.

b. Find the impulse response and plot it. Explain the oscillations.

c. Assuming zero initial conditions, find $x(k)$ if $u(k)=\delta(k)$. Also, plot the state sequence in the (x_1, x_2) plane.

d. Assuming zero initial conditions, find the step response of the system and plot $y(k)$.

e. Find the step response by solving the state equations directly in time domain assuming zero initial conditions. List $x(k)$ for a few values and plot $x(k)$ in the (x_1, x_2) plane.

9.12 Consider the following system:

$$T(s) = \frac{2\,s^2 + 0.1\,s + 0.4}{s^2 + 0.2\,s + 1}$$

Let the sampling period $T = 0.1$ sec. Obtain the state space formulas for Euler forward technique. Digitize the system using Euler forward and backward (you need to write functions for doing this), Tustin, and ZOH approximations. Obtain the step responses and Bode plots over the same range and determine the properties of each transform. Repeat the simulation for $T = 10$ and 0.01 sec.

9.13 Consider the following plant:

$$G(s) = \frac{4}{(s+1)^3 (s+2)^2}$$

a. Find the ZOH equivalent of $G(s)$ for the following sampling periods: $T = 0.5, 1, 4$ sec.

b. Find the poles and zeros $G(z)$. Note that even though $G(s)$ in minimum phase, $G(z)$ may turn out to be nonminimum phase depending on the choice of sampling period.

9.14 In this problem, we study the effects of the various digitization techniques applied to a continuous notch filter. In many control systems we wish to filter out a specific frequency; e.g., 60 Hz. The following continuous notch filter will provide 40 dB of attenuation at 60 Hz:

$$G(s) = \frac{s^2 + 1.2\pi s + (120\pi)^2}{s^2 + 60\pi s + (120\pi)^2}$$

a. Digitize this continuous filter at a sampling period of $T = 1$ msec using all of the *c2dm* methods (except *prewarp*). Show the Bode magnitude plots of the continuous and all of the digitized filters on the same graph.

b. Use the critical frequency warping technique (*c2dm* using *prewarp*) to digitize this filter. Compare the magnitude response of this digitization with the continuous filter.

9.15 Matched pole-zero is another technique used to convert from a continuous to a digital filter. Consider

$$G(s) = 100 \frac{s+10}{(s+1)(s+5)}$$

We can digitize this filter by replacing each finite pole or zero term $s + a$ with its discrete equivalent $z - e^{-aT}$, where T is the sample period. It has been found that this technique works best if we also consider the zeros at infinity. That is, if there are n poles and m zeros in the continuous transfer filter, we include the term $(z + 1)^{n-m}$ in the numerator of the digital filter. Finally we adjust the digital filter gain so that both digital and continuous filters have the same low frequency gain. This results in

$$G(z) = K \frac{(z+1)(z-e^{-10T})}{(z-e^{-T})(z-e^{-5T})} \qquad K = 100 \frac{(1-e^{-T})(1-e^{-5T})}{(1-e^{-10T})}$$

where K is chosen so $G(z)|_{z=1} = G(s)|_{s=0}$.

a. Find and display on single graphs, the Bode magnitude and phase plots for the continuous filter and the matched pole-zero for sample periods of $T = 0.5, 0.25, 0.1$ sec. You can use *c2dm* using the *matched* method.

b. Find and display on a single graph the step responses of the filters in part *a*.

9.16 We described, in the preceding problem, the matched pole-zero technique for simple pole and zeros. Derive the transformation for a second order pole or zero term:

$$s^2 + 2\zeta\omega_n s + \omega_n^2$$

a. Digitize the notch filter of problem 9.14 using the matched pole-zero technique. Compare the magnitude response of this filter with the continuous and critically warped notch filters.

9.17 Consider the following plant:

$$KG(s) = \frac{K}{(s+1)(s+2)}$$

Assuming a sampling period of 1 sec, use root locus and *rlocfind* to find the values of K for which the closed loop system remains stable.

9.18 Consider the following plant:

$$G(s) = \frac{2}{s(s+1)}$$

Let the sampling period be $T = 2$ sec. Design a cascade compensator to achieve a phase margin of 45 degrees. Use *w*-transform method.

9.19 Consider the following plant:

$$G(s) = \frac{1}{s(s+4)}$$

It is desired that the closed loop system follow unit ramp inputs with less than 5% error, have a bandwidth of at most 7 rad/sec, and have a phase margin of at least 45 degrees. Design a cascade compensator using w-transform method. You should select the sampling frequency to be at least 10 times the closed loop bandwidth.

9.20 We described the inverted pendulum in problem 7.6. We now wish to design a digital controller for this system. Determine the sampling rate by first finding the bandwidth your continuous design. Select the the sample rate to be 10 times this bandwidth.

9.21 The double inverted pendulum is created by hinging a second rod to the top of the rod described in problem 7.6. A digital controller for this system was presented by [ZZH87]. Their linear model used the six states defined by

$$x = [y, \theta_1, \theta_2 - \theta_1, \dot{y}, \dot{\theta}_1, \dot{\theta}_1 - \dot{\theta}_2]'$$

where y is cart position, θ_1 is the angle the bottom rod makes to the horizontal, and θ_2 is the equivalent angle of the top rod. The difference in the two angles measures the alignment between the rods, which we would like to maintain at a zero angle. The discrete model ($T = 20$ msec) was given as

$$x_{k+1} = \begin{pmatrix} A_{11} & A_{12} \\ A_{21} & A_{22} \end{pmatrix} x_k + b\, u_k$$

$$r_k = C\, x_k$$

where

$$A_{11} = \begin{pmatrix} 1.0 & -2.411E{-}4 & 1.152E{-}5 \\ 0 & 1.003 & -1.77E{-}3 \\ 0 & -3.95E{-}3 & 1.0074 \end{pmatrix}$$

$$A_{12} = \begin{pmatrix} 0.0148 & -3.08E{-}7 & -3.07E{-}7 \\ 2.65E{-}3 & 0.016 & 7.30E{-}3 \\ -3.07E{-}3 & 2.35E{-}5 & 0.016 \end{pmatrix}$$

$$A_{21} = \begin{pmatrix} 0 & -0.0294 & 1.4E{-}3 \\ 0 & 0.4244 & -0.221 \\ 0 & -0.492 & 0.924 \end{pmatrix}$$

$$A_{22} = \begin{pmatrix} 0.858 & -1.20E{-}4 & -4.11E{-}5 \\ 0.323 & 1.00 & 3.21E{-}4 \\ -0.374 & 1.62E{-}3 & 1.00 \end{pmatrix}$$

$$b = (7.53E–4, -1.715E–3, 1.99E–3, 0.0917, –0.209, 0.242)'$$
$$C = (I_3 \quad 0)$$

a. Find the eigenvalues of this system. Is it stable? Is it controllable?

b. Is the system observable for the given C? Find the minimal number of measurements we need to make to still have an observable system.

c. We want the closed loop system to have less than 10% overshoot and settle within 0.5 sec. Use this requirement to derive the desired closed loop dominant pole locations in the z-plane (remember, $T = 20$ msec). Choose four other pole locations and use *place* to design the digital controller gain.

d. Assuming full state feedback, find the discrete pulse response for your closed loop design.

Notes and References

For further information on digital control, refer to [PN90], [FPW90], [Ku80], [O87], [HL85], [K81], [J81], [AW90].

10

Algebraic Design

10.1 Introduction

One of the most intuitive design techniques that appeared on the scene in the 1950s was the algebraic, or analytical, method. The idea was to choose a desired closed loop transfer function and then algebraically solve for the compensator. Let $G(s)$ be the plant and $K(s)$ the compensator, and assume unity feedback configuration. The closed loop transfer function is

$$T_c(s) = \frac{K(s)\ G(s)}{1 + K(s)\ G(s)}$$

Assume we are given a desired closed loop transfer function, $T_d(s)$, to be realized. Letting $T_d(s) = T_c(s)$ and solving for the compensator, we get

$$K(s) = \frac{T_d(s)}{G(s)\ [\ 1 - T_d(s)\ ]}$$

This seems to be the end of our design. As you might have guessed, however, there are some serious flaws with such a simplistic approach. Implicitly assumed in the above approach is that we can realize any desired closed loop response for any plant using a simple unity feedback configuration. This suggestion is far-fetched, as you can see by choosing $T_d(s)$ to be equal to 1, the ideal response. This response would imply that the system can follow any command input instantaneously with zero error. To achieve the ideal response, however, we have the impossible condition that $K(s)$ would have to be infinite. Therefore, there must clearly be some restrictions to avoid ridiculous results. It turns out that with appropriate restrictions on the compensator, and the desired closed loop transfer function, it is possible to solve for the compensator algebraically.

Conceptually, the algebraic approach to design differs fundamentally from the classical approach. In the classical approach discussed in Chapter 7, the open loop transfer function is manipulated to achieve desired closed loop specifications. The form of the compensator is also restricted to specific lead-lag or PID types. We can meet limited objectives with relatively simple and low order compensators. For instance, in the root locus approach, a pair of complex conjugate poles can be assigned. The location of all other poles and zeros cannot be controlled, however. In essence, we work from inside out (outward approach); the open loop transfer function is shaped, but we have little control over the closed loop transfer function.

In algebraic design, we take an inward approach. First, we design a desired closed loop transfer function, and then we solve for the compensator. The poles and zeros of the compensator and, hence, the open loop transfer function cannot be controlled. Instead, we have more control over the closed loop poles and zeros. The lack of direct control over the open loop transfer function means we cannot meet any specified stability margin requirements without trial and error.

The ability to assign arbitrarily all poles of the system is reminiscent of state space design. In fact, transfer function analysis of observer-based designs led to the revival of the algebraic approach. Most of this chapter is based on the series of articles and books by C. T. Chen [C84, C87a, C87b, CS90a, CS90b] and T. Kailath [K80]. We will use Chen's notation and terminology in most cases.

To see how observer-based design leads to a transfer function design, consider the equations of a system with an observer-based compensator:

$$\dot{x} = A\,x + B\,u$$
$$y = C\,x$$

$$\dot{\hat{x}} = A\,\hat{x} + B\,u + L\,(\,y - C\,\hat{x}\,)$$

$$u = -\,K\,\hat{x} + r$$

Taking transforms and solving for $\hat{x}$, we get

$$\hat{x}(s) = (\,s\,I - A - L\,C\,)^{-1}\,[\,B\,u(s) + L\,y(s)\,]$$

Hence, the controller is given by

$$u(s) \;=\; -\,K\,(\,s\,I - A - L\,C\,)^{-1}\,B\,u(s)\; -\; K\,(\,s\,I - A - L\,C\,)^{-1}\,L\,y(s) + r$$

We recall that the inverse of a matrix is equal to the ratio of the adjoint over the determinant. Hence, we get

$$u(s) = -\left[\,\frac{L(s)}{A(s)}\;u(s)\; +\; \frac{M(s)}{A(s)}\;y(s)\,\right] + r \;=\; \frac{-1}{A(s)}\,[\,L(s)\,u(s) + M(s)\,y(s)\,] + r$$

where $A(s) = \det\,(\,s\,I - A - L\,C\,)$ and

$$L(s) = \text{Adj} \left[K (s\,I - A - L\,C)\,B \right], \quad M(s) = \text{Adj} \left[K (s\,I - A - L\,C)\,L \right]$$

The preceding suggests the *controller-observer* configuration shown in Figure 10-1.

Now, we turn things around and start with the above configuration. The problem can be formulated as

> Given the plant $G(s)$, find polynomials $\{A(s), M(s), L(s)\}$ such that the closed poles are placed at desired locations.

We already know from linear systems theory that this can be done using an nth order compensator (i.e., deg $(A(s))$ = system order = n), as long as the system is completely controllable and observable. Moreover, we know that we can also reduce the compensator order by one (single-output case), corresponding to using a reduced-order observer. We will see later that, in addition, we can place the closed loop zeros at desired locations (with some restrictions). We will also study other configurations.

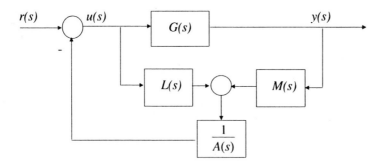

Figure 10-1 Controller-observer configuration.

10.2 Design Constraints

To achieve a compensator that works and can be realized physically (or in digital form), we have to place constraints on both the compensator and the desired closed loop transfer function. A desired closed loop transfer function, $T_d(s)$, is said to be *implementable* if there exists a configuration such that the transfer function between r (command input) and y (controlled output) is equal to $T_d(s)$ and meets the following four constraints:

1. The compensators are rational proper transfer functions.
2. The compensated system is well posed.
3 The compensated system is internally stable.
4. All forward paths from input to output pass through the plant.

The first constraint prevents the occurrence of pure differentiators as compensators. Pure differentiators amplify noise. The higher the noise frequency, the higher the amplification. This is a practical constraint, and most engineers are usually aware of it. The second constraint, well-posedness, ensures that all transfer functions between any pair of inputs and outputs are proper. This ensures that noise entering the system at any point will get filtered out by the system; i.e., the system itself does not act as a differentiator. It should be noted that the first two constraints are independent of each other. For instance, consider $G(s)$ and $K(s)$ below with unity feedback:

$$G(s) = \frac{s+1}{s-1} \quad \text{and} \quad K(s) = \frac{2-s}{2+s} \quad \rightarrow \quad \frac{GK}{1+GK} = \frac{(s+1)(2-s)}{2s}$$

We can see that, even though the individual subsystems are proper, the closed loop system is improper.

The third constraint, internal stability, means that the transfer function between *any pair of inputs and outputs* is stable. Note that this is a stronger condition than stability. It essentially prevents unstable pole-zero cancellations.

The fourth constraint requires all signals to pass through the system. If noise occurs at the input and does not pass through the loop, it is directly passed to the output. This condition prevents this from happening. All of the constraints are reasonable and are met in most cases. A design algorithm, however, must be such that it does not violate these constraints; otherwise, it will lead to unrealistic compensators.

Consider the following example. Given a plant, $G(s)$, and a desired closed loop transfer function, $T_d(s)$, we will blindly solve for a compensator:

$$G(s) = \frac{1}{s^2} \quad \text{and} \quad T_d(s) = \frac{1}{s^2+s+1}$$

We can solve for a feedback compensator (the compensator is in the feedback loop) to get

$$K(s) = \frac{1}{T_d(s)} - \frac{1}{G(s)} = s+1$$

which is not proper. Solving for a cascade compensator with unity feedback, we get

$$K(s) = \frac{G(s) - T_d(s)}{G(s) T_d(s)} = \frac{s}{s+1}$$

Although this is proper, it involves canceling the plant pole at the origin. The consequence of this is that if a disturbance input, d, enters between the compensator and the plant, its output will be

$$y(s) = \frac{s+1}{s\,(s^2+s+1)}\,d(s)$$

Hence any constant disturbance will grow unbounded with time and the system is not internally stable. The example shows that a blind approach is not appropriate.

10.3 Implementable Transfer Functions

Consider a proper plant, G, and a proper stable desired closed loop transfer function, T_d, where

$$G = \frac{N}{D} \quad \text{and} \quad T_d = \frac{N_d}{D_d}$$

Let $rd\,(G) = relative\ degree\ of\ G = degree\,(D) - degree\,(N)$.

A desired closed loop transfer function, $T_d\,(s)$, is said to be *implementable* for the plant, $G(s)$, if there exists a configuration such that the following two conditions are satisfied:

1. *Relative degree condition:* $rd\,(T_d) \geq rd\,(G)$.
2. *Nonminimum phase zero condition:* All RHP zeros of G must be retained in T_d.

   For example, consider the following plant and the proposed desired closed loop transfer functions:

$$G(s) = \frac{s-1}{s\,(s-2)}$$

$$T_1 = \frac{1}{s+1}, \quad T_2 = \frac{s-1}{s+1}, \quad T_3 = \frac{s-1}{s^2+2s+2}, \quad T_4 = \frac{-2\,(s-1)}{s^2+2s+2}$$

We see that T_1 violates condition 2, T_2 violates condition 1, whereas T_3 and T_4 are both implementable using some configuration. Note that T_4 corresponds to a Type 1 system, whereas T_3 is Type 0. It is also possible to track ramp inputs with zero steady state error (i.e., Type 2 system) by adding an additional zero to T_3 or T_4, but this would violate the first condition unless an additional pole is added.

10.4 Selection of Desired Closed Loop Transfer Function

The main step in the algebraic design is the appropriate choice of the desired closed loop transfer function. In fact, once this is determined, a simple program (similar to the ones provided in the Appendix) can produce the compensator. In general, several candidate transfer functions must be tested by simulation to come up with the final choice.

One approach is to choose a pair of dominant complex conjugate poles to meet transient step response requirements. The other poles and zeros can be chosen, subject to implementability conditions, to satisfy steady state error specifications. Careful attention must be given to the role of zeros, because they will affect the response (see Chapter 1). In fact, after adding poles and zeros to meet the implementability conditions, transient response properties may be lost. The location of the complex poles will have to be changed, and the whole process must be iterated to meet all objectives. One may wonder whether there exists a "best" location for the poles and zeros. The answer is "yes," depending on what one means by "best." This question has been answered many years ago by the control and filter community. Toward this end, we will present ITAE and Symmetric Root Locus methods later.

Other factors exist that one must consider in different situations. One is the problem of saturation and control energy. Most control systems contain electromechanical components that have physical limits on their behavior. One can pull a spring so much before it breaks. An electronic amplifier will saturate once its input passes certain levels. All of these properties will introduce undesirable nonlinearities into the system. This is related directly to control energy. For instance, one may be designing a disc drive controller for a laptop computer and then realize later that the motor needed is larger than the computer itself !

One way to check the control signal levels required is to compute the following transfer function (the transfer function between the command input and the control signal):

$$\frac{y}{r} = T_c \quad \text{and} \quad \frac{y}{u} = G, \quad \text{then} \quad \frac{u}{r} = \frac{T_c}{G} = T_u$$

Hence, for a given command input r, one can compute or plot u, to see if its maximum and minimum values violate any constraints on u. If u is monotonically decreasing, its maximum value can be computed using the Initial Value Theorem of Laplace transform:

$$u(0^+) = \lim_{s \to \infty} s\, U(s) = \lim_{s \to \infty} s\, R(s) \frac{T_c(s)}{G(s)} = \lim_{s \to \infty} \frac{T_c(s)}{G(s)} \quad \text{for a unit step input}$$

For example, for the previous plant G and T_3 and T_4, we compute

$$u(0^+) = \lim_{s \to \infty} \frac{T_3}{G} = \lim_{s \to \infty} \frac{s\,(s-2)}{s^2 + 2\,s + 2} = 1$$

$$u(0^+) = \lim_{s \to \infty} \frac{T_4}{G} = \lim_{s \to \infty} \frac{-2\,s\,(s-2)}{s^2 + 2\,s + 2} = -2$$

These numbers imply that the control signals will be bounded by 1 for T_3 and 2 for T_4.

Insight from results in optimal control theory indicate that the further the poles are pushed into the LHP, the higher is the control energy required. The Symmetric Root Locus (SRL) technique (to be discussed shortly), allows us to trade off control energy with speed of response.

Another issue is stability margin. Because concepts of gain and phase margin are based on open loop transfer function requirements, and we work with closed loop transfer functions here, meeting these requirements is difficult. One possibility is to use the formula for PM in Chapter 1, namely,

$$PM = 2 \sin^{-1} \frac{1}{2 \mid T(j\omega_{gc}) \mid}$$

Keep in mind that the above formula is for second order systems and the gain crossover frequency is unknown. If the bandwidth is specified, however, it could be used as an estimate of the gain crossover frequency and used in the above formula. Then the poles may be chosen to satisfy the phase margin requirement for the first iteration.

10.5 Optimal Transfer Functions: ITAE and Symmetric Root Locus

The problem of optimal transfer functions for a given response has been studied and solved in the 1950s. Suppose we want to design a filter of a given order that would track a unit step input with minimum error. The usual definition of error, $e(t)$, is the difference between input and output. One way to minimize the error is to minimize the area under it over all time. Mathematically, we define a *cost function,* which we attempt to minimize:

$$J = \int_0^\infty e(t) \, dt$$

Now, if the error is both positive and negative, the areas will cancel each other, resulting in zero cost despite large errors. One remedy is to use the absolute value of the error. This is called the Integral of Absolute Error (IAE) criterion. Another option would be to use the square of the error, the Integral of Square Error (ISE), criterion. This has the additional property of putting more emphasis on larger errors. Another popular measure is the Integral of Time Multiplied Absolute Error (ITAE) criterion:

$$J = \int_0^\infty t \mid e(t) \mid dt$$

ITAE has the advantage of putting more emphasis on steady state errors rather than transient errors, because t acts as a weighting factor. During transients, the value of t is small, whereas in steady state, t is very large, so error is heavily penalized in the steady state. ITAE turns out to be the most selective criterion, so it is the one used most often. Tables of transfer functions of different orders, tracking step, ramp, and parabolic inputs with associated plots for different criteria are available. Some control systems books have partial tables or plots for ITAE. See [C87a] and [FPE91]. For example, a third order Type 1 ITAE transfer function is given by

$$T_d(s) = \frac{\omega_0^3}{s^3 + 1.75\,\omega_o\,s^2 + 2.15\,\omega_0^2\,s + \omega_0^3}$$

The value of ω_0 can be chosen to meet other requirements, such as control energy. The ITAE program in the Appendix at the end of this chapter contains the numerator and denominator coefficients for systems of Type 0, 1, and 2. Example 10.3 will demonstrate the use of the ITAE approach.

Another approach to obtain a desired closed loop transfer function is to use basic results from optimal control, in particular, the SISO version of the LQR problem (discussed in Chapter 12). The applicable LQR objective function, a variation of the ISE criterion, is

$$J_{LQR} = \int_0^\infty [\,q\,(\,y(t) - r(t)\,)^2 + u(t)^2\,]\,dt$$

Minimizing this function minimizes the weighted energy of the tracking error and control. The parameter q allows us to trade off control energy against tracking error. Large values of q will place a heavy penalty on tracking error, resulting in a damped system with large control signals (possibly causing saturation problems). Small values of q will reduce control energy but will result in larger transient errors. The problem can be mathematically solved in the time or frequency domains. Once the optimal control is found and applied to the system, the optimal closed loop transfer function of the system can be obtained. It can be shown that controllers designed using the LQR approach will always be stabilizing.

The optimal closed loop transfer function corresponding to the LQR criterion for a unit step reference input (i.e., $r(t) = 1$, $t > 0$) is given by

$$T_{LQR} = \frac{q\,N(0)}{D_o(0)}\,\frac{N(s)}{D_o(s)} \quad \text{and} \quad G_e(s) = \frac{e(s)}{u(s)} = \frac{N(s)}{D(s)}$$

where $G_e(s)$ is the transfer function between the control signal and the tracking error. The polynomial $D_o(s)$ is the optimal characteristic polynomial and is the solution of

$$D_o(s)\,D_o(-s) = D(s)\,D(-s) + q\,N(s)\,N(-s)$$

Finding $D_o(s)$ from the preceding is called *spectral factorization* and is not an easy problem in general. We note, however, that if we divide the preceding equation by $D(s)D(-s)$, we get

$$D_o(s) \, D_o(-s) = 0 \quad \rightarrow \quad 1 + q \, \frac{N(s) \, N(-s)}{D(s) \, D(-s)} = 1 + q \, G_e(s) \, G_e(-s) = 0$$

The above is essentially the root locus form for the parameter q, where the appropriate transfer function is $G_e(s)G_e(-s)$. Because poles and zeros of this transfer function are symmetric with respect to the imaginary axis, its root locus will be symmetric about the same axes. The root locus is also symmetric with respect to the real axis; hence, this is called the Symmetric Root Locus (SRL) and is doubly symmetric about both axes and the origin.

To use the SRL, the root locus of the appropriate transfer function is obtained. There are two possibilities, 0-degree or 180-degree root loci. The appropriate root locus is the one that produces no poles on the imaginary axis (we already stated that LQR type compensators will always be stabilizing, so you cannot have closed loop poles on the imaginary axis).

For example, consider

$$G_e(s) = \frac{(s+1)}{s \, (s+2)} \quad \rightarrow \quad G_e(s) \, G_e(-s) = \frac{(s+1)}{s \, (s+2)} \, \frac{(-s+1)}{(-s) \, (-s+2)}$$

or

$$G_e(s) \, G_e(-s) = \frac{-(s+1) \, (s-1)}{s^2 \, (s+2) \, (s-2)}$$

You can verify that the 0-degree root locus will produce the correct result. Once the root locus is obtained, the optimal closed loop poles will correspond to the stable branches of the loci (the LHP ones). We can then select desired poles along these branches and choose q accordingly. This procedure is demonstrated in Example 10.4.

10.6 Unity Feedback Configuration

Unity Feedback Configuration (UFC) allows arbitrary pole placement for stable plants. Consider the following transfer functions:

$$G(s) = \frac{N(s)}{D(s)}, \quad K(s) = \frac{B(s)}{A(s)}, \quad T_d(s) = \frac{N_d(s)}{D_d(s)}$$

where G, K, and T_d represent the plant, compensator, and desired closed loop transfer functions, respectively. Setting the resulting closed loop transfer function equal to the desired one, we get (the dependence on s is suppressed)

$$T_d = \frac{N_d}{D_d} = \frac{B\,N}{A\,D + B\,N}$$

Equating the denominators, we get the *UFC Design Equation.*

$$\boxed{A\,D + B\,N = D_d}$$

Note that the numerator is fixed by N and B, where B is found by solving the Design Equation. This implies that, in general, assigning closed loop zeros is not possible using UFC. Because tracking properties (steady state errors to polynomial type inputs) depend on the coefficients of both the numerator and denominator of the closed loop transfer function, these requirements may not be met in general.

10.6.1 Solving the Design Equation

The Design Equation is a polynomial equation, with the unknowns A and B. Similar equations appear in number theory, where we try to solve for integer unknowns. For instance, consider

$$2\,x + 3\,y = 8 \quad \rightarrow \quad x = 1\ ,\ y = 2$$

The above equation is called the *Diophantine Equation* in number theory (finding the solutions is not as simple as it first appears). Because polynomials and integers share many algebraic properties, polynomial equations of the same form are also called by the same name. To get a feel for this equation, let us try a simple example.

Suppose the following plant is given, and we desire to move its poles to $\{-1 \pm j\}$; i.e.,

$$G = \frac{N}{D} = \frac{1}{s\,(s+1)} \quad \text{and} \quad \frac{N_d}{D_d} = \frac{1}{s^2 + 2s + 2}$$

The Design Equation becomes

$$A\,(s^2 + s) + B = s^2 + 2\,s + 2$$

If the compensator is a constant (i.e., A and B are constants), the above has no solutions. Trying polynomials of degree one for A and B, we get

$$A(s) = a_0 + a_1\,s\ ,\quad B(s) = b_0 + b_1\,s$$

$$(a_0 + a_1\,s)\,(s^2 + s) + (b_0 + b_1\,s) = s^2 + 2\,s + 2$$

Multiplying and equating coefficients of equal power, we get four equations and four unknowns:

$$\begin{bmatrix} 0 & 1 & 0 & 0 \\ 1 & 0 & 0 & 1 \\ 1 & 0 & 1 & 0 \\ 0 & 0 & 1 & 0 \end{bmatrix} \begin{bmatrix} a_0 \\ b_0 \\ a_1 \\ b_1 \end{bmatrix} = \begin{bmatrix} 2 \\ 2 \\ 1 \\ 0 \end{bmatrix} \rightarrow \begin{bmatrix} a_0 \\ b_0 \\ a_1 \\ b_1 \end{bmatrix} = \begin{bmatrix} 1 \\ 2 \\ 0 \\ 1 \end{bmatrix} \rightarrow K(s) = \frac{B}{A} = s + 2$$

As you can see, the equation has a solution, but the compensator is improper. Note that the system is second order, the compensator is first order, so in the absence of pole-zero cancellations, we should expect the closed loop transfer function to be third order. We also note from the Design Equation, that unless the right-hand side is third order, the coefficient a_1 will always be zero. Hence, it is clear that to obtain a proper compensator, we should specify a third order polynomial for $D_d (s)$. Toward that end, we introduce a third pole at $\{-3\}$ and solve for the compensator to get

$$K(s) = \frac{4s + 6}{s + 4}$$

This corresponds to a lead compensator, and could have been obtained using root locus design.

The preceding example demonstrates several points. First, polynomial Diophantine equations can be reduced to a set of simultaneous algebraic equations. Second, these equations do not always have unique solutions. Third, even when the equations have solutions, they do not necessarily result in proper compensators. Under mild conditions, however, it is possible to guarantee existence of a proper compensator to achieve arbitrary pole placement. These conditions are presented below.

Assume that the plant transfer function, G, is strictly proper (*deg (N) < deg (D)=n*) and *coprime* (i.e., there are no pole-zero cancellations), then there exists a compensator, K, of order $(n - 1)$, for any desired characteristic polynomial, D_d, of order $(2n - 1)$.

The general solution of the Diophantine equation is given below:

$$G = \frac{N}{D} = \frac{N_n s^n + N_{n-1} s^{n-1} + \dots + N_0}{D_n s^n + D_{n-1} s^{n-1} + \dots + D_0}, \qquad \text{where } N_n = 0$$

$$K = \frac{B}{A} = \frac{B_{n-1} s^{n-1} + \dots + B_1 s + B_0}{A_{n-1} s^{n-1} + \dots + A_1 s + A_0}$$

and $D_d (s) = F_{2n-1} s^{2n-1} + \dots + F_1 s + F_0$

Multiplying the appropriate terms and equating coefficients of equal power leads to the following set of simultaneous equations:

$$S(N, D) \, X = F$$

where
$$S(N,D) = \begin{bmatrix} D_0 & N_0 & | & 0 & 0 & | & | & 0 & 0 \\ D_1 & N_1 & | & D_0 & N_0 & | & \ldots & | & . & . \\ . & . & | & . & . & | & | & . & . \\ . & . & | & . & . & | & \ldots & | & 0 & 0 \\ D_n & N_n & | & D_n-1 & N_n-1 & | & | & D_0 & N_0 \\ 0 & 0 & | & D_n & N_n & | & | & D_1 & N_1 \\ . & . & | & 0 & 0 & | & \ldots & | & . & . \\ . & . & | & . & . & | & | & . & . \\ 0 & 0 & | & 0 & 0 & | & | & D_n & N_n \end{bmatrix}$$

and
$$X = \begin{bmatrix} A_0 \\ B_0 \\ A_1 \\ B_1 \\ . \\ . \\ . \\ A_{n-1} \\ B_{n-1} \end{bmatrix}, \quad F = \begin{bmatrix} F_0 \\ F_1 \\ F_2 \\ . \\ . \\ . \\ F_{2n-2} \\ F_{2n-1} \end{bmatrix}$$

The matrix $S(N, D)$ is called the *Sylvester matrix* and has order $2n$. It is a well-known fact in algebra that the Sylvester matrix is nonsingular if and only if the polynomials (N, D) are coprime. Note that in SISO systems, coprimeness of the plant transfer function is equivalent to controllability and observability. Therefore, the same condition that allows arbitrary pole placement using state feedback also allows pole placement using the polynomial or algebraic approach. This is the link between the state space and the transfer function approach.

The next example shows the application of this approach. Program 1 in the Appendix was used to solve the example.

Example 10.1 Unity Feedback Configuration

Consider the system transfer function used in the lead design in Example 7.4. It is repeated here for your convenience.

$$G(s) = \frac{400}{s(s^2 + 30s + 200)} = \frac{400}{s(s+10)(s+20)}$$

It is desired to place the dominant poles at $s_1 = -6.75 \pm j\,11.69$. Because the plant is third order, we can find a proper compensator by choosing five poles. We therefore choose three additional poles arbitrarily at $\{-10, -15, -20\}$. We next use the UFC program in the Appendix to solve for the compensator. The result is

b =
  1.0e+003 *
    0.0068   0.2050   1.3666
a =
    1.0000   28.5000 384.7186

Hence, the compensator is

$$K(s) = \frac{6.83\,(s+10)\,(s+20)}{(s+14.25+j\,13.47)\,(s+14.25-j\,13.47)}$$

We note that the compensator cancels the plant poles at {−10, −20}, and replaces them with complex poles.

The resulting closed loop transfer function becomes

$$T_c = \frac{2733.3\,(s+10)\,(s+20)}{(s+10)\,(s+20)\,(s+15)\,(s+6.75\pm j\,11.69)} = \frac{2733.3}{(s+15)\,(s+6.75\pm j\,11.69)}$$

The resulting step response, root locus and Bode plots are shown in Figures 10-2 and 10-3. We get a GM of 12 dB, PM of 59 degrees, and 9% overshoot and 14% steady state error to a unit ramp input. This is close to what we obtained using root locus lead design with a first order compensator.

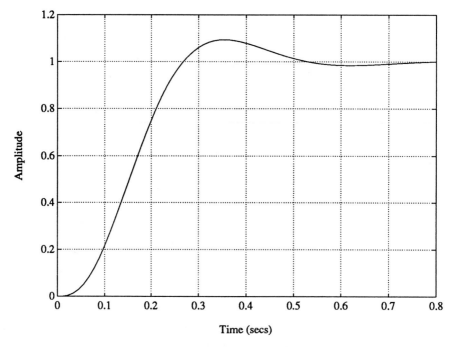

Figure 10-2 Step response for Example 10.1.

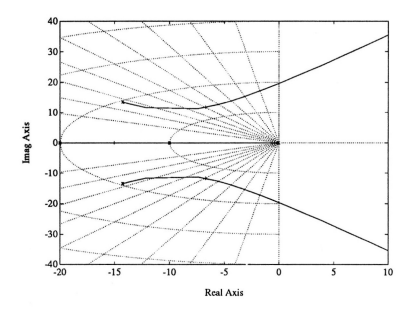

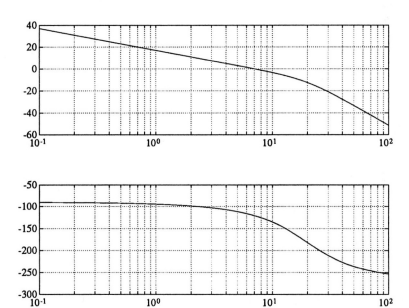

Figure 10-3 Root locus and Bode plots for Example 10.1.

Example 10.2 UFC Design of the Helicopter Problem

We now solve the helicopter problem introduced in Chapter 7. The plant transfer function is

$$G(s) = \frac{9.8\ (s - 0.25 \pm j\,2.49)}{(s - 0.118 \pm j\,0.367)\ (s + 0.656)}$$

We want the dominant poles to be placed at $\{-1 \pm j\}$ with three additional poles at $\{-2, -4, -5\}$. Using our program, we get

b =
  1.9210   2.6381   1.2193
a =
  1.0000 -6.2459 48.1889

$$K(s) = \frac{1.92\,(s + 0.68 \pm j\,0.4)}{(s - 3.12 \pm j\,6.19)}$$

Although the compensator is unstable, there has not been any unstable pole-zero cancellations. The resulting closed loop transfer function is

$$T_c(s) = \frac{18.82\,(s - 0.25 \pm j\,2.49)\,(s + 0.68 \pm j\,0.4)}{(s + 1 \pm j)\,(s + 2)\,(s + 4)\,(s + 5)}$$

The design meets all design constraints; the RHP zeros are retained, and the relative degree is 1. Note that even though the plant has both RHP poles and zeros, it is still possible to find a suitable unity feedback compensator to place the poles arbitrarily. The step response, root locus and Bode plots are shown in Figures 10-4 and 10-5. We get a GM of 13 dB, GRM of –8.5 dB, PM of 55 degrees, and 37% overshoot and 6% steady state error to a unit step input.

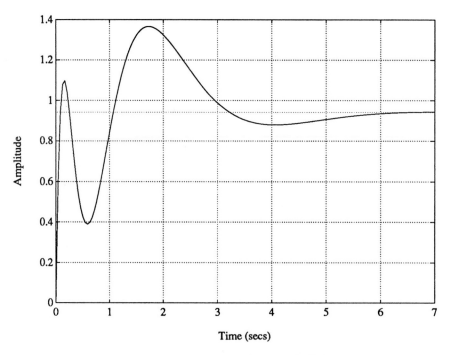

Figure 10-4 Step response for Example 10.2.

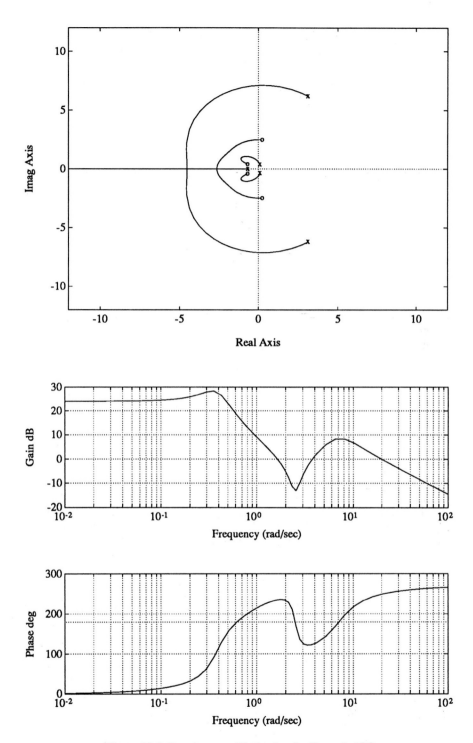

Figure 10-5 Root locus and Bode plots for Example 10.2.

10.7 Two-Parameter Configuration (RST Compensator)

The *two-parameter* configuration (also known as the *RST* compensator) is shown in Figure 10-6. It is a general configuration capable of arbitrary pole and zero assignment. The compensator equation is given by

$$R(s)\, u(s) = - S(s)\, y(s) + T(s)\, r(s)$$

where the name *RST* follows from the parameterization of the compensator and is fairly standard in the adaptive and digital control literature. The resulting closed loop transfer function is given by

$$T_c = \frac{N\,T}{S\,N + R\,D}$$

The following procedure guarantees realization of any desired closed loop transfer function for strictly proper and coprime plants.

Given $G(s)$, strictly proper and coprime, and an implementable $T_d(s)$, find a proper compensator to realize $T_d(s)$.

Solution: Consider

$$T_d(s) = \frac{N_d}{D_d} \quad \text{and let} \quad \frac{T_d}{N} = \frac{N_d}{D_d\,N} \triangleq \frac{N_p}{D_p}$$

Now, check the degree of D_p. If deg $D_p = p < 2n - 1$, where n is deg D, introduce a stable polynomial, $\overline{D}_p$, of degree $2n - 1 - p$; otherwise, set $\overline{D}_p = 1$. Multiply the numerator and denominator of the above by $\overline{D}_p$. Note that because this polynomial will be canceled, it is important that it be stable. We now have

$$T_d = \frac{N\,N_p\,\overline{D}_p}{D_p\,\overline{D}_p} \quad \text{letting } T_d = T_c\,, \text{ we get} \quad \frac{N_p\,\overline{D}_p}{D_p\,\overline{D}_p} = \frac{T}{S\,N + R\,D}$$

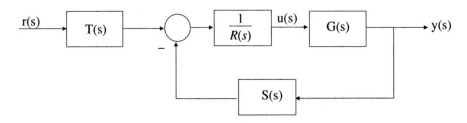

Figure 10-6 Block diagram of RST configuration.

Equating numerator and denominator terms determines the final Design Equations:

$$\boxed{\begin{aligned} T &= N_p \overline{D}_p \\ S\,N + R\,D &= D_p \overline{D}_p \overset{\Delta}{=} F \end{aligned}}$$

Note that the degree of F is $2n - 1$ and that of R and S is $n - 1$. Observe that the Design Equation is a Diophantine equation, and can easily be converted to the following form:

$$S(N, D)\, X = F$$

The matrix S is the same Sylvester matrix that appeared in the unity feedback design equation. The vectors X and F are defined as

$$X = \begin{bmatrix} R_0 \\ S_0 \\ R_1 \\ S_1 \\ \cdot \\ \cdot \\ \cdot \\ R_{n-1} \\ S_{n-1} \end{bmatrix} , \quad F = \begin{bmatrix} F_0 \\ F_1 \\ F_2 \\ \cdot \\ \cdot \\ \cdot \\ F_{2n-2} \\ F_{2n-1} \end{bmatrix}$$

10.7.1 Realization of the RST Compensator

Because the resulting RST compensator is in transfer function form, a question that may arise is how the compensator is actually realized. The answer is that the compensator is realized as one unit; i.e., as a system with two inputs and one output in state space form. We have

$$u = \begin{bmatrix} \dfrac{T}{R} & -\dfrac{S}{R} \end{bmatrix} \begin{bmatrix} r \\ y \end{bmatrix} = K(s) \begin{bmatrix} r \\ y \end{bmatrix} \quad \rightarrow \quad K(s) = \frac{1}{R}\,[\,T \quad -S\,]$$

To obtain the state space realization of $K(s)$, we use the *tf2ss* command.

The next example illustrates the procedure. The example was solved using the RST and ITAE programs (programs 2 and 4) in the Appendix.

Example 10.3 RST Compensator: ITAE Approach

We consider the following transfer function:

$$G(s) = \frac{(s-1)}{s\,(s-2)}$$

The above system has appeared in several papers and books and is well known for being difficult to control. It is an example of a system that requires an unstable compensator for stabilization. None of the traditional classical techniques apply to this plant. State space and the algebraic approach can easily handle this plant, however.

The first step is finding an appropriate desired closed loop transfer function. We will use the ITAE approach for demonstration. The transfer function must have relative degree of at least 1 and must retain the plant's RHP zero. We select a third order Type 1 transfer function (this will result in $\overline{D}_p = 1$):

$$T_d(s) = \frac{(s-1)(-\omega_0^3)}{s^3 + 1.75\,\omega_0\,s^2 + 2.15\,\omega_0^2\,s + \omega_0^3}$$

The only parameter to be determined is ω_0. One way to choose this is to simulate the step response of the transfer function between r and u, T_d/G, and choose the one resulting in smaller magnitudes for u.

After several trials, it appeared that larger values of ω_0 resulted in larger peak magnitudes for the control signal. We selected $\omega_0 = 1$, which ensured that $|u(t)| < 1$.

The compensator parameters are given by

```
R =
   1.0000  -6.9000
S =
  10.6500  -1.0000
T =
   -1
```

The compensator is realized in state space form as shown below:

```
>> [a1,b1,c1,d1]=tf2ss(T,R)

a1 =
   6.9000
b1 =
   1
c1 =
  -1.0000
d1 =
   0

>> [a2,b2,c2,d2]=tf2ss(-S,R)

a2 =
   6.9000
b2 =
   1
c2 =
  -72.4850
```

d2 =
 -10.6500

Because *tf2ss* handles SIMO systems, we will swap the *B* and *C* matrices to obtain our MISO compensator:

$$\dot{w} = 6.9\ w - r - 72.48\ y$$

$$u = w - 10.65\ y$$

The step response for *y/r* and *u/r*, the root locus, and Bode plots are shown in Figures 10-7, 10-8, and 10-9. The following data are obtained: GM = 1.25 dB, GRM = –1.34 dB, PM = –4.9 degrees, and the overshoot is about 3.8%. The closed loop poles are at {– 0.52 ± *j* 1.06 , – 0.708}. Note the very small stability margins for this design. The *rlocfind* command indicates the system is stable for the range of gain from 0.85 to 1.15. Because of the small stability margins, this design will be very sensitive to model errors. Although the design meets the specifications, it will most likely be unstable in practice.

It should also be pointed out that because of the numerator term, the selected transfer function is not truly ITAE optimal. Tables of ITAE optimal transfer functions do not have any entries with RHP zeros. What we did is very typical in engineering design; namely, we took the available tools and adapted them to our needs to satisfy the specifications as best as possible.

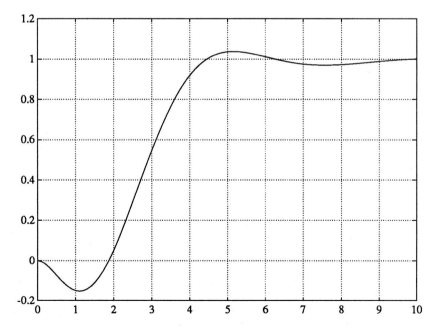

Figure 10-7 Output unit step response for Example 10.3.

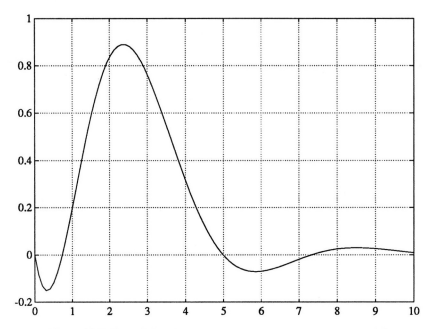

Figure 10-8 Control signal response to a unit step input in Example 10.3.

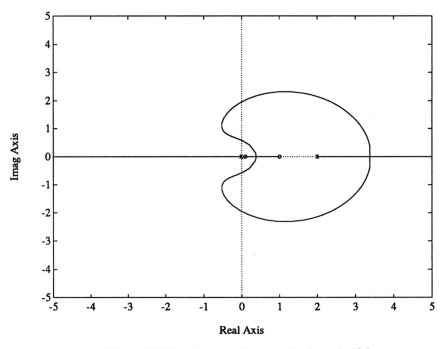

Figure 10-9 Root locus and Bode plot for Example 10.3.

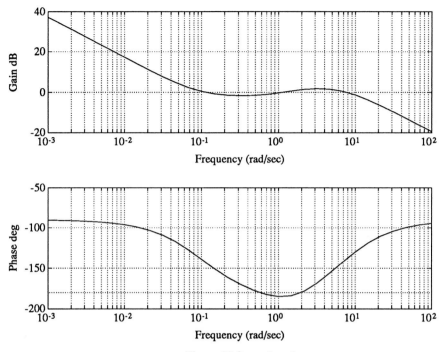

Figure 10-9 continued.

The next example illustrates the SRL approach.

Example 10.4 RST Compensator: SRL Approach

The previous example will be solved using the SRL approach. The first step is to obtain the root locus of

$$G(s)\,G(-s) = \frac{-(s+1)(s-1)}{s^2(s-2)(s+2)}$$

The SRL plots are shown in Figure 10-10. The 180-degree root locus has imaginary axis poles. The 0-degree root locus is the appropriate locus (of course, if you enter the above transfer function, the *rlocus* command gives the correct root locus plot).

Using the *rlocfind* command, the closed loop poles corresponding to the following three weights were selected: $\{q = 0.1, 1, 10\}$. Then three design iterations were performed, where, in each case, $\overline{D_p} = (s+1)$ was selected. Table 10-1 presents the data of our experiment. The output step response, control signals, and Bode plots are shown in Figures 10-11 through 10-13. From the data, the following observations can be made. As q increases (control becomes cheaper), closed loop poles are pushed deeper into the LHP, output becomes slightly more damped, control signal magnitudes increase, GM increases, GRM decreases, and PM changes slightly in each case. In Chapter 11, we will argue that some of these effects are expected in general.

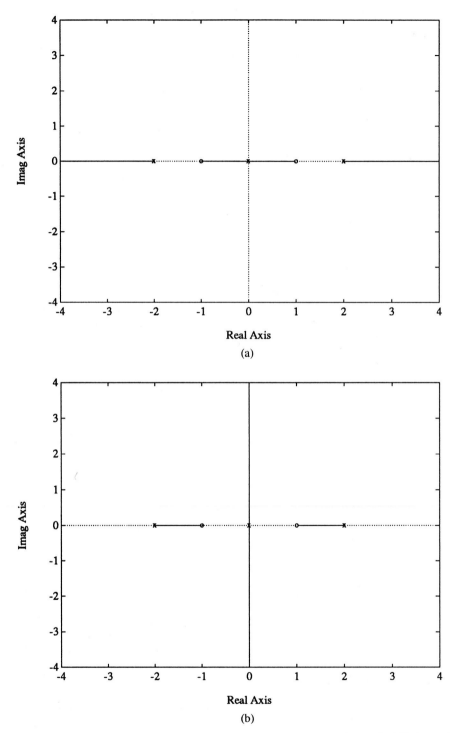

Figure 10-10 Symmetric Root Locus for Example 10.4. (a) 0-degree locus. (b) 180-degree locus.

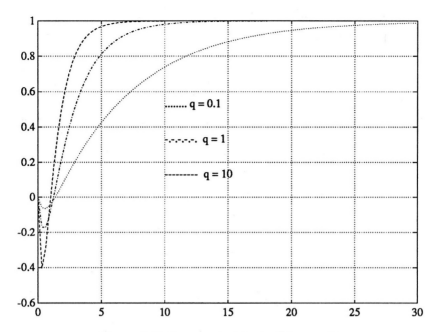

Figure 10-11 Step responses for the SRL example.

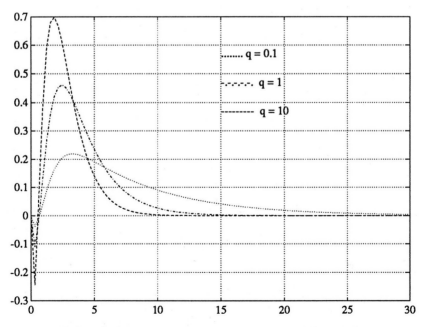

Figure 10-12 Control signal step responses for the SRL example.

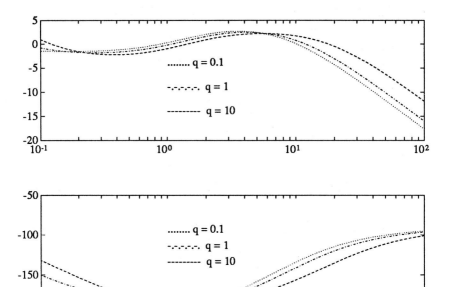

Figure 10-13 Bode plots for the SRL example.

Table 10-1 Results of RST-SRL Design Example

q	Desired Characteristic Polynomial	Closed Loop Poles	Y_{max}	U_{max}	U_{min}	GM	PM	Closed Loop Numerator and Denominator	R S T
0.1	1.00 2.17 .31	– .15 –1.00 –2.01	.98	.21	–.03	1.43 –2.35	9.74 46.66	– .31 .00 .31 1.00 3.17 2.49 .31 – .31 – .31	1.00 – 7.98 13.15 – .31 – .31 – .31
1	1.00 2.64 1.00	– .45 –1.00 –2.18	.99	.46	–.10	1.61 –2.17	– 9.51 44.83	–1.00 .00 1.00 1.00 3.64 3.64 1.00 –1.00 – 1.00	1.00 –10.29 15.93 – 1.00 –1.00 – 1.00
10	1.00 4.50 3.16	– .86 –1.00 –3.63	.99	.69	–.27	1.95 –2.00	41.76 –10.11 41.75	–3.16 .00 3.16 1.00 5.50 7.67 3.16 –3.16 – 3.16	1.00 –18.34 25.84 – 3.16 –3.16 – 3.16

10.8 Plant Input/Output Feedback Configuration

The Plant Input/Output Feedback Configuration (IOC) is precisely the configuration that results from an observer-based state feedback design. Therefore, arbitrary pole placement is possible. Using the polynomial approach simplifies the problem of zero assignment. This might be the only advantage over direct state space design. Of course, for implementation purposes, the compensator is converted to state space form.

The block diagram corresponding to the IOC is shown in Figure 10-1. As we can see the resulting closed loop transfer function is given by

$$T_c(s) = \frac{N\,A}{A\,D + L\,D + M\,N}$$

The following procedure guarantees realization of any desired closed loop transfer function for proper and coprime plants.

Given $G(s)$ strictly proper and coprime, find a compensator to realize $T_d(s)$. In addition, we also assume that the relative degree $(T_d(s))$ = relative degree $(G(s))$.

Solution : Consider

$$T_d(s) = \frac{N_d}{D_d} \qquad \text{and let} \qquad \frac{T_d}{N} = \frac{N_d}{D_d\,N} \overset{\Delta}{=} \frac{N_p}{D_p}$$

Now check the degree of N_p. If deg $N_p = p < n - 1$, introduce a stable polynomial, $\overline{D}_p$, of degree $n - 1 - p$; otherwise, set $\overline{D}_p$ equal to 1. Multiply the numerator and denominator of the above by $\overline{D}_p$. Note that because this polynomial will be canceled out, it is important that it be stable. We now have

$$T_d = \frac{N\,N_p\,\overline{D}_p}{D_p\,\overline{D}_p} \quad \text{letting } T_d = T_c, \quad \text{we get} \quad \frac{N_p\,\overline{D}_p}{D_p\,\overline{D}_p} = \frac{A}{A\,D + L\,D + M\,N}$$

Equating numerator and denominator terms determines the final IOC Design Equations:

$$\boxed{\begin{aligned} A &= N_p\,\overline{D}_p \\ L\,D + M\,N &= D_p\,\overline{D}_p - A\,D \overset{\Delta}{=} \quad F \end{aligned}}$$

The polynomial $\overline{D}_p$ plays the same role as the observer characteristic polynomial. Hence, the same judgment for choosing observer eigenvalues can be used to determine the roots of $\overline{D}_p$. Also, note that the compensator order will be $(n - 1)$, so this actually corresponds to a reduced order observer design. Finally, we note that the Design Equation is similar to the RST compensator; hence, the solution is given by (S is the same Sylvester matrix as in the unity feedback and RST designs)

$$S(N,D)\,X \;=\; F$$

$$
\text{where} \qquad X = \begin{bmatrix} L_0 \\ M_0 \\ L_1 \\ M_1 \\ \cdot \\ \cdot \\ \cdot \\ L_{n-1} \\ M_{n-1} \end{bmatrix}, \quad F = \begin{bmatrix} F_0 \\ F_1 \\ F_2 \\ \cdot \\ \cdot \\ \cdot \\ F_{2n-2} \\ F_{2n-1} \end{bmatrix}
$$

The next example illustrates the procedure.

Example 10.5 Input/Output Configuration: Helicopter Problem

The design problem discussed in Example 8.3 will be reexamined here. Using the IOC algebraic approach we will show that we get the same compensator here. The example was solved using the Input/Output program (program 3) in the Appendix; partial outputs of that program are displayed below. The plant transfer function is

$$
G(s) = \frac{9.8 \, (s - 0.25 \pm j\, 2.49)}{(s - 0.118 \pm j\, 0.367) \, (s + 0.656)}
$$

We first need to select a desired transfer function. For comparison, we will choose the final closed loop transfer function of Example 8.3. Hence, the following data are entered (actually the data from that example were first loaded, and then converted to transfer function form; this is what is displayed subsequently).

```
ng =
  9.8000  -4.9000  61.7400
dg =
  1.0000   0.4200  -0.0060   0.0980
Dd =
  1.0000  10.0000  48.0000  112.0000  132.0000  72.0000
Nd =
  1.0e+003 *
  0.0098  -0.0616   0.4446  -0.5342   2.2335
```

After forming ($N_d / D_d N$) and performing pole-zero cancellations, we get N_p and D_p.

```
np =
  1.0000  -5.7815  36.1758
dp =
  1.0000  10.0000  48.0000  112.0000  132.0000  72.0000
```

Note: Because of different algorithmic tolerances, these answers may vary with different hardware platforms. If you do not obtain the same answers, change the tolerance of the *minreal* command.

Because deg $N_p = p = 2$, then $\overline{D}_p = 1$ and $A = N_p$. After multiplying and subtracting the appropriate polynomials, we get F.

f =

    0   15.3615   14.2584   96.6735   132.7836   68.4548

Finally, we form the Sylvester matrix, reverse the elements of F, and solve the equation to get L and M.

l =

  1.0e-012 *

       0   -0.0072   0.189

m=

  1.5675   2.2387   1.1088

The compensator transfer function, in general, is given by (this can be derived by eliminating the feedback from u, see Figure 10-1).

$$K(s) = \frac{M}{L + A}$$

Computing the above, we get

$$K(s) = \frac{1.56\, s^2 + 2.23\, s + 1.10}{s^2 - 5.78\, s + 36.17} = \frac{1.56\,(s + 0.714 \pm j\,0.44)}{(s - 2.89 \pm j\,5.27)}$$

This is the same compensator obtained using reduced order observer-based controller design in Example 8.3.

The advantage of the algebraic approach is that tracking problems (e.g., introducing integral action) can be handled by modifying the desired closed loop transfer function. Although this can also be done using state space methods, those procedures are more complicated. Chen and Seo, [CS90a] and [CS90b], also discuss how disturbance rejection and internal model principle can be handled using simple modifications of the algebraic approach. The discrete version of the algebraic approach follows identically. Simply replace $G(s)$ by $G(z)$ where $G(z)$ is the pulse transfer function; i.e., the zero order hold equivalent or other discrete approximations of $G(s)$.

10.9 Appendix: Design Programs

1. Program for UFC Design

This program requires $G(s)=ng/dg$ and D_d. It returns, B and A where $K(s) = B / A$.

```
function [b,a]=ufc(ng,dg,Dd)
%     Dd = Denominator of Desired Transfer Function.
%     B = Numerator of compensator.
%     A = Denominator of compensator.
```

```
f = Dd;
m=length(ng);
nn=length(dg); n=nn-1; n2=2*n;
% n is the order of dg and n2 is the length of f
padzero=zeros(1,nn-m);
ngpad=[padzero ng];
% Degree of f is 2n-1 where n is the order of the plant.
S_col12=flipud([dg' ngpad']);
% sylv is the Sylvester Matrix
sylv=zeros(2*n);
for i=1:2:2*n-1,
    bgnrow=(i+1)/2;
    sylv(bgnrow:bgnrow+n,i:i+1)=S_col12;
end;
delta=flipud(Dd')
x=sylv\delta;
for i=1:2:2*n-1,
    r=(i-1)/2;
    a(n-r)=x(i); a=real(a);
    b(n-r)=x(i+1); b=real(b);
end;
```

2. Program for RST Compensator Design

This program requires G(s)=ng/dg, and the desired closed loop transfer function, T_d =Nd / Dd.

It returns the polynomials R, S and T. The program uses function kz, which removes leading zeros from polynomials.

```
function [R,S,T]=rst(ng,dg,Nd,Dd)
%     Nd = Numerator of Desired Transfer Function.
%     Dd = Denominator of Desired Transfer Function.
ngdd=conv(ng,Dd);
[np,dp]=minreal(Nd,ngdd);np=kz(np);
m=length(dg);
padzero=zeros(1,m-length(ng));
ngpad=[padzero ng];
n=m-1; p=length(dp)-1;
% n is the order of dg and p is the order of dp
% Note: The degree of dpbar=2n-1-p
if (p*n-1)
    ndpb=2*n-1-p;
    disp(' Please enter your Dp-bar (Order is on line below):')
    ndpb
    dpbar=input(' ');
else dpbar=1;
end;
T=conv(np,dpbar);
f=conv(dp,dpbar);
```

```
mt=2*n;
% mt is the length of f, deg of f is 2n-1, n is the plant order.
S_col12=flipud([dg' ngpad']);
% sylv is the Sylvester Matrix
sylv=zeros(mt);
for i=1:2:2*n-1,
   bgnrow=(i+1)/2;
   sylv(bgnrow:bgnrow+n,i:i+1)=S_col12;
end;
delta=flipud(f');
x=sylv\delta;
for i=1:2:2*n-1,
   j = (i-1)/2;
   R(n-j)=x(i);  R=real(R);
   S(n-j)=x(i+1);  S= real(S);
end;
```

3. Program for Input/Output Design

This program has the same inputs as RST, but will return the Input/Output compensator parameters L, M, and A. The program uses function kz, which removes leading zeros from polynomials.

```
%function [l,m,a] = io(ng,dg,Nd,Dd)
ngdd=conv(ng,Dd);
[np,dp]=minreal(Nd,ngdd);np=kz(np);
m=length(dg);
n=m-1; p=length(np)-1;
% n is the order of dg and p is the order of dp
% Note: The degree of dpbar = 2n-1-p
if (p   n-1)
   ndpb=n-1-p;
   disp(' Please enter your Dp-Bar (Order is on line below):')
   ndpb
   dpbar=input(' ');
else dpbar=1;
end;
a=conv(np,dpbar);
ftemp1=conv(dp,dpbar); ftemp2=conv(a,dg);
nft1=length(ftemp1); nft2=length(ftemp2);
ftemp2=[zeros(1,nft1-nft2) ftemp2];
f=ftemp1-ftemp2;
mt=2*n;
% n is the plant order and mt is the size of f
% Degree of f is 2n-1 where n is the order of the plant.
padzero=zeros(1,m-length(ng)); ngpad=[padzero ng];
S_col12=flipud([dg' ngpad']);
```

```
% sylv is the Sylvester Matrix
sylv=zeros(2*n);
for i=1:2:2*n-1,
   bgnrow=(i+1)/2;
   sylv(bgnrow:bgnrow+n,i:i+1)=S_col12;
end;
delta=flipud(f');
x=sylv\delta;
for i=1:2:2*n-1,
   r=(i-1)/2;
   l(n-r)=x(i);
   m(n-r)=x(i+1);
end;
```

4. ITAE Program

This program requests order, type, and wo, and will output the corresponding ITAE transfer function.

```
function [n,d]=ITAE(type,wo,order);
p=[1 1.4 1.75 2.1 2.8 3.25 4.475 5.20;0 1 2.15 3.4 5.0 6.6, ...
10.42 12.8; ...
0 0 1 2.7 5.5 8.60 15.08 21.60;0 0 0 1 3.4 7.45 15.54 25.75;...
0 0 0 0 1 3.95 10.64 22.20;0 0 0 0 0 1 4.58 13.30;...
0 0 0 0 0 0 1 5.15;0 0 0 0 0 0 0 1];

% ZERO-VELOCITY-ERROR SYSTEMS
v=[3.2 1.75 2.41 2.19 6.12;1 3.25 4.93 6.50 13.42;...
0 1 5.14 6.30 17.16;0 0 1 5.24 14.14;0 0 0 1 6.75;0 0 0 0 1];

% ZERO-ACCELERATION-ERROR SYSTEMS
a=[2.97 3.71 3.81 3.93;4.94 7.88 9.94 11.68;...
1 5.93 13.44 18.56;0 1 7.36 19.3;0 0 1 8.06;0 0 0 1];

            if type==1, x=p; i=order;    end
            if type==2, x=v; i=order-1; end
            if type==3, x=a; i=order-2; end
            d=x(:,i);
            j=length(d);
            while d(j)==0,
               j=j-1;
               end
            d=d(1:j);
            for i=1:j
               d(i)=d(i)*wo^i;
               end
            d=[1 d'];
            n=j+1;
            n=d(n-type+1:n);
```

5. The kz Progam

This program removes leading zeros from polynomials. It is used in the RST and IO programs.

```
function p_=kz(p)
ind=find(p~=0);p_=p(ind(1):length(p));
```

10.10 Problems

Note: Problems 10.1–10.8 are adapted from the papers by Chen and Seo [CS90a], and [CS90b].

10.1 *Internal Model Principle.*

Consider the plant

$$G(s) = \frac{2}{s\,(s^2 + 0.25\,s + 6.25)}$$

The desired closed loop transfer function is

$$T_d(s) = \frac{20}{(s + 10)\,(s^2 + 2\,s + 2)}$$

a. Design an RST compensator (choose the observer poles at –20, and –40).

b. Find and plot the step response of the system.

c. Suppose a step disturbance, d, is introduced such that plant input is the compensator output plus the disturbance. Find the transfer function, $H(s)$, between the disturbance and the plant output y.

d. Find the condition imposed on the compensator parameters to achieve disturbance rejection; i.e., $H(0)=0$.

e. We can achieve disturbance rejection by increasing the order of the compensator. In this problem, this can be done by increasing the order of the observer:

Choose $\overline{D}_p = (s + 20)^3$

Now, find the new RST compensator parameters.

f. Verify tracking and disturbance rejection properties of the system by finding unit step responses to the reference input and the disturbance.

10.2 Consider the same plant as in the previous problem. The desired closed loop transfer function in this case was chosen according to the dominant pole criteria.

a. Design an ITAE optimal desired closed loop transfer function satisfying the actuator magnitude constraint of $|u(t)| \leq 10$ for all $t \geq 0$.

b. Repeat the design using the SRL approach.

c. Plot step responses for the ITAE, SRL, and the dominant pole transfer function of the previous problem. Compare the three responses in terms of speed of response and overshoot.

d. Which technique gives the best response for this plant?

10.3 Consider the plant

$$G(s) = \frac{s-1}{s\,(s-2)}$$

a. Design an ITAE optimal closed loop transfer function satisfying the actuator limits: $|u(t)| \leq 10$

b. Repeat the design using the SRL approach.

c. Obtain the step responses and compare the results.

10.4 Consider the plant

$$G(s) = \frac{s+3}{s\,(s-1)}$$

In each of the following cases, we would like to achieve zero steady state error to unit step inputs and satisfy actuator magnitude constraint of $|u(t)| \leq 10$.

a. Design an optimal transfer function, $T_{d1}(s)$, using SRL approach.

b. Design an ITAE optimal transfer function, $T_{d2}(s)$.

c. Design a second order transfer function, $T_{d3}(s)$, with a damping ratio of 0.9 and natural frequency of 28.

d. Consider the following Type 1 transfer functions:

$$T_{d\,4}(s) = \frac{100}{s+100}\,, \quad T_{d\,5}(s) = \frac{10}{s+10}$$

e. Plot and compare the step responses in each case.

f. Plot and compare the actuator signals in each case.

10.5 Consider the plant in the previous problem.

a. Design a unity feedback compensator to place closed loop poles at $\{\,-2, -2 \pm j2\,\}$.

b. Plot the step response of the system. Does the response correspond to what would be expected from the closed loop poles? If not, explain why.

10.6 Consider the plant in the problem 10.4, and the following desired closed loop transfer functions.

$$T_{d\,1}(s) = \frac{600.25}{(s+3)\,(s^2 + 34.3\,s + 600.25)}\,, \quad T_{d\,2}(s) = \frac{10\,(s+13)}{s^2 + 12.7\,s + 30}$$

a. Design an RST compensator in each case and compare the designs.

b. Repeat the design using Input/Output Configuration.

10.7 *Extension of the RST Configuration*

One restriction imposed in the design for RST was that the desired closed loop transfer function had to be strictly proper. This restriction can be removed by changing one of the design steps. The change is as follows:

If *deg* $\overline{D}_p = p \leq 2n$, introduce an arbitrary polynomial $\overline{D}_p$ of degree $2n - p$.

Consider the plant $G(s)$,

$$G(s) = \frac{(s+1)^2}{s\,(s+3)}$$

Let the desired closed loop transfer function be $T_d(s) = 1$.

a. Generalize the RST program in the Appendix to handle this more general case.

b. Use your program to design a compensator.

10.8 *Choosing $\overline{D}_p(s)$ in the RST compensator*

There are various guidelines for choosing observer poles. One is to choose them at least two to three times faster than the fastest closed loop poles. Another guideline, suggested by recent results in optimal control, is to place the observer poles at the stable plant zeros and the remaining ones far in the LHP.

Consider the plant $G(s)$ and desired closed loop transfer function $T_d(s)$:

$$G(s) = \frac{s+3}{s\,(s-1)}\,, \quad T_d(s) = \frac{10\,(s+13)}{s^2 + 12.7\,s + 30}$$

We would like to study the effects of $\overline{D}_p(s)$ on disturbance rejection properties of the system. Consider the following choices for $\overline{D}_p(s)$:

$$\overline{D}_{p1}(s) = s + 3\ ,\ \overline{D}_{p2}(s) = s + 30\ ,\ \overline{D}_{p3}(s) = s + 300$$

a. Find the RST compensator in each case. Plot and compare the step responses for the transfer functions between disturbance $d(s)$ and output $y(s)$, and $d(s)$ and plant input $u(s)$.

b. Plot and compare the frequency responses in each case. The appropriate transfer function is $y(s)/d(s)$ in all cases.

c. To study the robustness of the designs, in each case, let the plant pole at $s = 1$ be replaced by $s = a$. In each case, find the range of a over which the system remains stable.

10.9 Consider the plants and the specifications in problem 7.5, repeat the designs using the algebraic apoproach. Choose any configuration you desire.

10.10 Consider the inverted pendulum problem discussed in problem 7.6. Design a compensator using the algebraic approach.

Notes and References

The algebraic approach is discussed fully in [C87a]. For a more advanced treatment including proofs, see [C84]. More recent tutorials, and extensions appear in [C87b], [CS90a], and [CS90b]. Evolution of the method from the state space viewpoint appears in [K80]. The method is also treated briefly in [FPE91] and [FPW90].

11

Random Signals
and Systems Analysis

11.1 Introduction

A fundamental exercise in control systems engineering is to design a system that performs optimally in an uncertain environment. By an uncertain environment, we mean systems with uncertain models subjected to uncertain, possibly random or stochastic, disturbances. One method of tackling this problem is to assume a perfect model for the plant and model the disturbances as random noise. This is the approach that evolved during the 1960s and culminated in the Linear Quadratic Gaussian (LQG) solution. Since that time, other approaches have been developed, such as Robust Control, Adaptive Control, Fuzzy Control, and Quantitative Feedback Theory.

The estimation problem culminated in the celebrated Kalman-Bucy filter theory, which has found numerous applications in control, communications, and signal processing. Because we will be presenting the Kalman-Bucy filter and the LQG solution in the next chapter, and these problems require some background in random processes, we will present a brief introduction to stochastic processes in this chapter. Because the subject of stochastic processes is quite involved and extensive, our discussion will be limited to definitions, terminology, relevant formulas, interpretations, and basic results that are needed for the next chapter. Relevant MATLAB signal processing commands will also be introduced.

11.2 Stochastic (Random) Processes

A stochastic process is a family of random variables denoted by $x(t,\omega)$. For a fixed time, $t = T$, $x(T,\omega)$ is a random variable called the *sample function*. For a fixed $\omega = \omega_0$, $x(t,\omega_0)$ is a time function called the *realization*. To simplify our notation, we will drop the dependence of $x(t,\omega)$ on ω.

We denote the probability density function of a process by $p(x(t))$; a process is completely characterized by its density function. Several (or vector) processes are characterized by their joint density functions. There are various statistical measures one can use to describe a process. The nth *moment* of a process is defined by

$$E \left[x^n (t) \right] = \int_{-\infty}^{\infty} x^n (t) \, p \left(x (t, \zeta) \right) d \zeta$$

The first moment, $n=1$, is the *mean* (also called *ensemble average* or *expected value*). The second moment is the *mean square value*. The nth *central moment* is defined by $E \left[x (t) - m (t) \right]^n$, where $m(t)$ is the mean. The second central moment is the *variance*, and its square root is the *standard deviation*. The first moment, or the mean, describes how the process behaves on the average, and the other moments are measures of variability. In most cases, all we may know about a process are its first and second order statistics. Processes that are completely characterized by these statistics are called *second order processes*. Note that in the above definition of ensemble average, we are integrating over random variables.

It is also possible to define *time averages* by

$$< x^n (t) > = \lim_{T \to \infty} \frac{1}{2T} \int_{-T}^{T} x^n (t) \, dt$$

For some processes, time averages and ensemble averages are equal. These processes are called *ergodic*. Because, in practice, we can have access to only one realization of the process, it is the time average that we can realistically compute. The ergodicity assumption is almost always made. It simply implies that one sample of the process represents the whole family, and we can replace ensemble averages by time averages, when needed.

The *(auto)correlation function* describes how different points in the process are related to each other; i.e., how similar $x(t_1)$ is to $x(t_2)$. It is defined by

$$R_x (t_1, t_2) = E \left[x(t_1) \, x (t_2) \right]$$

The correlation function is roughly a measure of randomness. Loosely speaking, if the correlation function is small, it means the process is "very random." Temporal relation between two processes is measured by their *cross-correlation function*, defined by

$$R_{xy} (t_1, t_2) = E \left[x(t_1) \, y(t_2) \right]$$

The *covariance function* is similar to the correlation function except that the means are subtracted out. It is defined by

$$\text{Cov} (x) = C_x (t_1, t_2) = E \left[(x(t_1) - m_1) (x(t_2) - m_2) \right]$$

where m_i is the mean of $x(t_i)$. *The cross-covariance* between two processes is defined similarly. The *correlation coefficient* is defined by

$$\rho_{xy} = \frac{Cov(x,y)}{\sigma_x \, \sigma_y}$$

where σ_x and σ_y are the standard deviations of x and y, respectively. The correlation coefficient is a scalar quantity bounded by 1. Given two processes, we say they are *statistically independent* if their joint density function is the product of their individual density functions. A process is said to be *stationary* if

$$p\,(x\,(t + \tau)) = p\,(x(t)) \quad \text{for all } t \text{ and } \tau$$

This implies that the density function and all statistics are functions of the time difference, τ, rather than the individual times. This is usually a strong assumption and is not needed for second order processes. A weaker assumption one can make is that the process is *stationary in the wide sense* (*w.s.s.*), defined by the following two conditions:

$$E\,[x(t)] = m\,, \quad \text{where } m \text{ is constant}$$

$$R_x\,(t_1,t_2\,) = E\,[x(t_1)\,x\,(t_2)] = R_x\,(t_1 - t_2) = R_x\,(\tau)\,, \quad \text{where } \tau = t_1 - t_2$$

Unless specified otherwise, we assume our processes are second order, ergodic, and stationary in the wide sense.

If the process has zero mean, then $Cov\,(x) = R_x(\tau)$. For $\tau = 0$,

$$R_x(0) = E\,[x^2(t)] \;=\; \text{mean square value}$$

$$C_x\,(0) = E\,[\,(x - m)\,^2] = \sigma^2 = \text{variance of } x$$

The most famous stochastic process is the *Gaussian* or *Normal* process. It is so called because its underlying density function is Gaussian (the famous bell-shaped curve). A very important property of a Gaussian process is that it is completely characterized by its mean and covariance. The Gaussian assumption is commonly made (as in LQG) in control design. In most cases, this assumption is made for mathematical convenience and, in fact, the mean or the variance of the process may not even be known. These quantities may be statistically estimated or even pulled out of a hat to render a rational synthesis method. The numbers can then be changed until some specifications are met, as in the LQG/LTR technique (see Chapter 12).

If two w.s.s. processes are also independent, then we have

$$R_{xy}\,(\tau) = E\,[x(t)]\,E\,[y(t + \tau)] = m_x\,m_y$$

The converse of the preceding is only true for Gaussian processes. Two processes are said to be *uncorrelated* if their cross-covariance is identically zero, which implies that

$$E\,[x(t)\,y(t)] = E\,[x(t)]\,E\,[y(t)]$$

Note that this is a weaker assumption than statistical independence. Two processes are said to be *orthogonal* if they are uncorrelated and have zero mean; i.e.,

$$E\,[x(t)\,y(t)] = 0$$

Frequency domain description of w.s.s. stochastic processes are obtained by taking the Fourier transform. The Fourier transform of the correlation function is called the *power spectral density* (PSD) function and is defined by

$$S_x(\omega) = F\,[\,R_x(\tau)\,] = \int_{-\infty}^{\infty} R_x(\tau)\,e^{-j\omega\tau}\,d\tau$$

$$R_x(\tau) = F^{-1}\,[\,S_x(\omega)\,] = \frac{1}{2\pi}\int_{-\infty}^{\infty} S_x(\omega)\,e^{j\omega\tau}\,d\omega$$

We make the following simple but important observation

$$R_x(0) = \text{mean square value of } x = E\,[\,x^2(t)\,] = \frac{1}{2\pi}\int_{-\infty}^{\infty} S_x(\omega)\,d\omega$$

Therefore, the area under the PSD is proportional to the mean square value of the process and represents its average power. It can also be shown that the PSD is an even function of frequency. The *cross-spectral density function*, $S_{xy}(\omega)$, is defined as the Fourier transform of the cross-correlation function.

11.3 Vector Processes

Consider the stochastic process $x(t,\omega)$, where x is an n-dimensional vector. The process is characterized by its joint density function for all time. The first and second order statistics for the process are defined subsequently, where we will assume ergodicity and stationarity in the wide sense.

The mean is defined component-wise; i.e., it is a column vector where each element is the mean of the individual elements of the process. The *(auto)correlation matrix* is defined by

$$R_x(\tau) = E\,[\,x(t)\,x'(t+\tau)\,]$$

We note that diagonal elements of the correlation matrix are the autocorrelation functions, whereas the off-diagonal elements are cross-correlation functions. The (*auto*) *covariance matrix* is defined by

$$C_x(t) = E[(x(t) - m)(x(t) - m)'] = E[x(t) x'(t)] - m m'$$

The diagonal elements of the covariance matrix are the variances of individual elements, and the off-diagonal elements are cross-covariance functions of different elements; i.e.,

$$C_{ii} = \sigma_i^2 \quad \text{and} \quad C_{ij} = \rho_{ij} \sigma_i \sigma_j$$

Note that if the process has zero mean, we have $C_x(t) = R_x(0)$. Also, if the covariance matrix is diagonal, the process is uncorrelated.

A process is said to be *white Gaussian* if its underlying density function is Gaussian and its PSD is constant for all frequencies, or equivalently, its autocorrelation function is an impulse. For our purposes, we will typically assume that stochastic disturbances and measurement noise are zero mean white Gaussian processes. Another important use of white noise is that many processes can be generated by passing white noise through a linear system called a *shaping filter*. In subsequent sections we will designate Gaussian (Normal) processes as $v \sim N(m, W)$ where m is the mean and W is the covariance of v.

11.4 Response of Linear Systems to Random Inputs

Consider the following linear time-invariant system, with transfer function $H(s)$ and state space representation given by

$$\dot{x} = A x + B u$$
$$y = C x$$

where $u \sim N(0, V)$. The mean (m) and covariance (P) of the states satisfy the following differential equations:

$$\dot{m} = A m \qquad\qquad m(0) = E x(0)$$

$$\dot{P} = AP + PA' + BVB' \qquad\qquad P(0) = Cov(x(0))$$

The above equations describe how uncertainties with respect to initial states and the random input propagate through the system. If there is no random input (i.e., $V = 0$), we still have uncertainty because of the initial states. Assuming the system is asymptotically stable, the mean approaches zero in steady state, and the covariance matrix will satisfy the following algebraic equation called the *Lyapunov* equation:

$$AP + PA' + BVB' = 0 \quad \rightarrow \quad P = \int_0^\infty e^{At} \, B \, V B' \, e^{A't} \, dt$$

The output covariance matrix is given by

$$\text{Cov}(y) = CPC'$$

Frequency domain descriptions in terms of power spectral densities are given by

$$S_x(\omega) = \Phi(j\omega) \, BVB' \, \Phi'(-j\omega), \quad \text{where} \quad \Phi(\omega) = (j\omega I - A)^{-1}$$

$$S_y(\omega) = H(j\omega) \, S_u(\omega) \, H'(-j\omega) = H(j\omega)VH'(-j\omega)$$

$$S_{xy}(\omega) = H(j\omega)V$$

Note that if the input is white noise with unit intensity (i.e., $V = I$), then the system frequency response is given by the cross-spectral density function. This is sometimes used to identify system dynamics. We can intuitively think of PSD's as transforms of inputs and outputs and the cross spectral density as the stochastic analog of the concept of the transfer function in deterministic systems. An alternate expression for P in terms of PSD is given by (using *Parseval's Theorem*)

$$P = \frac{1}{2\pi} \int_{-\infty}^\infty \Phi(j\omega) \, BVB' \, \Phi'(-j\omega) \, d\omega$$

11.5 MATLAB Signal Processing Commands

The appropriate commands for generating and analyzing random signals, and computing the response of linear systems to random inputs are described next. An example demonstrating the use of the commands will follow.

```
>> rand
```

The *rand* command in various forms generates random numbers. Typing *rand* by itself returns a random number from a uniform distribution between 0 and 1 (the default distribution), *rand (m,n)* returns an *m* by *n* random matrix, and *rand (a)* returns a random matrix with the same size as matrix *a*; *rand('normal')* switches to the normal distribution with mean 0 and variance 1, *rand('seed',n)* resets the seed to a value of *n*, and *rand('seed',0)* resets the seed to 0. This is used when we wish to repeat a series of experiments using the same random numbers.

```
>> fft
```

The *fft (Fast Fourier Transform) command provides an efficient algorithm for computing the Discrete Fourier Transform* (DFT) of a time domain signal. The definition of an N-point DFT is given by (in the standard definition, the indices of x and X start at zero):

$$X(i+1) = \sum_{k=0}^{N-1} x_{k+1} e^{-2\pi j \frac{ik}{N}} \qquad \text{for } i = 0, \dots, N-1$$

The syntax for *fft* is

```
>> xf=fft(x,m)
```

where x is a time domain signal that can be a row or a column, real or complex vector. The output, xf, is the DFT of x and, in general, is a complex vector. The length of xf will be equal to the length of x. The integer m is optional, and is the length of the desired DFT. If m is larger than the length of x, the sequence is padded with trailing zeros; if it is smaller, the sequence is truncated. If the input argument is a matrix, we get the DFT of the columns. The *fft* command uses a fast algorithm if the length of the input sequence is a power of 2; otherwise, a slower algorithm is used.

Note that for real data, the N-point DFT is symmetric around the (N/2) point, so for plotting purposes, it is sufficient to plot the first half of the DFT, which corresponds to positive frequencies. Recall also that peaks in the plot of DFT indicate the frequency components present in the signal. A rapidly fluctuating signal may have several peaks in the high-frequency region. A random signal with periodic components may have a random looking FFT with distinct peaks at the periodic component frequencies. The inverse DFT transform is obtained by the *ifft* command, which has similar syntax.

The power spectral density (PSD) of a signal, a measure of signal energy at different frequencies, is given by

$$PSD(x) = \frac{1}{n} |X|^2 = \frac{1}{n} X X^* \text{ where } X = DFT[x] \text{ and } * \text{ stands for complex conjugate}$$

The PSD can be computed as (n is the length of the DFT)

```
>> PSDx=X.*conj(X)/n
```

Standard statistical functions are *mean, median,* and *std* (standard deviation). For matrix input arguments, the commands compute the mean, median, and standard deviation of columns.

```
>> cx=cov(x)      or    cov(x,y)
>> rx=corrcoef(x)  or    corrcoef(x,y)
```

The *cov* command computes the covariance matrix. If its input is a vector, it computes the variance (square of the standard deviation). If the input is a matrix (with its rows corresponding to observations and its columns corresponding to variables), it returns the covariance matrix (denoted earlier by C_x). Recall that the diagonal elements will be the variances of each variable. The command can be used with two arguments as $cov(x,y)$; in this case, it would be equal to $cov([x,y])$. The correlation matrix of the matrix x (denoted by R_x) is given by the *corrcoef* command.

```
>> xcorr(x)    or    xcorr(x,y)
>> xcov(x)     or    xcov(x,y)
```

These commands (in the Signal Processing Toolbox) compute the correlation and covariance sequences for random processes. For a real discrete stationary random process, the autocorrelation sequence is defined by $E[x_n x_{n+m}]$. Because we have only access to finite data segments, the correlation sequence has to be estimated. An estimate is given by the *xcorr* command, which computes

$$R_x(m) = \sum_{n=0}^{N-m-1} x(n)\, x(n+m)$$

The *xcov* command computes the autocovariance sequence defined by

$$C_x(m) = E[(x_n - \bar{x})(x_{n+m} - \bar{x})], \qquad \bar{x} = \text{mean of } x$$

The two-argument syntax forms compute the cross-correlation and cross-covariance respectively.

```
>> [Q,P]=covar(a,b,c,d,V)
>> P=covar(num,den,V)
```

The *covar* command (in the Control System Toolbox) computes the covariance of the states of a linear system driven by white noise with intensity V. The outputs of the command are output covariance Q (equal to CPC'), and state covariance P. The root-mean-square (RMS) response can be found from the square root of the output covariance. The output RMS response is a measure of the average power at the system output. The *covar* command actually solves the algebraic Lyapunov equation introduced in the last section (also discussed next). Note the difference between the *cov*, *xcov*, and *covar* commands. The former two use observation data for computation, whereas the latter uses the dynamical equations of a linear system along with the input noise covariance to compute the output covariance. The *cov* and *xcov* differ in that *cov* computes the zero-th lag [i.e., $C_x(0)$] of the covariance function divided by $n - 1$, where n is the data length:

```
>> p=lyap(a,q)
```

The *lyap* command solves a special form of the algebraic Lyapunov equation (ALE) defined by

$$AP + PA' + Q = 0$$

The above equation appears in several places in control theory. In steady state stochastic analysis, the solution of ALE describes the state covariance, P, of an asymptotically stable LTI system driven by zero-mean white noise input with covariance V ($Q = BVB'$ in this case). In filtering applications, P may stand for the error covariance and is a measure of filter performance. In stability theory, it is known that for an asymptotically stable LTI system, the ALE in the form

$$A'P + PA + Q = 0$$

has a positive definite solution for any given positive definite Q (you should replace A by A' in the command in this case). The syntax form of the *lyap* command

```
>> X=lyap(A,B,C)
```

solves the general form of the ALE equation given by

$$AX + XB + C = 0$$

where $A = m \times m$, $B = n \times n$, $C = m \times n$.

```
>> P=spectrum(x,m)     or     spectrum(x,y,m)
>> specplot(P,Fs)
```

The *spectrum* command computes the power spectrum of a signal. The inputs are the signal x and the number of points m. Its outputs are two columns (PSD of x and its standard deviation). With three inputs, it computes several quantities: PSD of x, PSD of y, cross PSD of x and y, the estimate of the transfer function from x to y (it returns the frequency response), the coherence function and confidence limits of estimation. Although power spectrum is defined as the DFT of the correlation sequence, the *spectrum* command uses a special method (Welch method) for computation that uses windowing techniques. Hence, if you find the DFT of the correlation sequence, it will not be equal to the results of the *spectrum* command. The *specplot* command automatically plots the outputs of the *spectrum* command (PSD of x, PSD of y, transfer function magnitude and phase, and the coherence function).

The spectrum of a signal shows the frequency contents of that signal. A rapidly fluctuating signal may have many high frequency components; this is indicated by a "high pass" spectrum. Peaks in the spectrum correspond to periodic components in the signal.

Both autospectra and cross-spectra can be used to estimate the transfer function of a linear time invariant system using the relations below:

$$S_y(\omega) = |H(j\omega)|^2 S_x(\omega)$$

$$S_{xy}(\omega) = H(j\omega) S_x(\omega)$$

Let *sy* and *sx* denote the output and input spectra (obtained using the *spectrum* command), then *h* is the estimate of the square of the magnitude of the underlying system transfer function. Note that the autospectrum is real, and, therefore, this estimate ignores phase information. The magnitude of the transfer function can be estimated by the following:

```
>> h=sy(:,1)./sx(:,1); h=sqrt(h)
```

The above estimate will be very close to the magnitude of the fourth column of the output of the *spectrum* command:

```
>> P=spectrum(x,y,m); h=abs(P(:,4))
```

The following example will demonstrate the use of the above commands.

Example 11.1 Stochastic Analysis

We consider two second-order systems with different bandwidths. Both systems are driven by white noise. The following responses are obtained and compared for both systems: time response, Fourier transform of input and outputs, autocorrelation functions, and power spectral densities. The systems are given by

$$G_1(s) = \frac{2}{s^2 + 2s + 2}, \qquad G_2(s) = \frac{25}{s^2 + 25\sqrt{2}\,s + 625}$$

The bandwidths of the systems are $\sqrt{2}$ and 25, respectively. It is naturally expected that the first system will filter high frequency noise much better than the second one.

The first step is to set the random number generator to *Normal* with zero mean, unit intensity white noise; we will also reset the seed to zero. The number of points generated is 128, a power of 2, which is recommended for some of the commands.

```
>> dt=0.01; t=[0:127]'*dt; rand('normal'); rand('seed',0);
>> in1=rand(t);
```

The systems are then defined and simulated with the noise input:

```
>> n1=2; d1=[1,2,2]; n2=625; d2=[1,sqrt(2)*25,625];
>> y1=lsim(n1,d1,in1,t); y2=lsim(n2,d2,in1,t);
```

The inputs and the responses are shown in Figure 11-1. We observe that the outputs are smoothed versions of the input, where y1 is much smoother than y2. This is due to the fact that both systems are low pass with the second system having a higher bandwidth. This result is verified by looking at the DFT of the time domain signals:

```
>> in1f=fft(in1); y1f=fft(y1); y2f=fft(y2);
```

The plots of the first 64 points of the magnitude of the DFT corresponding to positive frequency versus the frequency axis, in units of Hertz, are shown in Figure 11-2. These plots verify the low pass characteristics of the systems. The absence of any distinct peaks indicates lack of any periodic components. We will compute the autocorrelations next:

```
>> ruu=xcorr(in1); ryy1=xcorr(y1); ryy2=xcorr(y2;
```

The plots are shown in Figure 11-3. Note that the auto-correlations are symmetric about the vertical axis—an even function; the input autocorrelation is almost impulsive (nonideal white noise) and that there is more correlation in the first system than in the second one. This is a measure of variability in the signals. The more fluctuation in a signal, the less correlation between the neighboring points and, hence, the more impulsive looking the autocorrelation appears. We will compute the PSD of the signals and plot them using the *specplot* command at the top of page 358.

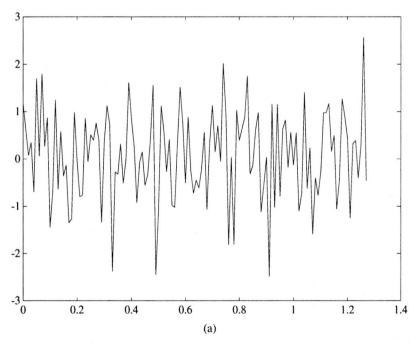

(a)

Figure 11-1 Time responses to noise. (a) Noise input. (b) y_1. (c) y_2..

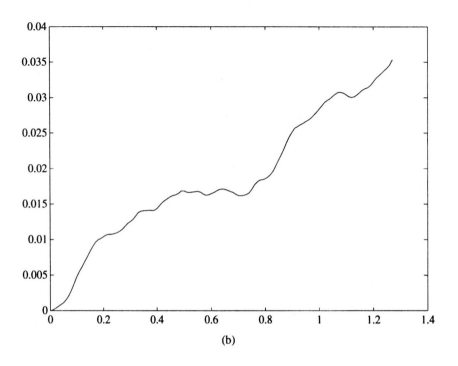

(b)

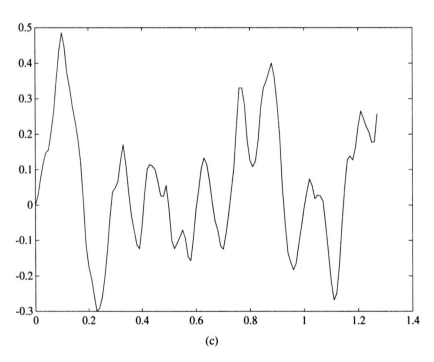

(c)

Figure 11-1 continued.

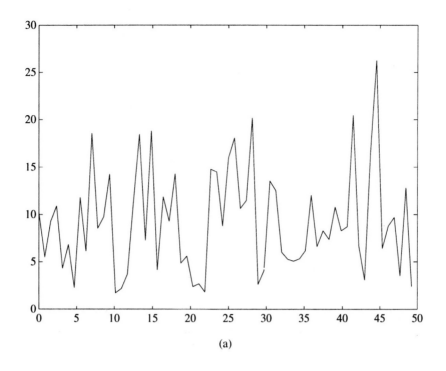

(a)

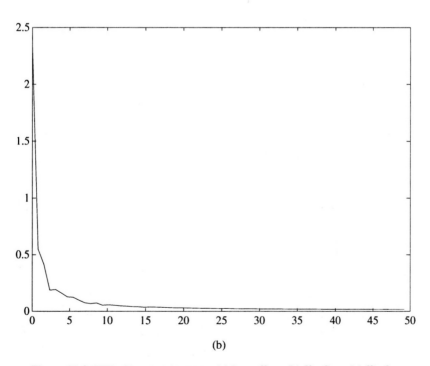

(b)

Figure 11-2 FFT of input and outputs. (a) Input fft.   (b) fft of y_1.   (c) fft of y_2.

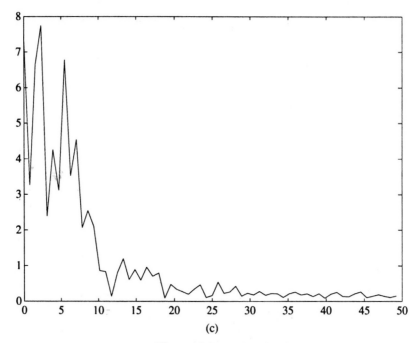

(c)

Figure 11-2 continued.

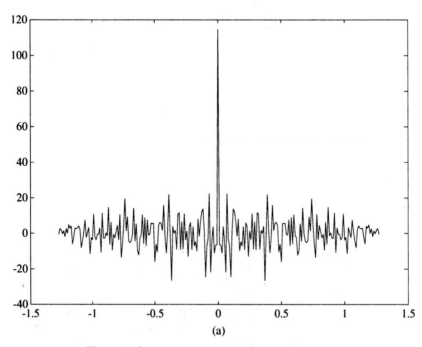

(a)

Figure 11-3 Autocorrelations. (a) Input. (b) y_1. (c) y_2.

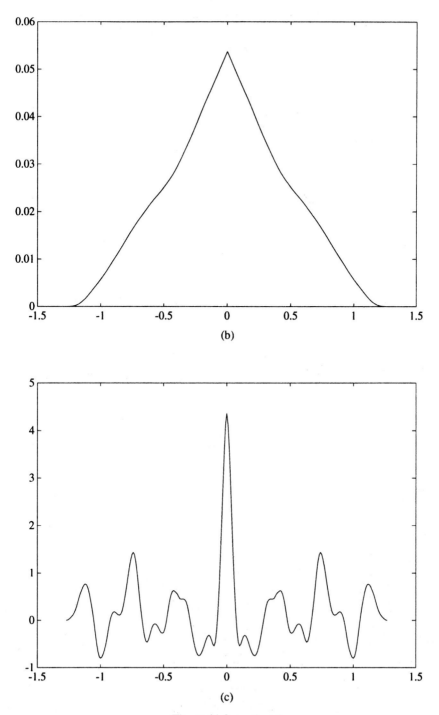

(b)

(c)

Figure 11-3 continued.

```
>> psdu=spectrum(in1,128); psdy1=spectrum(y1,128);
>> psdy2=spectrum(y2,128);
>> specplot(psdu,1/dt), specplot(psdy1,1/dt), specplot(psdy2,1/dt)
```

The PSD plots are shown in Figure 11-4. The plots reconfirm the conclusions from the DFT analysis. Note that the plots are somewhat similar to the DFT plots (the *specplots* are semilog, whereas the *fft* plots are straight magnitudes). All of the plots confirm the fact that a system with a higher bandwidth passes more noise and its output is more random. From a time domain point of view, the system with a higher bandwidth is faster and hence is more responsive to a jerky input such as white noise.

The state covariance and the output RMS values are now obtained (state space form of the system are needed at this point). The matrix p1 can also be computed using the *lyap* command:

```
>> [ycov1,p1]=covar(a1,b1,c1,D1,1), yrms1=sqrt(ycov1)
>> [ycov2,p2]=covar(a2,b2,c2,D2,1), yrms2=sqrt(ycov2)
```

```
ycov1 =
   0.5000
p1 =
   0.2500   0.0000
   0.0000   0.1250
yrms1 =
   0.7071


ycov2 =
   8.8388
p2 =
   0.0141   0.0000
   0.0000   0.0000
yrms2 =
   2.9730
```

Finally, the *cov* command is used to compute the covariance matrix for inputs and outputs:

```
>> sys_cov=cov([in1,y1,y2])
```

```
sys_cov =

   0.8968  -0.0003  -0.0249
  -0.0003   0.0001  -0.0001
  -0.0249  -0.0001   0.0310
```

Note that the output RMS values are the square roots of the output covariances. The higher RMS value in the second system indicates the higher average power of noise at the system output. The diagonal elements of the sys_cov matrix are the variances of the input and outputs. You can see the filtering action as the output variances are smaller.

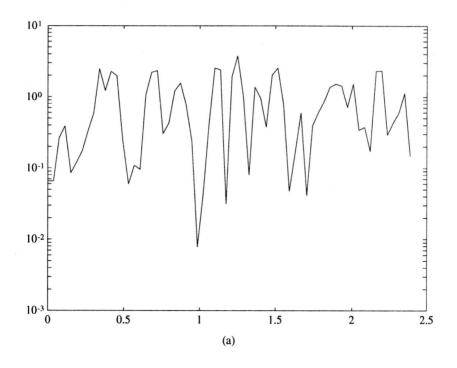

(a)

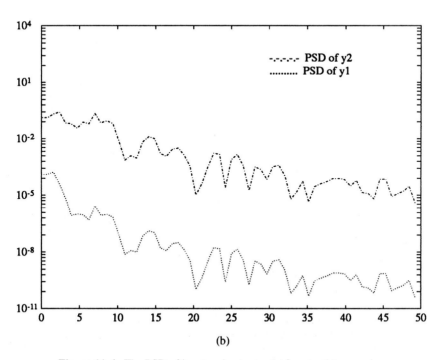

(b)

Figure 11-4 The PSD of input and outputs. (a) Input. (b) y_1 and y_2.

The Signal Processing Toolbox of MATLAB has a host of commands for analyzing and designing analog and digital filters. Analog filter prototypes such as Butterworth, Chebyshev, and elliptic filters are present. There are commands for designing IIR and FIR filters along with several popular windowing options. There are tools for filter transformations (low pass to high pass, bandpass, etc.). Several analysis tools for computing frequency response, group delay, and spectrum analysis are at hand. The following example is used as a vehicle to introduce and demonstrate a few of these commands.

Example 11.2 Digital Filter Analysis

We will start with a digital filter and show its frequency characteristics in both the time and frequency domain. We arbitrarily select an eighth order bandpass Butterworth filter. The filter is to pass frequencies between 100 to 300 Hz. This filter is given by the *butter* command with the following syntax:

```
>> [b,a]=butter(n,wn)    or    butter(n,wn,'type')
```

The command inputs are: n=filter order, wn=cutoff frequency. The default filter type is low pass. If wn is a two-element vector, it will correspond to a bandpass filter (the filter order will be automatically doubled). For high pass and bandstop filters, use the second form with the string option 'high' or 'stop', respectively. The cutoff frequency must be normalized to between 0 and 1 (1 corresponds to half the Nyquist frequency). The digital filter coefficients are returned in the following form:

$$ H(z) = \frac{b(z)}{a(z)} = \frac{b_1 + b_2 z^{-1} + \ldots + b_{n+1} z^{-n}}{1 + a_2 z^{-1} + \ldots + a_{n+1} z^{-n}} $$

Note that the above form for discrete transfer function representation is different from the Control System Toolbox.

Assuming a sampling frequency of 1000 Hz (Nyquist frequency = 500 Hz), our bandpass filter is given by (the cutoff frequencies are normalized by the Nyquist frequency)

```
>> [b,a]=butter(4,[100,300]/500);
```

The *z*-domain frequency response is computed by the *freqz* command:

```
>> [h,w]=freqz(b,a,2^7);
```

The inputs are the filter coefficients and the number of points (use a power of 2). The outputs are the complex frequency response and the set of frequencies. The magnitude response versus normalized frequency is shown in Figure 11-5.

```
>> f=w*500/pi; plot(f,abs(h))
```

We next generate a sinusoidal input with frequencies 50, 150, and 400 Hz:

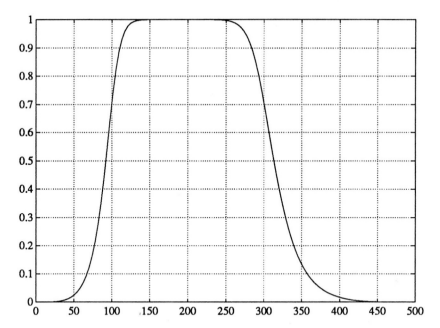

Figure 11-5 The magnitude of the Butterworth bandpass filter.

```
>> t=0:0.001:0.6; x=sin(2*pi*150*t)+cos(2*pi*400*t)+sin(2*pi*50*t);
```

We then corrupt the input signal with normally distributed white noise:

```
>> rand('normal'), xn=x+2*rand(t);
```

The first 100 points of the inputs are shown in Figure 11-6. The noise free input clearly shows periodic components, the noisy input, however, appears quite random. We next obtain the DFT and PSD of both inputs:

```
>> X=fft(x,512); Xn=fft(xn,512);
>> Px=X.*conj(X)/512; Pxn=Xn.*conj(Xn)/512;
>> ff=1000*(0:255)/512; plot(ff,Px(1:256)), plot(ff,Pxn(1:256))
```

The plots in Figure 11-7 clearly show the three frequency components present in both inputs. The inputs are then filtered using the *filter* command. The first two input arguments of this command are the filter coefficients, the third argument is the input data:

```
>> y=filter(b,a,x); yn=filter(b,a,xn);
```

Because the filter bandpass is between 100 to 300 Hz and the input frequencies are 50, 150, and 400 Hz, only the 150 Hz component should be present in the output. The first 100 points

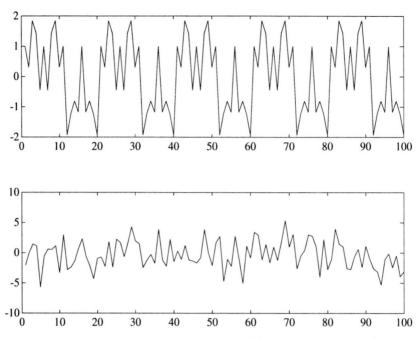

Figure 11-6 The noise-free input (top plot), and the noisy input (bottom plot).

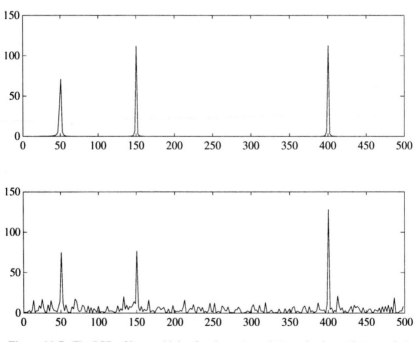

Figure 11-7 The PSD of inputs. Noise-free input (top plot); noisy input (bottom plot).

362

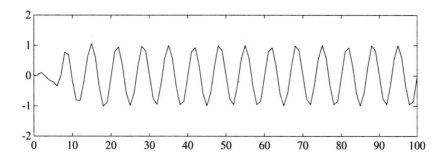

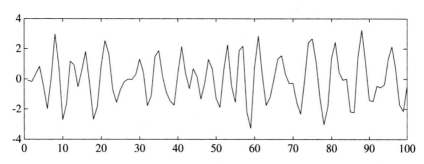

Figure 11-8 Filtered data. Filtered noise-free input (top plot), filtered noisy input (bottom plot).

of the filtered data are shown in Figure 11-8. The top plot (noise free input) clearly shows that only one harmonic is present. This is not clear in the noisy input case.

The PSD of the outputs in Figure 11-9 also show the presence of the 150 Hz harmonic in the output, confirming that the filter is clearly bandpass.

```
>> Y=fft(y,512); Py=Y.*conj(Y)/512;
>> Yn=fft(yn,512); Pyn=Yn.*conj(Yn)/512;
```

Finally, the impulse response of the filter is obtained. The *dimpulse* command uses a different form for the transfer function. It is easier to generate an impulse and run it through the filter directly. The plot is shown in Figure 11-10.

```
>> imp=[1,zeros(1,19)]; yi=filter(b,a,imp);
>> comb(yi), hold on, plot(yi,':'), hold off
```

Note the use of the *comb* command that is popular for displaying discrete sequences. We have intentionally used the *plot* command with a line style option for an interesting effect.

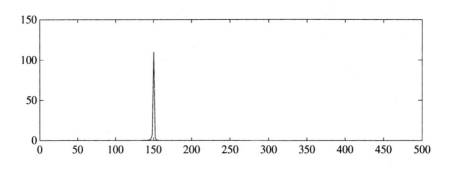

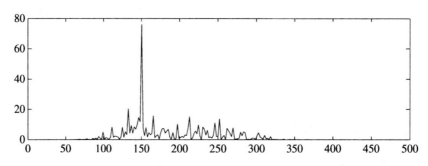

Figure 11-9 The PSD of filtered data. Noise-free input (top plot); noisy input (bottom plot).

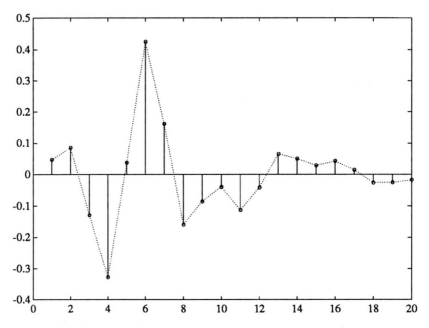

Figure 11-10 The impulse response of the Butterworth filter.

11.6 Appendix: Example Program

This is the program used for Example 11.1

```
dt=0.01; t=[0:127]'*dt; rand('normal'); rand('seed',0)
in1=rand(t);
n1=2; d1=[1 2 2]; n2=625; d2=[1 sqrt(2)*25 625];
y1=lsim(n1,d1,in1,t); y2=lsim(n2,d2,in1,t);
plot(t,in1), plot(t,y1) ,plot(t,y2)
in1f=fft(in1); y1f=fft(y1); y2f=fft(y2);
hz=[0:length(t)/2-1]'/(length(t)*dt);  %frequency axis
plot(hz,abs(in1f(1:64))), plot(hz,abs(y1f(1:64))),
plot(hz,abs(y2f(1:64)))
ruu=xcorr(in1); ryy1=xcorr(y1); ryy2=xcorr(y2);
tt=-flipud(t(2:128));tt=[tt;t];
plot(tt,ruu), plot(tt,ryy1), plot(tt,ryy2)
psdu=spectrum(in1,128); psdy1=spectrum(y1,128);
psdy2=spectrum(y2,128);
specplot(psdu,1/dt), specplot(psdy1,1/dt), specplot(psdy2,1/dt)
[a1,b1,c1,D1]=tf2ss(n1,d1); [a2,b2,c2,D2]=tf2ss(n2,d2);
[ycov1,p1]=covar(a1,b1,c1,D1,1), yrms1=sqrt(ycov1)
[ycov2,p2]=covar(a2,b2,c2,D2,1), yrms2=sqrt(ycov2)
sys_cov=cov([in1,y1,y2])
% you can also use the lyap command.
%p1=lyap(a1,b1*b1'), p2=lyap(a2,b2*b2')
%yrms1=sqrt(c1*p1*c1'), yrms2=sqrt(c2*p2*c2')
```

Notes and References

For additional information on stochastic analysis, see [Pa91] and [KS72].

12

Linear Quadratic Control

Linear Quadratic Control (LQ) refers to a body of techniques developed since the 1960s for control systems design. The LQ problem itself is an important subset of the powerful machinery of optimal control. The plant is assumed to be a linear system in state space form, and the objective function is a quadratic functional of the plant states and control inputs. The problem is to minimize the quadratic functional with respect to the control inputs subject to the linear system constraints. The problem can also be formulated and solved in the frequency domain using transfer functions [C61].

The advantage of LQ formulation of problems is that it leads to linear control laws that are easy to implement and analyze. Other problems of interest are: minimum time control, minimum fuel control (solution requires nonlinear on-off type controllers which are easy to implement using relays and switches but are more difficult to analyze due to nonlinearities), and other ITAE type criteria discussed in Section 10.5. There are many variations and extensions of the LQ problem, some of which will be discussed in this chapter.

We will restrict our attention to regulator type problems. The system is assumed to be at equilibrium, and it is desired to maintain the equilibrium—or set-point—despite disturbances. Hence, the objective is to minimize the effects of disturbances on the system. This is to be contrasted with tracking or servomechanism type problems, where the goal is to track a given reference or external input. It can be shown that tracking problems can be converted to regulator type problems.

We will also primarily consider the steady state case. In this case the optimization horizon is allowed to extend to infinity. It is known that in this case, the control law is a linear time invariant function of the states or outputs of the system. Finite horizon type problems lead to linear time varying controllers that are more difficult to implement and analyze. Actual implemented control systems, as of the early 1990s, which have been designed using LQ methods are few in number, but they will inevitably increase as more engineers are adequately trained in these techniques.

366

12.1 The Linear Quadratic Regulator Problem

Consider the linear system and the quadratic objective function (or cost function)

$$\dot{x} = A\,x + B\,u$$
$$y = C\,x$$

$$J = \frac{1}{2}\int_0^T (x'Q\,x + u'R\,u)\,dt$$

The problem is to minimize J with respect to the control input $u(t)$. This is known as the linear quadratic regulator (LQR) problem. A simple interpretation of the cost function is as follows. If the system is scalar (i.e., first order), the cost function becomes

$$J = \frac{1}{2}\int_0^T (q\,x^2 + r\,u^2)\,dt$$

Now we see that J represents the weighted sum of energy of the state and control. If r is very large relative to q, the control energy is penalized very heavily. This physically translates into smaller motors, actuators, and amplifier gains needed to implement the control law. Likewise if q is much larger than r, the state is penalized heavily, resulting in a very damped system that avoids large fluctuations or overshoots in system states. In the general case, Q and R represent respective weights on different states and control channels. Note that the main design parameters are Q and R. How these are chosen will be dealt with later, but, in general, several design iterations are necessary to obtain a stable optimal system with "good" response. Note that we require that Q be symmetric positive semidefinite (written as $Q \geq 0$) and R symmetric positive definite ($R > 0$) for a meaningful optimization problem.

12.1.1 LQR Solution Using the Minimum Principle

Optimal control problems can be solved using a variety of techniques. Among them are *Euler-Lagrange* equations, *Hamilton-Jacobi-Bellman* theory, and *Pontriagin's minimum principle*. We will present the latter.

To arrive at the *minimum principle*, we must first form the so-called *Hamiltonian*

$$\boldsymbol{H}(x, \lambda, t) = \frac{1}{2}(x'Q\,x + u'R\,u) + \lambda'(Ax + Bu)$$

The minimum principle states that the optimal control and state trajectories must satisfy the following three equations:

$$\dot{x} = \frac{\partial H}{\partial \lambda} \qquad x(0) = x_o \qquad \text{state equations}$$

$$-\dot{\lambda} = \frac{\partial H}{\partial x} \qquad \lambda(T) = 0 \qquad \text{costate or adjoint equations}$$

$$\frac{\partial H}{\partial u} = 0$$

Using rules for differentiation of matrices and vectors, the preceding equations for the LQR case become:

$$\dot{x} = A x + B u \qquad x(0) = x_o$$

$$-\dot{\lambda} = Q x + A' \lambda \qquad \lambda(T) = 0$$

$$u^* = - R^{-1} B' \lambda \qquad \text{u* is the optimal control}$$

The above coupled linear differential equations form a *two point boundary value problem (TPBVP)*, which, because of mixed boundary conditions, is difficult to solve numerically. Note that R has to be positive definite for its inverse to exist. Substituting the optimal control into the state equation we get

$$\begin{bmatrix} \dot{x} \\ \dot{\lambda} \end{bmatrix} = \begin{bmatrix} A & -BR^{-1}B' \\ -Q & -A' \end{bmatrix} \begin{bmatrix} x \\ \lambda \end{bmatrix} \overset{\Delta}{=} H \begin{bmatrix} x \\ \lambda \end{bmatrix}$$

The above matrix, H, is called the *Hamiltonian* matrix and plays an important role in LQR theory. It turns out, however, that we do not have to solve the *TPBVP* after all. To see this, let us make the following substitution

$$\lambda = P x$$

Differentiating both sides with respect to time and substituting for λ we get

$$\frac{d\lambda}{dt} = \frac{dP}{dt} x + P \frac{dx}{dt} = \frac{dP}{dt} x + PA x - PBR^{-1}B'P x = - Q x - A'P x$$

The above equation must hold for any x, hence a sufficient condition for optimal control is that P must satisfy

$$-\frac{dP}{dt} = A'P + PA + Q - PBR^{-1}B'P, \qquad P(T) = 0$$

The above is the celebrated *Riccati* differential equation. It is a *nonlinear* first order differential equation that has to be solved backwards in time. Recall that the *TPBVP* is a *linear* second order differential equation with mixed boundary conditions. It is usually the Riccati equation form of the LQR solution that is used.

The above formulation and solution of the LQR problem is known as the finite time (or finite horizon) problem. It results in a linear *time varying* controller of the feedback form

$$u(t) = -K(t)\,x(t) \quad \text{where} \quad K(t) = R^{-1}B'\,P(t)$$

For the infinite time LQR problem, we let T approach infinity. Of course, now one runs into the question of the convergence of the cost function and, hence, the existence of the optimal controller. Even if the optimal control exists, it does not necessarily result in a stable closed loop system. It turns out that under mild conditions, $P(t)$ approaches a constant matrix P (hence $dP/dt \rightarrow 0$), and the positive definite solution of the *algebraic Riccati equation (ARE)* results in an asymptotically stable closed loop system.

$$A'P + PA + Q - PBR^{-1}B'P = 0 \qquad (ARE)$$

$$u = -Kx, \qquad K = R^{-1}B'P$$

The exact conditions for the above to hold are the following. The pair (A, B) are stabilizable, $R > 0$, and Q can be factored as $Q = C'_q C_q$, where C_q is any matrix such that (C_q, A) is detectable. These conditions are necessary and sufficient for existence and uniqueness of an optimal controller that will asymptotically stabilize the system.

12.1.2 Generalizations of LQR

The LQR formulation can be generalized along many lines. We mention two of them, namely, cross-product terms in the cost function and regulators with a prescribed degree of stability [AM90].

Cross-product Terms

Consider the more general cost function

$$J = \frac{1}{2} \int_0^\infty \begin{bmatrix} x \\ u \end{bmatrix}' \begin{bmatrix} Q & N \\ N' & R \end{bmatrix} \begin{bmatrix} x \\ u \end{bmatrix} dt = \frac{1}{2} \int_0^\infty (x'Q\,x + u'R\,u + x'N\,u + u'N'x)\,dt$$

The preceding cost function is obtained when nonlinear systems are linearized or a nonlinear cost function is approximated by a quadratic one. It also is used when power into a system is to be penalized. Another common case is when the cost function contains the term

$$y'y \quad \text{where} \quad y = Cx + Du$$

The appropriate Riccati equation and optimal controller for this general cost function are given by

$$A'P + PA - (PB + N)R^{-1}(PB + N)' + Q = 0$$

$$u = -Kx, \qquad K = R^{-1}(B'P + N')$$

where conditions for existence and uniqueness of the stabilizing optimal control are the following: *(A, B)* controllable, *(A − BR⁻¹N′, W)* detectable, where *W* is any matrix such that $WW' = Q - NR^{-1}N'$ holds.

Regulators with Prescribed Degree of Stability

It is possible to design a regulator and prescribe the poles to be located α units to the left of the imaginary axis where α is a positive scalar. This can be done by considering the following modified cost function:

$$J = \frac{1}{2} \int_0^\infty e^{2\alpha t}(u'Ru + x'Qx)\, dt$$

It can be shown that the optimal control is given by the same control gain *K* as the standard LQR where *P* is the solution of a modified Riccati equation given by

$$(A + \alpha I)'P + P(A + \alpha I) + Q - PBR^{-1}B'P = 0$$

The conditions for existence and uniqueness of the stabilizing optimal control are the same as the standard LQR problem with the exception that *A* is replaced with *(A + αI)*.

12.1.3 MATLAB Implementation

The commands *lqr* and *lqry* solve the LQR problem directly. The syntaxes for these commands are given by

```
>> [K,P,ev]=lqr(A,B,Q,R,N)
>> [K,P,ev]=lqry(A,B,C,D,Q,R)
```

where ev stands for the optimal closed loop eigenvalues. Inclusion of N, the weight for the cross-product term, is optional. The *lqry* command solves the special case where the outputs instead of the states are weighted; i.e., the cost function is $y' Q y + u' R u$. The discrete version of the *lqr* command is *dlqr* with the same syntax.

The command *are* solves a general form of the algebraic Riccati equation given by

$$A' X + XA - XBX + C = 0$$

```
>> X=are(A,B,C)
```

It returns a positive definite solution if one exists (the conditions are: B is symmetric and non-negative definite, and C is symmetric).

Because LQR results in a state feedback controller, we can apply the approach in Chapter 8 to find root locus and Bode plots and find stability margins. A simple program for design and analysis is provided in the Appendix.

12.1.4 LQR Properties with Classical Interpretations

LQR has many desirable properties. Among them are good stability margins and sensitivity properties. We will also discuss the effects of weights in the LQR setting. Most of these properties can be derived using the *return difference inequality* derived by Kalman [K64].

Return Difference Inequality

The algebraic Riccati equation, under mild assumptions, can be manipulated to arrive at the relations presented next. Suppose y denotes the output measurements, and z denotes the controlled (or regulated) outputs. These quantities may be different. You may be measuring some or all of the states, but you may wish to control or regulate a different set (or combination) of states. In general, we let

$$y = C x \quad \text{and} \quad z = C_q x$$

which results in two transfer functions

$$G(s) = C \Phi(s) B \quad \text{and} \quad G_q(s) = C_q \Phi(s) B \qquad \text{where} \quad \Phi(s) = (sI - A)^{-1}$$

$G(s)$ is the transfer function between the input and the measurements and $G_q(s)$ is the transfer function between the input (possibly disturbances) and the regulated outputs.

Let $L(s)$ denote the (open) loop transfer function, and consider the block diagram in Figure 12-1; also let $Q = C'_q C_q$ and $R = 1$ for the ensuing discussion.

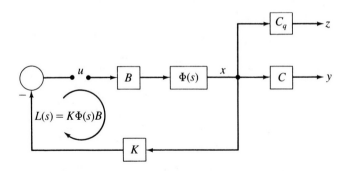

Figure 12-1 Block diagram for the LQR problem.

Return Difference Equality: SISO Case

$$| 1 + k\ \Phi(j\omega)\ b |^2 = 1 + | G_q(j\omega) |^2$$

or

$$| 1 + L(j\omega) |^2 = 1 + | G_q(j\omega) |^2$$

where $L(s) = k\ \Phi(s)\ b$.

Because the right-hand side of the return difference equality (RDE) is always larger than 1, the following inequalities hold.

Return Difference Inequality: SISO Case

$$| 1 + k\ \Phi(j\omega)\ b | \geq 1 \quad \text{or} \quad | 1 + L(j\omega) | = | J(j\omega) | \geq 1 \quad \text{or} \quad | S(j\omega) | \leq 1$$

where $J(s)$ stands for the return difference, i.e., $J(s) = 1 + L(s)$ and $S(s)$ stands for sensitivity, which is defined as the inverse of the return difference (see Section 1.6).

The preceding return difference inequality (RDI) implies that for all frequencies, the Nyquist plot of the open loop transfer function of an LQR based design always stays outside of a unit circle centered at $(-1,0)$. A typical Nyquist plot of a system stabilized by the LQR method is shown in Figure 12-2. The Nyquist plot clearly stays out of the circle centered at $(-1,0)$. Because the magnitude of the sensitivity is also always less than unity, the optimal system will have good feedback properties. Recall from the discussion in Section 1.6 that this implies good disturbance rejection and tracking properties.

LQR Stability Margins

The RDI along with simple geometric arguments can be used to derive the following stability margins for LQR in the SISO case:

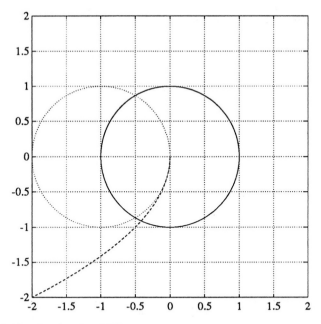

Figure 12-2 Nyquist plot of an LQR system demonstrating the return difference inequality.

  1. **GM: [0.5 , ∞)**
  2. **PM ≥ 60 °**

Note that the upper GM of infinity and the PM of 60 degrees are actually an overkill because most systems do not require such large margins. The lower gain margin (or gain reduction margin; GRM) is 0.5 (or –6 dB). One consequence of the infinite GM is the minimum phase property of the loop transfer function $L(s)$. This can be shown in several ways, but simple root locus argument reveals that if the system had not been minimum phase, at least one branch would have had to enter the RHP and approach a zero. Of course in that case, the system would not have infinite upper GM.

High Frequency Roll-off Rate

Consider the complementary sensitivity $T(s)$, which can be shown to be equal to

$$T(s) = I - S(s) = - k \, (j\omega - A + b \, k)^{-1} \, b$$

It then follows that

$$\lim_{\omega \to \infty} T(j\omega) = \frac{-1}{j\omega} \, k \, b = \frac{-1}{j\omega} \, R^{-1} \, b'Pb \; \leq \; 0$$

The preceding implies that $|T(j\omega)|$ drops as $1/(j\omega)$ in the SISO case, indicating a roll-off rate of -20 dB per decade at high frequencies. This, of course, affects the noise suppression properties of the optimal system and as such is not very good. It can be argued that this defect is the result of excessive stability margins. It is possible to trade off stability margins with high frequency roll-off rate using variations of LQ techniques known as *frequency shaping* and *loop transfer recovery* procedures [M89].

Time Delay and Nonlinearity Tolerance

If some time delay of the form $e^{-j\omega\tau}$ is inserted in the loop, we can show that the maximum amount of time delay that the system can tolerate and still remain stable is given by

$$\tau < \frac{\pi}{3\,\omega_x}, \quad \text{where } \omega_x \text{ is the highest gain crossover frequency}$$

Asymptotic stability of LQR can even be maintained when there are certain sector type time-varying nonlinearities inserted at the input of the plant. Observe that in these cases the LQR control gain is no longer optimal. Hence, other LQR properties like the stability margins may be lost; only stability is guaranteed [AM90].

Symmetric (Optimal) Root Locus

We will show that a special choice of Q and R allows us to investigate the effects of weights on the location of closed loop poles. Let us assume that Q and R are given by

$$Q = C'_q\, C_q \quad \text{and} \quad R = \rho\, I \quad \text{where } \rho \text{ is a positive scalar}$$

The cost function for $D = 0$ becomes

$$J = \frac{1}{2} \int_0^\infty (z'\,z + \rho\, u'\, u)\, dt$$

so we are minimizing the system (regulated) output and control energy. The Hamiltonian matrix, in this case, is given by

$$\mathsf{H} = \begin{bmatrix} A & -\dfrac{1}{\rho}\, B\, B' \\ -C'_q\, C_q & -A' \end{bmatrix}$$

The closed loop poles are the eigenvalues of the Hamiltonian matrix; i.e., they are the roots of the following characteristic polynomial $\Delta_c = |\,sI - \mathsf{H}\,|$.

After a series of matrix manipulations, we arrive at the following equation.

$$\Delta_c(s) = (-1)^n \, \Delta(s) \, \Delta(-s) \, \left| \, I + \frac{1}{\rho} \, G_q(s) \, G_q(-s) \,' \, \right| \, , \quad \text{where} \quad \Delta(s) = | \, sI - A \, |$$

Limiting ourselves to the SISO case, let us define the following:

n = number of poles, m = number of zeros, with $m < n$, r = *relative degree* = $n - m$, and $G_q(s) = \dfrac{n_q(s)}{\Delta(s)}$

The above equation simplifies to

$$(-1)^n \, \Delta_c = \Delta(s) \, \Delta(-s) \, [\, 1 + \frac{1}{\rho} \, G_q(s) \, G_q(-s) \,] = \Delta(s) \, \Delta(-s) + \frac{1}{\rho} \, n_q(s) \, n_q(-s)$$

Note the above equation has the standard root locus form. It implies the optimal closed loop poles can be obtained from the root locus of $G_q(s) \, G_q(-s)$. Such root loci are generally called *symmetric root locus* (SRL), as discussed in Chapter 10. By increasing ρ, we can minimize control energy. Note that the transfer function $G_q(s)$ is a function of C_q, which affects its numerator $n_q(s)$; because this term can be selected by the designer, we have control over the open loop zeros. The root locus gain ρ is then adjusted to place the closed loop poles. We will discuss the effects of limiting values of ρ.

Minimum Energy Control Case

$$\text{As } \rho \to \infty \quad \Rightarrow \quad (-1)^n \Delta_c(s) \quad \to \quad \Delta(s) \, \Delta(-s)$$

Because the optimal closed loop poles are always in the LHP (LQR guarantees closed loop stability), we conclude that as the control weighting is increased, the stable open loop poles will remain where they are, and the unstable poles will be reflected across the imaginary axis. This property can be used as a guideline for pole placement (e.g., in Chapters 8 and 10). For instance, if the open loop poles are at -10 and $+1$, a minimum energy controller will suggest that the closed poles be located at -10 and -1.

Cheap Control Case

$$\text{As } \rho \to 0 \quad \Rightarrow \quad \text{closed loop poles} \to n_q(s) \, n_q(-s) \quad \text{for finite } s$$

Hence, the closed loop poles approach the plant finite zeros or their stable images. For values of s approaching infinity, the closed loop poles will approach zeros at infinity in the famous *Butterworth pattern*.

$$\text{for } |s| \to \infty, \quad s = \left(\frac{\alpha_m{}^2}{\rho}\right)^{\frac{1}{2r}} e^{j\frac{\pi k(r+1)}{2r}} \quad k = \text{odd integer}$$

where α_m in the preceding is the coefficient of the highest order term in $n_q(s)$. We summarize our conclusions in the Table 12-1.

Table 12-1 Summary of Effects of Varying Control Weight on Pole Locations		
Control Energy Weight	**Open Loop Poles**	**Closed Loop Poles**
Minimum energy control $\rho \to \infty$	Stable poles	Will remain in original place
	Unstable poles	Will be reflected about the imaginary axis
Cheap control $\rho \to 0$	m poles	Will approach m finite zeros or their stable images
	$(n - m)$ poles	Will go to zeros at infinity in Butterworth pattern

Example 12.1 LQR Design

Using LQR design, we will investigate the solution of Example 8.1, control of longitudinal motion of a helicopter near hover. Moreover, we would like to determine the effects of weighting matrices Q and R on various quantities and also verify the LQR properties we discussed in this section.

Toward this goal, we will separate the effects of Q and R. In one set of simulations, $R = r$, where the scalar parameter r is fixed at a value of $\{1\}$ and $Q = q$ I, where the scalar parameter q is allowed to vary over the range $\{1, 10, 10^2, 10^3, 10^6\}$. In another set, q is fixed at $\{1\}$, and r is allowed to vary over the same range. Hence, we can compare the cheap control and minimum energy control cases.

The state space equations and the transfer function are repeated below for convenience.

$$\dot{x} = \begin{bmatrix} -0.4 & 0 & -0.01 \\ 1 & 0 & 0 \\ -1.4 & 9.8 & -0.02 \end{bmatrix} x + \begin{bmatrix} 6.3 \\ 0 \\ 9.8 \end{bmatrix} u$$

$$y = [\, 0 \ \ 0 \ \ 1 \,] x$$

$$G(s) = \frac{9.8 \, (s - 0.25 \pm j\, 2.49)}{(s + 0.65) \, (s - 0.11 \pm j\, 0.36)}$$

Case I : Cheap Control: $Q = q$I

We will first investigate the cheap control case, where the ratio r/q approaches zero. The control gain vector, step response characteristics (percent overshoot, rise time, 2% settling time and peak time), along with stability margin measures (GMs and PMs and their frequencies) are listed in Table 12-2. Note that the control gain tends to increase. This is expected, because the control cost is relatively decreasing, so larger gains are used. This may cause saturation problems in practice.

Table 12-2 Data for Varying q			$Q = q\mathbf{I}$, $R = r = 1$								
q	Control gain vector			POS	Tr	Ts	Tp	GM	PM	wgc	wpc
1	0.52	4.38	0.99	18.6	1.2	5.2	2.0	-15.8	83.8	12.7	2.0
10	1.12	11.89	3.15	19.0	1.2	5.1	1.9	-22.9	88.2	37.9	2.12
10^2	3.13	35.73	9.98	19.1	1.2	5.1	1.9	-30.8	89.4	117.4	2.15
10^3	9.53	111.15	31.57	19.1	1.2	5.0	1.9	-40.7	89.8	369.4	2.16
10^6	296.36	3489.23	998.39	19.1	1.2	5.0	1.9	-70.6	–	–	2.17

The PM is larger than 80 degrees in all cases (for $q = 10^6$, there was no gain crossover frequency over the selected range for the Bode plot). The negative GMs indicate by how much the gain can be reduced before instability occurs. It is at least -15 dB and increases with q. Using the gain crossover frequency as an approximate measure of the bandwidth, we observe that as the stability margins increase, bandwidth increases.

The complex closed loop poles (shown in Table 12-3) approach the stable images of the plant zeros, and the remaining real pole approaches the zero at infinity along a line corresponding to the Butterworth pattern. Because the complex poles are dominant and remain fixed, no appreciable effect on the step response is expected.

The step response, open loop Bode plots, and the closed loop Bode magnitude plot for all cases are shown in Figure 12-3. Note the -20 dB roll-off rate of the closed loop magnitude plot at high frequencies.

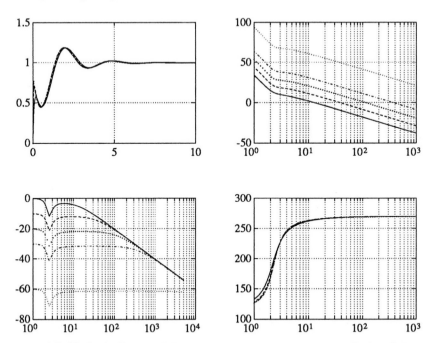

Figure 12-3 Clockwise from top left: step response, open loop Bode magnitude and phase, and closed loop magnitude plots. Legend: q=1, solid; q=10, dash; q=100, dots; q=10^3, dash-dot; q=10^6, small dots.

Table 12-3 Closed Loop Poles for Varying q			$Q = q\mathbf{I}$, $R = r = 1$		
q	1	10	10^2	10^3	10^6
Closed loop poles	-0.73 + 2.14i	-0.73 + 2.17i	-0.73 - 2.18i	-0.73 + 2.18i	-0.73 - 2.18i
	-0.73 - 2.14i	-0.73 - 2.17i	-0.73 + 2.18i	-0.73 - 2.18i	-0.73 + 2.18i
	-12.0	-36.9	-116.5	-368.4	-11650.3

Case II : Minimum Energy: $R = r\mathbf{I}$

Now, we will study the minimum energy control case. The ratio of q / r is allowed to approach zero. The values of control gain vector, step response characteristics, and stability margin measures are shown in Table 12-4. Note that, as expected, the gain decreases with higher values of r.

The step response characteristics indicate that with larger values of r, the overshoot decreases, whereas all speed of response measures will increase, resulting in a well damped and slow system. The margins indicate that the lower GM and PM are pushed to their limits of –6 dB and 60 degrees with increasing r. The bandwidth decreases as the margins are reduced, but the roll-off rate remains at –20 dB per decade, as shown in the plots of Figure 12-4.

The closed loop poles displayed in Table 12-5 verify that with larger values of r, the unstable plant poles at $(0.11 \pm j\, 0.36)$ are reflected to $(-0.15 \pm j\, 0.38)$, and the stable pole at (-0.65) stays close to its original position (-0.66).

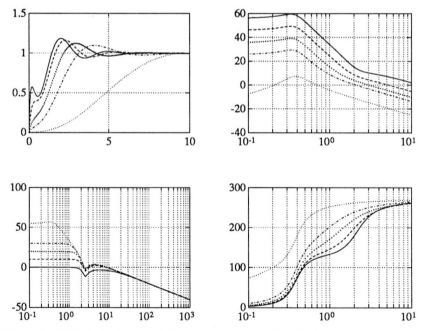

Figure 12-4 Clockwise from top left: step response, open loop Bode magnitude and phase, and closed loop magnitude plots. Legend: r=1, solid; r=10, dash; r=100, dots; r=10^3, dash-dot; r=10^6, small dots.

Table 12-4 Data for Varying r			$R = r\mathbf{I}, Q = \mathbf{I}$							
r	Control Gain Vector			POS	Tr	Ts	Tp	GM	PM	wgc	wpc
1	0.52	4.38	0.99	18.6	1.2	5.2	2.0	-15.0	___	___	2.0
10	0.39	1.96	0.31	16.3	1.4	4.6	2.3	-11.8	71.2	5.2	1.6
10^2	0.35	0.98	0.09	12.8	1.8	5.6	2.9	-12.6	61.9	3.1	1.1
10^3	0.28	0.48	0.02	09.9	2.2	7.8	4.1	-14.0	60.5	2.1	0.7
10^6	0.08	0.06	0.0002	0.018	5.4	8.8	9.9	-7.2	60.7	0.7	0.4

Table 12-5 Closed Loop Poles for varying r			$R = r\mathbf{I}, Q = \mathbf{I}$		
r	1	10	10^2	10^3	10^6
Closed loop poles	-0.73 + 2.14i	-0.72 + 1.95i	-0.66 + 1.50	-0.54 + 1.05i	-0.15 + 0.38i
	-0.73 - 2.14i	-0.72 - 1.95i	-0.66 - 1.50	-0.54 - 1.05i	-0.15 - 0.38i
	-12.00	-4.50	-2.27	-1.39	-0.66

12.2 Optimal Observer Design—Kalman-Bucy Filter

Estimation theory and the now famous *Kalman-Bucy filter* have a long history and wide variety of applications in control and communications. In fact, there are many more reported applications of the Kalman-Bucy filter than LQR theory. Our purpose in this section is to briefly describe the filter as an integral part of an optimal compensation scheme. The basic premise is that the LQR solution requires that all states be available for feedback. In reality, what we have are noise-corrupted measurements. The optimal estimation problem is to obtain the best estimate of the states from a record of noisy measurements. It turns out that under certain assumptions on the system and noise statistics, the optimal estimator (filter or observer) is a linear system that has the same structure as the standard Luenberger observer discussed in Chapter 8. We will first formulate the problem, present the solution, then show how to implement and simulate the filter using MATLAB.

12.2.1 Problem Formulation and Solution

Consider the system represented in state space form

$$\dot{x} = A\,x + B\,u + \Gamma\,\omega$$

$$y = C\,x + \nu$$

where ω represents random noise disturbance input and ν represents random measurement (sensor) noise. We have to assume some statistical knowledge of the noise processes. It is assumed that both are white Gaussian zero-mean stationary processes with known covariances given below.

$$E\{\omega(t)\} = 0, \qquad E\{v(t)\} = 0$$

$$E\{\omega(t)\,\omega(t+\tau)'\} = Q_o\,\delta(t-\tau)$$

$$E\{v(t)\,v(t+\tau)'\} = R_o\,\delta(t-\tau)$$

$$E\{\omega(t)\,v(t+\tau)'\} = 0 \quad \text{for all } t \text{ and } \tau$$

For those unfamiliar with stochastic processes, we refer the reader to Chapter 11 where a brief review with relevant commands is provided.

The problem is to obtain an estimate of $x(t)$ based on noise-corrupted measurements such that the variance of the error is minimized. Let us denote the estimate by $\hat{x}(t)$ and the error by $\tilde{x}(t)$, then the cost function to be minimized is given by

$$J_o = E[\tilde{x}(t)'\,\tilde{x}(t)] = \text{error variance}$$

where $\tilde{x}(t) = x(t) - \hat{x}(t)$.

The following assumptions are needed to obtain an asymptotically stable minimum variance filter. The pair (C, A) is detectable, the matrix R_o is positive definite, there exists H_0 such that $H_o H_o' = Q_o$, and (A, H_o) is stabilizable. Under the above assumptions, the optimal estimator (*Kalman-Bucy filter*) is given by

$$\dot{\hat{x}} = A\hat{x} + Bu + L(y - C\hat{x})$$

$$L = \Sigma\,C'\,R^{-1}$$

where Σ is found from

$$A\Sigma + \Sigma A' + \Gamma Q_o \Gamma' - \Sigma C' R_o^{-1} C \Sigma = 0$$

It turns out that Σ, the solution of the filter algebraic Riccati equation, is the estimation error covariance. It is known that the trace of the error covariance is the error variance; i.e.,

$$tr\,\Sigma = tr\,E[\tilde{x}(t)\,\tilde{x}(t)'] = E[\tilde{x}(t)'\,\tilde{x}(t)]$$

Therefore, the trace of Σ indicates how well the filter is performing.

Cross-correlated Noise

One assumption that can be relaxed to obtain a more general filter is the cross correlation between the noise processes. If we assume that the disturbance and measurement noise are correlated, then we can define a general covariance matrix as

$$E \left\{ \begin{bmatrix} \omega(t) \\ v(t) \end{bmatrix} [\omega(t)' \; v(t)'] \right\} = \begin{bmatrix} Q_o & N_o \\ N_o' & R_o \end{bmatrix} \delta(t - \tau)$$

The solution in this case becomes

$$L = (\Sigma C' + N_o) R_o^{-1}$$

$$A \Sigma + \Sigma A' + \Gamma Q_o \Gamma' - (\Sigma C' + N_o) R_o^{-1} (\Sigma C' + N_o)' = 0$$

Control and Estimation Duality

Close observation of the LQR solution and the optimal estimator solution indicates that the two problems are duals of each other. The duality was also pointed out in Chapter 8, where we discussed pole placement using observers. Duality implies that if we make the following substitutions in the LQR solution, we get the optimal filter solution:

$$A \to A', \; B \to C', \; Q \to Q_o, \; R \to R_o, \; N \to N_o, \; K \to L', \; P \to \Sigma$$

12.2.2 MATLAB Implementation

The *lqe* and *estim* commands are used to find the filter parameters, and form the filter equations, respectively. The syntaxes for both commands are given by

```
>> [L,Sig,ev]=lqe(A,GAMMA,C,Qo,Ro,No)
>> [Af,Bf,Cf,Df]=estim(A,B,C,D,L)
```

where the input No (cross-correlated noise case) is optional. The output ev stands for the optimal estimator eigenvalues. Because of duality, the *lqe* command uses the *lqr* command for computation. The *estim* command takes the system equations and the filter gain to compute the following filter equations.

$$\dot{\hat{x}} = (A - LC)\hat{x} + Ly$$

$$\begin{bmatrix} \hat{y} \\ \hat{x} \end{bmatrix} = \begin{bmatrix} C \\ I \end{bmatrix} \hat{x}$$

As discussed in the previous section, sometimes we distinguish between measured outputs (sensor outputs) and regulated outputs. In addition, a system may have other known external inputs that must be fed to the filter (such as deterministic control inputs or external command inputs), but were not used in the filter design stage (using *lqe*). The more general form of the *estim* command given next handles this case.

```
>> [Af,Bf,Cf,Df]=estim(A,B,C,D,L,sensors,known)
```

The input arguments, known and sensors, are vectors containing the indices for the external inputs and sensor (measured) outputs.

The next example illustrates an application of the above commands. Notice that most of the effort is spent on doing a valid simulation, and the filter design step is simply an application of the *lqe* command. Following the example, in the next section we will use the optimal estimator to estimate the states and use the estimates in lieu of the actual states for the LQR problem.

Example 12.2 Kalman-Bucy Filter Simulation

We will demonstrate how to simulate a Kalman-Bucy filter using the following system: a double integrator plant stabilized by a lead compensator.

$$G(s) = \frac{1}{s^2} \quad \text{and} \quad H(s) = \frac{18(s+1)}{(s+10)}$$

After cascading the plant with the compensator and closing the loop with unity feedback, we get the system matrices a, gamma, c, d. We will determine the number of inputs and outputs

```
>> dimgam=size(gamma); noinp=dimgam(2); dimc=size(c); noout=dimc(1);
```

We assume the input noise is a white Gaussian process with zero mean and variance 1, and the measurement noise has variance 0.01. Recall that if $z = \sigma x$, and $x \sim N(0,1)$, then $z \sim N(0,\sigma^2)$; where the notation $N \sim (\mu,\sigma)$ stands for Normal process with mean μ and variance σ. We must, therefore, multiply the measurement noise by 0.1 ($\sqrt{0.01}$) to produce noise with variance 0.01. We first reset the random number generator to normal for Gaussian white noise with zero mean and unity variance; then the system response to process noise is obtained; we then add measurement noise to the output.

```
>> rand('normal')
>> qo=1; w=sqrt(qo)*rand(100,noinp);
>> ro=0.01; nu=sqrt(ro)*rand(100,noout);
>> t=[0:0.1:(100-1)*0.1]';
>> [y,x]=lsim(a,gamma,c,d,w,t); y=x*c'+nu;
```

Note the order of multiplication in the last statement where noise is added to the output. We next find the filter gain.

```
>> [l,sig,ev]=lqe(a,gamma,c,qo*eye(noinp),ro*eye(noout));l,sig,ev

l =
   9.0499
   1.0840
   0.0491
```

sig =
```
   0.1089   0.0059   0.0001
   0.0059   0.0021   0.0002
   0.0001   0.0002   0.0000
```
ev =
```
-10.2766 + 8.6090i
-10.2766 - 8.6090i
 -1.0065
```

Now let us take a closer look at the results. The filter form is (note that the control term is zero)

$$\dot{\hat{x}} = A\hat{x} + L(y - C\hat{x})$$

It is known in general that if the measurements are too noisy (R_o large), and the input noise intensity is small (Q_o small), the filter relies on the system model for estimates and chooses L to be small; this results in a slow filter as measured by the location of its eigenvalues. If Q_o approaches infinity, the filter poles approach the stable images of plant zeros. Conversely, if the measurements are good and the input noise intensity is large, the filter relies on the measurements and chooses L to be large, resulting in a fast filter with high bandwidth. In our example, R_o is ten times smaller than Q_o, so we expect a large L and a fast filter. Indeed, the complex poles of the filter are about ten times faster than the system poles (the real part of the system complex poles is –0.98). Note that only the first component of L is large and the rest are much smaller. To explain this, take a closer look at the system itself:

$$\begin{aligned}
\dot{x}_1 &= -18\,x_2 + 162\,x_3 + \omega \\
\dot{x}_2 &= x_1 \\
\dot{x}_3 &= x_2 - 10\,x_3 \\
y &= 18\,x_2 - 162\,x_3 + \nu
\end{aligned}$$

Input noise is fed directly into x_1, so x_1 is quite noisy, but x_2 is the integral of x_1 and x_3 is a filtered version of x_1 and x_2. We can see that the noise gets filtered heavily by the time it reaches x_3. This is why the second and third components of L are much smaller than the first component. In a sense, the measurements are mainly used to estimate the noisier state and the system model is used to estimate the cleaner states. Inspection of the diagonal elements of Σ (sig) also indicates poorer performance with respect to the first state (largest component). The plots in Figure 12-5 also verify the above conclusions.

We now use the *estim* command to form the filter and use *lsim* to compute the state estimates using noisy measurements previously generated.

```
>> [af,bf,cf,df]=estim(a,gamma,,c,d,1);
>> xhat=lsim(af,bf,cf,df,y,t);
```

The states and their estimates are plotted in Figure 12-5. Note that although the estimation errors in the plots of x_2 and x_3 are very similar, the vertical scales are different. The plots of estimation errors verify this. The error in x_3 is at least ten times smaller than the error in x_2 and 100 times smaller than the error in x_3 (in the combined plot it appears as 0).

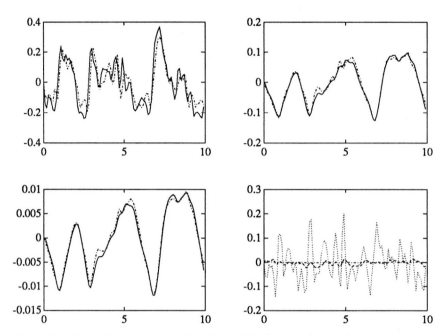

Figure 12-5 Plots of states versus their estimates. Top left, top right, and bottom left are x_1, x_2, and x_3. The solid lines are the states. The bottom right plot shows the errors.

12.3 The Linear Quadratic Gaussian Problem

Optimal control of a linear system with respect to the quadratic objective function under incomplete measurements corrupted by white Gaussian noise is generally referred to as the linear quadratic Gaussian (LQG) problem. The optimal control is a linear function of the state estimates obtained from the Kalman-Bucy filter. The LQR is a state feedback problem, whereas LQG is an output feedback problem, which is more realistic. The steady state formulation and solution of the problem are presented next.

12.3.1 LQG Problem Formulation and Solution

Consider the linear system driven by white Gaussian noise, with noise-corrupted measurements, and the quadratic objective function.

$$\dot{x} = A\,x + B\,u + \Gamma\,\omega$$

$$y = C\,x + v$$

$$J = \lim_{T \to \infty} \frac{1}{2T}\,E\left\{\int_{-T}^{T}(x'\,Q\,x + u'\,R\,u)\,dt\right\}$$

The problem is to find the optimal control that will minimize the *average cost*. Note that because the states and the control are both random, the cost function will be random, so we minimize it on the average. Using the same notation and under the same combined assumptions of the LQR and optimal estimation problem, the solution is given by the following:

$$u = -K \, \hat{x}(t)$$

$$K = R^{-1} B' P$$

$$A'P + PA - PBR^{-1}B'P + Q = 0$$

$$\dot{\hat{x}} = A\hat{x} + Bu + L(y - C\hat{x})$$

$$L = \Sigma C' R^{-1}$$

$$A\Sigma + \Sigma A' - \Sigma C' R_o^{-1} C\Sigma + \Gamma Q_o \Gamma' = 0$$

Note that the same Riccati equations for the LQR and Kalman-Bucy filter are used here. The solution satisfies the *separation principle*, which states that the problem can be solved in two separate stages. This can also be shown by the same procedure described for the observer-based compensator design, which is the deterministic version of the problem described here; i.e., the eigenvalues of the closed loop system are the union of the eigenvalues of the controller and the estimator.

$$\text{Closed loop eigenvalues} = \lambda(A - BK) \cup \lambda(A - LC)$$

The generalization of the LQG to the cross-correlated noise case with cross terms in the cost function is also straightforward. To study the effects of the four weights $\{Q, R, Qo, Ro\}$, we will consider the following example, that is, the LQG version of Example 12.1.

Example 12.3 LQG Design

We will investigate the effects of the four weights $\{Q, R, Qo, Ro\}$ on the time and frequency responses of the helicopter example. The simulations will be done by fixing three of the weights at unity and varying the fourth one over the range $\{1, 10, 10^2, 10^3, 10^6\}$. We will soon see that, in general, LQG does not have the same properties as LQR, and, in fact, most of the LQR properties are lost when a Kalman-Bucy filter is introduced.

It has been well known that uncertainties in the initial state, system input noise, and measurement noise increase the overall cost function value and, in fact, these costs can be computed and separated. What was later demonstrated by counterexamples, however, was the fact that the LQR robustness and stability margins are also lost. This renders LQG designs very susceptible to model uncertainties, which are always present; hence, a design based on LQG has to be treated with care and tested for robustness. Doyle and Stein [DS79] also developed a method called *loop transfer recovery (LTR)*, which allows one to recover LQR properties, asymptotically.

Stability margins measured by GM and PM are computed for each case in this design. In addition, we also compute the following: the minimum distance between the loop gain and the (–1) point, i.e., the minimum of the return difference is also computed as a measure of robustness (denoted by robust stability measure [RSM]); the peak in the closed loop transfer function (resonant peak [M_r]), which can also be used as a measure of relative stability; the control and (the transpose of) filter gain vectors; and closed loop poles.

Most data are truncated by one or two digits to reduce clutter. The plots of open loop magnitude and phase, closed loop magnitude, and step response are provided. The programs that generated the data and plots are presented in the Appendix.

Case I: Varying $Q = q$ I

From Table 12-6, we see that increasing q does not have an appreciable effect on any of the stability margins. Control gain increases. Filter gain is, of course, independent of Q. Note that the upper GM is reduced to about 6 (LQR has infinite GM), and the lower GM is between –12 to –15, which is better than LQR. The fact that RSM is smaller than 1 indicates the Nyquist plot enters the unit circle centered at (–1); i.e., the RDI does not apply in the LQG case. This indicates that LQR has better input disturbance rejection properties. The PM varies from 29 to 33 degrees, which is smaller than LQR. The plots are shown in Figure 12-6.

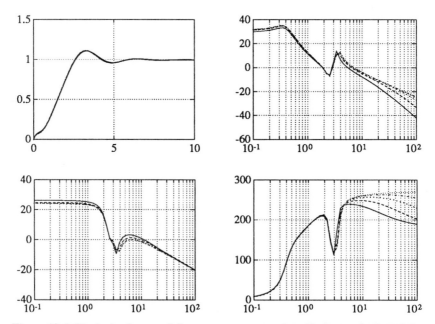

Figure 12-6 Clockwise from top left: step response, open loop Bode magnitude and phase, and closed loop magnitude plots. Legend: q=1, solid; q=10, dash; q=100, dots; q=10^3 , dash-dot; q=106, small dots.

Table 12-6 Data for Varying Q		$Q = q\mathbf{I}$						
q	Gain Margin	Phase Margin	RSM	M_r	Control Gain			Filter Gain
1	-13.5 6.4 -12.8	29.5 -64.0 59.0	0.46	26.1	0.5 4.4 1.0			0.6 0.8 3.9
10	-14.6 6.5 -12.8	31.8 -62.4 67.0	0.49	24.7	1.1 11.9 3.2			0.6 0.8 3.9
10^2	-14.9 6.6 -13.2	32.6 -62.1 72.9	0.50	24.3	3.1 35.7 10.0			0.6 0.8 3.9
10^3	-15.0 6.7 -13.3	32.9 -62.1 75.3	0.50	24.1	9.5 111.2 31.6			0.6 0.8 3.9
10^6	-15.1 6.7 -13.3	33.0 -62.1 76.4	0.51	24.1	296.3 3489.3 998.4			0.6 0.8 3.9

Table 12-7 shows that the closed loop poles appear fixed except for one that gets pushed far out into the LHP. The plots indicate a bandwidth of about 2.5 rad/sec and a roll-off rate of 20 dB/dec, which is the same as LQR for this particular system.

Table 12-7 Closed Loop Poles for Varying Q			$Q = q\mathbf{I}$		
q	1	10	10^2	10^3	10^6
Closed loop poles	-2	-2	-2	-2	-2
	-1 + 2i	-1 + 2i	-1 + 2i	-1 + 2i	-1 + 2i
	-1 - 2i	-1 - 2i	-1 - 2i	-1 - 2i	-1 - 2i
	-1 + 2i	-1 + 2i	-1 + 2i	-1 + 2i	-1 + 2i
	-1 - 2i	-1 - 2i	-1 - 2i	-1 - 2i	-1 - 2i
	-12	-37	-117	-368	-11650

Case II: Varying $R = r\mathbf{I}$

From Table 12-8, we make the following observations. Increasing r reduces the lower GM from −13.5 to −5.1 dB, but increases the upper gain margin from 6 to 13 dB. The PM initially goes down from 29 to 22 but later goes up to 38 degrees. This variation is also indicated by RSM. The control gain decreases (minimum energy control).

Table 12-8 Data for Varying R		$R = r\mathbf{I}$,						
r	Gain Margin	Phase Margin	RSM	M_r	Control Gain			Filter Gain
1	−13.5 6.4 −12.8	29.5 −64.0 59.0	0.47	26.1	0.5 4.3 0.9			0.6 0.8 3.9
10	−12.2 5.3	25.0 −84.3 63.6	0.39	29.7	0.3 1.9 0.3			0.6 0.8 3.9
10^2	−10.8 5.6	22.4	0.36	35.3	0.3 0.9 0.09			0.6 0.8 3.9
10^3	−10.4 7.0	23.9	0.39	41.7	0.2 0.4 0.02			0.6 0.8 3.9
10^6	− 5.1 13.7	−46.7 38.2	0.65	60.8	0.08 0.06 0.0003			0.6 0.8 3.9

The closed loop poles (presented in Table 12-9) are the union of the filter and controller poles. We see that because the filter gain is fixed, the first three poles (filter eigenvalues) remain unchanged. The controller poles move toward the stable images of the plant poles. The result is that increasing r will decrease the speed of response considerably. Likewise the bandwidth is also reduced to below 1 rad/sec. The plots for this case, presented in Figure 12-7, show that the high frequency roll-off rate is still about −20 dB/dec.

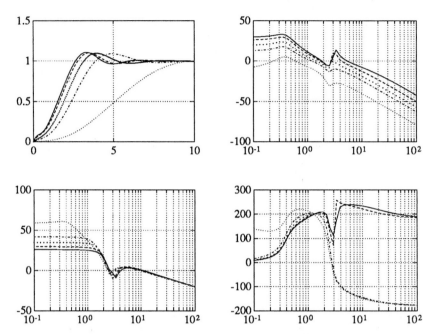

Figure 12-7 Clockwise from top left: step response, open loop Bode magnitude and phase, and closed loop magnitude plots. Legend: r=1, solid; r=10, dash; r=100, dots; r=10^3 dash-dot; r=10^6, small dots.

Table 12-9 Closed Loop Poles for Varying *R*			$R = r$ **I**		
r	1	10	10^2	10^3	10^6
Closed loop poles	-1.1 + 1.8i	-1.1 + 1.8i	-1.1 + 1.8i	-1.1 + 1.8i	-1.1 + 1.8i
	-1.1 - 1.8i	-1.1 -1.8i	-1.1 - 1.8i	-1.1 - 1.8i	-1.1 - 1.8i
	-2.1	-2.1	-2.1	-2.1	-2.1
	-0.7 + 2.1i	-0.7 + 1.9i	-0.6 + 1.5i	-0.5 + 1.0i	-0.1 + 0.3i
	-0.7 - 2.1i	-0.7 - 1.9i	-0.6 - 1.5i	-0.5 - 1.0i	-0.1 - 0.3i
	-12	-4.5	-2.2	-1.3	-0.6

Case III: Varying $Q_o = q_o I$

Table 12-10 shows that in this case, the lower GM varies from approximately –13 to –2 dB. The upper GM is between 6 and 8 dB. The PM again goes up and then comes down to 18 degrees. This is also verified from the RSM. The rather small margins for large values of q_o are also clear from the step response, which shows wild fluctuations.

Table 12-11 on page 390 shows that the first three closed loop poles are unchanged because the control gain is independent of q_o (separation property). Filter modal properties are duals of LQR modal properties and show the same pattern. The appropriate transfer function is the transmission between the input noise and the output.

$$G_{KF}(s) = C\ \Phi(s)\ \Gamma = C\ (sI - A)^{-1}\ \Gamma = \frac{-1.4\ (s-7)}{(s-0.118 \pm j0.36)\ (s+0.65)}$$

For large values of input noise intensity, q_o, m filter poles (at -5.6) approach the stable image of finite zeros of G_{KF} (at 7), and the rest go to zeros at infinity in a Butterworth pattern. For large values of measurement noise intensity, r_o, filter poles approach the stable images of plant poles (see Table 12-13).

Table 12-10	Data for Varying Q_o		$Q_o = q_o I$				
q_o	Gain Margin	Phase Margin	RSM	M_r	Control Gain	Filter Gain	
1	-13.5 6.4 -12.8	29.5 -64.0 59.0	0.4	26.1	0.5 4.3 0.9	0.6 0.8 3.9	
10	-14.8 5.9 -7.2	33.5 -46.7 48.0	0.5	22.5	0.5 4.3 0.9	1.2 1.3 4.8	
10^2	-16.1 6.2 -4.8	39.8 -36.7 39.4	0.5	18.9	0.5 4.3 0.9	2.2 2.1 5.9	
10^3	-20.7 6.8 -3.5	47.1 -30.2 32.5	0.5	15.2	0.5 4.3 0.9	4.2 3.4 7.3	
10^6	-40.2 8.5 -1.8	67.5 -21.5 18.2	0.2	14.4	0.5 4.3 0.9	26.0 13.8 14.0	

As we increase q_o relative to r_o, the filter places more confidence in the measurements by increasing the gain. This, in effect, produces a faster filter with higher bandwidth. When r_o is increased, the filter deemphasizes the measurements (lower filter gain) and uses the system model for estimation. The filter then trades off speed of response with more filtering action. The plots for this case are shown in Figure 12-8.

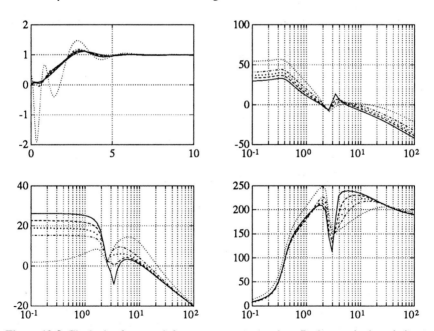

Figure 12-8 Clockwise from top left: step response, open loop Bode magnitude and phase, and closed loop magnitude plots. Legend: $q_o=1$, solid; $q_o=10$, dash; $q_o=100$, dots; $q_o=10^3$ dash-dot; $q_o=10^6$, small dots.

Table 12-11 Closed Loop Poles for Varying Q_o $Q_0 = q_0 I$

q_0	1	10	10^2	10^3	10^6
Closed loop poles	-0.7 + 2.1i	-0.7 + 2.1i	-0.7 + 2.1i	-0.7 + 2.1i	-0.7 + 2.1i
	-0.7 - 2.1i	-0.7 - 2.1i	-0.7 - 2.1i	-0.7 - 2.1i	-0.7 - 2.1i
	-12.0	-12.0	-12.0	-12.0	-12.0
	-1.1 + 1.8i	-1.3 + 2.2i	-1.6 + 2.7i	-2.0 + 3.2i	-4.3 + 5.9i
	-1.1 - 1.8i	-1.3 - 2.2i	-1.6 - 2.7i	-2.0 - 3.2i	-4.3 - 5.9i
	-2.1	-2.5	-3.0	-3.6	-5.6

Case IV: Varying $R_o = r_o I$

As mentioned earlier, the filter poles approach the stable images of plant poles. The PM, upper GM, and RSM improve as r_o is increased. Also, the bandwidth and speed of response are reduced. The data are tabulated in Tables 12-12 and 12-13. The plots are given in Figure 12-9.

Table 12-12 Data for Varying R_o $R_0 = r_0 I$

r_0	Gain Margin			Phase Margin			RSM	M_r	Control Gain			Filter Gain		
1	-13.5	6.4	-12.8	29.5	−64.0	59.0	0.4	26.1	0.5	4.3	0.9	0.6	0.8	3.9
10	-12.2	7.0		28.3	−137.1	98.0	0.4	33.5	0.5	4.3	0.9	0.1	0.3	2.5
10^2	-10.8	8.2		33.5			0.5	41.2	0.5	4.3	0.9	0.03	0.1	1.6
10^3	-9.3	11.8		40.7			0.6	49.1	0.5	4.3	0.9	0.001	0.05	1.0
10^6	-5.1	15.8		6-48.4	47.7		0.7	61.1	0.5	4.3	0.9	−0.004	0.01	0.4

Table 12-13 Closed Loop Poles for Varying R_o $R_0 = r_0 I$

r_0	1	10	10^2	10^3	10^6
Closed loop poles	-0.7 + 2.1i	-0.7 + 2.1i	-0.7 + 2.1i	-0.7 + 2.1i	-0.7 + 2.1i
	-0.7 - 2.1i	-0.7 - 2.1i	-0.7 - 2.1i	-0.7 - 2.1i	-0.7 - 2.1i
	-12.0	-12.0	-12.0	-12.0	-12.0
	-1.1 + 1.8i	-0.7 + 1.2i	-0.5 + 0.8i	-0.3 + 0.5i	-0.1 + 0.3i
	-1.1 - 1.8i	-0.7 - 1.2i	-0.5 - 0.8i	-0.3 - 0.5i	-0.1 - 0.3i
	-2.1	-1.4	-1.0	-0.7	-0.6

We note that overall, LQG has consistently lower stability margins than LQR. Its sensitivity properties are also worse than LQR. In all cases, in this nonminimum phase example, the closed loop system is conditionally stable. By repeated simulations, one can determine an appropriate choice of weights. It can be shown that by an appropriate choice of weights, it is possible to recover the desirable properties of LQR asymptotically. This is called *loop transfer recovery* (*LTR*). Another extension of the LQG design methodology is the choice of frequency dependent weights (*frequency shaped LQG*). From this view

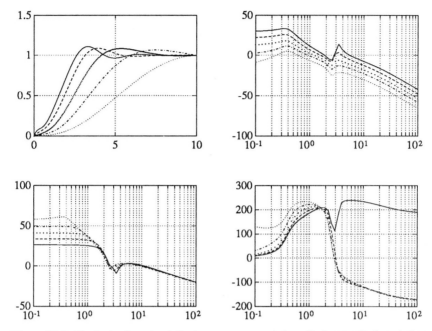

Figure 12-9 Clockwise from top left: step response, open loop Bode magnitude and phase, and closed loop magnitude plots. Legend: r_o=1, solid; r_o=10, dash; r_o=100, dots; r_o=10^3, dash-dot; r_o=10^6, small dots.

point, one can take a purely frequency domain approach to design and modify the frequency domain properties of the system in the multivariable case directly.

Other frequency domain techniques for designing robust controllers for multivariable systems are H_∞ and μ–synthesis. It has been shown that these methods can be derived from a time domain LQG type approach. Hence, state space algorithms can be used to solve frequency domain MIMO problems. Refer to [M89] and [F87] for further study. Commands for performing LTR, frequency-shaped LQG, H_∞ and μ–synthesis are available in the Robust Control Toolbox and the μ-Analysis and Synthesis Toolbox of MATLAB.

12.4 Appendix: Design Programs

Programs to generate the data appearing in the tables of this chapter are included in this Appendix. Although it is possible to write one program that will generate all of the data for LQR (LQG) for various cases considered, the workspace used may exceed the memory limitations in your version of MATLAB. Therefore, a separate program was written in each case. The programs for one case (varying q) are listed below. Programs for other cases will be almost identical.

1. Program to Generate LQR Example Data for Varying *q* (Example 12.1)

```
bsize=size(b); noinp=bsize(2); csize=size(c); noout=csize(1);
r=1; qq=[1 10 100 1000 1000000];
for i=1:5
q=qq(i);
[gain,p]=lqr(a,b,q*eye(a),r*eye(noinp));
cgh=gain; dgh=zeros(noinp); %a,b,cgh,dgh are open loop system matrices
at=a-b*gain; bt=b; ct=c; dt=zeros(noout,noinp);
out=step(at,bt,ct,dt,1,t); out=out/out(length(out));
[mag,phase]=bode(a,b,cgh,dgh,1,woq);
[cmag,cphase]=bode(at,bt,ct,dt,1,wcq);
kq(i,:)=gain; clpq(:,i)=eig(a-b*gain);
yq(:,i)=out; moq(:,i)=mag; poq(:,i)=phase; mcq(:,i)=cmag;
end
```

2. Program to Generate LQG Example Data for Varying *q* (Example 12.3)

Note: In this program, we have used the *reg* command. It forms the compensator equations and its syntax is similar to the *estim* command. It could also have been used in the observer design program of Chapter 8.

```
gamma=[1;0;0];
q=[1 10 1e2 1e3 1e6];r=1; qo=1; ro=1;
dimgam=size(gamma);noinp=dimgam(2);
dimc=size(c);noout=dimc(1);
for i=1:5
  [kqq,p]=lqr(a,b,q(i)*eye(a),r);
  [lqq,p]=lqe(a,gamma,c,qo*eye(noinp),ro*eye(noout));
  [ahq,bhq,chq,dhq]=reg(a,b,c,d,kqq,lqq);
  [aghq,bghq,cghq,dghq]=series(a,b,c,d,ahq,bhq,chq,dhq);
  [mqq,pqq]=bode(aghq,bghq,cghq,dghq,1,w);
  [atq,btq,ctq,dtq]=feedback(a,b,c,d,ahq,bhq,chq,dhq);
  [mcqq,pcqq]=bode(atq,btq,ctq,dtq,1,w);
  [nghq,dghq]=ss2tf(aghq,bghq,cghq,dghq,1);
  fq=freqs(nghq,dghq,w);
  retqq=abs(ones(w)+fq);
  mq(:,i)=mqq; pq(:,i)=pqq; mcq(:,i)=mcqq; retq(:,i)=retqq;
  [gmm,pmm,wpcm,wgcm]=margin(mqq,pqq,w);
  if length(gmm)==0, gmm=nan; wpcm=nan; end
  if length(pmm)==0, pmm=nan; wgcm=nan; end
  gmq(i,:)=gmm; pmq(i,:)=pmm; wgcq(i,:)=wgcm; wpcq(i,:)=wpcm;
  rsmq(1,i)=min(retqq); mrq(:,i)=max(mcqq);
  out=step(atq,btq,ctq,dtq,1,t); out=out/out(length(out));
  yq(:,i)=out; kq(i,:)=kqq; lq(:,i)=lqq; clpq(:,i)=eig(atq);
  end
marginq=[gmq pmq], rsmq, mrq, kq, lq, clpq
```

3. Program for LQG Design

This program can be used to design an LQG compensator. It computes open loop and closed loop Bode plots, step response, margins, minimum of the return difference, resonant peak, and closed loop poles.

The program requires: t,w;a,b,c,d; gamma, q, r, qo, ro

```
dimgam=size(gamma);noinp=dimgam(2);clear dimgam
dimc=size(c);noout=dimc(1);clear dimc
[k,p]=lqr(a,b,q,r);
[l,evf]=lqe(a,gamma,c,qo*eye(noinp),ro);
[ak,bk,ck,dk]=reg(a,b,c,d,k,l);
[agk,bgk,cgk,dgk]=series(a,b,c,d,ak,bk,ck,dk);
[m,p]=bode(agk,bgk,cgk,dgk,1,w);
[at,bt,ct,dt]=feedback(a,b,c,d,ak,bk,ck,dk);
[mc,pc]=bode(at,bt,ct,dt,1,w);
[ngk,ddgk]=ss2tf(agk,bgk,cgk,dgk,1);
f=freqs(ngk,dgdk,w); ret=abs(ones(w)+f);
[gm,pm,wpc,wgc]=margin(m,p,w), rsm=min(ret), mr=max(mc);
y=step(at,bt,ct,dt,1,t);y_norm=y/y(length(y)); clp=eig(at)
```

12.5 Problems

12.1 Consider the double-integrator system given by

$$G(s) = \frac{1}{s^2} \quad \text{or} \quad \dot{x} = \begin{bmatrix} 0 & 1 \\ 0 & 0 \end{bmatrix} x + \begin{bmatrix} 0 \\ 1 \end{bmatrix} u \quad, \quad y = [1 \quad 0] \, x$$

Let $\quad Q = \begin{bmatrix} 1 & 0 \\ 0 & 0 \end{bmatrix} \quad$ and $\quad R = 1$

a. Obtain the LQR solution, i.e., solve the Riccati equation to find P; find the optimal control gain K; find the optimal closed loop eigenvalues.

b. Find the open loop transfer function to obtain the root locus, open loop Bode plots, gain and phase margins. Also, obtain the Nyquist plot to show that it stays outside the unit circle centered at -1.

c. Obtain the closed loop Bode magnitude plot and verify the high frequency roll-off rate.

12.2 Consider the system in the preceding problem. Add process and measurement noise to the system. The plant equations are given by

$$\dot{x} = A\,x + B\,u + \omega$$

$$y = C\,x + v$$

Design a Kalman filter for this system. Assume the noise intensities are given by

$$Q_o = \begin{bmatrix} 1 & 0 \\ 0 & 1 \end{bmatrix} \quad \text{and} \quad R_o = 1$$

a. Find the solution of the filter Riccati equation Σ, and the optimal filter gain L; find the optimal LQG closed loop eigenvalues.

b. Find the LQG compensator transfer function. Use this to obtain the root locus, open loop Bode plots, gain and phase margins. Also obtain the Nyquist plot to confirm that it does enter the unit circle centered at (-1,0).

c. Obtain the closed loop Bode magnitude plot and check the high frequency roll-off rate.

d. Compare the properties of the LQR design of Problem 12.1 and the LQG design.

12.3 Repeat Problem 7.5 using LQG. Study the effects of various weights used to optimize the robust stability measures (RSM) that were defined in Example 12.3.

12.4 Repeat Problem 7.6 using LQG. Study the effects of various weights used to optimize the robust stability measures (RSM) that were defined in Example 12.3.

12.5 Solve the wedge control problem discussed in Problem 8.6 using the LQG approach. Refer to Section 1.6 for a review of feedback properties, and to Section 5.6 for computation of sensitivity and complementary sensitivity matrices. Recall that these quantities are related to disturbance rejection and noise suppression properties of systems. Study the effects of weights on these measures. Do this by obtaining the frequency response of the sensitivity and complementary sensitivity transfer functions. Use the peak value in these frequency responses as a measure of the size of these responses.

12.6 Repeat the preceding problem using the double inverted pendulum model introduced in Problem 9.21.

Notes and References

For more information about optimal control and the LQ problem, refer to the following texts: [L86a], [K70], [BH75], [KS72], [M89], [SW77], [AM90], [AF66], [E84], [O78], and [S86]. Textbooks in the area of estimation and Kalman-Bucy filtering are: [L86b], [AM79], [G86], [BH75], and [M87].

13

Robust/H∞ Control

13.1 Introduction

In the previous chapters, compensators are designed to satisfy specified requirements for steady state error, transient response, stability margins, or closed loop pole locations. Meeting all objectives is usually difficult because of various tradeoffs that have to be made, and the limitations of the design techniques. For example, classical Bode design allows us to satisfy phase margin and steady state error requirements, but the step response characteristics may not be desirable. Root locus design places a pair of complex conjugate poles to meet transient response specifications, but we have little control over the location of the other closed loop poles and zeros. Moreover, classical design is limited to SISO systems.

Although engineers have been applying classical techniques successfully, even for MIMO (multivariable) systems, the design requires many trial and error iterations in the hands of an experienced designer.

State space observer-based techniques (see Chapter 8) allow arbitrary pole placement, and are applicable to MIMO systems, but classical requirements such as stability margins cannot be controlled directly. In fact, the design may result in dangerously low stability margins. As mentioned in Section 8.5, there are also questions about the choice of pole locations. In the MIMO case, the controller gain K (similarly the observer gain) is non-unique. Its determination requires solving simultaneous nonlinear algebraic equations with possibly an infinite number of solutions. Although several techniques have been developed to tackle this issue (eigenstructure assignment, projective control, or the *place* command in MATLAB), they may not result in satisfactory performance.

The LQ formulation is a MIMO design technique that resolves some of the problems with observer-based control. The problem is recast in an optimization framework resulting in unique controller/filter gains. The pole selection task is also converted to the selection of optimization parameters (Q, R, etc.). The attractive properties of the LQR methodology were discussed in the previous chapter. It is known, however, that most of these attractive properties are lost when an estimator is introduced to estimate the unavailable states (LQG case).

None of the techniques discussed so far addresses practical issues such as model uncertainty. In addition, none of the techniques results in the best possible performance in the face of uncertainty. In this chapter we address some of these issues.

13.1.1 Critique of LQG

Early pioneers of control, particularly H. W. Bode and I. M. Horowitz, studied and delineated most of the properties of feedback. In the early sixties, with the birth of modern control, optimality and design of optimal control systems became the dominant paradigm. The solution of the LQG problem was probably the highlight of this era. The LQG paradigm failed to meet the main objectives of control system designers, however. That is to say, LQG control failed to work in real environments. The major problem with the LQG solution was lack of robustness. In a series of papers, researchers showed that LQG-based designs could become unstable in practice as more realism was added to the plant model. The same kinds of failures were also observed in industrial experiments with LQG. It became apparent that too much emphasis on optimality, and not enough attention to the model uncertainty issue, was the main culprit. During the eighties, much of the attention was shifted back to feedback properties and frequency-domain techniques (which were the main features of classical control), and their generalization to multivariable systems.

In this chapter we will discuss the *Loop Transfer Recovery* (LQG/LTR) and H_∞ techniques. These methods maintain the LQG machinery, but modify the design procedure to address some of the shortcomings of the original LQG approach. Before these design techniques are introduced, a brief introduction to the concept of robustness and uncertainty modeling is provided.

13.2 Performance Specifications and Robustness

The ultimate goal of a control system designer is to build a system that will work in the real environment. Because the real environment may change with time (components may age or their parameters may vary with temperature or other environmental conditions), or operating conditions may vary (load changes, disturbances), the control system must be able to withstand these variations. Even if the environment does not change, another fact of life is the issue of model uncertainty. Any mathematical representation of a system often involves simplifying assumptions. Nonlinearities are either unknown and hence un-modeled, or modeled and later ignored to simplify analysis. Different components of systems (actuators, sensors, amplifiers, motors, gears, belts, etc.) are sometimes modeled by constant gains, even though they may have dynamics or nonlinearities. Dynamic structures (e.g., aircrafts, satellites, missiles) have complicated high frequency dynamics that are often ignored at the design stage. Because control systems are typically designed using much-simplified models of systems, they may not work on the real plant in real environments.

The particular property that a control system must possess for it to operate properly in realistic situations is called *robustness*. Mathematically, this means that the controller must perform satisfactorily not just for one plant, but for a family (or set) of plants. Let us be more specific. Suppose the following plant is to be stabilized:

$$G(s) = \frac{1}{s-a}$$

It is suspected that the value of the parameter a is equal to 1, but this value could be off by 50%. If we design a controller that will stabilize the system for all values of $0.5 \leq a \leq 1.5$, we say the system has *robust stability*. If, in addition, the system is to satisfy performance specifications such as steady state tracking, disturbance rejection, and speed of response requirements, and the controller satisfies all requirements for all values of a in the specified range, we say the system possesses *robust performance*. The problem of designing controllers that satisfy robust stability and performance requirements is called *robust control*. A variety of approaches to this problem was investigated intensely during the 1980s and is still under investigation by many researchers.

The underlying concept within control theory that has made it into a field of science is feedback. The study of feedback and its properties is responsible for the rapid growth of this field. There are two important properties that a feedback system possesses that an open loop system cannot have. These are sensitivity and disturbance rejection. By sensitivity it is meant that feedback reduces the sensitivity of the closed loop system with respect to uncertainties or variations in elements located in the forward path of the system. Disturbance rejection refers to the fact that feedback can eliminate or reduce the effects of unwanted disturbances occurring within the feedback loop. An open loop system can also eliminate certain disturbances (an input is generated that subtracts off the measurable disturbance), but it requires full knowledge of the disturbance, which is not always available. Feedback is also used to stabilize unstable systems, but feedback itself is frequently the cause of instability. The stabilizing effects of feedback are emphasized so much in most texts that its other important properties are forgotten by beginning (or even experienced) students of control. Feedback can also improve the command performance of systems. Although this can be accomplished by an open loop system, the desired effect is lost if the plant is different from its model. A feedback system is much more tolerant of model errors and its performance will degrade less in such cases, however.

13.2.1 Nominal Performance of Feedback Systems

A feedback control system must be stable and satisfy certain performance specifications, called nominal performance; it must also maintain these properties despite model uncertainties. These properties are called robust stability and robust performance, respectively. We wish to set specifications for a "good" feedback system. Towards this end, consider the feedback system in Figure 13-1. The system has the following inputs:

$r(s)$ = command (or reference) input. This is the input which the system must be able to follow or track.

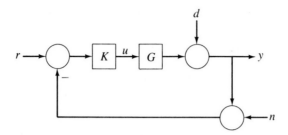

Figure 13-1 Block diagram of a feedback control system including disturbance and
measurement noise inputs.

$d(s)$ = disturbance input, which are known or unknown inputs that the system must
be able to reject. Disturbances may represent actual physical disturbances acting on
the system such as wind gusts disturbing aircrafts, disturbances owing to actuators
such as motors, or uncertainties resulting from model errors in plant or actuator.
Model uncertainties may include neglected nonlinearities in plant or actuator, and
neglected or unknown modes in the system.

$n(s)$ = sensor or measurement noise, which is introduced into the system via sensors
that are usually random high frequency signals.

A properly designed control system must track command inputs with small error and
reject disturbance and noise inputs. The contribution of general disturbances to the output
must be small.

The total output of the closed loop system in Figure 13-1 is given by

$$y(s) = \frac{g(s)k(s)}{1 + g(s)k(s)}\, r(s) + \frac{1}{1 + g(s)k(s)}\, d(s) - \frac{g(s)k(s)}{1 + g(s)k(s)}\, n(s)$$

Recall the following terminology introduced in Chapter 1:

$L = gk$ = (open) loop transfer function or loop gain
$J = 1 + gk$ = return difference
$S = 1 / (1 + gk)$ = sensitivity transfer function
$T = gk / (1 + gk)$ = complementary transfer function (also the closed loop transfer
function from r to y).

Note that for all frequencies, the following equality holds

$$S(s) + T(s) = 1$$

1. **Command Response**: Assuming that $d = n = 0$, then $y(s) \approx r(s)$ for a given range
    of frequencies when $S(s)$ is small, or equivalently when gk is large. Common

command inputs such as steps, ramps, and sinusoids are usually in the low frequency range.

2. **Disturbance Rejection**: $S(s)$ must be kept small to minimize the effects of disturbances. Again, this is equivalent to large loop gain; i.e., gk is large at the frequency range where the disturbances have their major energy content. If the disturbances are low frequency signals (which is usually true), we can see that command response and disturbance rejection are compatible requirements.

3. **Noise Suppression**: $T(s)$ must be kept small to reduce the effects of sensor noise on the output. From the definition of T, this is met if the loop gain gk is small.

Putting these effects together, we arrive at a general desired shape for the loop gain of a properly designed feedback system. This is shown in Figure 13-2. The general features of this loop gain are that it has high gain at low frequencies (for good tracking and disturbance rejection), and low gain at high frequencies (for noise suppression). Another reason for keeping the loop gain low at high frequencies can be arrived at by examining the control signal

$$u(s) = \frac{k(s)}{1 + g(s)k(s)} [r(s) - d(s) - n(s)]$$

For large loop gain, $u(s)$ is proportional to $1/g(s)$. At high frequencies $g(s)$ will roll off, resulting in large control activity $u(s)$. Hence, the loop gain must be kept small at large frequencies to minimize control energy.

Intermediate frequencies typically control the gain and phase margins. Bode has shown that for a stable system, the slope of the magnitude plot should not exceed -40 dB/dec near the gain crossover frequency, i.e., the transition from low to high frequency range must be smooth (e.g., -20 dB/dec). Desirable shapes for sensitivity and complemen-

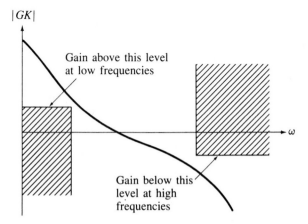

Figure 13-2 Desirable shape for the open loop transfer function of a feedback system.

tary sensitivity transfer functions are shown in Figure 13-3. Note that S must be small at low frequencies and roll off to 1 (0 dB) at high frequencies, whereas T must be at 1 (0 dB) at low frequencies and get smaller at high frequencies.

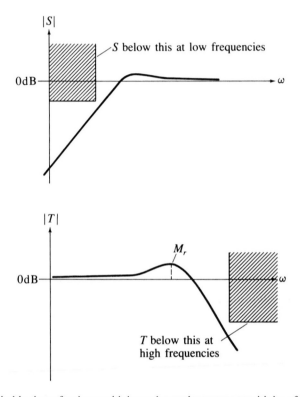

Figure 13-3 Desirable shape for the sensitivity and complementary sensitivity of a feedback system.

13.2.2 Nominal Performance: Multivariable Case

Nominal performance sets limits on the size of the sensitivity and complementary sensitivity transfer functions or, equivalently, on the size of the loop gain. For SISO systems, the transfer function size is measured by its magnitude. In the MIMO (multivariable) case, we deal with transfer function matrices (i.e., matrices whose elements are transfer functions). There are a variety of methods for measuring the size of matrix. One measure that has gained acceptance is the singular value of a matrix. The concept of singular values and its properties is discussed in the Appendix (sections 13.7.1 and 13.7.2) at the end of this chapter. Singular values, denoted by σ, of a matrix A are defined by

$$\sigma_i (A) = [\lambda_i (A^*A)]^{\frac{1}{2}} \qquad \text{where} \quad A^* = \text{complex conjugate of } A$$

The largest singular value, $\bar{\sigma}$, and the smallest singular value, $\underline{\sigma}$, are measures of amplification and attenuation of the matrix, respectively.

In the feedback system of Figure 13-1, all transfer functions are matrices and all inputs and outputs are vectors in general. The output of the system is given by

$$y = GK(I + GK)^{-1} r + (I + GK)^{-1} (d - n)$$

The derivation of the preceding expression is straightforward. Watch for the order of multiplication and remember to use matrix inversion for division. S and T are similarly defined by

$$S = (I + GK)^{-1} , \qquad T = GK (I + GK)^{-1}$$

Although the following can be proven mathematically, it seems plausible that good command response and disturbance rejection require small S, whereas noise suppression requires small T. In addition, large loop gain (GK) implies small S and small loop gain implies small T.

Because transfer function matrices are functions of s, their singular values are frequency dependent. Consequently, singular values evaluated at $s = j\omega$ can be plotted versus frequency, resulting in plots reminiscent of Bode magnitude plots. In fact, singular value plots are the generalizations of Bode magnitude plots for MIMO systems. These plots have quickly become one of the most valuable tools for analysis of multivariable systems. Singular value plots can be obtained using the *sigma* command in the Control System Toolbox (CST).

The nominal performance specifications for a feedback system (SISO/MIMO) are summarized in Table 13-1.

Table 13-1 Loop Transfer Function Properties		
	Low Frequency	**High Frequency**
Command Performance (r)	$\lvert gk \rvert \gg 1$ or $\lvert S \rvert \ll 1$	
MIMO Case	$\underline{\sigma}(GK) \gg 1$ or $\bar{\sigma}(S) \ll 1$	
Disturbance Rejection (d)	$\lvert gk \rvert \gg 1$ or $\lvert S \rvert \ll 1$	
MIMO Case	$\underline{\sigma}(GK) \gg 1$ or $\bar{\sigma}(S) \ll 1$	
Noise Suppression (n)		$\lvert gk \rvert \ll 1$ or $\lvert T \rvert \ll 1$
MIMO Case		$\bar{\sigma}(GK) \ll 1$ or $\bar{\sigma}(T) \ll 1$

13.2.3 Novel Formulation of Classical Problems

Characterization of nominal performance of feedback systems indicates that system performance can generally be translated into specifications on the sensitivity S and complementary sensitivity transfer functions T. We will see in the next section that robustness characterization also imposes similar conditions on the shape of S and T. A novel methodology for control system design consists of determining appropriate bounds on S and T, and adding compensators to the plant to shape S and T in such a way that they remain within the set bounds. This procedure is called *loop shaping*. Of course, loop shaping has been known to classical designers for a long time; the modern contribution to loop shaping is that it can now be applied to multivariable systems. In that case, we shape the singular values of S and T. Moreover, we shall see that LQG type algorithms can be applied to optimize the system's performance. Figure 13-4 shows the block diagram for loop shaping problem formulation.

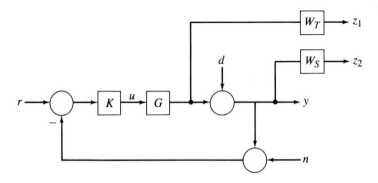

Figure 13-4 Block diagram of a feedback system for the loop shaping problem.

From the block diagram we obtain

$$z_1 = W_s (1 + GK)^{-1} d \quad \text{or} \quad z_1 = W_s S d$$

$$z_2 = W_T (1 + GK)^{-1} GK n \quad \text{or} \quad z_1 = W_T T n$$

Also note that $z_2 = W_T T r$

The transfer functions W_S and W_T are weights that are used to bound S and T. Typical shapes are given in Figure 13-5. The resulting problems are

$$|S| \le W_S^{-1} \quad \text{or} \quad |W_S S| \le 1 \quad \text{for all } \omega \qquad \textit{weighted sensitivity problem}$$

$$|T| \le W_T^{-1} \quad \text{or} \quad |W_T T| \le 1 \quad \text{for all } \omega \quad \textit{weighted complementary sensitivity problem}$$

Simultaneous satisfaction of both constraints is called the *mixed sensitivity problem*.

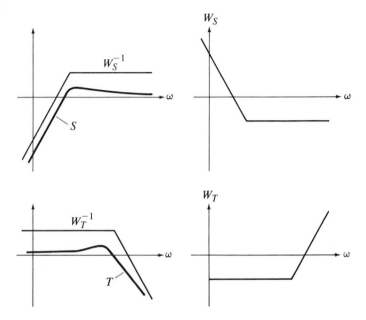

Figure 13-5 Typical shapes for S and T and their corresponding weights.

13.2.4 Modeling Uncertainty

To this point we have discussed performance specifications for a stable feedback system. A stable system is not our final objective, however, robustness is; stability must be maintained despite model uncertainties. Model uncertainty is generally divided into two categories: *structured uncertainty* and *unstructured uncertainty*. Structured uncertainty assumes that the uncertainty is modeled, and we have ranges and bounds for uncertain parameters in the system. For example, we may have a valid transfer function model of a system, but have some uncertainty about the exact location of the poles, zeros, or gain of the system. In the case of an RLC circuit, we know that it can be adequately modeled by a second order transfer function (in a given frequency range), but the components may have up to 20-30% tolerance. These kinds of uncertainties are structured. Unstructured uncertainties assume less knowledge of the system. We only assume that the frequency response of the system lies between two bounds. Both kinds of uncertainties are usually present in most applications. We will only discuss unstructured uncertainty (dealing with structured uncertainty is still under investigation; due to the complexity of the problem and our space limitations we will not discuss this case).

Unstructured uncertainty can be modeled in different ways. We will discuss *additive* and *multiplicative* uncertainty. Suppose we model a system by $G(s)$, where the actual system is given by $\tilde{G}(s)$

$$\tilde{G}(s) = G(s) + \Delta_a(s)$$

where the model error, or the additive uncertainty, is given by

$$\Delta_a(s) = \tilde{G}(s) - G(s)$$

Additive uncertainty can be used to model errors in high frequency dynamics that are neglected either due to ignorance or model reduction.

In the multiplicative uncertainty case, we assume the true model, $\tilde{G}(s)$, is given by

$$\tilde{G}(s) = (1 + \Delta_m(s))\, G(s)$$

where the uncertainty, or the model error, is given by

$$\Delta_m(s) = \frac{\tilde{G}(s) - G(s)}{G(s)}$$

This form of uncertainty can be used to model errors due to actuator or sensor dynamics.

Block diagram representations of these uncertainty models are shown in Figure 13-6. Because multiplicative uncertainty represents the relative error in the model, whereas additive model represents absolute error, the multiplicative model is used more often.

As an example, consider the following double integrator system stabilized by a lead compensator.

Example 13.1 Uncertainty Models

The nominal plant model (including the lead compensator) consists of the rigid mode (the two poles at the origin), and is given by

$$G(s) = \frac{10(s+1)}{s^2\,(s+5)}$$

The flexible mode is given by

$$\text{flexible mode} = \frac{s^2 + 2(0.1)(12)s + 12^2}{s^2 + 2(0.05)(10)s + 10^2} \frac{10^2}{12^2}$$

The true plant model, $\tilde{G}(s)$, must also include the flexible mode

$$\tilde{G}(s) = \frac{10(s+1)}{s^2\,(s+5)} \frac{s^2 + 2(0.1)(12)s + 12^2}{s^2 + 2(0.05)(10)s + 10^2} \frac{10^2}{12^2}$$

Modeling the flexible mode as additive uncertainty, we get

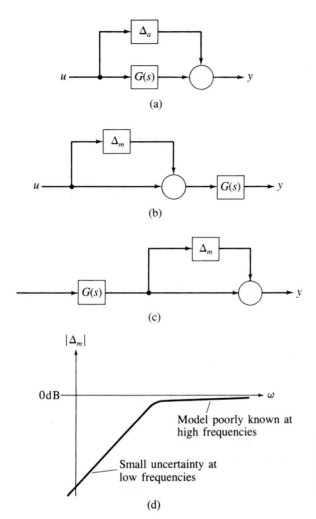

Model poorly known at
high frequencies

Small uncertainty at
low frequencies

(d)

Figure 13-6 (a) Additive uncertainty. (b) Multiplicative uncertainty at the plant input. (c) Multiplicative uncertainty at the plant output. (d) Typical shape for multiplicative uncertainty.

$$\Delta_a(s) = \tilde{G}(s) - G(s) = \frac{-3.05\,(s+1)\,(s-2.18)}{s\,(s+5)\,(s^2+s+1)}$$

Using the multiplicative model, we obtain

$$\Delta_m(s) = \frac{\tilde{G}(s) - G(s)}{G(s)} = \frac{-3.05(s-2.18)\,s}{s^2+s+1}$$

13.2.5 Robust Stability

Consider a feedback system containing a plant and a compensator. Suppose the compensator stabilizes the nominal plant model $G(s)$. We say the compensator robustly stabilizes the system if the closed loop system remains stable for the true plant $\tilde{G}(s)$. Most of the results and conditions for robust stability can be derived from variations of the Nyquist stability criterion or the following very powerful result, called the *small-gain theorem.*

Small-Gain Theorem

Consider the feedback system in Figure 13-7. Assume the plant and the compensator are stable. Then the closed loop system will remain stable if

$$|G(s)K(s)| < 1$$

Also, because of the following inequality

$$|G(s)K(s)| \leq |G(s)| \, |K(s)|$$

closed loop stability can be guaranteed if

$$|G(s)| \, |K(s)| < 1$$

In essence, the small-gain theorem states that, for closed loop stability, the loop gain must be small. The Nyquist stability criterion can be used to justify the validity of this theorem. Because we require the open loop transfer function to stay inside the unit circle centered at the origin, there can be no encirclements of the $(-1,0)$ point. In addition, we are assuming the system is open loop stable; it follows from the Nyquist stability criterion that the system has no closed loop RHP poles and is, therefore, closed loop stable. We should also add that the small-gain theorem guarantees internal stability; i.e., all possible closed loop transfer functions are stable, and all internal signals will remain bounded for bounded inputs.

Recall that for command performance and disturbance rejection, the loop gain must be much larger than one in the low frequency range. Hence, a system satisfying this theorem will have very poor performance. We will see, however, that it is possible to make the small-gain theorem work for additive and multiplicative uncertainties.

We can use the small gain theorem to answer two kinds of questions about robust stability. First, if a given uncertainty is stable and bounded, will the closed loop system be stable for the given uncertainty? Second, for a given system, what is the smallest uncertainty that will destabilize the system? To use the small-gain theorem, it is helpful to convert our system block diagram to a two-block structure shown in Figure 13-7. Let us now derive the condition for robust stability under multiplicative uncertainty. Consider the feedback system shown in Figure 13-8a. To obtain the two-block structure in Figure 13-7, we need to find the transfer function seen by the uncertainty block. The input and output of this

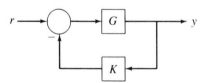

Figure 13-7 Block diagram of a feedback control system.

block are shown at the indicated points in Figure 13-8b, and its transfer function (see Figure 13-8c) is

$$M(s) = \frac{-G(s)K(s)}{1 + G(s)K(s)}$$

By the small-gain theorem, if the above transfer function and the uncertainty transfer function are stable, the closed loop system will be robustly stable if

$$\left|\Delta_m\right| < \frac{1}{\left|GK(1 + GK)^{-1}\right|}$$

Observe that the denominator of the right-hand side of the above inequality is the complementary sensitivity, T, so the robust stability condition becomes

$$\left|\Delta_m\right| < \frac{1}{|T|}$$

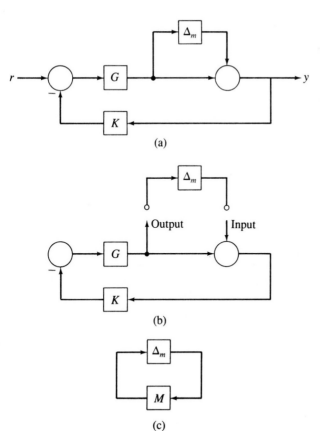

(a)

(b)

(c)

Figure 13-8 (a) Feedback system with multiplicative uncertainty. (b) Obtaining the transfer function seen by the uncertainty. (c) The system as seen by the uncertainty.

An alternative form for the above condition is

$$\left|\Delta_m\right| < \left|1+(GK)^{-1}\right|$$

where the expression on the right-hand side is the magnitude of the so-called *inverse return difference*. Note that this is different from inverse of the return difference, which is the sensitivity transfer function, S.

We can use this result to answer the two earlier posed questions. Suppose the stable uncertainty is bounded by

$$\left|\Delta_m\right| < \gamma$$

Then the closed loop system will be stable if

$$|T| < \frac{1}{\gamma} \quad \text{or} \quad |\gamma T| < 1$$

To answer the second question, we are interested in finding the size of the smallest stable uncertainty that will destabilize the system. Because the uncertainty must be smaller than $1/T$, it must be smaller than the minimum of $1/T$. To minimize the right-hand side of the preceding inequality, we must maximize T. The maximum of T over all frequencies is its peak value (also called the *resonant peak* for second order systems, see Figure 13-3). Hence, the smallest destabilizing uncertainty (we call this the *multiplicative stability margin* or MSM) is given by

$$\text{MSM} = \frac{1}{M_r} \quad \text{where} \quad M_r = \sup_{\omega} \ |T(j\omega)|$$

The symbol "sup" in the above stands for the *supremum* of the function (see Appendix, section 13.7.3, for the definition of supremum). The supremum is equal to the maximum of the function when the maximum is attained. In the MIMO case, the size of the smallest multiplicative uncertainty which destabilizes the system is given by

$$\overline{\sigma}[\Delta_m(j\omega)] = \frac{1}{\overline{\sigma}[T(j\omega)]}$$

An important point in the MIMO case is that we need to distinguish between input and output multiplicative uncertainties. The definitions of S and T are different in both cases. The preceding definitions are for output uncertainties as in Figure 13-6c. For uncertainties at the input, as in Figure 13-6b, S and T are given by

$$S = (I+KG)^{-1} \quad \text{and} \quad T = KG\,(I+KG)^{-1}$$

These distinctions are important because for certain systems the singular values of S and T at the input are quite different from the ones at the output. In such cases, we may obtain good robustness at the input, but poor robustness at the output, or vice versa. It can be shown that the condition number of the perturbed plant model ($\kappa(\tilde{G}) = \overline{\sigma}(\tilde{G})/\underline{\sigma}(\tilde{G})$) plays a key role. If the condition number is close to 1 (i.e., the system is *round*), we obtain good robustness estimates from the singular value measures; otherwise, singular value measures become very conservative. Because *gk* and *kg* are identical for SISO systems, this issue does not arise in that case. See [SD91] for further discussion.

The condition for robust stability under additive uncertainty modeling can be derived using the same approach. The transfer function seen by this uncertainty is given by

$$M(s) = \frac{-K(s)}{1 + G(s)K(s)}$$

Hence, the closed loop system will be robustly stable if

$$\left| \Delta_a \right| < \frac{1}{\left| K(1 + GK)^{-1} \right|} \quad \text{or} \quad \left| \Delta_a \right| < \frac{1}{\left| KS \right|}$$

If the uncertainty is stable and bounded by

$$\left| \Delta_a \right| < \gamma$$

then we can guarantee closed loop stability if

$$\left| KS \right| < \frac{1}{\gamma} \quad \text{or} \quad \left| \gamma KS \right| < 1$$

We can also define the *additive stability margin* (ASM) by

$$\text{ASM} = \frac{1}{\sup_{\omega} \left| K(j\omega) \, S(j\omega) \right|}$$

In the MIMO case, the size of the smallest additive uncertainty which destabilizes the system is given by

$$\overline{\sigma}[\Delta_a(j\omega)] = \frac{1}{\overline{\sigma}[K(j\omega) \, S(j\omega)]}$$

Note that for increased protection against destabilizing multiplicative uncertainties, MSM must be large, implying that the complementary sensitivity must be small. This is compatible with good noise suppression, but conflicts with tracking and disturbance rejection. Small loop gain at high frequencies will protect against multiplicative uncertainties in the high frequency range, however, without detracting from low frequency tracking or disturbance rejection. Similarly, observe that the appropriate transfer function for ASM is the same transfer function that determines control energy (actuator limits). Therefore, these requirements are compatible. Let us apply these results to an example.

Example 13.2 Robust Stability

Consider the compensated plant and the uncertainty models given in Example 13.1. The relevant models are repeated in the following:

Nominal plant model:
$$G(s) = \frac{10(s+1)}{s^2(s+5)}$$

True (or perturbed) plant model:
$$\tilde{G}(s) = \frac{10(s+1)}{s^2(s+5)} \frac{s^2 + 2(0.1)(12)s + 12^2}{s^2 + 2(0.05)(10)s + 10^2} \frac{10^2}{12^2}$$

Additive uncertainty model:
$$\Delta_a(s) = \tilde{G}(s) - G(s) = \frac{-3.05(s+1)(s-2.18)}{s(s+5)(s^2+s+1)}$$

Multiplicative uncertainty model:
$$\Delta_m(s) = \frac{\tilde{G}(s) - G(s)}{G(s)} = \frac{-3.05(s-2.18)s}{s^2+s+1}$$

The root loci for the nominal and the perturbed models are shown in Figure 13-9. Note that the nominal model is stable for all gains, whereas the perturbed model becomes unstable for very low or very high gains. The open loop Bode plots of both models are shown in Figure 13-10. The nominal model has a phase margin of 42 degrees and infinite gain margin, whereas the perturbed model has a gain margin of 10.6 dB with approximately the same phase margin. The step responses for both models are shown in Figure 13-11; note the ringing or oscillations due to the flexible modes. The plots for S and T are shown in Figure 13-12. MSM is obtained as the inverse of the peak value in T; ASM is the inverse of the peak value in S. The GM, MSM, and ASM (the numbers are not in dB) have the following values:

$$\text{MSM} = 0.64 \quad \text{ASM} = 0.66 \quad \text{GM} = 3.38$$

Note that MSM and ASM are more conservative measures of stability margin than the traditional GM. The gain margin is the factor by which the gain can be increased before instability occurs. This assumes no phase change, which implies that the gain margin is a measure of tolerance of pure gain uncertainty. Likewise, the definition of phase margin assumes that the gain is fixed, so phase margin is a measure of tolerance of pure phase uncertainty. MSM allows simultaneous gain *and* phase changes, however. It is, therefore, more general than GM and PM and it is also known as the *gain-phase margin*.

To determine robust stability with respect to multiplicative uncertainty model, we plot the magnitude of the inverse return difference $1 + (GK)^{-1}$ and Δ_m. The plot is shown in Figure 13-13. Robust stability is verified by noting that the magnitude of the inverse return difference always lies above the magnitude of the multiplicative uncertainty. Robust stability for the additive uncertainty mode is verified by plotting the magnitude of the return difference $1 + GK$ and Δ_a. The plot in Figure 13-14 verifies robust stability.

A point that needs to be emphasized is the fact that the small gain theorem is only a sufficient condition; i.e., even if it is violated, the system can still be stable. For example, if the nominal plant mode is changed to

$$G(s) = \frac{32(s+1)}{s^2(s+2)}$$

the robust stability tests fail as indicated in Figures 13-15 and 13-16. The system, although very lightly damped (as shown in Figure 13-17), is clearly stable, however.

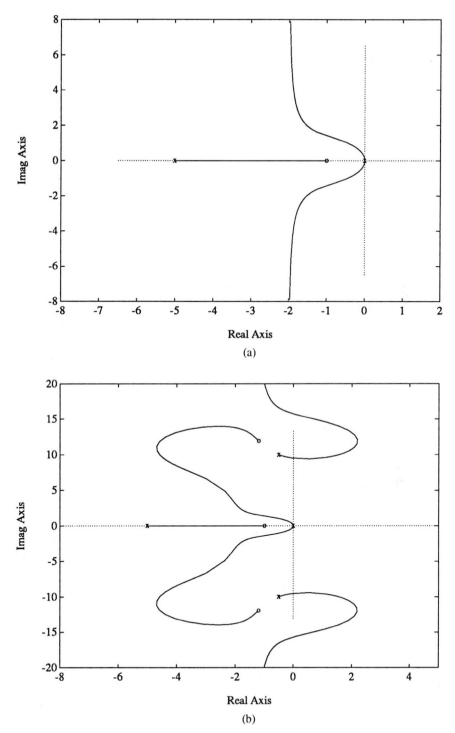

(a)

(b)

Figure 13-9 (a) Root locus for the nominal model in Example 13.1. (b) Root locus for the perturbed model.

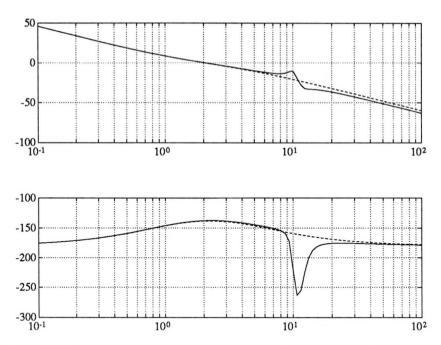

Figure 13-10 Bode plots for the nominal and perturbed (solid line) models in Example 13.1.

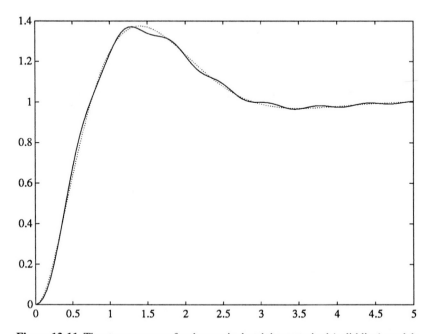

Figure 13-11 The step responses for the nominal and the perturbed (solid line) models.

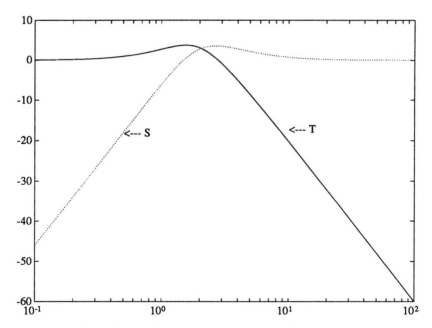

Figure 13-12 Plots of S and T (solid line) for Example 13.1.

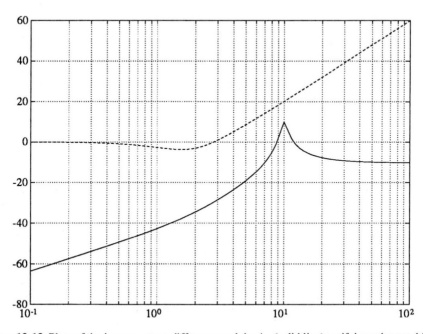

Figure 13-13 Plots of the inverse return difference and the Δ_m (solid line) verifying robust stability.

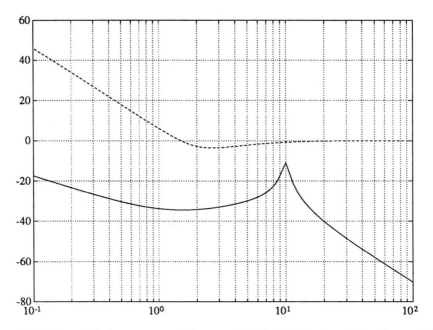

Figure 13-14 Plots of the inverse return difference and the Δ_a (solid line) verifying robust stability.

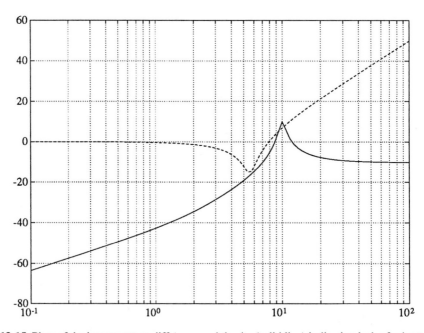

Figure 13-15 Plots of the inverse return difference and the Δ_m (solid line) indicating lack of robust stability.

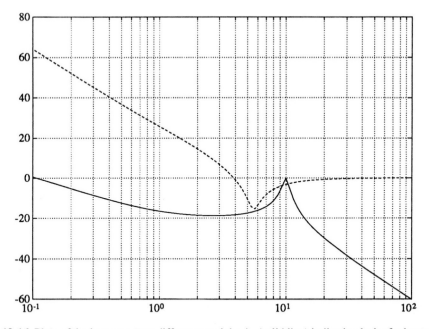

Figure 13-16 Plots of the inverse return difference and the Δ_a (solid line) indicating lack of robust stability.

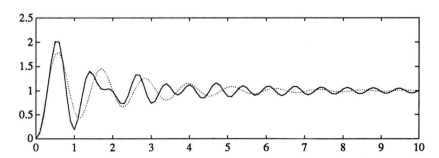

Figure 13-17 Step responses for the nominal and the perturbed (solid line) model.

13.3 H₂ Optimization and Loop Transfer Recovery (LTR)

13.3.1 H₂ Optimization

In the preceding sections we discussed the properties of a "good" feedback loop. Specifically, we obtained the total output of a system due to disturbance, noise, and command inputs as

$$y = T(r - n) + S d$$

We concluded that for good command performance and disturbance rejection, S must be small at low frequencies. Robust stability and noise suppression require that T be small at high frequencies. Because of the following identity

$$S(s) + T(s) = I \qquad \text{for all frequencies}$$

we therefore need to trade off between these two objectives. To perform this trade off in a systematic manner, the problem is posed as a frequency domain optimization problem.

Consider the following matrix inequality

$$\bar{\sigma}^2(M) \le tr(M M^*) \qquad \text{for any matrix } M$$

where tr denotes the trace of a matrix (sum of the diagonal elements) and $*$ stands for the conjugate transpose. Because of this inequality, if we minimize the trace, the singular values will be minimized. To emphasize the relative importance of S and T over a desired frequency range, we will select a frequency dependent weighting matrix $W(s)$. The following is the objective function we wish to minimize:

$$J_{H_2} = \frac{1}{2\pi} \int_0^\infty [tr(SWW^*S^*) + tr(TT^*)]\, d\omega$$

We wish to find a stabilizing compensator that will minimize the objective function for a given S, T, and W. This is called the H_2 optimization problem; the name will be explained when we discuss H_∞ optimization.

If we define $M(s)$ by

$$M(s) = [\, S(s)W(s) \qquad T(s)\,]$$

we can see that J can be written as

$$J_{H_2} = \frac{1}{2\pi} \int_0^\infty [tr(MM^*)]\, d\omega$$

By proper choice of the weighting matrix $W(s)$, we perform loop shaping. In essence, what we have presented is a frequency domain method for designing multivariable control systems. We point out that since the 1960s control designers have been seeking to extend classical frequency domain methods (i.e., Bode or Nyquist type techniques) to multivariable systems. Hence, this goal has now been attained (with singular value plots replacing Bode plots). We will not solve this problem directly, though. It can be shown that by proper choice of weights, the LQG method solves the H_2 problem in the limit. Therefore, the LQG method, which is a time domain optimization problem (with a time domain objective function), is essentially shaping S and T, when viewed from a frequency domain perspective. The modified LQG method is called *loop transfer recovery* (LQG/LTR).

13.3.2 Loop Transfer Recovery (LTR) Method

It was discussed earlier that the LQR solution has excellent stability margins (infinite gain margin and 60 degrees phase margin); we know that LQR is usually, but not always, considered impractical because it requires that all states be available for feedback. Doyle and Stein [DS79] showed, under certain conditions, that LQG can asymptotically recover the LQR properties. One of the problems with LQG is that it requires statistical information of the noise processes. In most cases, however, this information is either unavailable or is costly and impractical to obtain. Mathematical arguments and simulations had shown that the LQG design parameters (Q, R, Q_o, and R_o) have a strong influence on the performance of the system. It was suggested that because Q_o, and R_o are not usually available, they should be used instead as tuning parameters to improve system performance.

Consider the block diagrams in Figure 13-18. With the loop broken at the indicated point, the (open) loop transfer function of the LQR is given by

$$L(s) = K \Phi(s)B \qquad \text{where} \quad \Phi(s) = (sI - A)^{-1}$$

The loop transfer function for LQG is likewise given by

$$L(s)_{LQG} = K(sI - A + BK + LC)^{-1} L \, C\Phi(s)B$$

Under the following two conditions

1. $G(s)$ is minimum-phase (i.e., it has no zeros in the RHP)
2. $R_o = 1$ and $Q_o = q^2 BB'$

It can be shown that

$$\lim_{q \to \infty} L(s)_{LQG} = L(s)$$

The preceding suggests the following procedure for design. Choose the LQR parameters such that the LQR loop transfer function (also called the target feedback loop or TFL) has desirable time and/or frequency domain properties. Design an observer with parameters specified in (2) above. Increase the tuning parameter, q, until the resulting loop transfer function is as close as possible to the TFL. Because the loop transfer function of LQG approaches that of LQR, it will asymptotically recover its properties. A more detailed procedure follows.

In many situations, the variable that is measured is different from the variable we want to control. For example, we may want to control thrust in a jet engine, but we can

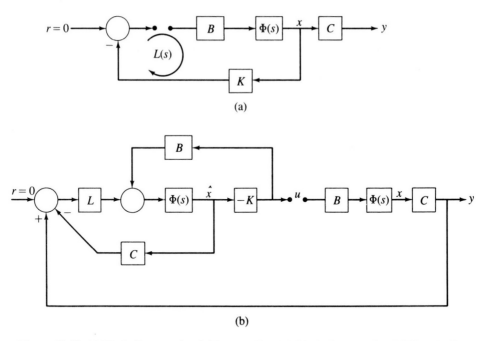

(a)

(b)

Figure 13-18 (a) Block diagram of an LQR controller. (b) Block diagram of an LQG controller.

only sense temperature and turbine speed. Let y denote the measured states, and z denote the controlled states, then

$$y = C x \quad \text{and} \quad z = C_q x$$

Loop Shaping Step

1. Determine the controlled variables (which may, or may not, be the same as the measured variables) and set

$$Q = C' C \quad \text{or} \quad Q = C'_q C_q$$

2. Convert the design specifications into a desired TFL. At this stage, if the system is type 0 and we want a type 1 system, we can add an integrator to the system.

3. Vary the parameter R until the resulting loop transfer function is similar to the TFL. One may use the RSL approach here. Also, check the sensitivity and complementary sensitivity transfer functions (S and T) to make sure they have desirable shapes.

Recovery Step

4. Select a scalar, q, and solve the filter Riccati equation

$$A\Sigma + \Sigma A' + q^2 BB' - \Sigma C' C\Sigma = 0 \quad \text{and set} \quad L = \Sigma C'$$

Increase q until the resulting loop transfer function is close to the TFL.

The higher the value of q, the closer the LQG system comes to LQR performance. It should be noted that the value of q should not be increased indefinitely, because this may lead to unreasonably large values for the filter gain L. Also, because LQR has a -20 dB/dec slope at high frequencies, large values for q will also recover this slow roll-off rate. Smaller values for q will tend to trade off lower stability margins with higher roll-off rates at high frequencies (for improved noise suppression and robust stability).

Example 13.3 LTR Design

We will now use the LTR technique on the double-integrator system to recover the LQR properties. Because LTR requires solving the Riccati equation a number of times, you have to solve the problem on the computer. First, we choose the LQR loop transfer function as the TFL. Therefore, our objective is to recover the LQR loop transfer function. We next let the parameter q vary over the range (1, 10, 100, 1000). The plots for the closed loop step response and open loop Bode plots for the LQR and LTR, for the specified values of q, are shown in Figure 13-19.

Note how the step response approaches the LQR case for increasing values of q. Also, as q increases, the low frequency gain of the system goes from 28 dB to 40 dB while the high frequency gain goes from -110 dB to -40. The values for the filter gain, L, its eigenvalues, and the stability margins (GM and PM) are tabulated in Table 13-2.

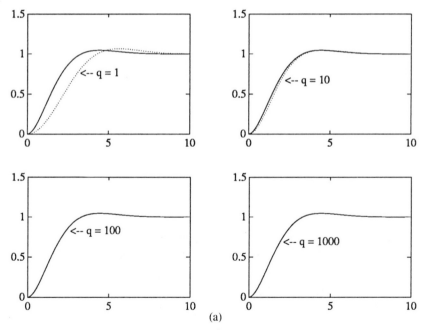

(a)

Figure 13-19 Step response, and Bode plots for LTR using $q = (\,1,\,10,\,100,\,1000)$. (a) Closed loop step response. (b) and (c) Open loop magnitude and phase Bode plots.

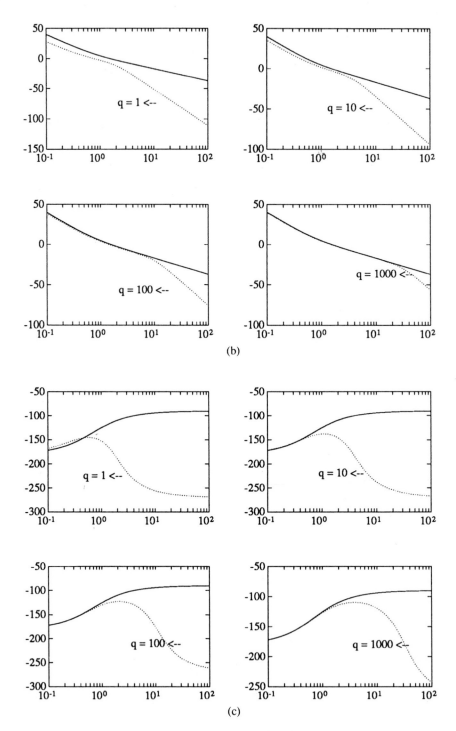

(b)

(c)

Figure 13-19 continued.

Table 13-2 Data for the LTR example				
q	1	10	100	1000
PM	32.6	41.9	55.0	61.7
GM	9.5	13.0	21.1	30.4
L	1.4 1.0	4.5 10.0	14.1 100.0	44.7 1000.0
Filter poles	-0.7+0.7j -0.7-0.7j	-2.2+2.2j -2.2-2.2j	-7.0+7.0j -7.0-7.0j	-22.3+22.3j -22.3-22.3j

The data show that the LQR phase margin is recovered. By increasing q, the gain margin increases from 10 to 30 dB. Note that increasing the margins will cost us in terms of higher values for the filter gain L, higher gain crossover frequency and lower high frequency gain, however. This will make the system more sensitive to noise and uncertainties at high frequencies. It appears that a value of q between 100 and 1000 is a reasonable compromise.

Note that the above procedure uses the machinery of LQG (i.e., two Riccati equations) and its guaranteed stability. It allows us to work strictly with Bode plots of various transfer functions, and to satisfy frequency domain measures (similar to classical control), however. Therefore, LTR can be considered a frequency domain design procedure that uses state space equations for computation. This is the common feature of control system design after LQR/LQG, sometimes called post-modern control; i.e., frequency domain techniques that use state space machinery for computation.

13.4 H∞ Control

13.4.1 A Brief History

One of the major challenges in control has been the analysis and design of multivariable (MIMO) control systems. This is a difficult problem because the transfer function of a MIMO system is a matrix. Even very basic concepts such as system order, poles, and zeros create difficulty in this case. For instance, there are five to ten different definitions of zeros of a multivariable system! Successful concepts and tools of classical control such as root locus, Bode plots, Nyquist stability criterion, and gain and phase margins initially ran into difficulty when applied to multivariable systems. State space techniques, based in the time domain, avoided the complexities of transfer function matrices, and provided tools for analysis and design of MIMO systems. Within the state space framework, the only difference between a SISO system and a MIMO system is the number of columns of the B matrix (number of inputs) and the number of rows in the C matrix (number of outputs). Note that in all of the techniques that we have discussed, these dimensions play no part. In fact, the most important feature of LQR/LQG is that they are systematic methods for designing MIMO systems.

At about the same time that most researchers were developing, extending, and refining time domain optimal control methods, researchers, mostly in Britain (A. G. J. MacFarlane and H. H. Rosenbrock) were busy extending classical control tools to the multivariable case. They were largely successful in these endeavors. Classical tools such as root locus (renamed *characteristic locus*), Nyquist techniques (renamed *Nyquist arrays*), and Bode plots (renamed *singular value plots*) were extended to the multivariable case. As the shortcomings of LQG methods became more apparent in the 1970s, more attention was paid to classical control concepts and concerns.

During the 1980s a new paradigm emerged, H_∞ control. This control problem was first formulated by G. Zames. It was essentially a frequency domain optimization method for designing robust control systems. Robustness became the main concern in the control community, and other techniques for designing robust multivariable control systems soon followed: H_∞ control by many researchers, μ-synthesis by J. Doyle (simultaneously introduced by M. Safonov as k_m-synthesis), Quantitative Feedback Theory (or QFT for short) by I. Horowitz, and methods based on the Kharitonov's theorem for structured uncertainty. All of these techniques are still being developed and refined today.

Our purpose in this section is to present a brief introduction to H_∞ control. Although this is a powerful technique for the MIMO case, our presentation is limited to the SISO case. The transition to the MIMO case is straightforward (in theory, but not necessarily in practice).

13.4.2 Notation and Terminology

H_∞ control has developed its own terminology, notation, and paradigm. For example, the classical block diagram has been modified to handle more general types of problems. Also, because the design equations are very lengthy, some shorthand notation is introduced to simplify the presentation. Because these notations have become standard in the literature, and the fact that they could be confusing to the novice, we will introduce and use them in this discussion to ease the transition for the reader to more advanced books and the literature.

We will first discuss the name. H_∞ refers to the space of stable and proper transfer functions. We generally desire that the closed loop transfer functions be proper (i.e., the degree of the denominator $\geq$ the degree of the numerator) and stable (poles strictly in the LHP). Instead of repeating these requirements, we say $G(s)$ is in H_∞. The basic object of interest in H_∞ control is a transfer function. In fact, we will be optimizing over the space of transfer functions. Optimization presupposes a cost (or objective) function, because we want to compare different transfer functions and choose the best one in the space. In H_∞ control, we compare transfer functions according to their ∞-norm (see the Appendix Section A.4 of this chapter for norms). The ∞-norm of a transfer function is defined by

$$\|G\|_\infty = \sup_\omega \ |G(j\omega)|$$

This is easy to compute graphically, it is simply the peak in the Bode magnitude plot of the transfer function (it is finite when the transfer function is proper and has no imaginary poles). We have already seen this quantity before in the robust stability Section 13.2.5. For instance, the multiplicative stability margin (MSM) can be written as

$$MSM = \frac{1}{\| T \|_\infty}$$

In H∞ control, the objective is to minimize the ∞-norm of some transfer function. So, we actually minimize the peak in the Bode magnitude plot (or the singular value plot in the MIMO case). Note that this will increase the robust stability margin of the system.

A notation which is rapidly becoming popular is the *packed-matrix* notation introduced in Chapter 5 and used in Chapters 8 and 12. Recall that the transfer function of a system with state space matrices $\{A, B, C, D\}$ is given by

$$G(s) = C(sI - A)^{-1} B + D$$

This transfer function in packed-matrix notation is written as

$$G(s) = \left[\begin{array}{c|c} A & B \\ \hline C & D \end{array} \right]$$

It should be emphasized one more time that the above is not a matrix in the ordinary sense, it is a shorthand notation for the previous expression for $G(s)$.

The solution to the H∞ control problem contains very messy Riccati equations; the following notation is introduced to simplify solution representation. Consider the following Riccati equation:

$$A' X + XA - XRX + Q = 0$$

The stabilizing solution of this equation will be denoted by $X = \text{Ric} (H)$, where H is the following *Hamiltonian* matrix.

$$H = \begin{bmatrix} A & -R \\ -Q & -A' \end{bmatrix} \quad \text{and} \quad (A - RX) \text{ is stable}$$

Instead of writing the Riccati equation, we will specify its associated Hamiltonian matrix and the reader can create the appropriate Riccati equation.

Finally, we introduce the more general *two-port block diagram* representation of control systems shown in Figure 13-20.

The two-port diagram is able to represent a variety of problems of interest. The diagram contains two main blocks, the plant and the controller. The plant section has two inputs and two outputs. The plant inputs are classified as control inputs and exogenous inputs. The control input, u, is the output of the controller, which becomes the input to the actuators driving the plant. The exogenous input, w, is actually a collection of inputs (a

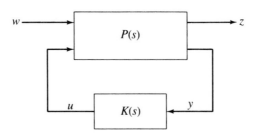

Figure 13-20 The two-port block diagram for H_∞ control.

vector). The main distinction between w and u is that the controller cannot manipulate exogenous inputs. Typical inputs that are lumped into w are external disturbances, noise from the sensors, and tracking or command signals. The plant outputs are also categorized in two groups. The first group, y, are signals that are measured and fed back. These become the inputs to the controller. The second group, z, are the regulated outputs. These are all the signals we are interested in controlling or regulating. They could be states, error signals, or control signals. Even if the original system is SISO (i.e., u and y are scalars), the new formulation is essentially MIMO. Most realistic control system problem formulations are of the MIMO kind.

A transfer function representation of the system is given by

$$
\begin{aligned}
z &= P_{zw}\, w + P_{zu}\, u \\
y &= P_{yw}\, w + P_{yu}\, u \\
u &= K\, y
\end{aligned}
$$

The closed loop transfer function between the regulated outputs and the exogenous inputs is obtained as follows. First, we substitute for u in the equation for y,

$$
y = P_{yw}\, w + P_{yu}\, Ky
$$

and solve for y

$$
(I - P_{yu}\, K)\, y = P_{yw}\, w \qquad \rightarrow \qquad y = (I - P_{yu}\, K)^{-1}\, P_{yw}\, w
$$

Therefore, u becomes

$$
u = K\, y = K\, (I - P_{yu}\, K)^{-1}\, P_{yw}\, w
$$

Substituting this into the equation for z, we get

$$
z = P_{zw}\, w + P_{zu}\, K\, (I - P_{yu}\, K)^{-1}\, P_{yw}\, w = [\, P_{zw} + P_{zu}\, K\, (I - P_{yu}\, K)^{-1}\, P_{yw} \,]\, w
$$

Finally

$$z = T_{zw}\, w \qquad \text{where} \qquad T_{zw} = P_{zw} + P_{zu}\, K\, (I - P_{yu}\, K)^{-1}\, P_{yw}$$

The above expression for the closed loop transfer function T_{zw} is called the *linear fractional transformation (LFT)*.

The plant can also be represented in state space form as

$$\dot{x} = A\,x + B_1\,w + B_2\,u$$
$$z = C_1\,x + D_{11}\,w + D_{12}\,u$$
$$y = C_2\,x + D_{21}\,w + D_{22}\,u$$

Using the packed-matrix notation, we get

$$P(s) = \left[\begin{array}{c|c:c} A & B_1 & B_2 \\ \hline C_1 & D_{11} & D_{12} \\ \hdashline C_2 & D_{21} & D_{22} \end{array}\right]$$

13.4.3 The Two-port Formulation of Control Problems

Some examples of standard problems, including the LQG problem, will now be cast into the two-port framework. Consider the classical regulator problem using unity feedback structure shown in Figure 13-21a. The objective is to keep the plant output small despite disturbances acting on the system and measurement noise. It is also desired to keep the actuator effort down to conserve control energy. The block diagram can be redrawn as shown in Figure 13-21b. In this diagram, the disturbance and measurement noise inputs are exogenous inputs that are pulled out to the left as w; the outputs we wish to regulate are the plant and controller outputs that are pulled out to the right as z. The input-output relations of the system are

$$y_p = G\,d + G\,n$$
$$u = u$$
$$y = -G\,d - n - G\,u$$

Now let

$$w = \begin{bmatrix} d \\ n \end{bmatrix}, \quad z = \begin{bmatrix} y_p \\ u \end{bmatrix} \quad \text{and} \quad P = \begin{bmatrix} P_{zw} & P_{zu} \\ P_{yw} & P_{yu} \end{bmatrix}$$

we get

$$P_{zw} = \begin{bmatrix} G & 0 \\ 0 & 0 \end{bmatrix}, \quad P_{zu} = \begin{bmatrix} G \\ 1 \end{bmatrix}, \quad P_{yw} = [\,-G \quad -1\,], \quad \text{and} \quad P_{yu} = -G$$

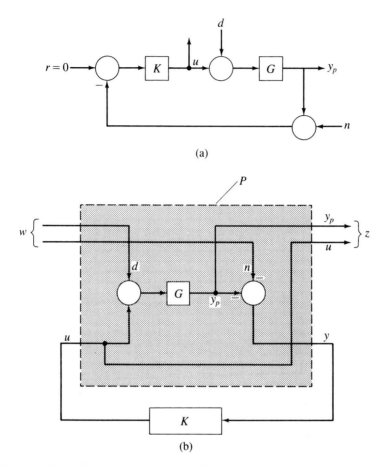

Figure 13-21 (a) Classical regulator problem. (b) The two-port formulation of the regulator problem.

Hence the LFT (closed loop transfer function from w to z) is

$$T_{zw} = \begin{bmatrix} SG & -T \\ -T & -T/G \end{bmatrix} \quad \text{where} \quad S = \frac{GK}{1+GK} \quad \text{and} \quad T = 1 - S$$

Note the appearance of S and T in these transfer functions. Recall that we wish to make these two quantities small in their appropriate frequency ranges. In H_∞ control, we will make the size (i.e., the norm) of this transfer function small, and hence regulate all outputs of interest.

The two-port representation of the LQG problem is shown in Figure 13-22. Note that the variance of z is given by

$$\text{Var}(z) = \text{E}\,[z'\,z] = E\,[x'Qx + u'Ru]$$

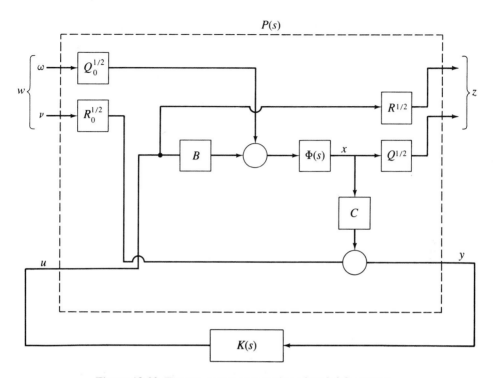

Figure 13-22 The two-port representation of the LQG problem.

In a properly posed problem, the optimal closed loop system will be stable. Hence, the control and state vectors will be stationary processes; the preceding equation is then a valid representation of the LQG objective function. Note that the LQG cost function is the weighted 2-norm of the states and control. If the inputs are unit intensity white processes, we see that the LFT will be equal to the LQG cost function. Hence, the LQG problem can be restated as

$$\underset{K(s) \text{ stabilizing}}{\text{Min}} \quad \| T_{zw} \|_2$$

Therefore, the main difference between the LQR/LQG/LTR and H_∞ control is the norm that is used. The former uses the 2-norm and the latter uses the ∞-norm. The main properties and advantages of the ∞-norm over the 2-norm are the following:

1. The ∞-norm is a gain (the L_2 gain of the system). It can also be interpreted as the energy gain of the system. The 2-norm is not a gain.
2. The ∞-norm minimizes the worst case RMS value of the regulated variables when the disturbances have unknown spectra. The 2-norm minimizes the RMS values of the regulated variables when the disturbances are unit intensity white processes.

3. H_∞ control results in guaranteed stability margins (i.e., it is robust), whereas LQG has no guaranteed margins.

13.5 H_∞ Control: Problem Formulation and Solution

13.5.1 Problem Formulation and Assumptions

The H_∞ control problem is formulated as follows: consider the two-port diagram in Figure 13-20, and find an internally stabilizing controller, $K(s)$, for the plant, $P(s)$, such that the ∞-norm of the closed loop transfer function, T_{zw}, is below a given level γ (a positive scalar). This problem is called the *standard H_∞ control problem*. The *optimal H_∞ control problem* is

Optimal Problem $\displaystyle \operatorname*{Min}_{K(s)\ \text{stabilizing}}\ \| T_{zw} \|_\infty$

Standard Problem $\displaystyle \operatorname*{Find}_{K(s)\ \text{stabilizing}}\ \| T_{zw} \|_\infty \le \gamma$

The standard problem is more practical. In practice, control system design is more like a balancing act of tradeoffs, and a mathematically optimal solution may not be so desirable after all the other real life constraints are taken into account. To solve the optimal problem, we start with a value for γ and reduce it until the problem fails to have a solution. As a starting value for γ, we can solve an LQG problem; find the peak in the resulting closed loop transfer function and use this value. To lower γ, we can use a search algorithm (such as a binary search) to reach the optimal value. This procedure is called γ-*iteration*.

For the problem to have a solution, certain assumptions must be satisfied. They are listed below after the dimensions of the various variables are given.

Dimensions: $\dim x = n$, $\dim w = m_1$, $\dim u = m_2$, $\dim z = p_1$, $\dim y = p_2$

1. The pair (A, B_2) is stabilizable and (C_2, A) is detectable. Recall from Chapter 8 that these are weaker versions of controllability and observability conditions. This assumption is necessary for a stabilizing controller to exist. It simply guarantees that the controller can reach all unstable states, and these states show up on the measurements.

2. rank $D_{12} = m_2$, rank $D_{21} = p_2$. These conditions are needed to insure that the controllers are proper. It also implies that the transfer function from w to y is nonzero at high frequencies. Unlike the first assumption, which is usually satisfied, this assumption is frequently violated (for example if the original plant is strictly proper; i.e., if it has more poles than zeros, this condition will be violated) unless the problem is formulated such that this condition is satisfied.

3. rank $\begin{pmatrix} A - j\omega\,I & B_2 \\ C_1 & D_{12} \end{pmatrix} = n + m_2$ for all frequencies.

4. rank $\begin{pmatrix} A - j\omega I & B_1 \\ C_2 & D_{21} \end{pmatrix} = n + p_2$ for all frequencies.

5. $D_{11} = 0$ and $D_{22} = 0$. This assumption is not needed, but it will simplify the equations for the solution. It also implies that the transfer functions from w to z and u to y roll off at high frequencies, respectively.

Before we present the solution, it should be pointed out that the solutions of the H_∞ and LQG problems are very similar to each other. They both use a state estimator and feed back the estimated states. The controller and estimator gains are also computed from two Riccati equations. The differences are in the coefficients of the Riccati equations, and the fact that the H_∞ state estimator contains an extra term. The compensator equations follow.

13.5.2 Problem Solution

The controller is given by (K_c corresponds to K, the controller gain, in the LQG case)

$$u = -K_c \hat{x}$$

and the state estimator is given by

$$\dot{\hat{x}} = A\hat{x} + B_2 u + B_1 \hat{w} + Z_\infty K_e (y - \hat{y})$$

$$\text{where} \quad \hat{w} = \gamma^{-2} B'_1 X_\infty \hat{x} \quad \text{and} \quad \hat{y} = C_2 \hat{x} + \gamma^{-2} D_{21} B'_1 X_\infty \hat{x}$$

We can also write this in packed matrix notation as

$$K(s) = \left[\begin{array}{c|c} A - B_2 K_c - Z_\infty K_e C_2 + \gamma^{-2} (B_1 B'_1 - Z_\infty K_e D_{21} B'_1) X_\infty & Z_\infty K_e \\ \hline -K_c & 0 \end{array} \right]$$

The extra term, $\hat{w}$, is an estimate of the worst case input disturbance to the system, and $\hat{y}$ is the output of the estimator. The estimator gain is $Z_\infty K_e$ (K_e corresponds to L in the LQG case). The controller gain, K_c, and estimator gain, K_e, are given by

$$K_c = \tilde{D}_{12} (B'_2 X_\infty + D'_{12} C_1) \quad \text{where} \quad \tilde{D}_{12} = (D'_{12} D_{12})^{-1}$$

$$K_e = (Y_\infty C'_2 + B_1 D'_{21}) \tilde{D}_{21} \quad \text{where} \quad \tilde{D}_{21} = (D_{21} D'_{21})^{-1}$$

The term Z_∞ is given by

$$Z_\infty = (I - \gamma^{-2} Y_\infty X_\infty)^{-1}$$

The terms X_∞ and Y_∞ are solutions to the controller and estimator Riccati equations; i.e.,

$$X_\infty = \text{Ric} \begin{bmatrix} A - B_2 \tilde{D}_{12} D'_{12} C_1 & \gamma^{-2} B_1 B'_1 - B_2 \tilde{D}_{12} B'_2 \\ -\tilde{C}'_1 \tilde{C}_1 & -(A - B_2 \tilde{D}_{12} D'_{12} C_1)' \end{bmatrix}$$

$$Y_\infty = \text{Ric} \begin{bmatrix} (A - B_1 D'_{21} \tilde{D}_{21} C_2)' & \gamma^{-2} C'_1 C_1 - C'_2 \tilde{D}_{21} C_2 \\ -\tilde{B}_1 \tilde{B}'_1 & -(A - B_1 D'_{21} \tilde{D}_{21} C_2) \end{bmatrix}$$

where $\tilde{C}_1 = (I - D_{12} \tilde{D}_{12} D'_{12}) C_1$ and $\tilde{B}_1 = B_1 (I - D'_{21} \tilde{D}_{21} D_{21})$

The closed loop system becomes

$$\begin{bmatrix} \dot{x} \\ \dot{\hat{x}} \end{bmatrix} = \begin{bmatrix} A & -B_2 K_c \\ Z_\infty K_e C_2 & A - B_2 K_c + \gamma^{-2} B_1 B'_1 X_\infty - Z_\infty K_e (C_2 + \gamma^{-2} D_{21} B'_1 X_\infty) \end{bmatrix} \begin{bmatrix} x \\ \hat{x} \end{bmatrix} + \begin{bmatrix} B_1 \\ Z_\infty K_e D_{21} \end{bmatrix} w$$

$$\begin{bmatrix} z \\ y \end{bmatrix} = \begin{bmatrix} C_1 & -D_{12} K_c \\ C_2 & 0 \end{bmatrix} \begin{bmatrix} x \\ \hat{x} \end{bmatrix} + \begin{bmatrix} 0 \\ D_{21} \end{bmatrix} w$$

As we had promised, the equations are quite complicated and messy!

Finally, it can be proved that there exists a stabilizing compensator if and only if there exist positive semi-definite solutions to the two Riccati equations and the following condition:

$$\rho(X_\infty Y_\infty) < \gamma^2$$

where $\rho(A)$ = spectral radius of A = largest eigenvalue of $A = \lambda_{max}(A)$.

The block diagrams of the LQG and H_∞ control systems are shown in Figure 13-23. Compare these diagrams to see the similarities and differences between them.

It should be fairly obvious that H_∞ problems cannot be solved manually. Computer programs such as MATLAB, Program CC, MATRIX$_X$ and Ctrl-C have special functions and utilities for solving these problems. For every value of γ, two Riccati equations must be solved. In addition, even if the plant is first order, we still may need to add weights to the system to either satisfy design requirements or satisfy the necessary assumptions for a feasible solution. This increases the order of the equations and makes manual solution almost impossible. A summary of the steps is given below.

1. Set up the problem to obtain the state space representation for $P(s)$.
2. Check if the assumptions (the rank conditions) are satisfied. If they are not, reformulate the problem by adding weights or adding (fictitious) inputs or outputs.
3. Select a large positive value for γ.

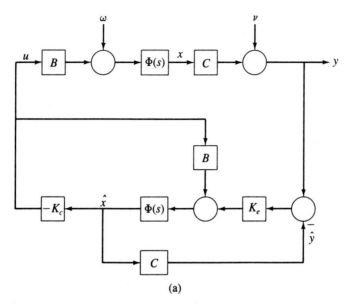

(a)

Figure 13-23 (a) The LQG controller block diagram. (b) Block diagram showing the
structure of the H_∞ control system. Continues on page 432.

4. Solve the two Riccati equations. Determine if the solutions are positive semi-definite; also verify that the spectral radius condition is met.

5. If all the above conditions are satisfied, lower the value of γ. Otherwise, increase it. Repeat steps 4 and 5 until either an optimal or satisfactory solution is obtained.

13.5.3 Weights in H_∞ Control Problems

Practical control problems require weighting the inputs and outputs. There are a few reasons for using weights. Constant weights are used for scaling inputs and outputs; they are also used for unit conversions. Transfer function weights are used to shape the various measures of performance in the frequency domain. In H_∞ control problems, weights are also used to satisfy the rank conditions. These assumptions are frequently violated unless appropriate weights are selected. In fact, the weights are the only parameters that the designer must specify. Proper selection of these weights depends a great deal on the experience of the user and on his/her understanding of the physics of the problem and other practical engineering constraints.

Tracking and disturbance rejection require that the sensitivity transfer function be small in the low frequency range. This can be formulated as specifying that the sensitivity remain below a given frequency dependent weight, i.e.,

$$|S| \leq W_s^{-1} \quad \text{or} \quad \left| W_s S \right| \leq 1$$

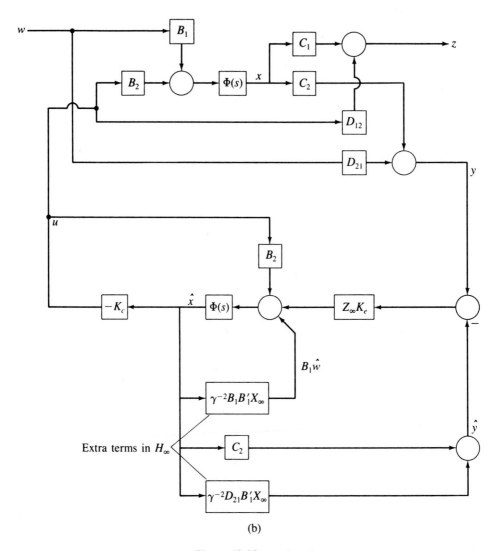

(b)

Figure 13-23 continued.

Similarly we can specify that the complementary sensitivity be kept below a given weight in the high frequency range, i.e.,

$$|T| \leq W_t^{-1} \quad \text{or} \quad |W_t T| \leq 1$$

Finally, both requirements can be satisfied by solving the so-called mixed sensitivity problem.

Example 13.4 *H*∞ **Control Design**

As an example, we will design a controller for a double integrator system using the *H*∞ approach. The first step is setting up the problem appropriately. The plant equations are given by

$$\dot{x}_1 = d + u$$
$$\dot{x}_2 = x_1$$

The new term that we have added is the disturbance term, *d*; this term corresponds to either an actual disturbance or to unmodeled dynamics in the system. The regulated outputs are x_2 and *u*. Hence, the two-port input *w* and output *z* are

$$w = \begin{bmatrix} d \\ n \end{bmatrix} \quad \text{and} \quad z = \begin{bmatrix} x_2 \\ u \end{bmatrix}$$

It is important that the control signal be included in the regulated outputs so that we can bound its magnitude to prevent saturation problems. This is also needed to insure that the rank condition on D_{12} is satisfied or the problem would fail to have a solution. The measurement equation is given by

$$y = x_2 + n$$

The noise term, *n*, is either actual sensor noise or is a representation of high frequency unmodeled dynamics. It is also needed to insure that the rank condition on D_{21} is met. Collecting these equations, we obtain the system equations in packed-matrix notation as

$$P(s) = \left[\begin{array}{c|c|c} A & B_1 & B_2 \\ \hline C_1 & D_{11} & D_{12} \\ \hline C_2 & D_{21} & D_{22} \end{array} \right] = \left[\begin{array}{cc|cc|c} 0 & 0 & 1 & 0 & 1 \\ 1 & 0 & 0 & 0 & 0 \\ \hline 0 & 1 & 0 & 0 & 0 \\ 0 & 0 & 0 & 0 & 1 \\ \hline 0 & 1 & 0 & 1 & 0 \end{array} \right]$$

The block diagrams of the system in the usual form and its two-port *H*∞ form are shown in Figure 13-24.

This problem was solved using H-infinity program in Section 13.6. After several trials, we found that the value of γ could not be reduced below 2.62 (the optimal value of γ can be found using the *hinfsyn* command of the μ-Tools or the *hinfopt* command in the RCT). Hence, we conclude that 2.62 is the optimal value (note that the solution of the optimal *H*∞ control problem involves a search over γ, and we can get as close to it as possible but not achieve it). The following are the relevant data obtained.

$$\gamma = 2.62, \quad X_\infty = \begin{bmatrix} 1.59 & 1.08 \\ 1.08 & 1.47 \end{bmatrix}, \quad Y_\infty = \begin{bmatrix} 1.47 & 1.08 \\ 1.08 & 1.59 \end{bmatrix}$$

$$K_c = [1.59 \quad 1.08], \quad K_e = \begin{bmatrix} 1.08 \\ 1.59 \end{bmatrix}$$

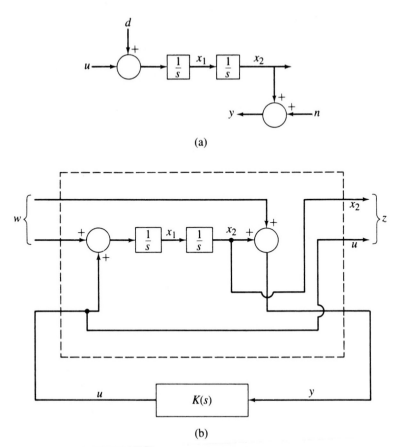

(a)

(b)

Figure 13-24   (a) The block diagram for the double-integrator system. (b) The two-port
H_∞ block diagram.

The transfer function of the compensator and the resulting closed loop poles are given by

$$K(s) = \frac{-578.3(s + 0.39)}{(s + 2.33)(s + 220.72)}, \quad \text{closed loop poles} = \{-0.71, -0.81 \pm 0.91j, -220.7\}$$

Note that this compensator is a lead compensator with a pole added at -220 to improve the
high frequency attenuation. The Bode and Nyquist plots of the system are shown in Figure
13-25. We have obtained a gain margin of 44 dB and phase margin of 45 degrees. Note that
the Nyquist plot does enter the unit circle centered at $(-1,0)$.

Finally, we will compare the robust stability of the H_∞ compensator with the lead
compensator of Example 13.2. The same flexible mode is used to perturb the plant. The plots
for S and T, inverse return difference versus Δ_m and Δ_a, are shown in Figure 13-26 for both
cases. The stability margin data presented in Table 13-3.

The data indicates that the H_∞ compensator has better stability margins. In particular,
it has more tolerance for the unmodeled flexible mode.

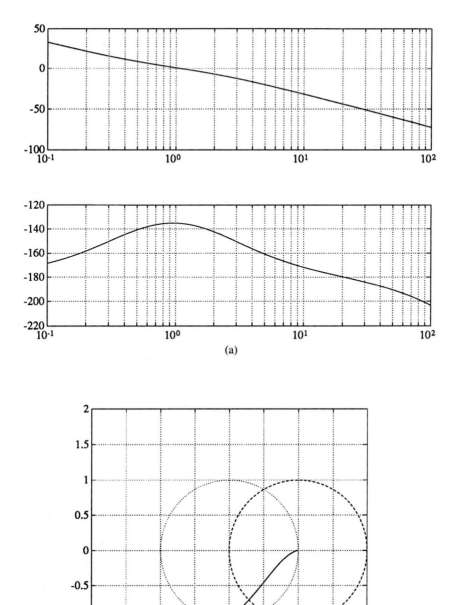

Figure 13-25 (a) Bode plots for Example 13.4. (b) Nyquist plot for Example 13.4.

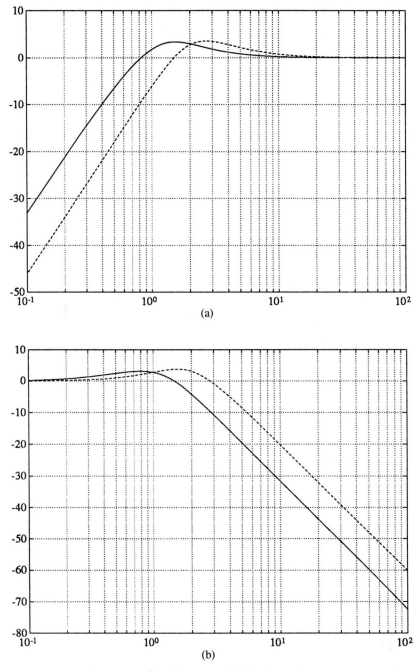

Figure 13-26 (a) The plot for S. (b) The plot for T. (c) Inverse return difference and Δ_m. (d) Inverse return difference and Δ_a. Solid lines are for the H_∞ compensated system in all cases.

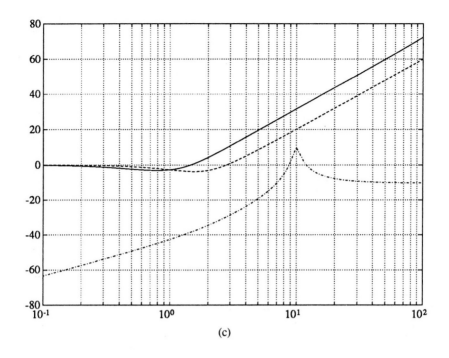

(c)

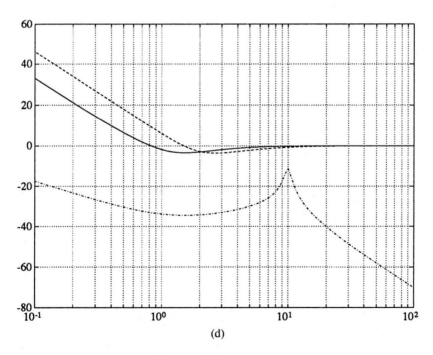

(d)

Figure 13-26 continued.

Table 13-3 Comparison of stability margins of lead and H_∞

	GM	PM	GM with flexible mode	PM with flexible mode	MSM = 1/‖ T ‖$_\infty$	ASM = 1/‖ S ‖$_\infty$
Lead (Ex. 13.2)	∞	41.6	11.1	42.5	0.64	0.66
H_∞ (Ex. 13.4)	44.3	44.6	22.8	45	0.70	0.67

We will end our brief introduction to H_∞ control by pointing out that this subject is still very novel and is rapidly progressing. We have also limited our discussion to the treatment of unstructured uncertainty, and have presented only one of the approaches to robust control. The different approaches, however, have one feature in common; i.e., they are all frequency domain computer assisted tools for design of MIMO systems satisfying practical constraints. For this reason, H_∞ control is expected to find a permanent place among the control engineer's toolbox.

13.6 Programs

1. Program for Robustness Analysis (for Example 13.2)

Use the program either as a function or as a script file. The compensator is attached to the plant, so GK is assumed to be the plant.

Program Inputs: Compensated plant and the time axis.

Program Outputs: Step response, Bode plots and margins for the nominal and perturbed models. S, T, $1 + GK$, $1 + (GK)^{-1}$, and their singular values are computed. Also, equivalent additive (multiplicative) uncertainties and their singular values are computed.

```
function [svcsi,svdm,svr,svda,svs,svt]=rob(ng,dg,nk,dk,t)
[ngk,dgk]=series(ng,dg,nk,dk)
% closed loop step response for GK
[nt,dt]=cloop(ngk,dgk); yt=step(nt,dt,t);
ndel=(100/144)*[1 2*.1*12 144]; ddel=[1 2*.05*10 100];
[ngkd,dgkd]=series(ngk,dgk,ndel,ddel)
[mgk,pgk]=bode(ngk,dgk,w); [mgkd,pgkd]=bode(ngkd,dgkd,w);
[gm,pm]=margin(mgk,pgk,w); gm=20*log10(gm);
[gmd,pmd]=margin(mgkd,pgkd,w); gmd=20*log10(gmd);
% closed loop step response for the perturbed model GK~
[ngtd,dgtd]=cloop(ngkd,dgkd); ytd=step(ngtd,dgtd,t);
% Additive uncertainty model
[nda,dda]=parallel(ngkd,dgkd,-ngk,dgk); [nda,dda]=minreal(nda,dda)
% Multiplicative uncertainty model
ddm=conv(ngk,dgkd); ndm=conv(dgk,ngkd)-conv(ngk,dgkd);
% Remove leading 0's in the polynomials
ind=find(ndm~=0); ndm=ndm(ind(1):length(ndm));
ind=find(ddm~=0); ddm=ddm(ind(1):length(ddm));
```

```
[ndm,ddm]=minreal(ndm,ddm);
% Compute return difference 1+GK and its singular value (sv)
[a,b,c,d]=tf2ss(ngk,dgk);
[as,bs,cs,ds]=parallel(a,b,c,d,[],[],[],1);
svr=sigma(as,bs,cs,ds,w); svr=20*log10(svr);
% Use sigma with the 'inv' option to get sv of S=(1+gk)^-1
svs=sigma(as,bs,cs,ds,w,'inv'); MSM=1/max(svs);
svs=20*log10(svs);
% Compute sv of T=GK(1+GK)^-1
[at,bt,ct,Dt]=tf2ss(nt,dt);
svt=sigma(at,bt,ct,Dt,w); ASM=1/max(svt);
svt=20*log10(svt);
% Compute the sv of the inverse return difference 1+[(GK)^-1]
svcsi=sigma(at,bt,ct,Dt,w,'inv'); svcsi=20*log10(svcsi);
% Compute sv of both uncertainties
[adm,bdm,cdm,Ddm]=tf2ss(ndm,ddm); svdm=sigma(adm,bdm,cdm,Ddm,w);
svdm=20*log10(svdm);
[ada,bda,cda,Dda]=tf2ss(nda,dda);svda=sigma(ada,bda,cda,Dda,w);
svda=20*log10(svda);semilogx(w,svda,w,svr)
```

2. LTR Program (for Example 13.3)

Program Inputs: System eq {a,b,c,d} and tuning matrices {r,qo,ro} and LTR parameter vector {q} and w and t.

Program Outputs: Bode and step responses. Stability margins. Control and filter gains and the compensator.

```
% ********** Start LQR ****************
dimb=size(b);noinp=dimb(2);
dimc=size(c);noout=dimc(1);clear dimc
k=lqr(a,b,c'*c,r);
% LQR Bode and step response
[m,p]=bode(a,b,k,0,1,w);m=20*log10(m);
y=step(a-b*k,b,c,0,1,t);y=y/y(length(y));
% ******* Start LTR ********************
dimlq=length(q);
for i=1:4,
        [l,evf]=lqe(a,eye(2),c,q(i)*q(i)*b*b',ro);
        [ak,bk,ck,dk]=reg(a,b,c,d,k,l);
        [agk,bgk,cgk,dgk]=series(a,b,c,d,ak,bk,ck,dk);
        [mgk,pgk]=bode(agk,bgk,cgk,dgk,1,w);
        [at,bt,ct,dt]=feedback(a,b,c,d,ak,bk,ck,dk);
        [at,bt,ct,dt]=minreal(at,bt,ct,dt);
        [gm,pm,wpc,wgc]=margin(m,p,w);
        yt=step(at,bt,ct,dt,1,t);yt=yt/yt(length(yt));
        mgg(:,i)=mg;pgg(:,i)=pg;ygg(:,i)=yg;
end
```

3. Program for H-infinity design (for Example 13.4)

Program inputs are: System equation = {a,b1,b2,c1,c2,d11,d12,d21,d22} & gam.
      Program outputs: Ric. Eq. solutions {xi,yi} and H-infinity compensator {ak,bk,ck,dk} and closed loop eigenvalues {clpoles} and the open loop transfer function.

```
% *************** checking conditions **************
n=size(a); n=n(1); m1=size(b1); m1=m1(2); m2=size(b2); m2=m2(2);
p1=size(c1); p1=p1(1); p2=size(c2); p2=p2(1); gam2=1/(gam*gam);
rank1=rank([a b2;c1 d12]);
 if rank1~=n+m2, disp('rank1 fails: no solution'),end
rank2=rank([a b1;c2 d21]);
 if rank2~=n+p2, disp('rank2 fails: no solution'),end
%*** Forming the Hamiltonian matrix and solving the Riccati eq ****
d21_=inv(d21*d21');d12_=inv(d12'*d12);
c1_=(eye(p1)-d12*d12_*d12')*c1;
b1_=b1*(eye(m1)-d21'*d21_*d21);
ahx=a-b2*d12_*d12'*c1;
bhx=gam2*b1*b1'-b2*d12_*b2';
chx=-c1_'*c1_;
ahy=(a-b1*d21'*d21_*c2)';bhy=gam2*c1'*c1-c2'*d21_*c2;chy=-b1_*b1_';
dhy=-ahy';
xi=are(ahx,-bhx,-chx)
yi=are(ahy,-bhy,-chy)
% *************** Checking conditions *******************
xeig=min(real(eig(xi))); if xeig, disp(' x  0  no solution'),end
yeig=min(real(eig(yi))); if yeig, disp('y  0   no solution'),end
rho=max(real(eig(xi*yi)));
if rho > (gam*gam), disp('rho fails:  no solution'),end
%********** Compute gains and the compensator ************
kc=d12_*(b2'*xi+d12'*c1)
ke=(yi*c2'+b1*d21')*d21_
zi=inv(eye(n)-gam2*yi*xi);
ak=a-b2*kc-zi*ke*c2+gam2*(b1*b1'-zi*ke*d21*b1')*xi ; bk=zi*ke;
ck=-kc; dk=0*ones(m2,p2);nsk=n;
[z_k,p_k,g_k]=ss2zp(ak,bk,ck,dk)
%****************** Closing the loop *******************
acl=[a , -b2*kc;
zi*ke*c2 , a-b2*kc+b1*b1'*xi*gam2-zi*ke*(c2+d21*b1'*xi*gam2)];
bcl=[b1;zi*ke*d21];
ccl=[c1 -d12*kc];
clpoles=eig(acl)
% ********** Find the loop trannsfer for classical analysis ******
[agk,bgk,cgk,dgk]=series(a,b2,-c2,d22,ak,bk,ck,dk);
```

13.7 Appendix

13.7.1 Singular Value Decomposition (SVD)

In control theory, transfer function poles and the eigenvalues of the A matrix in the state space representation have played key roles in stability analysis. Similarly, the notion of singular values plays a key role in robust stability analysis of multivariable systems.

Consider a rectangular matrix A with rank ρ, then A can be decomposed as

$$A = U \hat{\Sigma} V^* \quad \text{where} \quad A = m \times n, \quad U = m \times m, \quad V = n \times n$$

U and V are unitary matrices, i.e., $\quad U^* U = I_m \quad$ and $\quad V^* V = I_n$

Note that U^* stands for the conjugate transpose of U. The matrix $\hat{\Sigma}$ is defined by

$$\hat{\Sigma} = \begin{cases} [\, \Sigma \mid 0 \,] & \text{if } n > m \\[2mm] \left[\dfrac{\Sigma}{0} \right] & \text{if } n < m \end{cases} \quad \text{and} \quad \Sigma = \begin{bmatrix} \sigma_1 & & & \\ & \sigma_2 & & \\ & & \ddots & \\ & & & \sigma_\rho \end{bmatrix}, \quad \rho = \min\{m, n\}$$

The above representation of A is called the *singular value decomposition* (SVD) of A. The singular values satisfy

$$A^* u_i = \sigma_i v_i$$
$$A v_i = \sigma_i u_i$$

It then follows that

$$(A^* A) v_i = \sigma_i^2 v_i$$
$$u_i^* (AA^*) = \sigma_i^2 u_i^*$$

which implies that v_i are the right eigenvectors of $A^* A$ and u_i^* are the left eigenvectors of AA^*. The vectors v_i and u_i are called the *right and left singular vectors* of A, respectively. Note that these vectors must be normalized first, before they are used to form the columns of V and U, respectively. *Singular values* (sometimes called *principal gains*) of A are defined by

$$\sigma_i = [\, \lambda_i (A^* A) \,]^{1/2}$$

Singular values are nonnegative real numbers and are usually ordered as

$$\sigma_1 \geq \sigma_2 \geq \dots \geq \sigma_\rho$$

The largest and the smallest singular values are denoted by $\overline{\sigma}$ and $\underline{\sigma}$, respectively. Also, another way to express the SVD of A is

$$A = \sum_{i=1}^{\rho} \sigma_i u_i v_i^*$$

Singular values, particularly $\overline{\sigma}$ and $\underline{\sigma}$, have many properties and applications. Before we discuss these properties, let us work an example.

Consider the following matrix

$$A = \begin{bmatrix} 1 & 0 & -1 \\ 0 & 1 & 0 \end{bmatrix}$$

The *svd* command in MATLAB returns the singular value decomposition.

```
>> [u,s,v]=svd(a)

u =
   1   0
   0   1
s =
   1.4142      0         0
      0     1.0000       0
v =
   0.7071      0      -0.7071
      0     1.0000       0
  -0.7071      0      -0.7071
```

The following statements result in zero vectors, verifying that v_i and u_i are the eigenvectors of A^*A and AA^*, respectively.

```
>> a'*a*v(:,1)-2*v(:,1)
>> a'*a*v(:,2)-1*v(:,2)
>> a'*a*v(:,3)
>> u(:,1)'*a*a'-2*u(:,1)'
>> u(:,2)'*a*a'-u(:,2)'
```

13.7.2 Singular Values and Matrix Norms

The Euclidean or 2-norm of a matrix is defined by

$$\| A \|_2 = \max_{x \neq 0} \frac{\| Ax \|_2}{\| x \|_2} = \max_{\| x \|_2 = 1} \| Ax \|_2 = \overline{\sigma}(A)$$

Note, if you imagine a matrix as a system with x as its input and Ax as its output, then the 2-norm has a gain interpretation. Moreover, the largest singular value corresponds to the maximum gain. The smallest singular value can similarly be defined as

$$\underline{\sigma}(A) = \min_{x \neq 0} \frac{\| Ax \|_2}{\| x \|_2} = \min_{\| x \|_2 = 1} \| Ax \|_2$$

If A is nonsingular, the following equalities can be obtained:

$$\underline{\sigma}(A) = \frac{1}{\| A^{-1} \|_2} \quad \text{and} \quad \overline{\sigma}(A^{-1}) = \frac{1}{\underline{\sigma}(A)}$$

Another useful concept is the *condition number* of a matrix, defined by

$$\text{cond}(A) = \kappa(A) = \| A \| \, \| A^{-1} \| = \frac{\overline{\sigma}(A)}{\underline{\sigma}(A)} \geq 1$$

The third equality is valid if the 2-norm of the matrix A is used. The smallest singular value is a measure of singularity of a matrix. The smaller it is, the closer the matrix gets to being singular. In numerical computations, due to round-off error, singular matrices may have nonzero determinants, and therefore appear to be nonsingular. A small $\underline{\sigma}$ is an indication that the matrix is nearly singular. The condition number is a measure of relative distance to singularity. A large condition number indicates a nearly singular matrix. The MATLAB command, *cond*, computes the condition number of a matrix.

Because of the preceding properties of extremal singular values, they are used extensively for robust stability analysis.

13.7.3 The Supremum of Functions

The *supremum* (or *least upper bound*) of a function is its maximum possible value, even if it is not attained. This definition is needed for mathematical reasons because we frequently encounter transfer functions that have no maximum. For instance, the following transfer function (a lead network)

$$G(s) = \frac{s + 1}{s + 5}$$

has no maximum (if you take the derivative of its magnitude and set it equal to zero, you will get the minimum value of 0.2). However, a glance at its frequency response shows that it approaches the value of 1 as the frequency approaches infinity. But, because we never reach the infinite frequency, we never reach the maximum value (although we get very close to it). That is why it does not have a maximum. In these situations, we use the notion of the supremum (or *sup* for short). We have

$$\sup_{\omega} \frac{|j\omega + 1|}{|j\omega + 5|} = 1$$

The equivalent generalization for minimum is the *infimum* (or *greatest lower bound*), or *inf* for short.

13.7.4 Norms and Spaces

The concept of norm is the mathematical equivalent of the ordinary notion of size. It is one of the most important mathematical constructs because it enables us to compare different objects. Every object can be thought of as a member of a set. A set armed with some operations and properties is called a space. For instance, the space of n dimensional vectors (space R^n), space of continuous functions, space of stable transfer functions, etc.

There are a variety of norms for different objects. We will define norms for the following categories: constant vectors, constant matrices, time functions, frequency domain functions, and transfer functions (and their multivariable versions). Unless otherwise specified, all vectors are $n \times 1$ and matrices are $n \times n$.

Vector Norms

We introduce two norms, the 2-norm and the ∞-norm. They are defined by

$$\| x \|_2^2 = \sum_{i=1}^{n} |x_i|^2 \qquad \text{and} \qquad \| x \|_\infty = \max_i |x_i|$$

Matrix Norms

Matrix norms are usually defined in terms of vector norms (induced norms). The matrix 2-norm (also known as the *spectral norm*) was defined in section 13.7.2; it is equal to the largest singular value of the matrix. The ∞-norm is defined as the largest row sum of the matrix; i.e.,

$$\| A \|_\infty = \max_i \sum_{j=1}^{n} |a_{ij}|$$

The *Frobenius* (or *Euclidean*) norm is easy to compute; it is defined by

$$\| A \|_F = [tr(A^* A)]^{1/2}$$

The *spectral radius*, although not a norm, is frequently used as a norm; it is defined by

$$\rho(A) = \max_i |\lambda_i(A)|$$

Norms for Time Functions

For a given time function, $x(t)$, its square is a measure of instantaneous power (e.g., the power associated with a 1Ω resistor is $v \times i$ or v^2); its integral over time gives the signal energy. This is the 2-norm (or L_2 norm) of a signal.

$$\| x(t) \|_2^2 = \int_0^\infty x(t)^2 \, dt = \frac{1}{2\pi} \int_{-\infty}^\infty | X(j\omega) |^2 \, d\omega$$

The second equality is the statement of the Parseval's theorem. When the above norm is finite, the function is said to belong to the L_2 space (i.e., it is square integrable).

For signals that are bounded (in the L_∞ space), we can define the ∞-norm (or L_∞ norm) by

$$\| x(t) \|_\infty = \sup_{t \geq 0} | x(t) |$$

We can also have vectors whose components are time domain signals. In such cases, the norms are defined by

$$\| x(t) \|_\infty = \sup_{t \geq 0} \max_i | x_i(t) |$$

$$\| x(t) \|_2^2 = \int_0^\infty x(t)' x(t) \, dt = \frac{1}{2\pi} \int_{-\infty}^\infty X^*(j\omega) X(j\omega) \, d\omega$$

Vector norms can be weighted (e.g., for scaling purposes). The weighted 2-norm is

$$\| x(t) \|_Q^2 = \int_0^\infty x'(t) Q x(t) \, dt$$

Consequently, the LQR objective function is the weighted norm of the states and the control inputs.

System Norms

Optimization in the frequency domain requires norms for transfer functions. For instance, we may be interested in searching over all stable transfer functions, and select one that is optimal in some sense. Therefore, we need a norm for comparing systems. There are two important norms, H_2 and H_∞. The H_2 norm is defined by

$$\| G \|_2^2 = \frac{1}{2\pi} \int_{-\infty}^{\infty} |G(j\omega)|^2 \, d\omega$$

Recall from Chapter 11 that the PSD of the output of a system is given by

$$S_y(\omega) = |G(j\omega)|^2 S_x(\omega)$$

Therefore, the RMS value of the output is given by

$$y_{rms} = \left\{ \frac{1}{2\pi} \int_{-\infty}^{\infty} |G(j\omega)|^2 S_x(\omega) \, d\omega \right\}^{1/2}$$

For white noise inputs, $S_x(\omega) = 1$ for all frequencies. Hence, the system H_2-norm can be interpreted as the RMS value of the output when the system is driven by white noise input.

The H_∞ norm is defined as

$$\| G \|_\infty = \sup_{x \neq 0} \frac{\| Gx \|_2}{\| x \|_2} = \sup_\omega |G(j\omega)|$$

The second equality is valid when the system is stable. Note that the norm is defined as the ratio of the L_2 norms of the output over the input. Hence, it is also known as the L_2 *gain* of the system. It can also be shown that

$$\| G \|_\infty \geq \frac{\left\{ \int_{-\infty}^{\infty} S_y(\omega) \, d\omega \right\}^{1/2}}{\left\{ \int_{-\infty}^{\infty} S_x(\omega) \, d\omega \right\}^{1/2}} = \frac{y_{rms}}{x_{rms}}$$

Hence, this norm is bounded below by the *rms gain* of the system. The ∞-norm is important for several reasons. First, it is a gain, with the following important (submultiplicative) property

$$\text{If } \quad L = G K \quad \text{then} \quad \| L \|_\infty \leq \| G \|_\infty \| K \|_\infty$$

The preceding inequality is very useful for establishing robust stability results. Second, the ∞-norm is the peak in the Bode magnitude plot (or the largest distance from the origin in the Nyquist plot of G).

The multivariable versions of these norms are

$$\| G \|_2^2 = \frac{1}{2\pi} \int_{-\infty}^{\infty} tr \, G^*(j\omega) \, G(j\omega) \, d\omega = \frac{1}{2\pi} \int_{-\infty}^{\infty} \sum_i \sigma_i^2 \, [\, G(j\omega) \,] \, d\omega$$

$$\| G \|_\infty = \sup_\omega \overline{\sigma}[\, G(j\omega) \,]$$

Finally, we define the H_2 space as the space of transfer functions that are strictly **proper** with no imaginary poles, and the H_∞ space as the space of transfer functions that are **stable** and proper.

Computing the H_2 and H_∞ Norms

The H_2 norm can be computed using the following equality

$$\| G \|_2^2 = tr \, (B'W_o B) = tr \, (CW_c C')$$

where W_o and W_c are the *observability* and *controllability Grammians*, respectively. **These** Grammians are the solutions of Lyapunov equations given by

$$A'W_o + W_o A + C'C = 0$$
$$AW_c + W_c A' + BB' = 0$$

where A, B, and C are the state space matrices of the system.

The ∞-norm is more difficult to compute. In fact, it can only be numerically approximated. Consider the following Hamiltonian matrix and its associated Riccati equation:

$$H_\gamma = \begin{bmatrix} A & \dfrac{BB'}{\gamma} \\ \dfrac{-C'C}{\gamma} & -A' \end{bmatrix} \qquad \text{and} \qquad A'X + XA + \gamma^{-1}XBB'X + \gamma^{-1}C'C = 0$$

Then we have that

$$\| G \|_\infty < \gamma \quad \text{if and only if} \quad H_\gamma \text{ has no imaginary eigenvalues}$$

or equivalently

$$\| G \|_\infty < \gamma \quad \text{if and only if} \quad X > 0$$

The preceding suggests the following algorithm:

1. Choose γ.
2. Find the eigenvalues of the Hamiltonian.
3. If the Hamiltonian has no imaginary eigenvalues, lower γ and go to step 2; otherwise, increase γ.
4. Stop when $\gamma = \gamma_{min}$. Then, $\| G \|_\infty = \gamma_{min}$.

In step 3, various search rules can be used; the bisection rule is adequate in most cases. As an example, we can show that

$$\left\| \frac{1}{s+1} \right\|_\infty = 1$$

13.8 Problems

13.1 Consider the following system [DS79]

$$\dot{x} = \begin{bmatrix} 1 & 1 \\ 0 & 1 \end{bmatrix} x + \begin{bmatrix} 0 \\ 1 \end{bmatrix} u + \begin{bmatrix} 1 \\ 1 \end{bmatrix} \omega$$

Let the LQR parameters be

$$Q = q\, C'C, \ r = 1.$$

Let the filter parameters be

$$Q_0 = q_0 \begin{bmatrix} 1 \\ 1 \end{bmatrix} [1 \quad 1] \ , \ r_0 = 1$$

For each case below, compute gain and phase margins, compute MSM (peak value of the closed loop Bode plot), and draw the Nyquist plot overlaid on the unit circle centered at the origin.

a. $q = 10^6, 10^3, 1, 10^{-3}$ and $q_0 = 1$
b. $q_0 = 10^6, 10^3, 1, 10^{-3}$ and $q = 1$

Comment on the robustness of the LQG design. What are the effects of increasing q and q_0 on the robustness.

13.2 Consider the double-integrator plant compensated by a feedback lead compensator.

$$G(s) = \frac{1}{s^2}, \quad K(s) = \frac{20\,(s+1)}{s+10}$$

Suppose the actual plant model contains an additive uncertainty given by

$$\Delta_a(s) = \frac{-1}{s^2 + s + 1}$$

a. Determine if the compensator $K(s)$ stabilizes the plant model $G(s)$.

b. Determine if the compensator $K(s)$ stabilizes the actual plant model given by $\tilde{G}(s) = G(s) + \Delta_a(s)$.

c. Find $M(s)$, the transfer function "seen" by the uncertainty.

d. Draw Bode plots of $\Delta_a(s)$ and $M(s)$ to determine the robust stability of the system.

13.3 Consider the following system:

$$\dot{x} = \begin{bmatrix} 0 & 1 \\ -3 & -4 \end{bmatrix} x + \begin{bmatrix} 0 \\ 1 \end{bmatrix} u + \omega$$

Let $Q = C'_q C_q$ where $C_q = 4\sqrt{5}\,[\,\sqrt{35} \quad 1\,]$, $r = 1$, $C = [2 \quad 1]$

$$Q_0 = \begin{bmatrix} 35 \\ -61 \end{bmatrix}[35 \quad -61] \quad \text{and} \quad r_0 = 1$$

a. Find an LQR compensator $K(s)$. Compute the control gain K, the closed loop poles, GM and PM.

b. Design an LQG compensator. Compute GM and PM. Compare the stability margins with part a.

c. Design an LTR compensator by solving the following Riccati equation:

$$A\,\Sigma + \Sigma\,A' + (Q_0 + q^2\,BB') - \Sigma\,C'C\,\Sigma = 0$$

Increase the value of q from 1 to 10^6 in steps of 100 and observe the effects. Tabulate GM and PM for all values of q. Compare the margins with the LQR and LQG cases.

13.4 Note: As much as possible, try to solve this problem manually. Consider the first order system given by:

$$\dot{x} = x + u + d$$
$$y = x + n$$

Our objective is to regulate the state x and the control signal u in presence of disturbance d and noise inputs n.

Let $w = \begin{bmatrix} d \\ n \end{bmatrix}$ and $z = \begin{bmatrix} x \\ u \end{bmatrix}$

a. Obtain the plant equation, $P(s)$, in packed-matrix notation.

b. Draw the two-port block diagram of the system.

c. Verify that all the rank conditions are met.

d. Compute $\tilde{D}_{12}$, $\tilde{D}_{21}$, $\tilde{C}_1$, $\tilde{B}_1$

e. Find the controller Hamiltonian matrix and solve for X_∞ in terms of γ.

f. Repeat part e for the estimator, and solve for Y_∞ in terms of γ.

g. Compute the product $(X_\infty\, Y_\infty)$ in terms of γ. Find out if the spectral radius condition is met for $\gamma = 2$. Repeat for $\gamma = 3$. For the rest of the problem, let $\gamma = 3$.

h. Compute X_∞ , Y_∞ , Z_∞ , K_c , K_e.

i. Find the compensator transfer function and the closed loop poles.

j. Draw the Nyquist plot and obtain gain and phase margins.

13.5 Consider the system given by

$$\dot{x} = \begin{bmatrix} -54 & 2 & 10 \\ 2\text{E}{-}4 & -10\text{E}{-}3 & -5\text{E}{-}3 \\ -10\text{E}{-}3 & -24\text{E}{-}3 & -0.14 \end{bmatrix} x + \begin{bmatrix} -10\text{E}4 \\ 0.25 \\ -2 \end{bmatrix} u$$

$$y = [\,0 \quad 3 \quad 0.05\,]\,x$$

The open loop transfer function L must meet all of the following specifications:

i. $|L| > 20$ dB   for $\omega \le 0.1$ rad/s for good disturbance rejection and command performance.

ii. $|1 + L| \ge 25$ dB   for $\omega \le 0.05$ rad/s for insensitivity to parameter variations.

iii. $|L| \le -20$ dB   for $\omega \ge 5$ rad/s for adequate immunity to noise.

Use loop shaping and LTR to meet the specifications as closely as possible.

13.6 Consider the model in Problem 13.2. Suppose the actual plant is given by

$$\tilde{G}(s) = \frac{2\,(s + 1)}{s^2\,(s^2 + s + 1)}$$

a. Find a multiplicative uncertainty model for the system.

b. Find the transfer function $M(s)$ as seen by the multiplicative uncertainty.

c. Determine if the closed loop system is robustly stable under the multiplicative uncertainty computed in part a.

13.7 Adapted from[LR90]. Consider the single input, dual output plant shown in Figure 13-27.

The specifications are to have integral tracking performance for output y_l with a time constant of 0.6 sec. Both outputs y_1 and y_2 are available for feedback.

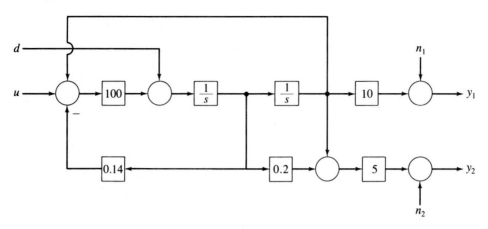

Figure 13-27 Block diagram for Problem 13.7

It has been suggested that for integral tracking, one should regulate the integral of the tracking error. Hence, we will introduce a command input y_c, and an integrator at $e = y_1 - y_c$ (before the entry of the noise source n_1).

In addition, all regulated outputs, the disturbance, and the noise inputs will be weighted. The new block diagram is shown in Figure 13-28 on page 452.

The following weights are suggested:

$$W_d = 0.1 \ , \ W_{n_1} = W_{n_2} = 1 \ , \ W_u = 1 \ , \ W_e = 0.5$$

By varying the weights, one can manipulate the performance of the system.

a. Verify that the plant equations are given by

$$\dot{x}_1 = -14\, x_1 + 100\, x_2 + 0.1\, d + 100$$
$$\dot{x}_2 = x_1$$
$$\dot{x}_3 = -10\, x_2 + y_c$$

$$z = \begin{bmatrix} 0.5 - x_3 \\ u \end{bmatrix}$$

$$y = \begin{bmatrix} x_3 + n_1 \\ x_1 + 5\, x_2 + n_2 \end{bmatrix}$$

b. Obtain the system equation in packed matrix form, $P(s)$.

c. For a value of $\gamma = 0.5922$ (the optimal value obtained by γ-iteration), find K_c, K_e and the compensator transfer function.

d. Draw the Nyquist plot, and compute the stability margins.

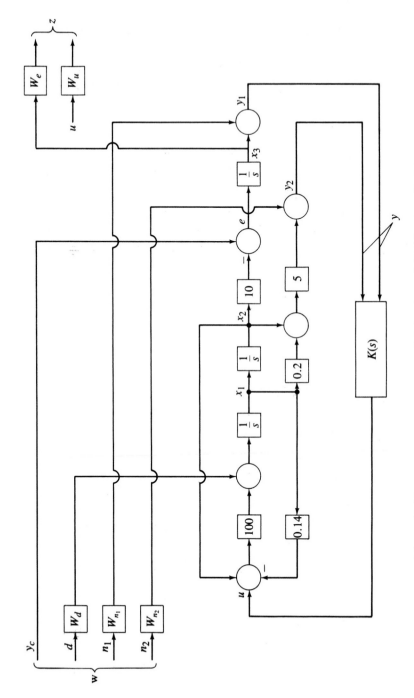

Figure 13-28 Block diagram for Problem 13.7 showing weighted inputs and outputs.

452

e. Plot the unit step response of the system. (Set all inputs to zero and let $y_c = 1$, then plot y_l.)

f. Verify that the above value of γ is optimal using γ-iteration.

Note: The (1,3) element of C_2 is incorrect in the original source.

13.8   Consider the plant given by

$$G(s) = \frac{s-1}{(s+1)\,(s^2+s+1)}$$

The specification is $|S| \leq 0.1$ for $\omega \leq 0.01$ rad/s.

This is a sensitivity minimization problem. The requirement means that we want to reject low frequency disturbances (or equivalently to reduce the system sensitivity to parameter variations or model uncertainties). To set up the problem for H_∞, consider the two-port block diagram of the system shown in Figure 13-29.

Note that we have

$$S = \frac{e}{d} = \frac{1}{1+GK}$$

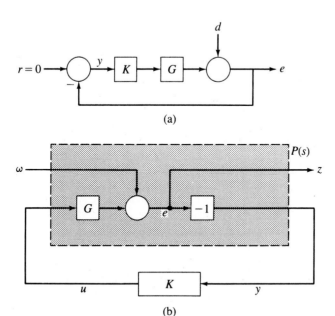

(a)

(b)

Figure 13-29 (a) Block diagram for Problem 13.8. (b) Two-port block diagram for sensitivity minimization.

a. Obtain the system matrix $P(s)$ and use γ-iteration to solve the problem.

b. Find the compensator $K(s)$ and plot the magnitude of S.

c. Plot the response of the system to a unit step disturbance.

Notes and References

For many original papers on robustness and LTR, see the special issue on Linear Multivariable Control Systems. IEEE Transactions on Automatic Control. Feb. 1981. LQ techniques are discussed in great detail in [AM90]. For lack of robustness of observers, see [DS79]. Current book about H_∞ control are [F87], [M89] and [BB91b]. Feedback control from a modern perspective is available in [DFT92]. For a comprehensive discussion of norms, the two-port representation, and a novel optimization technique, see [BB91a]. Recent MATLAB-based software is discussed in [BPGDS 91] and [CS91]. Software for LQ techniques and H_∞ control are: Robust Control Toolbox for MATLAB [CS88], μ-Analysis and Synthesis Toolbox for MATLAB [BDGPS91], MATRIX$_X$ Robust Control Module by Integrated Systems, Inc., and Program CC Version 4.0 [T88]. Other software products are also available; we have mentioned the ones we have tested and used.

Appendix

Hardware Design Projects

A.1 Introduction

Control theory and design, both classical and modern, are based on some abstract mathematical constructs. For this reason, many students do not have a clear idea of how the mathematics they perform with paper and pencil, or on the computer, corresponds to reality. Real control systems are composed of physical plants, actuators, sensors, electronic filters, and amplifiers. Real systems tend to be nonlinear. For these, the linear control systems that we design will work only for small signals.

To give the control student some appreciation for the practical application of control design, we have each of our control majors model, design a control system for, and actually build one of several hardware projects: magnetic levitation of a steel ball; inverted pendulum on a cart; and a ball-on-beam balancer. We will present a complete description for each of these hardware projects, including: system description; plant, actuator, and sensor models; control specifications; control law; the controller electronics; a parts list for the entire project; and the results. The projects we present were student designed and this appendix is based on their final reports. Although these projects worked, we make no claim that these are the most efficient designs possible.

A.2 Magnetic Levitation

The object of this project, described in a paper by Wong [W86], is to keep a metal ball suspended in midair by adjusting the field strength of an electromagnet. In the ideal situation, we can simply increase the electromagnet current until the magnetic force produced just counteracts the weight of the ball. In the real world, however, disturbances, such as variations in line voltage, will cause variations in the electromagnetic current. These current variations will cause the ball to either fall (current decreases) or attach itself to the electromagnet (current increases). We want, therefore, to incorporate a feedback signal to stabilize the ball in the face of such disturbances.

The feedback sensor here is a light source-photodetector pair. The photodetector is arranged so that when the ball drops, the detector output increases. The detector output is fed back to the current driver, which increases the coil current. The increased coil current strengthens the magnetic field, which raises the ball. The block diagram for this system is shown in Figure A-1. The models used for the plant and sensors are described next.

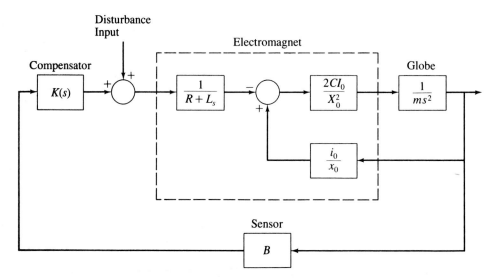

Figure A-1 Block diagram of the magnetic levitation system.

A.2.1 System Models

The equations describing the motion of a ferrous ball within an electromagnetically generated field are nonlinear. The variables of interest are the distance between the ball and the magnet, x; and current in the electromagnet coil, i. The force generated by the electromagnet, f, is given by

$$f = -\frac{i^2}{2}\frac{dL}{dx}$$

where L is the total inductance in the system. The suspended steel ball contributes to the inductance of the electromagnet coil. As the ball approaches the magnet, the total inductance goes up. As the ball moves farther from the magnet, the inductance decreases, reaching a minimal value as the ball approaches infinity. This minimum value is, of course, the inductance of the magnet. The total inductance is given by

$$L = L_1 + \frac{L_0\, x_0}{x}$$

where L_1 is the inductance of the coil in the absence of the ball, and L_0 is the additional inductance contributed by the ball.

If we take dL/dx of the preceding and substitute into the force equation, we get

$$f = -\frac{i^2}{2}\left(\frac{-L_0 x_0}{x^2}\right) = \frac{L_0 x_0}{2}\left(\frac{i}{x}\right)^2$$

If we now let $C = \dfrac{L_0 x_0}{2}$, we get the final force equation

$$f = C\left(\frac{i}{x}\right)^2$$

The actual value of C is determined experimentally.

To produce a tractable model, we linearize the force equation to get

$$f = C\left(\frac{I_0}{X_0}\right)^2 + \left(\frac{2CI_0}{X_0{}^2}\right)i - \left(\frac{2CI_0{}^2}{X_0{}^3}\right)x$$

where I_0 and X_0 are the equilibrium values for these variables, and i and x are understood to be incremental variables. At equilibrium, the magnetic force on the ball equals the gravitational force. Defining f_0 as the magnetic force at equilibrium, we get

$$f_0 = C\left(\frac{I_0}{X_0}\right)^2 = mg$$

where m is the mass of the ball. Note that this equation will allow us to experimentally determine C. Because we are interested in controlling the incremental magnetic force required to maintain the equilibrium position, we solve for $f_1 = f - f_0$.

$$f_1 = \left(\frac{2CI_0}{X_0{}^2}\right)i - \left(\frac{2CI_0{}^2}{X_0{}^3}\right)x$$

For the electrical equation, we assume that the electromagnet coil is adequately modeled as a series resistor-inductor combination. Note that the inductor includes the steel ball and has the total inductance described previously. The voltage-current relationship for the coil is

$$v = Ri + L(x)\frac{di}{dt}$$

This equation is actually quite complicated because of the nonlinear dependence of the inductor on the ball position. We can simplify the analysis by assuming that when the system is properly designed, the ball will remain close to its equilibrium position, i.e., $x = x_0$. This means that $L(x)$ is simply $L_1 + L_0$. We make the further simplifying assumption that the inherent inductance of the coil, L_1, is much larger than the inductive contribution of the ball, L_0, and get the final equation

$$ v = R i + L_1 \frac{di}{dt} $$

The equation of motion for the ball derives from the familiar relationship between the acceleration of a body and the total forces acting on the body

$$ m \ddot{x} = -f_1 $$

where m is the mass of the ball.

We choose to model the photodetector combination as a simple gain element, i.e.,

$$ v_s = \beta x $$

where v_s is the sensor output voltage, and β is the experimentally derived gain between the ball position and the output voltage.

We have, now, the equations needed to describe this system. We can either create a Laplace transform or a state space model. The transform equations are

$$ I(s) = \frac{V(s)}{R + sL_1} $$

$$ F_1(s) = \left(\frac{2CI_0}{X_0{}^2} \right) I(s) - \left(\frac{2CI_0{}^2}{X_0{}^3} \right) X(s) $$

$$ X(s) = -\frac{1}{ms^2} F_1(s) $$

$$ V_s(s) = \beta X(s) $$

The overall transfer function between the coil input voltage and the ball sensor output voltage is

$$ G(s) = \frac{V_s(s)}{V(s)} = \frac{-2\beta CI_0 / m L_1 X_0{}^2}{(s + R/L_1)(s^2 - 2CI_0{}^2 / mX_0{}^3)} $$

To form the state space representation, we use the electrical equation and combine the two force-position equations by eliminating f_1 as a variable. If we define the state vector as $w = [i, x, \dot{x}]'$ and define the output as $y = V_s(s)$, then

$$\dot{w} = \begin{pmatrix} -R/L_1 & 0 & 0 \\ 0 & 0 & 1 \\ -2CI_0/mX_0^2 & 2CI_0^2/mX_0^3 & 0 \end{pmatrix} w + \begin{pmatrix} 1/L_1 \\ 0 \\ 0 \end{pmatrix} v$$

$$y = (0 \quad \beta \quad 0) \, x$$

A.2.2 Parameter Determination

The parameters in the system equations are determined as follows. Coil resistance and inductance, R and L_1, can be measured with an ohmmeter and an inductance meter. A small metal globe is used for the ball; its mass, m, is measured on a scale. The desired initial ball distance, X_0, can be arbitrarily chosen as long as the ball intersects the light beam of the detector. To find I_0, use a pedestal to set the ball at the desired initial position and increase the coil current until the ball just lifts. This current is I_0. We can now find the constant C by using the previous equation for f_0

$$C = \left(\frac{X_0}{I_0}\right)^2 mg$$

The sensor constant, β, is found by displacing the globe a known distance and measuring the output of the photodetector.

A typical set of parameters is given in Table A-1. For these values, the open loop transfer function is

$$G(s) = \frac{-221457.6}{(s + 44.12)\,(s - 44.12)\,(s + 283.5)}$$

Table A-1 Parameters for the Magnetic Levitation System	
PARAMETER	VALUE
Equilibrium distance X_0	0.01 m
Equilibrium current I_0	0.125 A
Ball mass m	0.01058 Kg
Force constant C	6.5906 x 10^{-4} N-m^2/A^2
Coil resistance R	31.1 Ω
Coil inductance L	0.1097 H
Sensor gain β	156 V/m

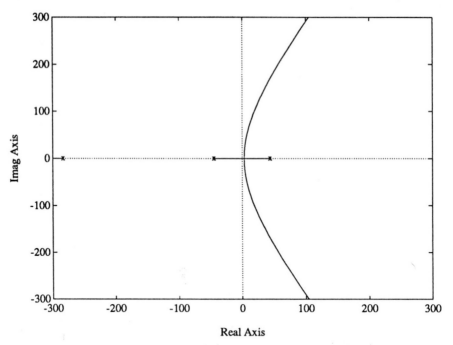

Figure A-2 Uncompensated root locus of the magnetic levitation system.

A.2.3 Controller Design

The uncompensated root-locus is shown in Figure A-2 above. This plot shows that the uncompensated system is unstable and cannot be stabilized by just changing the system gain. To pull the root locus into the left-hand plane, we need to add a compensator zero in the left-hand plane between the first left-hand plane pole and the origin. The necessary pole required for compensator realization is then placed deeper into the left-hand plane; this will minimize the impact of the compensator pole on the root locus.

While it seems reasonable to attempt pole-zero cancellation by placing the compensator zero at the system pole of –44.12, this is not a good idea. The system model is a linear approximation to a nonlinear system. If the actual system pole is to the right of –44.12, the compensator zero will not cancel the pole; the compensator zero will actually lie to the left of the system pole. In this case, stability will not be achieved. To provide some robustness in the face of system model uncertainties, the compensator zero is placed at –30.

The compensator pole is chosen to be a decade away from the compensator zero and, hence, is set to –300. These choices for zero and pole locations result in the compensator

$$K(s) \;=\; K_c \frac{s+30}{s+300}$$

The root locus for the compensated system, $K(s)G(s)$, given in Figure A-3, shows that the system will be stable for gains between 25 and 180. The Bode plots for the compensated system (gain = 50) are shown in Figures A-4 and A-5. The system has a GM of 11.3 dB, PM of 35 degrees, and GRM of –6 dB.

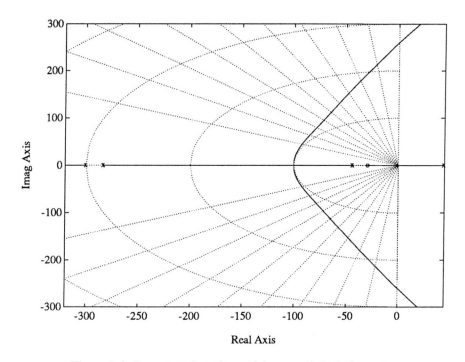

Figure A-3 Compensated root locus of the magnetic levitation system.

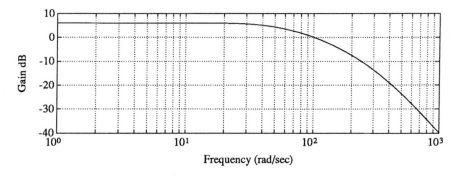

Figure A-4 Compensated Bode magnitude plot of the magnetic levitation system.

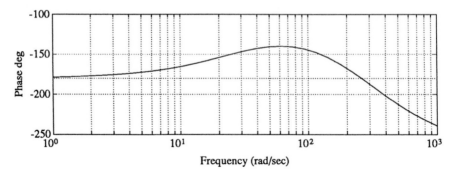

Figure A-5 Compensated Bode phase plot of the magnetic levitation system.

A.2.4 Circuit Construction

Figure A-6 shows the final circuit design and Table A-2 gives the parts list for this project. A brief discussion of the electronics follows.

Table A-2

Part	Number Used	Part	Number Used
Magnet coil	1	Capacitors 2200μF	2
TIP 31 Transformer	1	Steel globes	Assorted
LM741 Op Amp	1	Bread-board	1
Lamp/Base	1	Grid-board	1
Transformer	1	Platform	1
1N5400 Diodes	4	Plastic tubing	2
1N4004 Diodes	1	Assorted wiring	–
1K Ohm Potent.	1	Heat sink	1
Photoresistor	1	Cushion feet	Assorted
15 V/5W Zener	2		
LED	1		
Capacitor 0.1 μF	1		
Resistors			
47 Ohm	2		
50 Ohm	1		
1 Ohm	1		
10K Ohm	3		
27K Ohm	1		
3.5K Ohm	1		
1K Ohm	1		
330K Ohm	1		

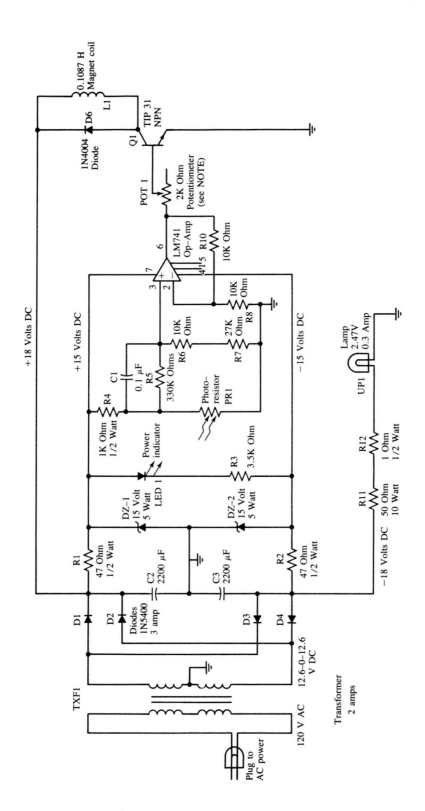

Figure A-6 Circuit schematic for the magnetic levitation system.

NOTE 1: Pot set at approx 360 Ohms to levitate med size globe.
NOTE 2: All resistors 1/4 Watt unless otherwise noted.

The transformer, diodes D1-D4, and capacitors C2 and C3 provide a filtered full-wave rectified DC voltage to the regulator zener diodes DZ1 and DZ2. The zener diodes provide the ± 15 V supply voltages to the circuit.

The power indicator, LED1, and the photoresistor, PR1, compose the ball position sensor discussed earlier. The photoresistor, PR1, forms a voltage divider with R4. As the ball changes position, the resistance of PR1 changes, which changes the voltage at the node between PR1 and R4. This voltage is the input to the compensator.

The compensator is an Op-Amp active filter composed of the Op-Amp, gain setting resistors R8 and R10, and the pole-zero setting resistors and capacitor R5, R6 in series with R7, and C1. The transfer function of the active filter is given by

$$K(s) \ = \ (1 + \frac{R10}{R8}) \ \frac{s + \dfrac{R6 + R7}{CR5(R6 + R7)}}{s + \dfrac{R5 + R6 + R7}{CR5(R6 + R7)}} \ = \ 2 \frac{s + 30.3}{s + 300.6}$$

This design, therefore, achieves the proper pole and zero settings and provides a gain of 2. The final gain is achieved in the next stage.

The transistor collector current supplies the driving current to the magnetic coil. The collector current is β_F times the base current, which is found by dividing the Op-Amp output voltage, V6, by the potentiometer resistance, POT1. The magnetic coil driving current is, therefore,

$$i \ = \ \beta_F \frac{V6}{POT1}$$

This relationship provides the final gain in the system. Because the β_F of any given transistor is not known, generally varying between 50 and 250, a potentiometer is used to adjust the gain experimentally.

Although the student who built this project did not experimentally determine the low frequency gain of the electrical system (i.e., the compensator), it can be found as follows: first, disconnect the photodetector from the circuit; next, inject a low frequency voltage signal into the input of the active filter and measure the AC voltage across the inductor. The ratio of these two signals will give you the electronic gain.

A.2.5 Results

The ball was successfully suspended between the magnetic poles. To test the efficacy of the feedback system, several disturbances were applied to the ball. A probe (actually, a finger) was used to displace the ball from its initial position. The feedback system was able to correct top or side displacements up to 5 mm. It was also found, serendipitously, that the feedback system would reject disturbances due to shaking or bumping of the structure.

The magnetic levitation system is a very unstable system. Because of the system nonlinearities and the low stability margins that are usually attained, the system is initially very difficult to tune. It usually does not work (as in most designs) the first time around, and many hours of gain adjustment and fine tuning are required for initial levitation. Careful modeling and parameter determination, coupled with maximized stability margins, will save a lot of time at the end. The use of heat sinks (or fans) is very important as the components can get very hot. Make sure the light source is not drawing too much current from the main circuit. You may want to provide a separate energy source (such as batteries) for the light source. Electromagnets can be purchased (about $40) or you can make your own. Cover the light source and the photoresistor using PVC pipes to minimize the effects of ambient lighting. Properly designed systems can levitate any metal object (keys, wrenches, etc.) that can cast a shadow.

The magnetic levitation system is an excellent learning experience. It demonstrates the effects of nonlinearities, model uncertainties, stability margins, and lead compensation. It can also be constructed within a reasonable period of an academic term (quarter or semester period) by one person or groups of two or three students.

A.3 Ball-on-Beam Balancer

The object of this project, described in a paper by Wellstead, et al. [WCFMR89], is to control the position of a ball that is free to move along a centrally hinged rigid beam. The job of the controller is to rotate the rigid beam to compensate for movement of the ball. The total system for this project is shown in Figure A-7.

The actuator in this system is a DC motor, $M(s)$, that is coupled through gearing to the beam shaft. The DC motor is controlled with a local feedback loop in which beam angular position is measured with a shaft-mounted potentiometer (K_p). The ball-on-beam dynamics are represented in the figure by $G(s)$. The ball movement sensor is a nichrome wire contact; changes in position of the ball along the nichrome wire change the effective length of the wire, which changes the resistance of the wire and the voltage across the wire (K_b).

A.3.1 System Models

Ball-on-Beam Dynamics $G(s)$

Figure A-8 shows schematic representations of the ball-on-beam problem. The Lagrangian approach was used to model the system. Because the actuator in this system is a DC motor, there is no elastance, and, hence, no potential energy in this system. The Lagrangian, therefore, is the kinetic energy, U, given by

$$U = \frac{1}{2}mv^2 + \frac{1}{2}I_b\omega^2 + \frac{1}{2}I_a\dot{\theta}^2$$

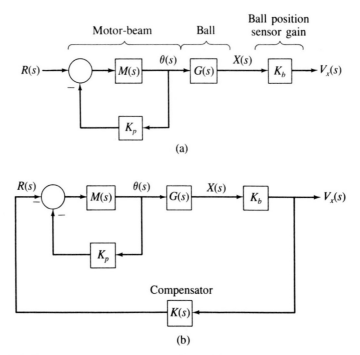

(a)

(b)

Figure A-7 Block diagram of the ball-on-beam problem. (a) open loop system. (b) closed loop system.

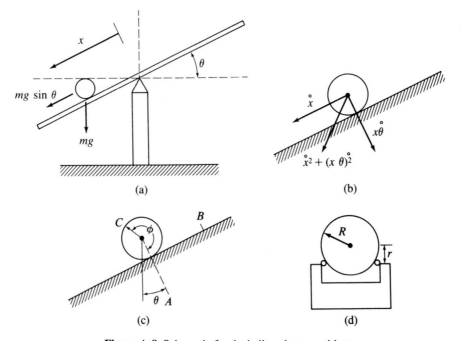

Figure A-8 Schematic for the ball-on-beam problem.

where m is the ball mass, v is the translational velocity of the ball, ω is the angular velocity of the ball, θ is the angle of the beam shaft, I_a is the beam inertia, and I_b is the ball inertia. Because the sensors in this system measure ball translational position, x, and shaft angular position, θ, we want to write the above equation in terms of just these two variables. Therefore, we now find relationships between v and ω, and x. We first note that the distance traveled by the ball is given by

$$x = r\,\varphi$$

where φ is the rotational angle of the ball with respect to the shaft and r is the rolling, or effective, radius of the ball (see Figures A-8a and d). The total angle of the ball is the sum of the angle of the ball with respect to the shaft, φ, and the angle of the shaft, θ. The rotational velocity of the ball, therefore, is given by

$$\omega = \dot{\varphi} + \dot{\theta} = \frac{\dot{x}}{r} + \dot{\theta}$$

The translational velocity of the ball, v, is given by (see Figure A-8b)

$$v = [\,\dot{x}^2 + (x\,\dot{\theta})^2\,]^{\,\frac{1}{2}}$$

Using the equations for rotational and translational velocities in the Lagrangian gives us

$$L = \frac{1}{2}\left\{ m\left[\dot{x}^2 + (x\,\dot{\theta})^2\right] + I_b\left[\frac{\dot{x}}{r} + \dot{\theta}\right]^2 + I_a\,\dot{\theta}^{\,2}\right\}$$

Lagrange's equation for the ball-beam system is

$$\frac{d}{dt}\left(\frac{d}{dx}L\right) - \frac{d}{dx}L = mg\sin\theta$$

Performing the indicated operations on L results in the non-linear differential equation

$$(m + \frac{I_b}{r^2})\,\ddot{x} + \left(\frac{I_b}{r^2}\right)\ddot{\theta} - mx\,\dot{\theta}^{\,2} = mg\sin\theta$$

To linearize this equation, we assume that the control system, for small disturbances, will act to return the ball to rest with minimal shaft movement. Therefore, the shaft angle and its derivatives are assumed to be small, and the dynamic equation becomes

$$\left(m + \frac{I_b}{r^2}\right)\ddot{x} = mg\,\theta$$

The plant model is found by taking the Laplace transform of the preceding

$$G(s) = \frac{X(s)}{\Theta(s)} = \frac{mg}{m + \dfrac{I_b}{r^2}} \, \frac{1}{s^2}$$

We can simplify this transfer function by substituting the following inertia relationship into the above equation.

$$I_b = \frac{2}{5} \, m \, R^2$$

This gives us

$$G(s) = \frac{X(s)}{\Theta(s)} = \frac{mg}{m + \dfrac{2}{5} \dfrac{mR^2}{r^2}} \, \frac{1}{s^2} = \frac{g}{1 + \dfrac{2}{5}\left(\dfrac{R}{r}\right)^2} \, \frac{1}{s^2}$$

Motor-Beam Dynamics $M(s)$

Because the motor is controlled by a feedback loop (see Figure A-7), the total motor-beam transfer function is given by

$$\frac{\Theta(s)}{R(s)} = \frac{M(s)}{1 + K_p \, M(s)}$$

If we assume that the motor dynamics are much faster than the overall system dynamics, we can model the motor-beam transfer function as a simple gain. That is,

$$\frac{\Theta(s)}{R(s)} = \frac{M(0)}{1 + K_p \, M(0)} = \alpha$$

Under this assumption, the uncompensated loop gain between $R(s)$ and the voltage output of the position sensor, $V_x(s)$, is, therefore,

$$\frac{V_x(s)}{R(s)} = \frac{\Theta(s)}{R(s)} \frac{X(s)}{\Theta(s)} K_b = \alpha \, G(s) \, K_b = \frac{\alpha \, g \, K_b}{1 + \dfrac{2}{5}\left(\dfrac{R}{r}\right)^2} \, \frac{1}{s^2}$$

where K_b is the ball position gain ($V_x(s) = K_b \, X(s)$), and is determined as discussed in the next section.

A.3.2 Parameter Determination

The appropriate ball radii r and R are measured directly and are

$$r = 0.00639 \text{ m} \quad \text{and} \quad R = 0.0127 \text{ m}$$

Ball position is measured as the output of a linear potentiometer. As the ball moves along the nichrome wire, which provides the runners for the ball, the total resistance of the wire increases linearly. Because the voltage applied across the nichrome runners is 1.193 V and the total length of the runners is 0.636 m, we find the ball position gain as

$$K_b = 1.193/0.636 = 1.875 \text{ V/m}$$

The last parameter to be determined is the motor gain α, which is the transfer function between the voltage input and the beam angle output. Remember, we assumed that the dynamics of the motor-beam feedback system are negligible. This is also a good time to double-check this assumption. To do this, we drive the motor-beam system, without the ball (this opens the outer loop), with a sinusoidal signal from a function generator and measure the potentiometer output. Curve fitting the resulting Bode plot from this experiment leads to

$$\frac{\Theta(s)}{R(s)} = \frac{37}{s^2 + 21s + 448}$$

where we have used our knowledge of the gain between potentiometer angle and potentiometer output voltage to write the transfer function in terms of beam output angle.

The undamped natural frequency and damping ratio are

$$\omega_n = 21.2 \text{ rad/s} \quad \text{and} \quad \zeta = 0.5$$

These numbers indicate a system that has a rise time of approximately 85 ms and a 2% settling time of 0.38 s. Because the total system is expected to be a lot slower than the motor-beam system, we are justified in our assumption to ignore the motor-beam system dynamics. The low frequency gain of the motor-beam system transfer function gives α

$$\alpha = \frac{37}{448} = 0.083 \text{ rad/V}$$

The final model for open loop transfer function of our system (see Figure A-7) is

$$\frac{V_x(s)}{R(s)} = \frac{0.588}{s^2}$$

A.3.3 Controller Design

To achieve reasonable robustness in the controller design, a lead compensator will be used to provide 45° phase margin. After some trial and error, the following compensator was chosen

$$K(s) = K_c \frac{s+1}{s+6}$$

The compensated root locus for this design is shown in Figure A-9. A gain of $K_c = 15$ places the closed loop poles at the spot corresponding to the desired phase margin. That the phase margin is actually achieved is confirmed in the Bode plots of the compensated system, as shown in Figure A-10.

The open loop and closed loop transfer functions (compensator in feedback) are

$$K(s)G(s) = 8.83 \frac{s+1}{(s+6)\,s^2}, \qquad T(s) = 0.5884 \frac{s+6}{s^3 + 6s^2 + 8.83s + 8.83}$$

The system has a damping ratio of 0.5 and natural frequency of 1.4. To predict the response of this closed loop regulator system, the system step response was found and displayed, as shown in Figure A-11. The overshoot and settling time are approximately 12% and 7 sec, respectively.

In addition, the ability of this design to reject disturbances was determined by injecting a 1 V, 10 Hz random signal into the motor controller. The output of this simulation (measured at x) is shown in Figure A-12a . While the disturbance caused some steady state error in the ball position, the amount of this displacement was small and did not follow the disturbance. Figure A-12b shows the result of the simulation with the beam dynamics included. The beam dynamics provides more filtering, resulting in improved disturbance rejection. Therefore, this design provides a reasonable amount of disturbance rejection.

A.3.4 Construction

The circuit schematic for this design is shown in Figure A-13. The parts list is given in Table A-3. A few points before we describe the behavior of the circuit. The students, because of cost and ease of implementation, decided to use a DC armature motor to drive the beam. As it turned out, DC motors exhibit nonlinear behavior; i.e., limit cycling, which was partially corrected by using a weak motor and through the electronic design. They concluded, that, in hindsight, a linear bidirectional actuator would have been a better solution. It also became clear through experimentation that the filter capacitor type had to be carefully chosen. An electrolytic capacitor did not prove to be linear, so the students used a more expensive mylar film capacitor.

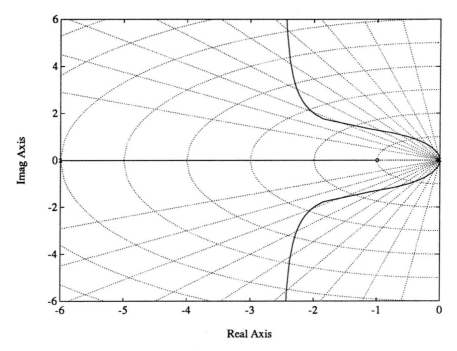

Figure A-9 Compensated root locus of the ball-on-beam problem.

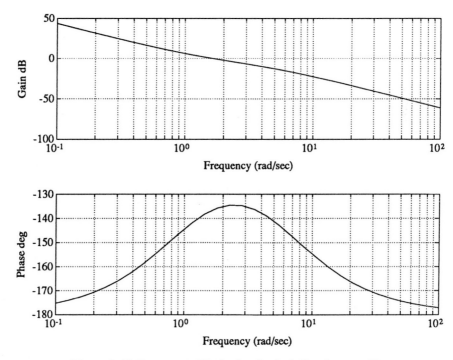

Figure A-10 Compensated Bode plots for the ball-on-beam problem.

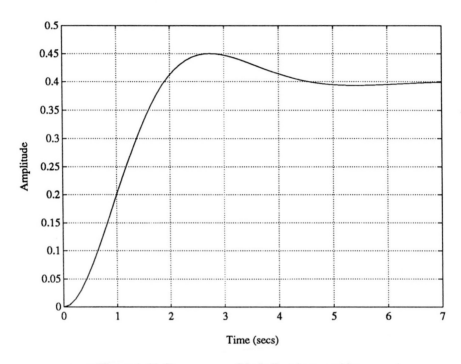

Figure A-11 Step response of the ball-on-beam problem.

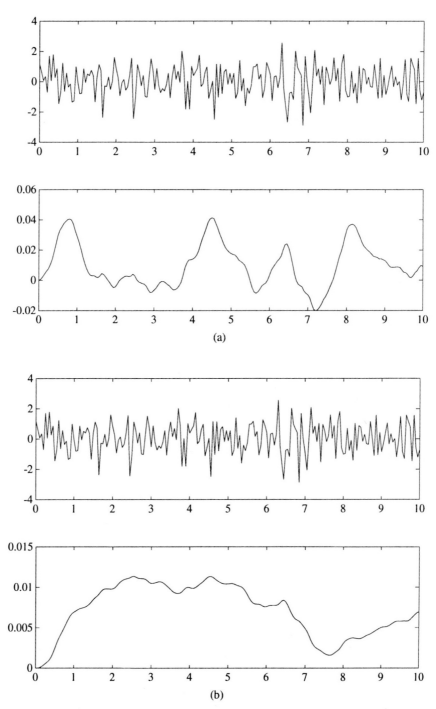

Figure A-12 Noise response of the ball-on-beam problem (a) without the beam dynamics. (b) beam dynamics included.

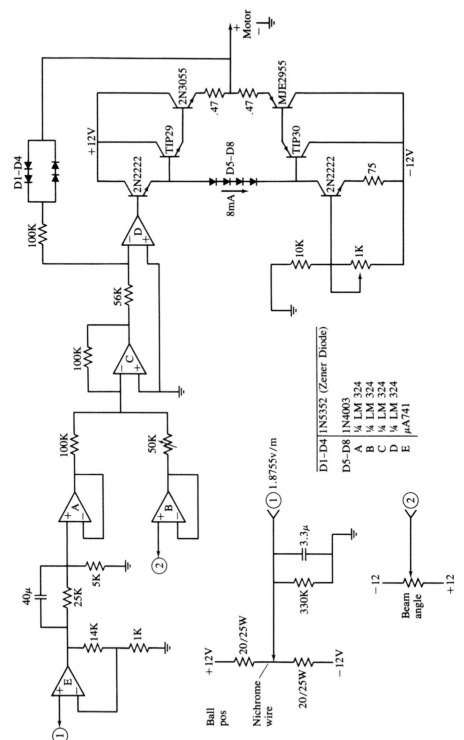

Figure A-13 Circuit schematic for the ball-on-beam problem.

Table A-3 Parts List

+/-12 v, 3 Amp Power Supply	
Motor Driver	**System**
Large heat sinks(2)	50kΩ potentiometer
2n3055	Nichrome Wire
mje2955	Misc. wood and metal
Lm324	Motor pod
PC Board	Axle
Resistors(6)	Aluminum sheet for motor pod
.47Ω/10W resistors(2)	Bushing
2n2222A(2)	48T gear
TIP 29	8T gear
TIP 30	12T/60T gear
1n5352 Diodes(4)	Brass tube
1n4003 Diodes(4)	

Compensator and Assorted Components

20Ω/25W resistors(2)
50kΩ potentiometer
Resistors(7)
μA741
40μF mylar film capacitor

The Op-Amps E and A and the RC filter compose the compensator that was designed earlier. The first Op-Amp, A, provides a gain of 15, while the second Op-Amp serves as a unity gain buffer. The filter has the transfer function

$$\frac{R_1}{R_1 + \dfrac{R_2}{sCR_2 + 1}} = \frac{s + 1/R_2C}{s + \dfrac{R_1 + R_2}{R_1 R_2 C}} = \frac{s + 1}{s + 6}$$

The input to the compensator comes from the output of the nichrome wire-ball linear potentiometer.

The beam angle measurement comes from the shaft-mounted potentiometer and is input to the system through the buffer Op-Amp B. The summing junction indicated in the feedback system shown in Figure A-7a is actually implemented with the single Op-Amp C.

The motor controller is implemented with the six transistors shown. The zener diodes, D1-D4, in conjunction with Op-Amp D, form a linearizing feed back loop that also corrects for the dead zone inherent in the permanent magnet DC motor.

A.3.5 Results

With the ball initially at rest in the center of the beam, the ball was struck to give it an impulse disturbance. The ball returned to rest in approximately 4 sec and exhibited less than 5% overshoot. The beam response showed no unusual distortions and no problems with noise were experienced.

The beam was then tilted up to 15° and the experiment repeated. It was found that, depending on tilt angle, the ball would stabilize at a given distance from the center of the beam.

The ball-on-beam project provides an excellent tool for studying electromechanical systems. Its double-integrator dynamics is used in many control system texts as an example. The compensator design is quite straightforward, and the system is easily stabilized. It provides a mechanism for learning about motor modeling, effects of neglected dynamics, effects of nonlinearities, and lead compensation. It also forces the students to consider system design issues such as using alternate types of motors, sensors, and discovering techniques (mechanical or electronic) for reducing the effects of nonlinearities. Finally, it is an ideal project for design courses that have both EE and ME students taking the course.

A.4 Inverted Pendulum on a Cart

The object of this classical problem is to maintain a rod in the upright position as the cart to which it is hinged moves horizontally (see Figure A-14). The cart is driven by an electric motor. Cart position and rod angle are measured with potentiometers.

A.4.1 System Models

The inverted pendulum has already been described in Problems 7.6 and 9.20. We present here the additional model components that describe this specific project. Specifically, we must include the dynamics of the permanent magnet DC motor that is used to drive the cart. The force on the cart that is due to the motor is derived from the following

$$T = K_1\, i_a, \qquad V_{emf} = K_2\, \Omega, \quad \text{and} \quad e - V_{emf} = R_a\, i_a$$

where T is the motor torque and is dependent on the armature current; V_{emf} is the back EMF induced in the armature and is dependent on motor rotational speed; the total voltage across the armature (applied voltage, e, minus back EMF) equals armature resistance times armature current.

The torque applied to a wheel is related to the force acting on the wheel by

$$T = r F$$

where r is the radius of the wheel. Combining all of these relationships gives us

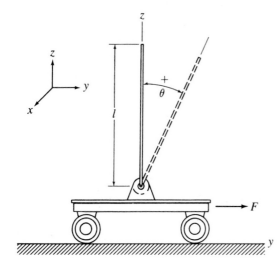

Figure A-14 Schematic of the inverted pendulum on a cart.

$$F = \frac{k_1 e - k_1 k_2 \Omega}{R_a r}$$

Now, shaft rotational speed, Ω, is related to horizontal displacement, $y(t)$, by

$$\Omega = \frac{\dot{y}}{r}$$

The linearized equations for the basic inverted pendulum are

$$F = (M + m)\ddot{y} + ml\ddot{\theta}$$

$$m\ddot{y} + ml\ddot{\theta} - mg\theta = 0$$

Substituting the motor force equation into the above and rearranging yields

$$\ddot{y} + \frac{k_1 k_2}{MR_a r^2}\dot{y} + \frac{mg}{M}\theta = \frac{k_1}{MR_a r}e$$

$$\ddot{\theta} - \frac{(M + m)g}{Ml}\theta - \frac{k_1 k_2}{MlR_a r^2}\dot{y} = -\frac{k_1}{MlR_a r}e$$

The final model will be cast in state space form. We will show this form in the next section, after the constants are determined.

A.4.2 Parameter Determination

The mass of the cart, M, the mass of the rod, m, the length of the rod, l, and the radius of the wheel, r, are all measured directly. The motor parameters, k_1, k_2, and R_a are measured with the experimental set-ups shown in Figure A-15.

The constant, k_1, is measured by attaching a rod of known mass and length to the motor shaft. A driving voltage is applied to the motor until the rod is held horizontally. At this point, the motor is producing a torque that equals the torque produced by the rod ($1/2mgl$). Measuring the current at this voltage allows us to find

$$k_1 = \frac{T}{i_a} = \frac{1/2mgl}{i_a}$$

Because the motor is connected to the cart wheel through a gear train, we must include the

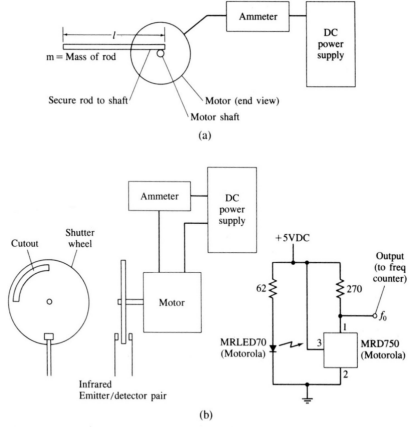

(a)

(b)

Figure A-15 (a) Test set-up for determination of the motor constant k_1. (b) Set-up for determination of the motor constant k_2.

gear train ratio in the above constant. For this project, the gear train ratio was 10.5:1, which means that we must multiply k_1 by this value.

To measure k_2, we must measure the speed of the motor for given applied voltages and take the average ratio of these values. In this project, motor speed was measured electro-optically with a shaft-mounted shutter and a photodetector (see Figure A-15b).

The last motor constant, the armature resistance (R_a), can be found from the same experiment that determines k_2. We simply measure armature current as well as armature voltage and take the average of voltage-to-current ratios.

Finally, we must find the sensor gains that convert rod angle and cart position to voltages. Because the rod angle is measured with a potentiometer, it is a simple matter to convert potentiometer shaft angle to voltage output. The rod angle sensor gain is found by dividing the applied voltage by the maximum potentiometer rotation angle; i.e.,

$$k_\theta = \frac{V_{max}}{350^o} = \frac{V_{max}}{0.97*2\pi} \text{ rad}$$

The cart position is measured with a ten-turn potentiometer that is coupled to a pulley that is arranged to roll along the surface as the cart moves. In this case, we must take the additional step of converting pulley rotation angle to cart horizontal position. This leads to

$$k_y = \frac{V_{max}}{3600^o} \frac{360^o}{\pi D}$$

where D is the pulley diameter. The parameters determined for this project are given in Table A-4.

Table A-4 Parameters for the Inverted Pendulum System		
PARAMETER	DESCRIPTION	VALUE
r	cart wheel radius	0.0198 m
M	cart mass	1.045 Kg
m	rod mass	0.024 Kg
l	rod length	0.622 m
k_1	motor torque-current constant	3.37 x 10^{-3} Nm/A
k_2	motor voltage-speed constant	3.41 x 10^{-3} V/rad/sec
R_a	armature resistance	2.28 Ω
k_θ	rod angle sensor gain	1.637 V/rad
D	pulley diameter	0.027m
k_y	cart position sensor gain	11.79 V/m

Using the parameter values given in Table A-4, the state space representation for the system is given by

$$\dot{x} = \begin{bmatrix} 0 & 0 & 1 & 0 \\ 0 & 0 & 0 & 1 \\ 0 & -0.225 & -1.354 & 0 \\ 0 & 660 & 89 & 0 \end{bmatrix} x + \begin{bmatrix} 0 \\ 0 \\ 0.373 \\ -24.6 \end{bmatrix} u$$

$$\begin{bmatrix} y \\ \theta \end{bmatrix} = \begin{bmatrix} 1 & 0 & 0 & 0 \\ 0 & 1 & 0 & 0 \end{bmatrix} x$$

where $x = (y \ \theta \ \dot{y} \ \dot{\theta})$ and $u = e$. The above equations include the gear train constant of 10.5 and the motor drive amplifier gain of 2.1. The plant eigenvalues for the inverted pendulum are $\{25.7, -25.7, 0, -1.32\}$. The eigenvalues indicate that the plant is unstable, which is expected with an inverted pendulum.

A.4.3 Controller Design

The controller for this project was designed using a modification of the LQG method discussed in Chapter 12. The modification was that a reduced order observer was used in place of a full order Kalman filter. The LQG methodology was used because of the multivariable nature of the problem (single-input two-output system). The motor is controlled by

$$u = -K \hat{x}$$

where K is the controller gain and $\hat{x}$ is the estimate of the states. The separation principle is used to independently determine the controller and observer gains. Because the actual controller is implemented with operational amplifiers, the final control equations are presented in state space form.

The controller gain was found with the *lqr* command using a state weighting of $Q = \text{diag}(1000, 1000, 1, 1)$ and the control weighting of $r = 1$. The resulting control gain is

$$K = [-31.62 \ -79.26 \ -22.39 \ -3.01]$$

The closed loop eigenvalues for this gain are

$$-31.49 \pm 5.36j \quad \text{and} \quad -1.98 \pm 1.87j$$

The control law stabilizes the plant and the dominant closed loop pole indicates that the system has a settling time of approximately 2 sec.

The next step is the design of the observer. Because we are directly measuring the rod angle and the cart position, we only need to estimate the remaining two states: the rod angular velocity and the cart velocity. In this case, we design a reduced order observer, as discussed in Chapter 8. In order to find the observer gain L, we again use the *lqr* command as shown next

```
>> l=lqr(a22',a12',qo,ro)
```

The matrices A_{22} and A_{12} are read off the 2×2 partitioning of the plant A matrix. These matrices play the role of the A and C matrices in the full order case. The weighting matrices Q_o and R_o are used to tune the observer. The selected weights, after several trials, are

$$Q_o = \begin{bmatrix} 1 & 0 \\ 0 & 500 \end{bmatrix}, \qquad R_o = \begin{bmatrix} 1 & 0 \\ 0 & 1 \end{bmatrix}$$

These weights were used to obtain desirable observer poles, and simultaneously come up with reasonable numbers for the observer parameters. It is desirable, from an implementation point of view, that the observer parameters not vary over a large range. The observer gain is

$$L = \begin{bmatrix} 0.19 & 0.65 \\ 0.65 & 24.83 \end{bmatrix}$$

This resulted in

$$w = \begin{pmatrix} -1.55 & -0.66 \\ 88.34 & -24.83 \end{pmatrix} w + \begin{pmatrix} -0.74 & -17.59 \\ 0.89 & 101.41 \end{pmatrix} y + \begin{pmatrix} 0.37 \\ -24.60 \end{pmatrix} u$$

where the observer poles of -22 and -4.4 indicate that the observer poles are greater than the system poles. This results in the observer having a settling time that is faster than the system.

The state estimate equation is

$$\hat{x} = \begin{pmatrix} 1 & 0 \\ 0 & 1 \\ 0.19 & 0.66 \\ 0.66 & 24.83 \end{pmatrix} y + \begin{pmatrix} 0 & 0 \\ 0 & 0 \\ 1 & 0 \\ 0 & 1 \end{pmatrix} w$$

Combining the control and estimator equations, we find the control as

$$u = 37.97x_1 + 168.7x_2 + 22.39w_1 + 3.01w_2$$

Signal flow graph of the compensator as actually implemented is shown in Figure A-16. The diagram includes the sensor gains k_y and k_θ, which multiply the feedback gains for x_1 and x_2. The impulse response of the system showing the cart position and pendulum angular velocity are shown in Figure A-17.

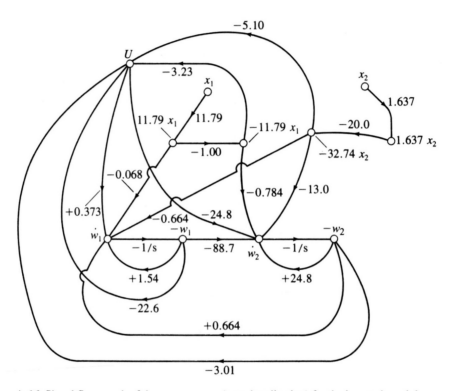

Figure A-16 Signal flow graph of the compensator (actual realization) for the inverted pendulum on a cart.

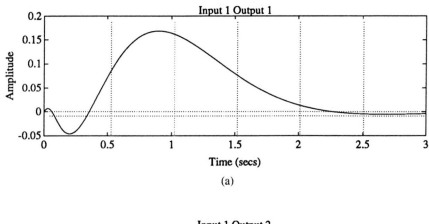

(a)

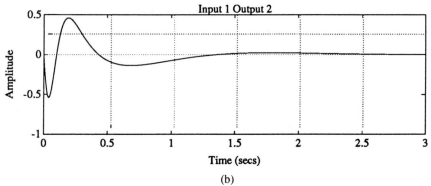

(b)

Figure A-17 Impulse response of the inverted pendulum on a cart. (a) Cart position. (b) Pendulum angle.

A.4.4 Construction

The cart was constructed from the chassis and power plant of a radio-controlled car. This reduced the time required to build the cart, allowing more time for compensator design. It was also a cheap way to go. The body and radio control electronics were removed and a platform was mounted to the remaining chassis. The pendulum was mounted directly to the servo potentiometer shaft. To keep the plant light, the motor control electronics were powered by a remote DC supply.

The schematics for the compensator and the motor controller are shown in Figures A-18 and A-19, respectively. The compensator was a direct implementation of the signal flow graph shown in Figure A-16. The motor amplifier is an H-bridge implementation of complementary bipolar devices and uses local feedback for gain control. A parts list for the project is given in Table A-5.

A.4.5 Results

The cart was able to compensate for disturbances to the rod as long as the initial rod deviation was less than 5°. The table that the cart rolled on was constructed so that it could be tilted. It also became necessary to add a material called "Rubber Tread" to the table surface to improve the traction between the wheels and the surface of the table. During table tilt, the cart would roll approximately 100 cm and would return to its rest position when the table was leveled. The controller was able to maintain the rod in the vertical position in spite of this movement.

Measurable noise was observed in the output of the sensors used in this project. Because the compensator was implemented with integrators, this noise was filtered out. The fact that sensors are always noisy is the reason that differentiators should not be used to create velocity measures. Even with the integrator implementation, the control bandwidth used did result in some vibration in the system, indicating that some of the sensor noise was getting through. A narrower control bandwidth might have further reduced this noisy behavior.

As commented by the student who designed the system, the system response seemed somewhat "nervous." After the fact, it had become clear to the student that the noise problem was most likely due to the use of the reduced order observer, which has a direct path from the measured output to the estimate.

The inverted pendulum on a cart provides another medium for learning about electromechanical systems. It is an unstable system and practically requires two output measurements. Its multivariable nature makes it suitable for applying state space design techniques. Its stabilization using classical control is also a challenging problem. Because of the number of components involved, its construction is more challenging than the other two projects. Inexpensive toy cars can be used as the cart, but their motors are usually too fast and have to be replaced. Another problem with toy cars is sensing their position, because positioning a potentiometer at the wheels is a challenging mechanical problem. It may be easier to build a cart from scratch. A new mechanism for the inverted pendulum has recently been suggested by Furuta, et al. [FYKN91].

Table A-5

CHASSIS

Radio Controlled Car
Potentiometer, 20k
Single Turn
Potentiometer, 10k
Ten Turn

MOTOR DRIVE AMPLIFIER

Op-Amp, Dual
A1, A2
TRANSISTOR, NPN, 80V ,.2A
Q1, Q7
TRANSISTOR, PNP, 80V, .2A
Q2, Q8
TRANSISTOR, NPN, 40V, 4A
Q3, Q5
TRANSISTOR, PNP, 40V, 4A
Q4, Q6
DIODE, 1 AMP 600V
CR3, CR4, CR9, CR10
RESISTOR, 0.22 Ohm 2W 5%
R11, R12, R13, R14
RESISTOR, 1.0 kOhm 1/4W 5%
R6, R7
RESISTOR, 4.7 kOhm 1/4W 5%
R4, R8, R24
RESISTOR, 10kOhm 1/4W 5%
R5, R9, R10, R17, R18
RESISTOR, 10.0 kOhm 1/10W 1%
R1, R2, R21, R22, R23
RESISTOR, 15kOhm 1/4W 5%
R24, R25
CAPACITOR, 39 µF / 20 VDC
C1, C2
CAPACITOR, 220 µF / 16 VDC
C3, C4
CAPACITOR, 0.033 µF / 100 VDC
C5, C6

COMPENSATOR

Op-Amp, Dual
A1, A2, A3, A4, A5, A6
DIODE, ZENER, 5.1V 1/2W
CR1, CR2
RESISTOR, 680 Ohm 1/4W 5%
R24

COMPENSATOR continued.

RESISTOR, 1.0 kOhm 1/4W 5%
R1, R2, R35, R43
RESISTOR, 4.7 kOhm 1/4W 5%
R15, R47, R50, R51, R52
RESISTOR, 10 kOhm 1/4W 5%
R18
RESISTOR, 1.0 Meg 1/4W 5%
R25, R26, R36, R37
RESISTOR, 1.00 kOhm 1/10W 1%
R19
RESISTOR, 1.33 kOhm 1/10W 1%
R40
RESISTOR, 3.57 kOhm 1/10W 1%
R20, R29
RESISTOR, 5.90 kOhm 1/10W 1%
R39
RESISTOR, 6.81 kOhm 1/10W 1%
R22
RESISTOR, 9.31 kOhm 1/10W 1%
R38
RESISTOR, 10.0 kOhm 1/10W 1%
R13, R14, R16, R27, R28, R41, R45, R47, R49
RESISTOR, 13.0 kOhm 1/10W 1%
R51
RESISTOR, 20.0 kOhm 1/10W 1%
R34
RESISTOR, 30.1 kOhm 1/10W 1%
R32, R33, R42
RESISTOR, 53.6 kOhm 1/10W 1%
R30
RESISTOR, 88.7 kOhm 1/10W 1%
R23
RESISTOR, 110 kOhm 1/10W 1%
R3, R4, R5, R6, R9, R10, R11, R12
RESISTOR, 113 kOhm 1/10W 1%
R21
RESISTOR, 200 kOhm 1/10W 1%
R17
RESISTOR, 294 kOhm 1/10W 1%
R31
TRIMPOT, 10 kOhm 20 TURN 68'
R19, R2, R21, R22, R23
CAPACITOR, 47 µF / 35 VDC
C1, C2, C3, C4
CAPACITOR, 1.0 µF / 50 VDC
C5, C6

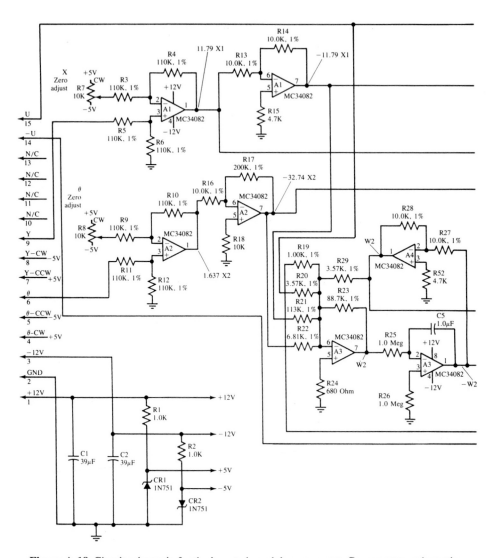

Figure A-18 Circuit schematic for the inverted pendulum on a cart. Compensator schematic.

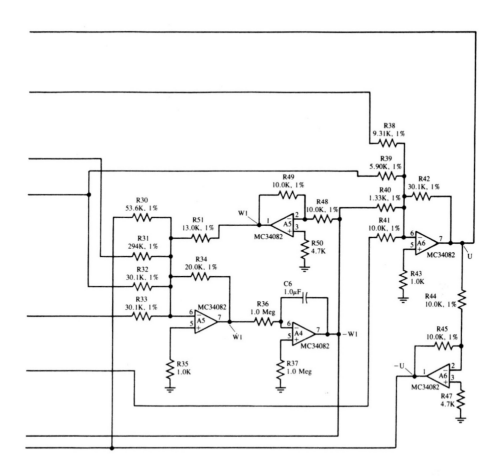

Figure A-18 continued.

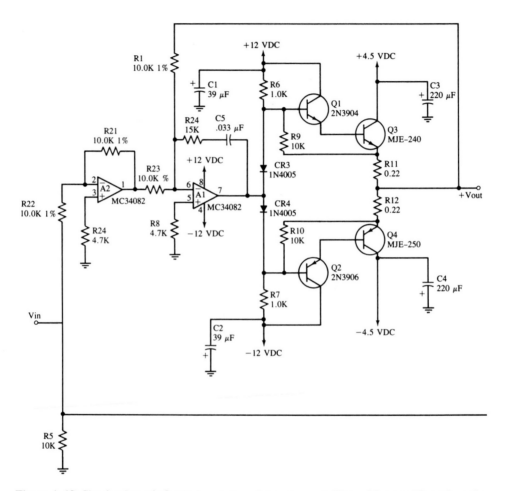

Figure A-19 Circuit schematic for the inverted pendulum on a cart. Motor drive amplifier schematic.

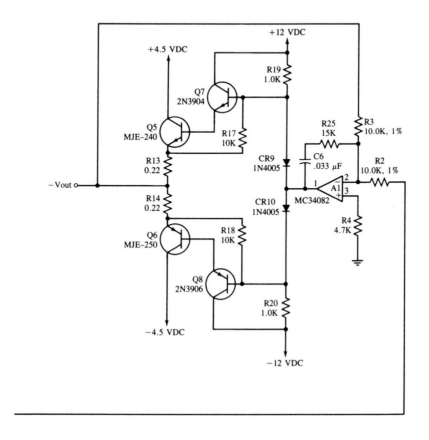

Figure A-19 continued.

Bibliography

[AF66] M. Athans and P. L. Falb. *Optimal Control.* McGraw-Hill, 1966.

[AH84] K. J. Astrom and T. Hagglund. A Frequency Domain Method for Automatic Tuning of Simple Feedback Loops. Proc. of the 23rd *Conference on Decision and Control*, Las Vegas, Nevada, 1984.

[AM79] B. D. O. Anderson and J. B. Moore. *Optimal Filtering.* Prentice Hall, 1979.

[AM90] B. D. O. Anderson and J. B. More. *Linear Optimal Control.* Prentice Hall, 1990.

[AW90] K. J. Astrom and B. Wittenmark. *Computer Controlled Systems:Theory and Design.* Prentice Hall, 2nd edition, 1990.

[B91] W. L. Brogan. *Modern Control Theory.* Prentice Hall, 3rd edition, 1991.

[BB91a] S. P. Boyd, and C. H. Barratt. *Linear Controller Design.* Prentice Hall, 1991.

[BB91b] T. Basar, and P. Bernhard. H∞-Optimal Control and Related Minimax Design Problems. Birkhauser Boston, 1991.

[BH75] A. E. Bryson, Jr. and Y. C. Ho. *Applied Optimal Control : Optimization, Estimation and Control.* Hemisphere Publishing Corporation, 1975.

[BDGPS91] G. J. Balas, J. C. Doyle, K. Glover, A. Packard, and R. Smith. *User's Guide to the μ-Analysis and Synthesis Toolbox for MATLAB.* MUSYN Inc. and The MathWorks, Inc. 1991.

[BPDGS91] G. J. Balas, A. Packard, J. C. Doyle, K. Glover and R. Smith. Development of Advanced Control Design Software for Researchers and Engineers. Proc. *American Control Conference*, Boston, MA, June 26–28, 1991.

[C84] C. T. Chen. *Linear System Theory and Design.* Holt, Rinehart and Winston, 1984.

[C87a] C. T. Chen. *Control System Design: Conventional, Algebraic and Optimal Methods.* Pond Woods Press, 1987.

[C87b] C. T. Chen. Introduction to Linear Algebraic Method for Control System Design. *IEEE Contr. Syst. Mag.*, vol. 7, no. 5, pp. 36–42, © 1987 IEEE.

[CS88] R. Y. Chiang and M. G. Safonov. *User's Guide to the Robust Control Toolbox* for MATLAB. The MathWorks, Inc., 1988.

[CS90a] C. T. Chen and B. Seo. Application of Linear Algebraic Method for Control System Design. *IEEE Contr. Syst. Mag.*, vol. 10, no. 1, © 1990 IEEE.

[CS90b] C. T. Chen and B. Seo. The Inward Approach in the Design of Control Systems. *IEEE Trans. on Educ.*, vol. 33, no. 3, pp. 270–278, © 1990 IEEE.

[CS91] R. Y. Chiang and M. G. Safonov. A Hierarchical Data Structure and New Capabilities of the Robust-Control Toolbox. Proc. *American Control Conference*, Boston, MA, June 26–28, 1991.

[De89] R. A. DeCarlo. *Linear Systems: A State Variable Approach with Numerical Implementation.* Prentice Hall, 1989.

[Do89] R. C. Dorf. *Modern Control Systems.* Addison-Wesley, 5th edition, 1989.

[DFT92] J. C. Doyle, B. A. Francis, and A. R. Tannenbaum, *Feedback Control Theory.* Macmillan, 1992.

[DH88] J. J. D'Azzo, C. H. Houpis. *Linear Control Systems: Analysis & Design.* McGraw-Hill, 3rd edition, 1988.

[DS79] J. C. Doyle and G. Stein. Robustness with Observers. *IEEE Trans. Automat. Contr.*, vol. 24, pp. 607–611, 1979.

[E84] T. F. Elbert. *Estimation and Control of Systems.* Van Nostrand, 1984.

[F86] B. Friedland. *Control Systems Design: An Introduction to State-Space Methods.* McGraw-Hill, 1986.

[F87] B. A. Francis. *A Course in H∞ Control Theory.* Springer-Verlag, 1987.

[FPE91] G. F. Franklin, J. D. Powell, A. Emami-Naeini. *Feedback Control of Dynamic Systems.* Addison-Wesley, 2nd edition, 1991.

[FPW90] G. F. Franklin, J. D. Powell, M.L. Workman. *Digital Control of Dynamic Systems.* Addison-Wesley, 2nd edition, 1990.

[FYKN91] K. Furuta, M. Ymakita, S. Kobayashi, and M. Mishimura. A New Inverted Pendulum Apparatus for Education. Preprints, *IFAC.Advances in Control Education.* pp.191–96, © 1991 IEEE

[F91] A. Feliachi. MS Curriculum National Survey. Proc. *American Control Conference*, Boston, MA, June 26–28, © 1991 IEEE.

[G86] A. Gelb. *Applied Optimal Estimation.* MIT Press, 1974.

[HW91] P. Hsu and J. Wendlandt. The Wedge-A Controller Design Experiment. Preprints, *IFAC Advances in Control Education*, pp. 169–174, © 1991 IEEE.

[H88] J. Hale. *Introduction to Control System Analysis and Design.* Prentice Hall, 2nd edition, 1988.

[HL85] C. H. Houpis and G. B. Lamont. *Digital Control System-Theory, Hardware, Software.* McGraw-Hill, 1987.

[HSS88] G. H. Hostetter, C. J. Savant, Jr. and R. T. Stefani, *Design of Feedback Control Systems.* Holt, Rinehart and Winston, 2nd edition, 1989.

[ISI90] Integrated Systems Inc. *User's Guide to the Robust Control Module* for MATRIX$_X$. Integrated Systems Inc., 1990.

[J81] R. Jaquot. *Modern Digital Control Systems.* Marcel Dekker, 1981.

[JH85] M. Jamshidi and C. J. Herget eds. *Computer-aided Control Systems Engineering.* Elsevier Science Publishers, 1985.

[K64] R. E. Kalman. When is a Linear Control System Optimal? *Journal of Basic Engineering. Trans. ASME D*, 86, pp. 51–60, 1964.

[K70] D. E. Kirk. *Optimal Control Theory: An Introduction.* Prentice Hall, 1970.

[K80] T. Kailath. *Linear Systems.* Prentice Hall, 1980. Reprinted by permission.

[Ku80] B. C. Kuo. *Digital Control Systems.* Holt, Rinehart and Winston. 1980.

[K81] P. Katz. *Digital Control Using Microprocessors,* Prentice Hall, 1981.

[K91] B. C. Kuo. *Automatic Control Systems.* Prentice-Hall, 6th edition, 1991.

[KS72] H. Kwakernaak and R. Sivan. *Linear Optimal Control Systems.* Wiley Interscience, 1972.

[L64] D. G. Luenberger. Observing the State of a Linear System. *IEEE Trans. Mil. Electron.*, MIL-8, pp. 74–80, 1964.

[L79] D. G. Luenberger. *Introduction to Dynamic Systems: Theory, Models & Applications.* Wiley, 1979.

[L86a] F. L. Lewis. *Optimal Control.* Wiley, 1986.

[L86b] F. L. Lewis. *Optimal Estimation: With an Introduction to Stochastic Control Theory.* Wiley, 1986.

[LR90] W. S. Levine, and R. T. Reichert. An introduction to H∞ Control System Design. *Proceedings of the 29th Conference on Decision and Control,* Honolulu, Hawaii, Dec. 1990. © 1990 IEEE.

[M84] R. J. Mayhan. *Discrete-Time & Continuous-Time Linear Systems.* Addison-Wesley, 1985.

[M87] J. Mendel. *Lessons in Digital Estimation Theory.* Prentice-Hall, 1987.

[M89] J. M. Maciejowski. *Multivariable Feedback Design.* Addison-Wesley, 1989.

[MJ73] J. L. Melsa and S. K. Jones. *Computer Programs for Computational Assistance in the Study of Linear Control Theory.* McGraw-Hill, 2nd edition, 1973.

[O78] D. H. Owens. *Multivariable and Feedback Systems.* Peter Peregrinus, 1978.

[O87] K. Ogata. *Discrete-Time Control Systems,* Prentice Hall, 1987.

[O90] K. Ogata. *Modern Control Engineering.* Prentice Hall, 2nd edition, 1990.

[Pa91] A. Papoulis. *Probability, Random Variables, and Stochastic Processes.* McGraw-Hill, 3rd edition. 1991.

[P91] G. K. H. Pang. Issues in the Development of the Interactive CACSD package SFPACK. Proc. *American Control Conference,* Boston, MA, June 26–28, 1991.

[PH88] C. L. Phillips and R. D. Harbor. *Feedback Control Systems.* Prentice Hall, 1988.

[PN90] C. L. Phillips and H. T. Nagle. *Digital Control System Analysis and Design.* Prentice Hall, 2nd edition, 1990.

[S86] R. F. Stengle. *Stochastic Optimal Control: Theory and Application.* Wiley Interscience, 1986.

[SD91] G. Stein and J. Doyle. Beyond Singular Values and Loop Shapes. *Journal of Guidance,* Vol. 14, No. 1, Jan.–Feb. 1991.

[SM67] D. G. Schultz and J. L. Melsa. *State Functions and Linear Control Systems.* McGraw-Hill, 1967.

[SW77] A. P. Sage and C. C. White. *Optimal Systems Control.* Prentice-Hall, 1977.

[TS86] J. M. T. Thompson and H. B. Stewart. *Nonlinear Dynamics and Chaos.* Wiley, 1986.

[T88] Peter Thompson. *Tutorial and User's Guide for Program CC, Version 4.* Systems Technology Inc., 1988.

[WCFMR89] P. E. Wellstead, V. Chrimes, P. R. Fletcher, R. Moody, and A. J. Robins. Ball and Beam Control Experiment. *Int. J. Elect. Eng. Educ.,* vol. 15, p. 21, 1989.

[W86] T. H. Wong. Design of a Magnetic Levitation Control System—An Undergraduate Project. *IEEE Trans. on Educ.,* vol. E-29, no. 4, pp. 196–200. 1986.

[ZN42] J. G. Ziegler and N. B. Nichols. Optimum Settings for Automatic Controllers. *Trans. ASME,* pp. 759–768, 1942.

[ZZH87] F. Zu-ren, Y. Zheng-qi and C. Hui-tang. Microprocessor-Based Controller for Double Inverted Pendulum. *IFAC 10th Trennial World Congress,* Munich, FRG, pp. 237–240, 1987.

IEEE Control Systems Magazine, Vol. 10, No. 6, p. 40, © 1990 IEEE.

Index

2-norm of matrix, 442

A

Ackermann's formula, 223
additive stability margin (ASM), 409
ALE, 351
algebraic Lyapunov equation (ALE), 351, 447
aliasing, 258
asymptotic stability, (*See stability*)
autocorrelation function, 344
autocorrelation matrix, 346
autocovariance matrix, 347

B

ball-on-beam project, 465
bandwidth (BW), 10, 12
BIBO stability, (*See stability*)
bilinear transform, 271
Bode plot of system with time delay, 107
Bode plot, 3
Bode plot, using MATLAB, 95
Butterworth pattern, 375

C

chaos, 160
characteristic equation, 2

command response, 398
complementary sensitivity, desirable shape, 400
complementary sensitivity, state space equation, 140
complementary sensitivity, 21, 398
condition number, of system, 409
condition number, 443
conditional stability, 229
controllability, 222
controllability and pole-zero cancellation, 223, 319
controllability matrix, 222
controller-observer configuration, 310, 332
convolution, 5
correlation coefficient, 345, 349
correlation function, 344
correlation matrix, 346
cost function, 314
   IAE, 314
   ISE, 314
   ITAE, 314, 325
   LQR, 315, 329
covariance function, 344
covariance matrix, 347, 351
cross-correlation function, 344
cross-spectral density function, 346
CST, (*See Control Systems Toolbox commands*)

D

delay time (T_d), 11
detectability, 232

M

MATLAB commands

503